The Human Core
The Intrapsychic Base of Behavior

VOLUME I
Action within the Structural View

The Human Core
The Intrapsychic Base of Behavior

VOLUME I
Action within the Structural View

by
Leo Rangell, M.D.

INTERNATIONAL UNIVERSITIES PRESS, INC.
Madison   Connecticut

Library of Congress Cataloging-in-Publication Data

Rangell, Leo.
    The human core : the intrapsychic base of behavior / by Leo
Rangell.
        p. cm.
    Includes bibliographical references.
    Contents: Vol 1. Action within the structural view — v. 2. From
anxiety to integrity.
    ISBN 0-8236-2365-3 (v. 1) — ISBN 0-8236-2366-1 (v. 2)
    1. Psychoanalysis. I. Title.
    [DNLM: 1. Behavior 2. Psychoanalytic Theory. WM 460 R196h]
RC504.R36 1990
150.19'5--dc20
DNLM/DLC
for Library of Congress   89-20046
                                                            CIP

Manufactured in the United States of America

This work, a distillate of half a century of immersion in the practice of psychoanalysis and concern for its theory, would not have been conceivable without the unfailing devotion and constant participation of my wife Anita. This book is dedicated to her.

CONTENTS

Volume I

ACTION WITHIN THE STRUCTURAL VIEW

Section I

THE INTRAPSYCHIC PROCESS: AN ORGANIZING CONCEPT OF BEHAVIOR

Section II

THE ETIOLOGICAL SEQUENCE

Section III

CHOICE AND RESPONSIBILITY

Contents Volume II: From Anxiety to Integrity

Section IV

THE PSYCHOANALYTIC CORE

Section V

APPLICATIONS TO TECHNIQUE

Section VI

THE INDIVIDUAL AND THE GROUP

Point of Entry

For the first 40 years of psychoanalysis, the new contributions had to do with the forces impinging upon the individual, from without and from within. The early discoveries moved from external forces resulting in traumatic conditions, to internal instinctual pressures causing the state of mounting tension from within. To both influences, the individual was in a passive, receptive position.

In the 1920s and 1930s, Freud added and refined the structural view, which centered on the role of the ego acting on the forces impinging upon it. This began a phase of psychoanalytic theory and understanding in which an active agency within the mind was "doing" something to the stimuli it was receiving, from both directions.

From then on through the 1960s this trend continued and expanded. Anna Freud elaborated on defenses. Hartmann expanded on the functions of the ego in conflict-free and conflictful behavior. Rapaport deepened the concept of ego autonomy and described the ego's role in affects and thinking. Other contributors to this expansion of ego functions included Kris, Loewenstein, Waelder, and Jacobson. Theoretical and

1

clinical advances up to the early years were summarized and systematized by Fenichel in 1940 and until his death in 1946.

Neither Hartmann nor Rapaport carried their contributions on autonomy and the conflict-free to the point of a psychoanalytic theory of action. Both inexplicably stopped short of this. Hartmann, who wrote of rational and irrational action, specifically stated that there was as yet no theory of action within psychoanalytic theory, by which he meant centrally its metapsychology. Rapaport came close to the subject in a paper on activity-passivity which he never published. Gill (1967), who included this paper in a volume he edited of Rapaport's works, writes of Rapaport's conflict about this subject which, with all his hesitations, "he regarded as at the very heart of an adequate conceptualization of the human psyche" (p. 531).

The papers I include in these two volumes were written in the spirit of Hartmann and Rapaport and others of their general thought. Selected from my writings, I consider them as an extension of the unfinished theme by both Hartmann and Rapaport. I did not write these papers consecutively or with this subject in mind. An overall theme evolved gradually from clinical material and my pursuit of a theoretical thread which became visible to me from one paper to another.

New subjects which evolved and were studied related to each other in a continuous line which gradually began to appear to me as constituting a psychoanalytic theory of action. Theoretical nodes upon this line included unconscious choice conflicts and unconscious decision-making. Various approaches from different directions, from studies of anxiety, intrapsychic conflict, or moral conflicts, converged into a sequence of intrapsychic activity which culminates in human decision and action. I called the ongoing unconscious mental activity from which these active products derive the "intrapsychic process." By a series of incremental theoretical steps, I came to look upon this process as the "human core." This unconscious intrapsychic activity culminating in action is encompassed within psychoanalytic theory, subsumed under and best explained by the structural and other metapsychological points of view. This is a central theme of this book.

These papers did not appear in a historical vacuum. The fate of this linear development of psychoanalytic theory is another datum explored and studied. Other large theoretical movements were taking place in the 1960s which affected not only the periphery of psychoanalytic thought but its "mainstream" as well. Following Rapaport's premature death in 1960, at the same early age of 49 as Fenichel had died in 1946, a strong and articulate group, who had worked in close intellectual unity with Rapaport during this creative period, questioned and discarded what they regarded as the abstract metapsychology of psychoanalytic theory, of psychic systems and structures, which came into being with Freud's additions to psychoanalytic theory and was carried so much further by Rapaport. Retaining only what they regarded as experience-near "clinical theory," George Klein, Schafer, Gill, and others reverted to a concept of the whole person, not a psychic system, the ego, as agent. A major work which emerged from this group was Schafer's "action language," which spelled out a new language for psychoanalysis as a theory of action outside of psychoanalytic metapsychology.

One can discern a similar backlash or at least loss of excitement or even acceptance of Hartmann's writings. From the 1960s on, group interest gradually turned elsewhere, away from the active developing "ego psychology." This has been the case in Europe for many years, but has been evident currently in the United States as well. At the same time, accompanying these strong currents against intrapsychic structural dynamics, which extend backward from Rapaport and Hartmann to Anna Freud and Freud's own later theories, other "alternative" theories evolved and commanded attention. Whether the modern theories of the self or the object, which are variations of previous interpersonal theories, these also center around psychologies of the whole rather than of structural parts or component psychic systems. Conflicts are between self and object, rather than intrapsychic, or, if intrapersonal, between

internalized self and object representations rather than interstructural.

In the wake of these strong currents, the steady linear
accretions to psychoanalytic theory represented by the continuously evolving concepts in the papers of these two volumes
were largely overshadowed with respect to group response and
discussion, and have never become part of what is loosely called
classical or mainstream psychoanalytic theory. Gray (1982)
described a developmental "lag" after the advent of "ego
psychology," characterized by a reluctance to apply the new
insights to the psychoanalytic therapeutic procedure. This lag
extends to a "block" in following through the implications of
structural psychology to its full range of mental functioning, up
to and including the unconscious initiation and execution of
action, in autonomous as well as conflictful mentation.

The reasons for this dissociated reaction between discoveries and effects are part of the contents of these papers. The
resistance to Freud's first psychoanalytic insights, to the reve-
lations that man was less in control of his motivations than he
thought, is now matched by an opposite resistance. With
unconscious decision, the fact that man acts and actively
controls more than he is consciously aware of is met with an
equal resistance from an opposite direction of narcissistic
defense. Much of what one says has been done to him, by other
people and other forces, it now turns out has been done by
himself.

The key is *unconscious* choice, *unconscious* decision, and
unconscious execution of intention into willed action. This
unconscious sequence is the psychoanalytic contribution to the
understanding of man's actions. With this addition, man is now
not less but more responsible for his actions than he thought.
More accurately, he is both less and more responsible simultaneously. That this is confusing and puzzling is no reason for it
not to be pursued and known. Psychoanalysis deals characteristically with such dichotomies, and starts from there to unravel
and understand them. These new insights have profound
applications in life about responsibility, whether for what one

chooses to do, or for what one chooses, equally actively, not to do. Examples range from allowing someone to be spoken ill of, to the crime of silence at more serious violence.

The formulations and concepts developed here are not related to specific nosologic entities, to borderline or narcissistic or any other diagnostic category, by apply across the spectrum of behavior. As such they serve to fulfill Hartmann's and Freud's goal of psychoanalysis as a general psychology. As will be seen, problems of integrity, vital in decisions, actions, and behavior, also find a place, on a par with neuroses; defenses against the superego operate as they do against the id.

Along with the neglect or avoidance of this advancing edge of psychoanalytic theory, and the diminution of structural theory in general, has been a pejorative trend based on a fusion of political terms with the scientific. This has been widespread and has invaded the most active and authoritative psychoanalytic levels. At a panel (1987) revisiting a "classic" paper of Loewald (1960) on the nature of therapeutic action, Cooper praises Loewald for his "radical" revision in having introduced the concept of the analyst as a new object, while criticizing him as "conservative" for continuing to use the traditional language of metapsychology. Theory which stresses the interactional over the intrapsychic is radical, i.e., positive, good; traditional is conservative, i.e., negative, bad. Not only the theory but the time period of its acceptance also is considered in the same political terms. At the same panel, Schafer refers to "the ultra-conservative Freudian audience that prevailed around 1960" (p. 11). From the "radical" discovery of the unconscious, to the "conservative" maintenance of the structural view, the Freudian revolution has come full circle.

These pejorative connotations, on a social or political basis, extend to other significant controversies as well. To the complex scientific question of one theory or many, eclecticism with respect to diversity of theories is seen as democratic, while a unitary theory, however multifaceted and inclusive its interior components, is regarded as authoritarian or isolationist, if not autocratic and dictatorial. The psychology of the whole is also given a humanistic meaning, in contrast to a supposedly mechanistic one when the whole is seen to be composed of parts. One theory is considered to respect the person as a whole, the other to see him fragmented, in a less empathic or humanistic way. The fact is that the self, and the object, as whole entities, have always had a firm place in central unified psychoanalytic theory. The obvious confluence and confusion of the scientific and political need to be undone, and the value systems of each kept separate.

The arguments and findings in these two volumes begin quietly and gain momentum, starting on a clinical base, and steadily accumulating a succession of theoretical formulations. The new fuller view, extending Hartmann and Rapaport to a theory of the intrapsychic roots of action, is not an extension of "ego psychology" but aims toward what I look upon as "total, composite psychoanalytic theory." It was never "ego psychology," even with Freud, parallel to or separate from a theory of drives, nor, as Schur pointed out, was there ever a separate "structural theory." Both of these are common misnomers. The structural point of view is one of the metapsychological points of view, all parts of psychoanalytic theory. To a discussant who commended a presentation of mine as an advance in ego psychology, I pointed out that my description of the intrapsychic process in ongoing mental operations is better called "an id-ego-superego-external world" psychological theory.

Reverting from a position of having defined the component parts, to giving them up and seeing only the whole again, is in my opinion a scientific regression, returning to what was scientifically the case before the advent of psychoanalysis. Far from having outlived its usefulness, psychoanalytic metapsychological theory is still to be utilized for its full significance as a theoretical guide to clinical data. I have often asked, without receiving a satisfactory reply, whether those who discard metapsychology dispense with all of its points of view, i.e., besides the structural, the dynamic, genetic, adaptive, etc., and, if so, with what do they replace them? In my opinion, more has been lost than gained by this development.

It would be well to reinstate the line of inspiration which has been allowed to disappear. The 1960s, with the forward movement of the study of the ego to complete and advance the totality of structural psychology, was still an inspirational period for psychoanalysis and for candidates entering the field at that time. This was the case for my generation starting to train in psychoanalysis in the early 1940s. The spirit was not interrupted by the war, where analytic thinking received another inspirational boost.

The consistent and cumulative directions of psychoanalysis were aborted and terminated prior to their fruition into a total theory of human behavior. Having reached an acme of achievement, a generation of psychoanalysts, trained during that period, began to practice in the flush of these ideas. Since then, the new attenuated and alternative systems, which some feel as exciting and others as reversing and sacrificing what had been amassed, have come to dominate, in numbers and interest, training, practice, and the psychoanalytic literature, to the extent that what is still called mainstream theory is no longer main, but is today a minority position.

I suggest we pick up the thread which has been lost or buried, and follow it and lead it, and guide it again to a total psychology of human behavior. The resistances which were met and dissolved to the first half of Freud's discoveries, which had to do with man's automatic behavior, will have to be exposed and equally resolved with respect to the total implications of the second half of Freud's discoveries, the unconscious roots of man's self-directive acts.

This book may not fulfill the goal of a total understanding of behavior and action, but I hope it will resume the movement toward it. The theme which evolves through these papers is the subtle combination of psychic determinism and the exercise of choice. Behavior is both automatic and self-directed. The ego will is as important as the instinctual wish. The automatic phrase "free will" is misleading and diverting. Will is both free and restricted. Within the channels defined by the drives and the superego, constitutional givens, and the constraints of the external world, the ego directs the self where it "wills."

Psychic outcomes stem from id, ego, and superego; from primary and secondary process mentation at unconscious as well as conscious levels. The unique combination of these passive and active forces characterizes the human species, and makes for human potential as well as limitations. The unconscious process which integrates the two levels of behavior and oversees its final external outputs is the "human core."

Section I

The Intrapsychic Process: An Organizing Concept of Behavior

Introduction

The first section starts with an overview of the general theme, introduces the concept of the intrapsychic process, and traces its evolution throughout these writings. As psychoanalytic theoretical writings in general, the actual material then starts upon a clinical base. In this case, a phobia of dolls is presented. The postulation of the phobic doll symptom as at the hub of a metaphoric wheel introduces the concept of a core intrapsychic base of behavior. In the next paper, setting out to differentiate the work of the psychoanalyst from other behavioral scientists, the core is extended to the area of unconscious intrapsychic conflicts. In this study, the central dynamic motivating processes are seen as constituting "the human core." The role of affects is described as a ubiquitous experience at this psychic human core.

In a study of the human affective state of poise, the relation of this state of desired balance is traced to the physiological state of repose or imbalance of the snout or perioral area. This psychological and somatic core, embryologically the rostral tip of the organism, is seen as the "window to the emotions." In a paper presented in honor of René Spitz, the

11

two major acquired words in the human vocabulary, "No" and "Yes," are studied in relation both to psychological developments and to the physiology of the musculature in this buccal-lingual-perioral core area of the human face. The final paper of this section studies the origins of both psychic and somatic structure formation in infancy, from the neonatal period into the first year of life.

CHAPTER 1

The Evolution of an Idea

The purpose of this book is to present a theme which has coursed its way through a group of papers which I have written over the past four decades. A major and consistent theme consists of the exercise of unconscious choice by the ego, during an ongoing core process of mental functioning. This change, or, to be more accurate, the inclusion of this new theoretical emphasis added to those which already exist, has far-reaching consequences to the understanding of human behavior.

There are two main thrusts to this contribution, in the relationship of figure to ground as it were. Each of these is an equal focus of theoretical study. The central armature of this conceptual frame revolves around the postulation of the "intrapsychic process." This comprises a linear series of unconscious psychic events, from the intention to discharge an instinctual impulse, through a number of intermediate scanning, testing, and contemplative steps, cognitive and affective, leading toward action, mood, or other final psychic outcomes.

I have called this center of psychic activity the "human core." This dynamic and structural interplay of forces is an ongoing mental process, with both short- and long-range goals,

13

and immediate and ultimate psychic products. These together, the process and its products, comprise the subject of this book. The analyst looks from the outside in, toward this core for explanations, and from the inside out, from this center to its derivatives.

Derivatives of this unconscious intrapsychic process, which emerge from it as figures from the ground, are the postulation of unconscious choice conflict and the contiguous concept of unconscious ego decision-making. This is a view of psychic conflict and its solutions quite different from the conventional type of oppositional conflict which leads to a solution by compromise formation. The operation of an active, though unconscious, ego decision and "will" in the final psychic outcome introduces a significant new dimension into psychoanalytic theory, the psychoanalytic therapeutic procedure, and the elusive questions of responsibility and accountability.

The central concept of a sequential series of intrapsychic events, from which intermediate and then final psychic products radiate to the periphery, converged from a continuous series of studies, first clinical, and then separate investigations over the years of various major nuclei of psychoanalytic theory, such as anxiety, conflict, and ego functioning, each from its own specific vantage point. The approach in each case was through a "microdynamic" examination of the underlying sequences taking place at the psychic core.

The aim of this book is not to present a collection per se of the papers contained within it. Of a bibliography approaching 300 publications, I have selected for these two volumes a group of papers which coalesce into this unified theme. The goal is to trace and study the development of this specific line of thought, how it emerged, developed, was understood and applied, and its significance for psychoanalytic theory and clinical psychoanalysis. The evolution of the idea, its course and fate, is as important as its summation, to transmit the impact of the altered emphasis which this lends to psychoanalytic theory and practice.

With many explanatory formulations, even purportedly

new theoretical "systems," the central concept often remains elusive and undefined. It has been said, for example, that Kohut never defined the "self," which was explicitly defined before Kohut's self psychology by Hartmann, Jacobson, and others. To obviate such a gap, I will describe and briefly summarize the intrapsychic process in a semidefinitional outline form, as it has evolved during the course of these studies (see the summary at the end of this chapter).

This pathognomonic, organizing sequence is a combination and elaboration of two of Freud's central concepts, signal anxiety and thought as experimental action. In my expanded version of this intrapsychic process, the two are combined and extended, to include steps preliminary to the receipt of the anxiety signal, and intrapsychic functions and activities subsequent to the results of the experimental thought. Encompassed within the total sequence are the anxiety signals, the contents of unconscious thought, and the activities of the ego toward achieving its aims.

This ongoing, intrapsychic, testing process is seen to contain and utilize within it all of the metapsychological points of view, the dynamic, genetic, topographic, adaptive, even the economic, the ego having to judge intensities of reaction, and centrally the structural. Far from moving away from metapsychology, the description of this underlying process fortifies it. All the points of view are concentrated here. This is without minimizing meaning and purpose, as some claim it does, which is then used as an argument against the retention of metapsychology. Indeed, the description of this underlying core process, with the unconscious logic that it encompasses, enhances and clarifies the purposeful nature of unconscious mental activity. For practical as well as theoretical reasons, I agree with Anna Freud (1936; Sandler and A. Freud, 1985), and with Eissler (1969), to retain all the metapsychological points of view, not just some, including, for example, the economic and topographic. Each adds a degree of understanding.

Encompassed within the boundaries of the intrapsychic sequence described, and deriving from it, a number of new formulations were arrived at, as well as new emphases not hitherto centered upon. These include: (1) Within the subject of unconscious conflict, there are new aspects of intrapsychic conflict, choice conflict, the facing of a dilemma, the being "in conflict," in contrast to the conventional oppositional type of conflict between ego and id. (2) Within ego functions, related to the above, there is a new unconscious decision-making function of the ego, not hitherto included within the ensemble of ego functions by Freud (1923a), Anna Freud (1936), Hartmann (1950a) or others. (3) Among the variety of final psychic outcomes, there is "the syndrome of the compromise of integrity," described as on a par with neuroses in human affairs. This results from intersystemic ego-superego tensions and conflicts, with compromises of the superego occurring, comparable to id-ego conflicts from which compromises of the id result. (4) Within the central activities of the ego, Hartmann's ego autonomy is extended to the exercising of the will, between decision and action, initiating movement on the path toward external action.

These themes did not arise by being conceived of and then pursued. That is, papers were not written to demonstrate the existence and workings of the unconscious intrapsychic process, nor of the unconscious decision-making function of the ego. Nor did they appear by serendipity, as it were, i.e., coming into appearance almost accidentally in the center of a variety of other subjects. My view is rather that these specific concepts, or this combined running insight, came to my attention successively and repetitively by virtue of their unfailing existence as explanatory backgrounds behind each psychoanalytic phenomenon I set out to study.

Anna Freud (1969) stated that psychoanalysis was not for creation but for discovery. Like Freud's metapsychological "points of view," which grew not because of an affinity to nineteenth-century neurology, as claimed by some, but because they best encompassed emerging and accumulating clinical experience, this underlying formulation gained for me increasing attention because it appeared empirically as the most regularly occurring background behind all observable phenomena being investigated. As such, it came to serve best as an explanatory model toward understanding anxiety, conflict or trauma, whether eventuating in normal outcomes or symptom formation.

Although this unconscious intrapsychic process and its derivatives are a unifying thread underlying human mentation, it does not constitute a new paradigm, as much as these are eagerly awaited to be followed by many. It is also not being presented as a new point of view of metapsychology. It is, in my opinion, an extension which is added to and comes to reside squarely within the body of existing psychoanalytic theory. This ongoing process and its derivatives, which lend a new emphasis to psychoanalytic thinking, constitute a major new branch stemming from the main trunk of psychoanalytic theory. This then acquires new branches with their own subsequent derivative offshoots.

In the midst of this microscopic pursuit of the intrapsychic process, anxiety theory has been advanced and a unitary theory of anxiety offered which fuses Freud's two theories of anxiety. Aspects of both of Freud's theories of anxiety are seen to exist and to be included within separate arcs of the intrapsychic sequence. The anxiety signal, Freud's second theory, is seen to occur at one stage of the process, and the tension state following unsuccessful defense, which is the phenomenological equivalent of the observations of Freud's which led to his first theory of dammed-up libido, is seen to occur at a later phase of the developing and ongoing intrapsychic process. Defense is now, however, against all instinctual drives, aggressive as well as libidinal impulses.

Each arc in this intrapsychic sequence fortifies the others, making for a mutually reciprocal process in all directions. The presence of a choice conflict makes a decision function of the ego necessary. The emphasis on the ego-superego contribution introduces the moral issue and the question of integrity or its absence. This in turn needs to be taken into account within the decision-making process. The introduction of the signal theory of anxiety made a choice conflict inevitable. The recognition of a tension state as one arc of the intrapsychic process made understandable Freud's first theory of anxiety which resulted from mounting tension.

As a test for the viability of a theory or part theory, its fecundity and usefulness come under question. The formulations arrived at and traced here, in their operations behind a variety of clinical phenomena and life events, are seen to shed light on mental processes within the psychic apparatus, derivative phenomena into the interior of the organism, psychic and somatic, and behavioral outcomes in the external world. The intrapsychic sequence comprises an organizing principle of all human behavior. Anxiety, choice, defense occur universally in normal operational intrapsychic dynamics. The same background process exists in common across the nosologic spectrum. What separates the course of conduct is the ingredients which confront the ego, and the solutions which the latter imposes to effect solutions.

Each segment of the sequence has external derivatives, from direct instinctual sequelae, to defense, to free-floating anxiety, to decision, or the ego state of indecision, to psychic tension or its somatic derivatives, external action, or a psychopathological outcome, neurotic, borderline, or a more severely pathological syndrome. All of the links, however, whether resulting in immediate phenomena close to the core, such as primitive affects, or more distant sequelae at the periphery, retain their contiguity and continuity. Most observable behavioral phenomena, clinically and in life, consist of a combination of fused and interacting elements, compromises, or even aggregates. Modulated affects seen in later normal life are composed of instinctual drives "tamed" by ego defenses (Fenichel, 1941a; E. Kris, 1950; Rapaport, 1950, 1953a; Jacobson, 1953a).

While I agree with Brenner (1982a) that the data of psychoanalysis are psychological in content, I also feel, as in the studies of Reiser (1984, 1985), that observations in psychoanalysis can point toward an interface with somatic phenomena and mechanisms. The existence within the intrapsychic process of the arc I describe as the tension state links to Freud's first (physiological) theory of anxiety, and provides such an interface and merging with somatic phenomena. This can be the dynamic connection linking psyche and soma, possibly via Selye's (1950) stress phenomena and adrenocortical response, to the kaleidoscopic variety of psychosomatic outcomes. These include phenomena deriving from or accompanying anxiety and those which eventuate from further development of symptomatology, whether conversion or psychosomatic derivatives in final mind-body outcomes.

Yet, though phenomenologically contiguous and even combined, the two systems remain theoretically separate. Kety (1960) has said that there may one day be a biochemistry of memory but never of memories. C. Fisher (1966, 1978) has said the same about sleep and dreams. Sleep and dreaming can be explained, but dreams will always require interpretations. Neurophysiology can explain the one, but the other will always require a hermeneutic approach. Both are necessary and each plays a part. Psychoanalysis can approach the psychosomatic synapse from its side, but a meeting with those coming from the other direction is necessary to restudy what Freud first approached in his Project (1895), which he thought to the end of his life would one day come about.

An important new concept for psychoanalytic discourse is that of human "will." Will has until now been ensnared in the automatic phrase "free will," from which it needs to be extracted. As I (1959) have previously separated "conversion" from "hysteria," so "free" needs to be separated from "will," and each considered on its own. Ego will is no more or less free than ego autonomy, both of which are relative, yet both of which are phenomenologically present and to be accounted for.

The implications of these new, or at least for psychoanalysis unfamiliar, theoretical foci, of choice, decision, will, need to be integrated with the basic psychoanalytic tenet of psychic determinism. The execution of will and of directing activity on the part of the ego does not speak against causation, and exists side by side with psychic determinism, both of which are soft and relative. Man's will, built upon constitutional givens, added to and further developed by acquired life experiences, joins the chain of causation and determinism which exists in nature. Man is subject to causation and determinism, yet can change. Both formulations fit empirical observations, and both are necessary to encompass the basic tenets upon which psychoanalysis is predicated—that man can influence and change the deterministic forces that guide him.

As we attend to the subject of unconscious ego will, hitherto avoided by psychoanalysis, analytic insights deepen the understanding of human psychic activity which has been stalemated and a subject of endless debate among philosophers and scientists from the beginnings of modern man. The positions I have taken extend the views arrived at by Freud. They indeed follow from Freud's (1923a, 1940) formulations of the unconscious ego, and the operation of secondary process mentation within the unconscious.

Purpose, intention, choice, decision are by these works included within structural, metapsychological, psychoanalytic theory. The omission of this stream of motivation from psychoanalysis, which has incorrectly led others to seek new theories to include them, has been obviated by the inclusion of this series of purposeful activities within total psychoanalytic theory. With an extension of ego autonomy into what I call "the executive functions of the ego," and a place given to ego will comparable to that of the instinctual wish, psychoanalysis joins other psychologies, academic and experimental psychology, learning theory and other disciplines, in including and encompassing purposeful action.

The description of this intrapsychic background base of behavior encompasses and contains all other partial and alternative theories, such as of the self, the object, the interpersonal, Kleinian, developmental theory, information processing, systems theories, the findings of direct infant observers, even the concepts of computer analysis, or of the brain as the largest and most complex of computers. Information is processed, the object is addressed, the self is preserved, the earliest and later inputs, pregenital and oedipal, are all given their due place, in the automatic scanning which is ongoing within the unconscious intrapsychic process described.

Our specifying and adding to this base, with the spectrum of its complex interactive elements, make many alternative theories unnecessary, such as those by G. Klein (1973, 1976) introducing purpose and intention, or Schafer's (1976) theory of action, Kohut's (1971, 1977) of the self, Atwood and Stolorow's (1984) on intersubjectivity, or Gedo's (1979) of the centrality of a hierarchy of values. Each of these is proffered at the expense of one or more elements of accumulated theory which are thereby discarded and needlessly lost. I have previously taken up the issue of alternate theories in papers on contemporary issues (see Chapter 22), and in others on the self (1982b), and the object (1985b) within total psychoanalytic theory. The Blancks (1986) are the most recent to postulate a "superordinate ego," but within a specific developmental object relations theory. Their description emphasizes the function of synthesizing rather than of deciding or choosing, more in the nature of "fitting together" (p. 36) than what I have described in the sense of "sticking out."

These contributions demonstrate advance by accretion rather than by repetitive new and partial theories, a method I consider to have advantages for a rational development of psychoanalytic knowledge and history. The march of new theories or explanatory systems, which have been alternative rather than additive to existing theory, have typically had a rapid rise accompanied by excitement and followed by a quiet decline and disappearance. During the years of their ascendancy, however, cumulative theory has been excluded or set back, usually for decades at a time. What may be absorbed from the new approaches, which in each case is some partial advance, could have been contributed without an eclipse, stagnation, or even regression of the total accumulated body of theory.

The present additions constitute a major branch, stemming from but not replacing the main trunk. Some analysts seem indeed to have feared that a deeper acknowledgment and understanding of the activities of the unconscious ego replace or diminish the roles of other aspects of traditional psychoanalytic theory, such as instinctual drives or psychic determinism, neither of which it does. Instead, more becomes known about the interactions between all psychic elements, and knowledge which accumulates is integrated with the whole.

These contributions are within the mainstream, but they are not automatically of the mainstream. The latter is not as monolithic as some think. The fusion of Freud's two anxiety theories presented in these papers is disagreed with by Waelder (1953) and Brenner (1953), who feel that Freud simply failed to discard his first theory after it had become obsolete. Fenichel's (1945) clinical and theoretical contributions support the views I have taken, as does Blau (1952, 1955), while Schur (1953) and Benjamin (1961a, 1963) retain divided opinions on the subject. The addition of another type of solution to conflict, other than that of compromise formation, has not been met with alacrity, nor has it taken its place automatically and energetically in psychoanalytic parlance. Brenner (1982a) emphasizes compromise formations exclusively and does not mention choice.

The introduction of intention, purpose, and decision, although into a field of such presumed hermeneutic emphasis, was so resisted within the field itself as to make room for others to create new psychologies to make the same point. Another, even more primary motive for most of these new systems of thought was to eliminate the mechanistic thinking which to the minds of their authors go with metapsychology. Yet hermeneutics and explanations, dynamics and structures, meanings and mechanisms are fused and integrated in total psychoanalytic theory. I have preferred the term "total" psychoanalytic theory throughout these and other writings. I have opposed the terms "classical" or "traditional," as referring ambivalently to feelings of respect, even awe, while at the same time also connoting the deteriorating and decrepit. The psychology of the self or of object relations is as much part of total general theory as is the theory of drives.

A block against these directing functions of the ego exists in many who espouse the ego and structures, as well as in those who stress purpose and intention in their alternate theories.

Just as an entire group rebelled and veered off from the previous teachings of Rapaport, including their own brilliant systematization with him of metapsychology, so do I now sense a similar aversion developing to Hartmann's ego psychology, and within it particularly to the role of the autonomous ego.

This applies to my extension of Hartmann's ego autonomy, and before that of Freud's unconscious ego, into the subject of the executive functions of the ego, and the exercise of ego decision and will. A visible group against Rapaport or now a discernible movement away from Hartmann can be partly attributed to an anti-intellectual bent, or a reaction against science, which asserts itself periodically in favor of humanism or the art of psychoanalysis, under the presumption that the two approaches are incompatible. A discussant who had previously leaned toward self and object psychology rather than structural theory stated that taken together these considerations I am proposing "humanize the ego."

Affective conflict leads to intellectual blurring. Intellect is confused with intellectualization as a defense. A fear of reification has led to an inhibition to following through to its ultimate explanatory value Freud's immensely useful division of the psychic apparatus into structural systems. If one fails to keep in mind their metaphoric nature and their conceptual base as clusters of functions, there is an ensuing confusion over the spurious question of homunculus. The system ego is confused with and fails to be differentiated from a shrunken-down but total "little man." Such a diminutive but reduced clone would still need division into structural systems. The ego, as the agent of responsibility, is not a smaller version of the total organism but the psychic executive system acting on the part of the organism as a whole.

Paradoxically, while it appears that I am presenting my ideas as new, these contributions are actually new-old, having been described more than 35 years ago. The ideas I am here developing are in continuity with and in the spirit of Freud, Anna Freud (1936), Hartmann (1939a, 1950a), Rapaport (1951a,b 1953a, 1958, 1960), Fenichel (1945), Jacobson (1964),

Spitz (1959), and Mahler (1968). A theory of action, considered by Hartmann (1947) to be absent from psychoanalytic theory, was initiated by the decision-making function of the ego within the structural view before Schafer (1976) felt it necessary to discard the structural view to bring this about. And intention and purpose had been similarly introduced into metapsychology years before G. Klein (1973) introduced his "clinical theory" to encompass these psychic activities.

Claiming that self psychology made room for these functions which had not existed in psychoanalysis before, Kohut, inexplicably, as late as 1977, wrote, "I could find no place [in traditional psychoanalytic theory] for the psychological activities that go by the name of choice, decision, and free will—even though I knew that these were empirically observable phenomena" (p. 244). These views are ahistorical and incomplete. Meissner (1986) similarly fails to take these previous contributions into account in agreeing with the need for a self psychology, joining Schafer at the same time, to institute a self-as-agent. The ego-as-agent and how this fits in with the center of structural theory are overlooked and again unacknowledged.

But strangely, the recognition of these inescapable phenomena, observable at will, and demanding to be encompassed within psychoanalytic theory, met resistance or inhibition in mainstream psychoanalysis as well as in the writings of Kohut, Schafer, and others. What Gray (1982) pointed out as a developmental lag, referring to the failure to include ego defenses into technique for a long period of time, proved to be a developmental block with regard to formulating a theory of ego decision and action. These subjects have been included in psychoanalysis for over a quarter of a century without having been sufficiently acknowledged or utilized operationally.

This empirical observation has been made in recent writings by other psychoanalytic contributors, such as Weiss et al., (1986) in San Francisco, and A. Kris (1977, 1984) in Boston. Weiss and Sampson, working from a long-term experimental approach to the psychoanalytic process, from which they come to focus on secondary process ego operations in the unconscious, and A. Kris, arriving at a concept of divergent or either/or conflicts from free associations and the therapeutic process, note the confluence of their theoretical formulations to the conclusions I am here reporting. Meeting a reception themselves of unexpected controversy and resistance, in societal discussions and editorial attitudes, these authors comment on the long existence of the theoretical advances made in these papers, without their having been adequately received or absorbed, either at the time of the various original presentations, or in subsequent psychoanalytic discourse and writings.

Such a block is not haphazard, but also has motivational, psychological meanings. One of Freud's remarkable achievements was to be able to observe and recognize resistances as data. In this instance, in addition to the general reaction away from scientism and intellectuality, a nidus of resistance is pointed out to be against an increase of responsibility. Whereas the earliest psychoanalytic insights wounded man's narcissism, in that man was shown to have less control over his actions than he knew, with the present additions the opposite is the case; i.e., with the introduction of unconscious choice and decision, man chooses and acts with more purpose and intention than he knows.

Responsibility, rather than being less, may paradoxically actually become greater than conventionally thought. The developmental block pointed to within as well as outside of psychoanalysis is now due to resistance against increased responsibility rather than decreased control. While the two concepts seem to be in contradiction, both dynamics coexist, as often turns out to be the case with seeming dualities in psychoanalysis. Legal and moral issues which follow become more, not less, complex. Of major interest and concern to humankind, this subject requires more definitive study and understanding in psychoanalysis as well. Such a formulation does not make for popularity or easy acceptance, but it is to be hoped that it will be proven and will endure from clinical validation throughout the analytic world. The issues to be further studied and made clearer, in which some of the dilemmas to these questions reside, have to do with the ratio or degree of automaticity versus control, of activity versus passivity, in opening up "the sluices to motility and action" (Rapaport, 1953b).

In this opening chapter, an overview will be given first, to present to the reader a map of the field to be studied. Individual sections can then be read with a better perspective in relation to the whole. The progression of papers in the successive chapters is not chronological but logical, tracing the origins and development of the concept of the unconscious intrapsychic human core and its derivatives. The sequence follows the evolution of the idea, its beginnings, modifications, and applications, the observations which led to it, the refinements of its understanding, and the insights to which it leads in return.

To give a brief overall perspective, the volumes of this book are composed of six sections. The first section of papers consists of the origins and development of the concept of a psychic core and of an ongoing unconscious intrapsychic process. The second develops the functioning of this core further, in the etiological sequence of anxiety, conflict, psychic trauma, and the steps leading to final psychic outcome, normal or pathological. The third, the final section of the first volume, describes an extension of Hartmann's ego autonomy into the unconscious decision-making function of the ego. Related to this are papers on integrity and will.

The fourth section, which begins volume 2, follows this core concept into psychoanalysis itself and the psychoanalytic method. The papers in this section deal with the description of the core of psychoanalysis and the psychoanalytic process, particularly as distinguished from other forms of psychotherapy and psychiatry. The fifth describes the vicissitudes and changes in the functioning of this core process in psychoanalytic therapy. The sixth and last section follows the role of this intrapsychic core process in shaping group relations, from diadic to the largest social groups.

The courses and succession of these papers to a degree trace my personal and professional developmental history. Since this happened to overlap with the scientific interests of the American and International Psychoanalytic Associations during the period of theses writings, a serendipitous contribution of these papers can be that they chronicle the scientific life of both associations during these years. Many of these papers were delivered to the panels of these Associations from the 1950s to the 1980s. Others were presidential addresses and honorary lectures of various institutes throughout the psychoanalytic world during this period.

As I reflect retrospectively over this collection of work, I am moved to comment that what I am presenting as suggested advances in psychoanalytic theory probes not only into areas of ambiguity but of seeming incompatibility.

Psychoanalysis deals with ambiguity, but we hope it does so clearly. Fenichel (1941b) stated that "the subject-matter not the method of psychoanalysis is irrational" (p. 13). Our goal is to apply rationality to the ambiguous, although it is also, as Loewald (1978) says, the reverse, to see and permit the life of the irrational in the rational. This leaves room for creativity and uncertainty in the promulgation of human affairs.

SUMMARY

THE INTRAPSYCHIC PROCESS

I will now recapitulate in skeletal outline the linear sequence of what I call "the intrapsychic process." The following sequential series can be said to take place in a model psychodynamic process operative moment by moment in everyday life.

1. On a baseline of quietude, homeostasis, and inactive behavior, the ego permits a tentative experimental discharge of an instinctual impulse, to sample the reactions of the superego and external world.

2. There is an automatic scanning by the ego of memories associatively connected with such intended action.

3. Based on this intrapsychic scanning of previous associated experiences, the ego receives a signal of safety, and freedom from anxiety, or danger, accompanied by the affect of anxiety.

4. If a safety signal is received, there is little or no conflict (I include "little" because experience has shown that there always needs to be a certain amount of vigilance), and channels are open to the ego for further development of direct external activities in thought, affect, or action. (External here includes not only the outer world but all that is external to the ego, i.e., in the body or mind, somatic or mental, on the surface or within the psychic interior.)

5. If the signal received is that of anxiety, the ego is confronted with the presence of conflict. I have called this the first tentative or experimental phase of intrapsychic conflict, from an intention and a small experimental dose of instinctual discharge. The experimental conflict ensuing at this stage is a dilemma or choice type of conflict. The ego must now decide what to do next, in terms of id versus superego or environmental demands.

6. If the anxiety is mild and encompassable, one choice can be to proceed as in the actions following the safety signal in 4 above. The small amount of controllable anxiety can in such case be bound and dealt with.

7. Anxiety of sufficient degree or of certain specific qualities leads to the decision to instigate defense. The employment of defense introduces what I have called the second phase of intrapsychic conflict. This is the more conventionally known oppositional conflict between ego and id.

8. There may now ensue a state of poised intrapsychic stability, with psychic forces deployed between ego and id in a state of sufficient balance and control.

9. If instinctual pressures continue or are too great, stability may not ensue but a state of increasing psychic tension. The id is stronger than the ego's capacity to contain it.

10. This state of increasing tension is associated with mounting anxiety, based on a fear of traumatic helplessness. The last two phases are the phenomenological occurrences or equivalents of Freud's original description of "actual neurosis." The anxiety is now *following* the attempts at repression (or other defense), after having previously caused these.

11. Following these phases, which is the segment always meant by conflict proper, the ego is now again confronted with a choice or dilemma type of conflict. This is the third stage of intrapsychic conflict, the need at this point to seek a resolution of the continuing unstable state.

12. The great variety of results which can now eventuate comprise the clinical phenomenology of psychopathology, i.e., "inhibitions, symptoms, and anxiety." (This was the original title of Freud's important treatise on anxiety, which was later changed to "the problem of anxiety." I believe that the first title had much to recommend it.) Symptoms, incidentally, include psychological and somatic, as well as combinations of the two.

Intrapsychic conflicts are seen to have progressed from choice to oppositional to choice or dilemma types again, and the psychic outcomes to include choices and compromise formations at various stages. Psychopathology, including typically the psychoneuroses, occur from the middle stages onward, from the time of failing defenses (phase 9 above), to the institution of neurotic symptomatology to stem the tide and produce stability again, however precarious this may turn out to be. Before that point in the sequential chain, anxiety, choice, and defense occur universally in normal operational intrapsychic dynamics. These involve conflict-free and conflictful situations in normal mentation. Neurotic conflict and pathological solutions enter the picture with the insufficiency of defenses and their incipient or threatened breakdown.

CHAPTER 2

The Analysis of a Doll Phobia

I

From the complex fabric of a case, only material relevant to the patient's phobia for dolls will be extracted. This too will, of necessity, be much condensed, and only the main streams indicated. The phobic symptom was greatly overdetermined, which accounted for its tenacity and long duration. The doll can be pictured as the hub of a wheel. From the hub there radiate outward numerous spokes, each representing an origin, a motive, a cause, or a historical determinant feeding into the hub doll. The various spokes also have interconnecting links, in irregular fashion, joining the various parts together into a network.

The phobia had existed for as long as the patient could remember, at least from his fifth year. What finally brought him into analysis at the age of 38 was an article in *Life* magazine to the effect that the age for analysis was up to 40. The patient, who had considered treatment on and off for many years, was

Awarded the Clinical Essay Prize of the British Institute of Psychoanalysis for 1951. Published in *Internat. J. Psycho-Anal.*, 33:43–53, 1952.

31

finally confronted with a deadline. At 38, figuring a few years for the analysis, he could just make it. This turned out, as could be predicted, to be a deep-rooted character trait of his.

It was interesting, through the eyes of a man who feared them, to discover how ubiquitous dolls are in our culture. When one chooses an object for a phobia, he in a sense becomes married to the object. In order to avoid it, his eyes seek it out. He finds it in obscure places, he sees it with his peripheral vision. The patient was afraid of any kind of three-dimensional figure, of dolls with which children play, of manikins, of window dummies used for display purposes, of puppets, of pieces of sculpture, of various *objets d'art* in the form of figurines. An ashtray or a lamp base might be carved as a figure, a bar of soap might be fashioned in the form of a little animal. Any such object was a threat, was his enemy, and provoked anxiety.

Gradually certain conditions or qualifying characteristics emerged which were of special importance, and which determined where in the scale of its ability to frighten a certain object stood. Some of these qualities or attributes were known to the patient from the start, while others crystallized out as the analysis progressed, so that even the symptom became clearer and more defined. Each condition had its specific dynamic meaning and history and became an integral part of the phobia to fulfill an unconscious requirement. To understand each prerequisite was to decipher a code which then acted as an accurate road sign pointing the way back to specific aspects of the infantile past.

Thus, the material of which the figure was made was important. Porcelain, plaster, china, were bad; metal, steel, tin, not so bad. Why? Because the former could break easily, were delicate, fragile, could shatter into small pieces. Metal was less likely to do this; it could dent, or bend, but not so readily break off. Something sticking out from a figure made it especially fearful. An arm or a leg outstretched, or separate little fingers, were bad, because a slight accident could break them off. The more lifelike a figure was, the worse it was; and it was particularly the moment of a figure "coming to life" or simulating movement which was the most frightening. From this standpoint rubber was bad, since it was smooth-flowing, regular, lifelike. Celluloid was very bad; it was also lifelike, and when wet it could curl and almost move. Wax figures, which could melt, or soap forms, which could actually change in shape and even disappear, could not be tolerated. A doll with a hollow inside, particularly a hollow head, was worse than a stuffed doll. For if it were shattered, there would be nothing left, just air, just a gaping hole. Maimed, broken, or melted dolls were especially frightening. Surprise was an undesirable element. If he saw what was coming, he could steel himself and meet the emergency. If he came upon a figure suddenly, he was unnerved. A window between him and a display figure was a protecting screen. To find the same figure in the open, as on the floor of a store, made him feel defenseless. To look at the doll was bad enough; to touch or be touched by it was frightening to conceive; to have it rub against his arm, even in thought, was enough to cause sweating and near panic. Human dolls were worse than animal ones; female ones worse than males; juvenile ones worse than adult; nude dolls worse than clothed ones.

Some of the recent technologically successful doll creations, such as the Baby Coo, Di-Dee-Doll (you feed it water and it wets), Betsy-Wetsy, etc., were anathema to him. Once, shortly after his marriage, while shopping with his wife in a department store, he stepped out of a elevator into the toy department, where he was suddenly confronted by what seemed to him row after row of toy models, masks, grimacing faces, moving and pointing figures, etc. He felt weak and sick, grabbed his wife's arm, and fortunately was able to make a hasty exit.

I will now give some brief pertinent background data for a general orientation, following which the various individual etiological streams or spokes will be traced longitudinally through the life history of the patient. Both parents were in their 80s, and live in an Eastern city where the patient was born.

The mother was American-born, always spoke well, was beautiful, red-headed, refined, calm, sweet; the patient was always proud of her. The father was foreign-born, spoke with a foreign accent, was always sentimental and sloppy; his eyes watered in the movies or when he swelled with pride; he was explosive, outspoken, unrefined; the patient was always ashamed of and guilty toward him. Only in recent years did the patient's opinion of his parents reverse; he then considered his mother empty, vacuous, shallow, ignorant; and his father shrewd, intelligent, and a good judge. He had a sister, 7 years his senior, the only living sibling. In addition, before the patient was born, the parents lost a little girl, aged 3, of meningitis. The mother was said never to have smiled during her pregnancy with the patient. The birth of a boy was a disappointment to her; but the father cried at the birth of his son, and announced, "All Philadelphia is mine." The mother kept him in long curls and frocks until 3 1/2 to 4. At 4 1/2 his father went bankrupt and their economic condition took a deep decline.

At the time he began analysis the patient was 38, married, and had one son aged 7. In addition to the phobia, another presenting complaint was the existence of chronic, severe, marital difficulties; they had separated four to five times, had talked of divorce; the patient had a long series of extramarital involvements. Since their marriage they lived with the patient's mother-in-law, in a house owned by the latter. This arrangement made for much friction and irritation to the patient, but in spite of his constant complaints he always found excuses for not altering the situation. The patient was personable, affable, and in appearance made a favorable impression. He spoke in a deep resonant voice which often provoked comments about its very masculine quality. He was fluent, witty, superficially aggressive, and forward. He was a statistical analyst, who worked at 'figures,' at which he was considered unusually proficient. He had always been adept with figures, was always first in mathematics at school, and had numerous systems with which to perform complicated figuring instantaneously in his head.

The patient was in his third year of analysis, with consistent

attendance except for the usual vacations, for a total of somewhat over 700 hours. The results and changes up to this point
will be given below.

II

The dynamic meanings of the phobia and the substructure
from which the symptom sprang and into which its roots
extended, gradually evolved during the course of the analysis.
Pieces of this structure were forthcoming from many different
directions, such as the content of the free associations, the
patient's daily activities, his character structure, his dreams, his
fantasies, the transference, even his motor activities on the
couch, etc.

Very early there poured out his enormous guilt and
conflict regarding masturbation, which always was his chief
form of sexual activity and gratification. Along with the phobia,
this had always been his most carefully guarded secret. Any
reference to the subject in his presence, in company or when
"out with the boys," created severe anxiety, the same as that
produced by the phobia, so that he would quickly and deftly
change the subject. One of his earliest memories was at the age
of 4, his mother and his aunt telling him to take his hands out
of his pockets. This aunt was gentle, delicate, soft-spoken,
pretty, looked "like a doll." At age 4 to 5, a very significant and
oft-repeated memory related to a glass curio cabinet which
contained their good Dresden china, fragile and breakable: his
mother would warn him, "Don't touch, it will break." At about
the same period, his father, holding the boy in his arms, would
playfully bring the patient's hand toward a bas-relief hanging
on the wall, then snap it back with "Cootchi-coo—mustn't
touch." The path for displacement was thus laid down, and the
nuclear idea for the phobia was born. "Don't touch" was
projected outward, displaced from the body to the external
world. Instead of not touching the penis, he would not touch
the china, the bas-relief, eventually the doll. The return of the
repressed is seen in the choice of object. The doll, though

inanimate, is again the human body. The doll is his penis, not to be touched.

The patient prided himself on being a stickler for authority. Particularly toward scientists and doctors: if it were prescribed that he take a medicine at 10, 2, 4, 6, he would not deviate a minute from the prescribed time, since that would nullify its effectiveness; he ascribed magical power to the dictates and advice of "big people." But this seeming obedience was a sham; he obeyed in small things strictly, in order to break the big rule brashly. "I will carry out conscientiously all your edicts, except, please, I will masturbate." The reaction-formation nature of this character trait was demonstrated by his consistent breaking of the analytic rules.

The glass protecting the Dresden china made its appearance later in its derivative, the store window between him and the display dummy.

The "it will break" half of these early warnings ushered in a very central chapter in the entire analysis, that of castration, the punishment feared for the forbidden act. The castration theme made its appearance on every front, but insight into it, and still more emotional acceptance of it and working through, was a slow, deliberate, and plodding process, beset with resistances of the strongest type. A remark was made to the patient, aged about 6, that someone, in taking a handkerchief out of his pocket, dropped a dollar bill. The patient since then, looked behind him whenever he took something out of his pocket, to make sure nothing dropped out. He could not leave anything incomplete or dangling. When, in reading, he came to the end of a sentence, or a paragraph, or a page, he must say to himself, "Period, end, finish," before going on, to make sure he left nothing out, or left no opening, or that it was all there, rounded, closed, and smooth. One of the earliest remembered instances of his present phobia occurred at age 5. Sitting in the bathtub he was playing in the water with a small celluloid toy fish, when the latter suddenly suffered a hole in it, swung around, and hissed in the water. The little boy was frightened. In recalling this, the patient first tried to pass it off as a meaningless, normal childhood fear, but soon saw its connections with his present symptom. The following events were temporally related to this incident and made its meaning clear:

1. Being told, "Don't play with fire or you will pee in bed."

2. Standing outdoors at night with his mother and father watching the huge fire of a near-by celluloid factory. He remembered the general tension and anxiety, but more specifically recalled his parents' fears, and then of course his own, that the factory might explode. These background events enabled us to translate his bathtub experience. He had not heeded the warning, he did play with fire, i.e., sexual heat and excitement (the identity of fire, heat, sexual excitement was clearly brought out in a number of dreams); the penis on fire did explode, castration did occur. The swishing fish, forerunner of the doll, was the peeing penis, detached from the boy and floating away. Note the quality celluloid, in both factory and figure. The sudden movement, the swish, and the lifelike quality reversed the process of projection. By threatening to bring the mechanical figure back to life, it stripped the symbol of its disguise, thereby provoking anxiety. Connected with this is the following dream:

I am in a bathtub. I have an erection and touch it. I show it to my wife, who wants to take a picture of it. Then my penis is detached, floating around. But I tell myself it is nothing, as this always happens.

The wife-mother saw the forbidden erection, and castration resulted. But the patient reassured himself, "It is nothing." The doll which was avoided was the detached penis, an unwelcome reminder of castration.

The presence of a strong anal component may already be suspected (reference to money above, the dollar bill, the compulsive ritual, the water, etc.). The patient looked at the toilet water compulsively to examine what flushed down. In fact, the following additional historical segment formed another sturdy base for the developing neurotic structure to lean upon. At the age of 3, the patient had a convulsion, which was diagnosed by the doctor who "saved his life" as having been due to constipation from eating too many biscuits. There was a vague memory, or perhaps he was told this later, of awakening from this convulsion on a rubber pad; he connected this rubber with the element of rubber in his phobia. To prevent a recurrence, his mother, on the doctor's advice, instituted treatment by enemas. From age 3 to 4 1/2, the patient received a daily enema from his mother. For a long time in the analysis he recalled only the discomfort and pain of this period, but then, after analysis of certain recurring anal behavior and characteristics, he remembered how, in the latency period, he had purposely "held it in" in order to induce his mother to administer an enema. He remembered and realized the pleasure of the retention, of the manipulation and attention by his mother, of the increasing tension by the water almost to the bursting point, and then the explosive expulsion. The phallic mother, the mother with the enema tip, the castrating woman, the woman who came in and took it out of him, became a dominant point of fixation in his sexual life. She became the ambivalently loved and hated object, the one most feared, and yet, by the repetition compulsion, a *sine qua non* of his sexual attainment. Anal erotism and anal threat became blended and highly developed. The possibility of real damage during this period was reinforced when one day the mother, in her haste to get the patient to the bathroom, fell and broke her ankle. The patient considered it his fault and feared retaliation. Some years later, he had a wish that his sister should be permanently crippled. A few hours later, he fell and broke his arm. He considered this a direct punishment for his hostile wish. In later years, he stubbed his toes and injured his fingers at every turn. He did it to himself, to prevent an outside person from doing it to him.

Through most of his adult years, and until analysis, the patient suffered from recurrent alternating diarrhea and constipation, and carefully correlated every vagary in his bowel habits with what he had eaten. His senior business partner, with whom he had a close and telling relationship throughout the entire analysis, a relationship which served as a barometer of what was happening to the patient, was a man with chronic ulcerative colitis. An "extra long, good bowel movement"often made the patient late, and sometimes he would "please" the analyst by giving it up at home, coming on time and doing it verbally, on the couch. Money and time were subjects of great preoccupation; they were treated as erratically, and with as much alternation in attitudes, as were his fecal contents. The connection between the two became clear to him by such associations as his concern over the "gold dust" on his shorts. He constantly argued about the fee, and about wanting time off for various reasons. He would frequently estimate what his annual income was going to be, and would "warn" the analyst of impending disaster. He was chagrined when his income doubled after the first year of analysis. He pictured the analyst as an extractor, and in this way he again enjoyed the mother with the enema tip. He counted the change in his pocket every morning and evening, and had to go over his daily transactions to the penny. Gnawing anxiety ensued when anything was missing, and he would spend hours trying to recover the error. When he added long columns of figures or money, he checked them three ways—up, down, and diagonally. Yet he threw away large chunks of analytic time by repeated lateness, and one day impulsively bought a big new convertible. There were certain daily obsessive-compulsive thoughts and actions, a habit of "getting stuck" on thoughts and being unable to let go, a tendency to procrastination, numerous perfectionistic traits, and yet a piling up and messiness on his desk.

Castration anxiety caused a regression to a previously strong point of anal fixation and regressively colored the latter. Each then confirmed and lent strength to the other. The earlier anal experiences made the later phallic castration possibilities more real, and the phallic dangers in turn revived and reinforced the earlier anal threats. The phallus, like the stool earlier, could be removed and broken off. The doll was both. In one dream the doll was associatively connected with ears of corn covered with brown gravy. In another dream, the patient was trapped in City Hall, to which he associated "shitty hall," and which he had entered by the back end. He once, in his work, had visited a window trim company, and was much afraid that in walking through the building toward the office he might suddenly come across a row of manikins lined up in some long dark hallway—the manikins=the stool; lined up in the hallway=in the rectum.

But the patient too was trapped, and he himself seemed to be equated to the doll. The connection between the patient— his own phallus, and in turn the doll—came out convincingly from many angles. On the couch he engaged in repeated automatic actions of lovingly stroking and fondling his abdomen, rubbing his hands regularly and rhythmically over the top of his head, stretching and then relaxing his entire body, and accompanying this with a rising crescendo of voice, ending in a violent yawn or sigh and then receding. While this was in part a resistance and a defiance of the analyst, there could be no mistaking its character as a masturbatory substitute and an avenue of libidinal gratification. Interpretation of this to the patient was, after some time, accepted and the behavior modified. He was using his whole body as a phallus. He would play 10 to 15 sets of tennis in a day, then come in and complain that his body was stiff, and "My head feels as if it is bloated and swelling up from within." When a pretty girl passed their office window, all the boys would stand up at attention. This equation, this interchangeability of the whole for one of its parts, also was seen in the symptom: the doll, a whole body, also stood for the penis. The patient =the doll = the penis = the stool.

The doll was a retreat into the mechanical. Reversal of this process, with the mechanical threatening to come to life again, threatened to undo this defense and provoked anxiety. The moment of its coming to life, the most feared, was also the most enjoyed; it was the beginning of the forbidden erection. The patient remembered lying on a couch and bringing about repeated erection and relaxation; it was the start of the erection which gave him the greatest pleasure. In his masturbation he employed "mechanical contrivances." The act was a production, lasting one to two hours, usually in the small hours of the morning, while the family was asleep. It took place in the bathtub (compare the "fish" episode above), where the water washed away the guilt. With a wet towel he bound himself tightly, sometimes imagining his genital to disappear. He rubbed soap bubbles around his anus (mother's soapsuds enema), and with a rubber hose played a stream of water around his anus or anteriorly. All this was accompanied by looking at pornographic picture books which he carefully bought and prepared; plus the accompaniment of vivid detailed fantasies.

These fantasies, taken together, were in significance like a crucial repetitive dream; they were condensed, symbolic, and revealed which pregenital and partial impulses were receiving expression. The recurring and fairly constant features were these: The patient was picked up and taken in tow by a dominant, aggressive woman, "The Queen," or "Her Highness," who then seductively exhibited herself to him. Variable forms of domination were practiced on the patient; sometimes he was bound, or blindfolded, or beaten with a whip. His clothes might then be cut off, and he was usually dressed up as a female. The leading lady, or else some of her assistants, then demonstrated to the patient how to seduce a man; oral practices were employed; the patient was supposed to follow suit. Finally fellatio and cunnilingus were performed on each other between the patient and the woman.

The oedipal character of his phallic strivings was evident. The women he chose, in reality as well as in pictures, were all red-heads. One of his favorite burlesque queens had a name very akin to his mother's. He recalled an early memory of being held in his mother's arms; she had a black lacy veil over her face and smelled of perfume. The patient now would sometimes wear his mother-in-law's black silk panties as a prelude to masturbation. His mother-in-law, from whose roof he could not move away despite his protestations, occupied a prominent position in his sexual fantasies. He married a second cousin. Many of his fantasies, and a number of his "affairs," were within the family. An early sexual fantasy was of a woman completely covered with a tight black garment, with only the genitals and nipple areas exposed. He was strongly impressed and early stimulated sexually by the story of Circe who turned Ulysses' companions into pigs—or by a fairy with a wand who could do magical things. She could make inanimate things come alive, and turn people into inanimate things (= mother with the enema tip, who could make his erection come to life, but could also turn his penis or stool into a doll; desired and exciting, yet feared and threatening at the same time).

A doll was something which was looked at as well as played with; behind the display window it was an object of exhibition. As such it played a part in connection with the patient's strong scoptophilic impulses. Looking at the lewd pictures comprised a prominent part of the masturbatory foreplay. These pictures were carried in a "dummy" folder, i.e., one which presumably contained his work papers. He treated it as "hot cargo, " as evidence for a crime; he felt anxiety in driving past a policeman when this folder was in the car. What if he should die and this be found among his possessions? His scoptophilic impulses were served in his daily routine; he had arranged his desk near a window where he watched women's legs pass by; he created elaborate fantasies concerning certain "regulars" in this passing parade, who subsequently found a way into his masturbatory fantasies as well. This office arrangement ceased during the analysis, cutting down his work day by several hours. (Note his position behind the window, in the place of the usual manikin. The latter was feared because she was looking back.)

When finished with a picture, he sometimes threw it down the toilet. Here it might curl when wet and begin to assume a three-dimensional look, provoking great anxiety in the patient. Thus up to a point, an object satisfied his impulses, i.e., as long as it was two-dimensional. Beyond that point, i.e., when depth was added, the same object became phobic. Among the visual pictures which early attracted him sexually and with which he masturbated were cut-out paper dolls, which his sister, and later he himself, made and played with. Sometimes these too would wave and become lifelike, and would then frighten him. These were a transition between impulse satisfaction and phobia. This connection, that the feared object was at another level desired, was understood in the reverse direction by the patient when, during the course of the analysis, in looking at a manikin one day from afar, he developed an erection.

His voyeurism was an attempt to deny castration. He remembered how once he saw his mother bending over after she had finished on the toilet, and that afterwards he told his grandfather that mother had hair around her behind. The pubic hair was displaced posteriorly, a falsification designed to maintain the illusion that in front there was still something, or that it was hidden under the hair. The patient spoke with warmth and affection of an aunt who, when scolded by his mother for appearing nude in front of the patient, replied casually, "Oh, it's nothing. All bodies are the same. It's all just skin." The patient repeated this statement with pride and as authority a number of times. When one day the analyst remarked, "But it isn't true," the patient reacted with sincere surprise, and realized how he had never wanted to question the accuracy of this statement.

He looked but he did not allow himself to see. With cunnilingus, in fact and in fantasy, he stopped short of seeing. He was ignorant of the anatomy of the vulva, and had the idea, even into analysis, that the clitoris was large and was inside, somewhere near the cervix. If there was no penis sticking out, there was still one inside. The analyst remarked how odd it was that the patient, who was a scholarly type and who, being related to doctors, had medical books available, had never looked at a picture in these books to satisfy his unanswered questions. He reacted with astonishment. "My God. I would move heaven and earth to find a misplaced comma, but would never lift a finger to find out where the clitoris was." He recalled as a boy, lying on the ground under a woman's skirt, how he had shut his eyes. He had always told himself that this was because he "was a gentleman," as compared with his friends. He had almost a fetishlike attitude toward a black silk stocking and a high heel, which was almost equated to woman for him. He would speak of seeing "a beautiful silk-stockinged leg with a high heel" walking down the street. He displaced downward (as well as in other connections upward); woman was not a castrated being; the high heel was a penis, mechanical again; and under the stocking on the thigh could be hidden a penis. In his sexual fantasies a woman would put her high heel in his face. One day the sudden sight of a man's completely bald head frightened him; it was like the "sheer nudity" which he most feared in the doll. Here was the perineum, from front to back, unequivocally exposed, and it was smooth; nothing was sticking out. His eyes were strongly libidinized. On the couch, he rubbed them constantly, with a regular rhythmical, almost ticlike pattern, which had an automatic and irresistible quality to it. Often the itching of his eyes alternated with itching of the testicles.

The doll was his mother, it was woman, it was the being without a penis. Dolls had no genitals. Female dolls scared him worse than male ones. Hollow dolls were empty, were holes. When a doll was shattered, it was air, it was nothing, it was castrated; it was the female genital. He could not contemplate seeing it; clothing on the doll made it easier.

Exhibitionistic tendencies, the counterpart of his scoptophilia, were also active, and were demonstrable in his general behavior, his Don Juan attitude toward women, his manner of speaking, his aggressive superiority toward his colleagues, and often a haughty and self-satisfied manner in the analysis. As a corollary to his avoidance of anything associatively connected with castration, there existed, and for the same reason, his need to exhibit in a positive way his still present and undamaged phallus. This too was achieved, characteristically, by displacement, and by the use of his entire body and performance as a substitute for the genital.

In addition to the role played by the doll in the service of autosexuality, and heterosexuality, it also served a function to the patient in relation to a strong unresolved homosexual conflict. The latter had been able to emerge into consciousness only recently, having previously been kept rigidly repressed, and any allusions to the subject attended with severe anxiety. A brief and transitory reference to his homosexual impulses occurred early in the analysis in conjunction with a dream in which he was chased by a number of men and turned and threw milk into their faces. His associating milk to semen provoked denial and fear on his part, following which the subject disappeared for a long time. Only in recent months, following analysis of his ambivalent relationship to his phallic mother, and in conjunction with a strong positive father transference, did his homosexual impulses and his deep attachment to his sentimental father come into their full light and were faced. From the age of 6 to 11, following economic reverses which forced them to move into a smaller apartment, the patient slept with his father, the latter hugging him close from behind. The patient remembered first his shame and guilt regarding this, his reluctance to admit it to his friends, and finally the pleasure he obtained from it. During late latency and early adolescence, there was mutual masturbation and "touching penises" with the boys. Much of his present-day behavior became understandable with the liberation of this phase of his repressed sexuality, which was still taking place and being worked through; such as his proclivity for working late with the boys, his long tennis sessions, his relation to his senior partner, his interest in stag parties, burlesque, etc. Many of his "heterosexual" interests and exploits were thinly veiled reactive defenses against homosexual impulses. In his sexual fantasies he fought, against obvious pressure, to prevent the appearance of homosexual object choices, which finally did break through on a few occasions. He was afraid that if he allowed them in fantasy, they might also occur in fact, as happened with cunnilingus and other fantasies. Other items belonging in this context were: his strong feminine identification, transvestite tendencies in masturbation and fantasies, oral receptive inclinations, anal erotic practices, and his passive masochistic impulses.

Just as his relationship to the phallic mother was a blend of desire and threat, so too was it in his relation with his father.

The feared castrator, heretofore the mother, was now brought out to be the father, in a dream in which the patient "is playing in a deep valley. A giant, with whiskers like the father's, comes threateningly down, chopping trees as he comes."

The patient's position, rooted in anal ambivalence, poised between heterosexuality and homosexuality, between active desires for his mother and passive desires for his father (and aggressive mother), and with corresponding inhibitions and fears in both directions, was expressed in the following dream (the detailed associations cannot be gone into):

My son has a .22 rifle which he is shooting at his mother. It is just a game. I have a 30–30 rifle, am behind him, and am also going to shoot at her. She wants it, but I think the shock will be too great. I go to the back door. A man is behind the glass door, and he scares me. I shoot at him. Is he friend or foe? I shouldn't have shot so quickly. But the bullet bounces off the glass and floats lazily away. I want to hit the man with the gun. I awake screaming with fear.

Here the doll behind the glass was a man, the homosexually desired father. The doll was not only his own penis, it also was another man's penis, his father's penis, the penis homosexually desired and therefore feared.

Connected with this was the fact that girls, not boys, played with dolls. His interest in the phobic object betrayed, and his avoidance of the doll denied, his passive feminine orientation. "Why can I not stand to see a little girl's doll melt away?" he once asked. Because the little girl's fantasied penis must remain intact. In this connection we recall the sister who died before the patient was born and whom he replaced. She was always said to have looked "like a little wax doll." If she had lived, said the doctor, she would have been damaged. The patient heard this repeatedly during his early years. The possibility of damage, of castration, even of death, existed then on a "real" base. The patient was living in her stead; the same could happen to him; he too could become inanimate, dead, a wax doll, and melt away (his convulsions, age 3). Or he could live and be, like her, feminine, damaged, castrated. His mother furthered this by keeping him in curls and dresses until 4 years.

To recapitulate, this section described the following main etiological spokes feeding into the central doll at the hub of the wheel: the doll represents, in turn and simultaneously, the patient's own penis, his stool, he himself *in toto*, his mother, woman in general, the female genital, another man's (father's) penis, the sister who died, the little girl's fantasied penis. There are other smaller secondary spokes; and all the spokes interconnect.

III

It is necessary to reaffirm at this time that the preceding material and content did not flow forth in an uninterrupted stream; rather, the sequence and rate were determined by the specific resistances and defenses and how they were dissolved. It is interesting in this connection to note that Freud in his *Studies on Hysteria* (1893–95) used an analogy very similar to the main structural analogy of the wheel used in this presentation. Regarding the pathogenic material as stratified in layers of different resistance potential, with the pathogenic nucleus at the core, Freud states that "the analyst should himself undertake the opening of the inner strata and the advancement in the radial direction, while the patient should take care of the peripheral extension."

While the phobic symptom, the high degree of symbolic representation, the hypersexualization of all activity and the phallic exhibitionism all point to a predominantly hysterical level, the analysis was nevertheless in most respects the analysis of a compulsive character. In line with this, the chief defenses were isolation and related mechanisms. The pathogenic early memories and infantile traumas were not long in being remembered, but they were stripped of emotional import, and their intimate connections with the main streams of symptom and character formation were obscured and denied for long periods of time. The patient intellectualized and rationalized freely; he "knew" things and adopted them readily, but they applied chiefly to others, or to himself in theory only, not to be seriously entertained or to be really translated into action. Thinking itself was highly libidinized, and his new-found insights were at first used exhibitionistically and aggressively both in the analysis and in his daily life. He translated into slogans, which on the one hand expressed the point but on the other kept him from getting too close to it. Thus, though he went with a procession of women, his behavior with them led him to see that "I am not an intercourser," a phrase which he then wore out until it lost its meaning. He defended by flippancy, by playing games: "the oedipus edifice which stands in my way," or, with reference to the body = phallus material which had been under discussion for some time, he once said, "If anyone else ever called me a prick as often as you do, I'd get mad."

Other defenses employed by him in his character make-up, as in his analysis, were reaction formation, displacement, and acting out. Even his deep and masculine voice was studied and cultivated; during moments of emotional excitement he would feel that his voice became high-pitched and shrill, which to him was feminine, Jewish, castrated. During one phase of the analysis, much of the libidinal energy was diffused out in rhythmical, automatic, muscular activities on the couch. When this was analyzed and worked through, and its substitute character appreciated, it was followed by a more detailed verbalization of the vivid sexual fantasy life. Many of his resistances were intended for impulse gratification as well. He "did" his analysis as he treated his impulses. The flow of material was alternately profuse and begrudging, in line with his bowel habits. At times it flooded the analysis, with a torrent of dreams, associations, and recollections; and at other times it was almost completely blocked, by lateness, a few missed hours, or by stretching and yawning on the couch. The significant material tended to be obscured in a flood of detail. In his masturbation, he liked to go "past the optimum point," i.e., beyond the point when he should have had orgasm, then recede, then come up again, and so on many times. He attempted to make the same use of analytic insight and interpretations, i.e., accumulate them "past the optimum point," beyond the point where they should have been effective, then let them recede into the background, and then he would be ready for more. This tendency to convert every activity and procedure into an instrument for pregenital impulse satisfaction was a maneuver which had to be attacked repeatedly to further the analytic work.

Just as a perversion, during the course of analytic therapy, is often first converted into a neurosis, so this patient's neurosis, during the course of therapy, took a temporary turn in the direction of perversion. That is, when, as a result of the analytic process, the strength of his punitive superego was diminished, the repressed polymorphous perverse impulses were able to come forth stronger and more openly. The patient repeatedly expressed the hope to be able to get rid of the phobia but to keep his "delicious" masturbation. The quest for satisfaction was seen too in the resistance of seeking transference gratification instead of insight.

The transference had a multiple character, varied in its manifestations, and served both to further insight and to defend against it. It was, as previously described, alternately a mother and a father transference, with ambivalent negative and positive aspects to each. Much of the advancement in the radial direction was achieved by analysis of the vicissitudes of the labile transference relationship. The analyst was reacted to mainly as the phallic mother or the sentimental father. One phase of the transference was a type of cross-identification, where the analyst became the patient and the patient became his own father. Thus, when the patient felt that the analyst was making a particularly poignant or discerning remark or interpretation, his eyes would moisten with pride instead of his absorbing what was being said. He became his father, beaming at his son.

The patient's present status was as follows: The bowel

symptoms cleared up very early, his ritualistic obsessive-compulsive behavior and symptoms were greatly modified. His work habits, interpersonal relationships, and use of his time showed considerable change in the direction of improvement. His marriage was on the road to being solidified. However, genital sexuality was not yet achieved. While the old neurotic defenses and solutions were altered, pregenitality still predominated in many respects, and progression forward, through an adequate oedipal solution, to genital attainment remained incomplete.

References to the status of the phobia were indirect, but for months all indications pointed to the fact that the substructure crumbled and that in large part it was the memory of the phobia which remained. Again and again the patient would allude to what should have been a phobic situation, and would "confess" to the absence or only minimal presence of anxiety or fear. But he hastened to find an excuse. There was not enough of a surprise element, or the material of this particular doll was not bad enough, or maybe this one never would have frightened him, etc. He was, in actuality, being conservative, and was only gradually feeling his way into the new world of figures. Once he went with his wife into a fur salon to buy her a fur coat (also a manifestation of the analysis); the only empty seat left for him was one immediately next to and under a manikin standing on the floor. He sat down. But, to me he said, "Don't take any credit. It was the only seat I could find." His mother-in-law had a sewing dummy hanging in her closet. When nobody was looking, the patient went in and stroked it in the dark closet. His wife saved the bride-and-groom figures from their wedding cake, and recently put them under a glass top in their bedroom; the patient tested himself, touched them, passed the test. At a bar, a prankster bartender bent down and came up suddenly with an artificial rubber hand attached over his own, and shook the patient's hand with it. This had all the worst elements in it; the patient was able to laugh it off. He visited homes with little girls in them, and allowed himself to be exposed with impunity to their dolls. He recently visited the

County Museum. There was a statue of Charles Chaplin, with hands outstretched, and a finger broken off. The patient shook hands with him. There were numerous other such incidents. Last Hallowe'en, hideous-looking rubber face masks appeared in every drug and toy store. The patient expected nightmares of trouble; instead he went through the season quite indifferent.

Phobic patients characteristically are reluctant to put to the test the results of their therapeutic labor, after having long been conditioned to the relationship between phobic object and the outbreak of anxiety. This is especially true where the phobia existed as in this patient, for virtually a lifetime. Years of such incrustation could not be shaken off lightly. The patient still was in the process of working through his liberation from the phobic object.

As a final addition, the following bit of clinical data will be offered as pertinent to and an interesting variation of the case under discussion. It has in common with my patient a use of the same object, but for quite different psychic purposes. The same qualities which make the doll suitable to my patient for phobic avoidance serve in this next example to qualify it as a means of sublimation. A well-known puppeteer made his living and also satisfied deep inner psychic needs by dolls and puppets. This man was an overt homosexual. The puppet represented his narcissistically highly overvalued penis. His entire life was devoted to making them, dressing them, playing with them, and exhibiting them. He lived in a room next to his prized and successful collection. He could make them male or female, at will; he was enraptured by them. After a performance, the audience was invited backstage to admire them, at which time this man sat on a chair nervously biting his nails, a study in mixed feelings. In him mingled great pride and satisfaction plus gnawing anxiety lest someone cause the slightest damage to his prized possessions.

The doll in both these cases was the concentrate of strong feelings and values emanating from the person's unconscious. In the one case, equilibrium was maintained by shunning this concentrated symbol; in the other, he was able to embrace and enjoy it.

A search of the literature failed to reveal any reports of a similar doll or related phobia. However, very relevant to this discussion is the material relating to the doll Olympia, in Hoffmann's story "The Sand Man," which reappears again in Offenbach's opera *Tales of Hoffmann* and which is described by Freud (1919b) in his paper "The Uncanny." The following features of the story and Freud's interpretation of it form a bridge to this case: The student Nathaniel is identified with the doll Olympia, whom he loves, and who represents his own feminine counterpart; his love for her is thus a narcissistic one. Nathaniel's father is ambivalently loved and feared; he is the potential castrator. The uncanny effect is considered to be due primarily to the dread of castration. The attention is shifted chiefly to the eyes, to which are displaced the genital interests and fears. The Sand Man removes the eyes of bad little children. The father is in part a mechanic; much of the emotional tone of the story is created by the intellectual uncertainty as to whether the doll is alive or not, whether the inanimate has become animate. The father dies in a chemical explosion. The many similarities with my patient's relation to dolls occur at once. The conflicts within Nathaniel, however, lead not to phobia, but to madness.

POSTSCRIPT

It would be of interest to add a brief note to describe the final course and termination of the analysis. This took place in roughly another year of treatment, at a slightly diminished intensity and frequency. The final work consisted not so much in the discovery or elucidation of new psychodynamic insights, of new spokes in the already complex wheel of causality, but rather in the digestion and working through of those which had already been uncovered, and the addition and delineation of the interconnecting links between the spokes, in a circular rather than in a radial direction.

Thus, as an example, the patient associated one day to the fact that Raggedy Andy dolls were not as bad to him as were stiff ones. He had awakened that morning with a "stiff erection"; he realized then again, as though for the first time and with sudden conviction, that the doll was equated to an erection. We had been talking for days about the constant and energetic stretching, stiffening, and then relaxing of his body which went on during the analytic hours. So the doll, the erection, was his whole body as well. He loved it, he rubbed and fondled it, he was narcissistically attached to it. Why was it endangered, why did he have to concentrate so on preserving it? A veritable orgy of current masturbatory fantasies and actions provided the links and the answers, for they emphasized and brought out into clear focus the strong tendencies to feminine identification. In these fantasies, the patient would be transformed into and dressed as a woman, and would then be forced into oral practices on both men and women. It was the strength of these bisexual impulses which made it so necessary to guard the integrity of the erect phallus, to prevent it from becoming hollow, as the inside of the doll. The homosexual object choice was narcissistically determined, and was a projection of the self. Thus did the movement proceed, with the ego wending its way in irregular circular fashion along the intercommunicating paths from one radial grouping to another, from phallus to body, to woman, to female genital, to homosexual object, back and forth and in all directions. Just as each lent support to the other, so did insight into one lead to a diffusion of the process of understanding into the other, thus facilitating the working through and eventual dissolution of all the various etiological spokes.

During this final phase, every reference to and contact with dolls were notoriously without anxiety or phobic reaction, so that by the end he had a number of times picked up and handled the previously phobic object with impunity. On one occasion he picked up a rubber figure quite casually and squeezed it so that is whistled and its tongue came out. Parallel to this development in the realm of the symptom, there was a steady and impressive progress in the underlying character structure toward increased solidity and maturity, showing itself clearly in his marriage, his work, and in his general life.

However, the final complete extrusion from the ego of even the outlines of the ego-alien phobic structure, as well as the process of termination of the analysis itself, was colored again by the remnants of all his well-known pregenital impulses and defense mechanisms, as though they were making a last stand. He "hung on" orally as long as he could, retaining the memory and threat of symptoms, trying "to get as much as he could" and to "suck the treatment dry." He compared himself in the last months with a drug addict being taken off the drug. New oral material emerged. His mother, mourning over her lost daughter when the patient was born, had been unable to give him the breast, and instead fed him by bottle. This, he observed, was the first "mechanical contrivance," the first substitute of the inanimate for the animate. Further dietary restrictions came about a few years later following the "constipation and convulsions." His anal desires to retain were also again at work, causing a prolongation of transference gratification and a resistance to its removal. Just as he had to tear up and destroy an envelope or piece of paper into many small pieces before discarding it, to make sure that he did not miss anything, so he clung to the analyst, and had to wring him out before letting go. And finally it was again castration fear which motivated his last grip on the symptoms and the analyst, for to let even them go would mean a revival of the sense of loss, a feeling of having dropped something, or of something having been torn away.

The final resolution, following the analysis of these lingering pregenital influences, came with the working through and solution of the oedipal conflict. This took place both on the levels of the transference and in his relationship with his senior partner, with primarily an identification with the father figure and the patient's rising to a new role of maturity. His final liberation from castration fear was emphasized in the following dream, which occurred in the last week of analysis:

I am driving a big long truck, with a supply of long steel bars sticking way out in the back. One short bar falls off—but I keep on going and don't care in the least. My father is with me and he seems to be worried about it—but I am not worried and I have a "So what?" feeling.

Indicative of his changed attitude and his new focus of attention was the following bit of material brought out in the last few days of treatment. In associating to the item of "circles" which had appeared in a dream, the patient commented that the circle was the perfect symbol of completeness, as exemplified in a wedding ring. But, he was reminded, this very symbol had until now been to him the perfect symbol of incompleteness, representing as it did the vagina, anus, or mouth, from which something, the penis or stool or breast, like the steel bar in the dream above, had been forcibly removed. But now his gaze had shifted from the opening in the circle to the periphery, the closed line. His point of view had changed, literally. And similarly the doll to him was now not the hollow inside but rather the complete and intact and therefore safe skin covering and body wall.

CHAPTER 3

Psychoanalysis, Affects, and the "Human Core"

I

In casting about for a central focus on the occasion of this fourth Franz Alexander Lecture, I found my interest coming back repeatedly to the unlikely sounding concept of the "human core " as this appears to the psychoanalyst. Since this has been a central interest of philosophers and other commentators on the human condition from the beginning of time, and since even in modern times it represents one of the two polar extremes which challenge man's intellect—that is, outer space and the inner core of the human mind—I must at once make powerful disclaimers. Not only am I naturally limiting myself to how this subject of perennial interest looks to the psychoanalyst, but even in this latter category I hasten to add that I am not aspiring to a statement that can claim any metapsychological

Delivered as the Fourth Franz Alexander Lecture of the Chicago Institute for Psychoanalysis, January 31, 1964. Published in *Psychoanal. Quart.*, 36:172–202, 1967.

comprehensiveness or scientific purity. I have selected only a few aspects of the subject which strike me as being of particular relevance.

By way of explanation and orientation, my interest in the 'core' stems from a recent period which I spent at what might be looked upon more as the periphery. I am referring to a year I spent (1962–1963) at the Center for Advanced Study in the Behavioral Sciences at Palo Alto, where, in contrast to the psychoanalyst, my co-workers and co-thinkers were largely those who study the external aspects of human behavior, its products, and their effects en masse. Fittingly enough to this occasion and to the person whom this lecture honors, Dr. Franz Alexander was the first representative of psychoanalysis at this Center of intellectual activity during the first year of its operation, from 1954 to 1955.

While before my year in this milieu my awareness of the enormous influence exerted by psychoanalysis on all of the intellectual disciplines had been general and impressionistic, I was able during the unusual experience of that year to savor more intimately its role, either actually or potentially, in sociology, history and philosophy, in law and political science, in anthropology, linguistics, art and biography, in English and comparative literature, and its relationships even to economics, mathematics, and autonomics. While the direct experience of such a panoramic view can lead almost to a sense of exhilaration, it also produces a sober humility and a distinct feeling of probing responsibility.

The mere contemplation of such activity on the part of an analyst divides my colleagues into two camps. On the one hand, in spite of a distinct shift in recent years, there are still those who view such "shoulder rubbing" with other disciplines with visible stiffness, if no longer with dismay, while on the other hand there are many who look toward such cooperative efforts for an immediate practical as well as theoretical panacea-providing amalgam. These opposing views are to me like the descriptions which one hears about a half glass of water. Some will describe it as half empty, while others as half full. Both are right. To me there was throughout the year a sense of excitement and satisfaction, of broad vistas, and an awareness of possibilities as well as challenges, but also a conviction of an unswerving necessity to keep a footing at all times in a solidly anchored psychoanalytic position.

The question which occurred to me therefore, and one never to lose sight of, was what marks the center of the psychoanalyst's unique and exclusive contribution to the discussions of such a group. What constitutes the *sine qua non* which only an analyst can add to this total effort, without which the latter cannot be complete and which cannot be added, at least as well, by anyone else? This was a challenge, it seemed to me, of orientation, of the perspective of our field in relation to the rest. It is to a few aspects of the results of this thinking and of the answers to this question to which I would like to address myself.

At the beginning of the year some of the Fellows were introducing themselves to each other in the informal way which characterized the Center. " What is your field?" inquired one of another. "Sociology, the queen of the behavioral sciences," came the answer. "Oh, I thought mine was!" said the first, "I am a historian, actually a historical biographer. Who better studies man than we?" I restrained myself, with the inner and reassuring feeling that we in our field had something good going for us in this discussion. But I wanted to figure out first just where we do fit in.

The answer in a general way, it became apparent to me during the course of the year, is that the psychoanalyst, and only the psychoanalyst, deals with what I came to think of, if somewhat loosely, as the " human core." This is his domain, his unique field of action, his acknowledged area of expertness. It is from here, and only from here, that the psychoanalyst qualifies in a specific way to add to an understanding of any level or any aspect of human behavior.

If you would listen in, for example, to the following random conversation which took place later in the year, perhaps a typical one, it might illustrate what I am trying to convey. At lunch a small group was discussing imperialism, the causes,

motives, and intricate historical backgrounds of that aspect of
human history in which the more powerful and advanced
nations appropriate for themselves and then proceed to help
what they euphemistically call "the underdeveloped countries."
A distinguished composite group, each contributed from his
own field an impressive array of facts, displaying in intimate
knowledgeable detail the economic, political, sociological, religious, military, industrial, geographic, and commercial aspects
of the phenomenon under discussion, providing in all an illuminating and dizzily instructive bird's-eye view of a large segment
of human behavior, not often the fare of a psychoanalyst. I
knew intuitively that something big was being left out, something which indeed I stood for and with which I had some
familiarity. It took no little courage at an opportune moment to
suggest, "What about human nature?" This was received with
some surprise but with interest and respect, and the conversation veered into new dimensions.

In a certain sense, if you will, we may consider this incident
a paradigm for applied psychoanalysis. It is to add and to
explain the inner nature of man which is the analyst's *raison
d'être*. "Explanations" of human nature vary at different levels
of sophistication and expectation. Even in the incident and
under the circumstances described above, the discussion
among these behavioral scientists went on to include such
concepts as man's aggressive drives, narcissistic strivings, and
acquisitive tendencies. To the colorful uncle of a patient of
mine, an old-time Damon Runyonish vaudeville actor with a
long and less than exemplary life behind him, it was much more
simple. On learning that his young nephew was already heavily
involved in guilt-producing extramarital activity, he mused
philosophically, "Oh, well, it happens to kings and queens.
That's human nature." But, as analysts and within our own
discipline, we aim to go farther and to be more precise. The
question follows, "What is this core to which we attend, this
human core, not as it appears to the philosophers but as it
presents itself to the psychoanalyst?" This is not the same
question as "What is psychoanalysis?" which many of us on

other occasions have set out to differentiate from other dynamic psychotherapies. It is rather a question of what comprises the indispensable contents with which the psychoanalytic method is concerned. How may we conceptualize this in psychoanalytic terms?

To answer this question, it is neither possible nor desirable to force an artificially succinct formulation with a claim to exclusiveness if it might better fit the facts to offer in a descriptive way as many nuclear aspects as may turn out to be necessary in characterizing such a hypothetical area. With this aim, I would first state that the realm of "unconscious intrapsychic conflicts" qualifies unequivocally to be at such a core of universal and persistent psychoanalytic interest. Each of these three words, moreover, possesses an equal valence and its share of literal and specific meaning. Thus, it is the unconscious rather than conscious, the intrapsychic rather than internal-external, and the conflictful rather than the conflict-free and autonomous, which I submit as the analytic focus.

This does not in any way run counter to the steady expansion of psychoanalysis from the pathological to the normal or from a theory of neurosis to a general psychology, so consistently pointed out by Hartmann (1939a,b), Rapaport (1951c, 1958), and others. Hartmann (1944), while giving due place to the role of the adaptive and conflict-free in psychoanalysis, points out that empirically psychoanalysis and social sciences have two "different centers." The former, he notes, deals mainly with areas of conflict, the unconscious and the irrational; the latter with the rational, the conscious and the external. The first, however, is not to be equated with the abnormal, since it is as much in the normal as in the symptomatic that analysis illuminates and demonstrates the role of the unconscious and the intrapsychic. It is, indeed, precisely here that analysis is enabled to meet the whole range of behavioral sciences. But at this juncture, quoting Hartmann (1944), "In applying psychoanalysis to sociological problems, the theory of human conflicts is its most important contribution to this science." Elsewhere, still with Hartmann (1956a), "we can say in retrospect that this emphasis on conflict, on defense, and on the dynamic unconscious was to become the cornerstone of analysis in its clinical and technical as well as theoretical aspect." And still in another place, "in all situations in which the id, the super-ego, or the unconscious part of the ego play an important role, statements will be reliable only if they are based on psychoanalytic findings" (1944). Robert Waelder (1963), approaching the same question from the standpoint of divergent theories, arrives at essentially the same conclusion about the center of analytic operations being in the area of unconscious conflicts. This is also consonant with the succinct expression of Ernst Kris (1947), who describes psychoanalysis as "the science of human behavior viewed as conflict."

Proceeding further with our descriptive attempts, it goes without saying that we do not have in mind any discrete or finite center with a hard core and definable borders. It is not so much a point, but a broad area of structural and energic interplay, a hierarchic spectrum of conflicts and their complex derivatives, and a stratification of anxiety signals, the dangers which they presage and the actions or other effects to which they lead (Schur, 1953, 1964; Rapaport, 1953a). Hartmann (1944) comes closest to sharing this concept of an inner core when he speaks of "the central structure" or "the nucleus of the personality." Although he does not define these directly, his discussion indicates that by these he means the types of mental structure and the ways in which conflicts are solved, both of which he contrasts to "the superficial layers of the personality." Loewald (1962) uses the term "ego core," but in a more limited and specific sense. Going from the periphery toward this hypothetical core, the path is toward and ever closer to the infantile neurosis. But just as Freud (1900) says about the dream that the associations to it lead to a nexus of obscurity, so do genetic reconstructions dwindle into a more and more obscure and unarticulated area of the earliest ontogenetic history. The rest we surmise when we come from the opposite direction by direct childhood observations and longitudinal developmental studies.

By both approaches, the study of ontogenesis is also a crucial one in itself with respect to arriving at the deepest sources. I quote Hartmann (1956b) again: "It is here, in the study of ontogenesis, that the mainsprings of psychoanalytic knowledge lie, and most of what we say analytically . . . about the special characteristics of the human mind and related questions, is ultimately traceable to what we know about ontogenesis."

To pinpoint further the activity of this central core, we may with still another approach borrow a page from Freud's final theory of anxiety. The ultimate anxiety with its associated basic danger is that, either by instinctual flooding from within or external stimulation from without, there will be an overthrow, extinction or annihilation of the ego, or more accurately of the self (Hartmann, 1950a, 1956a; Jacobson 1954, 1964). Conversely, from the adaptive point of view, the aim is to keep such a core cathected with at least a minimally sufficient amount of libido to preserve a "healthy narcissism." Lichtenstein (1964) discusses the role of narcissism in the emergence and maintenance of what he calls "a primary identity," a primary organizational principle without which psychological development proper cannot take place. Moreover, this struggle for ultimate preservation takes place not only in states of impending psychic helplessness or traumatic panic, but exists at the core behind all the subsequent external stratifications seen in normal daily life. I have studied these interrelationships in the state of social poise and the universal search for security and mastery which underlies it (see Chapter 4).

It is the dualism characteristic of this central inner core, universally operative, and a widespread, probably preconscious awareness which exists in the minds of people about the analyst's observing stance toward it, which is responsible for the common and well-known ambivalent reactions of the general public to psychoanalysis and analysts so often satirized in popular magazines and in the press. There is, to say the least, a vigilant interest, with alternating periods of coming toward and standing off. Nor were the distinguished academicians at the Center for Advanced Study an exception, although many of them, in spite of strong opinions pro and con, were meeting a psychoanalyst for the first time. We can understand this seemingly contradictory reaction only if we remain mindful of the dichotomous balance, the counterpoint between impulse and defense, as it exists at this central source.

It is only from here that we can make our unique contributions. Psychoanalysis itself is not centrally relevant to man's gnostic and intellectual achievements, his advances in knowledge per se, or even to the essence of his creative efforts, other than as these are influenced from this inner spring. While the body of psychoanalytic *theory* was enlarged, with immeasurable benefit and extension of scope, when it encompassed the adaptive and the conflict-free, the psychoanalytic *method* is incomplete if it does not make contact specifically with the conflictful unconscious from which psychoanalysis started. I am in agreement with Waelder (1961b) who stated that to the extent that we limit our observations to ego factors or to the conscious or the conflict-free, we have no claim over other disciplines. Such would be the case, for example, if perception, motility, or intelligence were to be studied only from their conscious, overt, or external manifestations. But for the influences which emanate from unconscious sources and from conflicting unconscious tendencies, others must look to us. These are the central concern of the psychoanalyst. Only with a root firmly maintained here can we hope to bridge the gap to other fields and offer the possibility of a wider application of psychoanalytic insights. Beres (1959), Kohut (1960), and others, addressing themselves to various aspects of the wide range of problems inherent in applied psychoanalysis, come to the same conclusions both as to the pitfalls as well as the desiderata.

II

Before turning to the next major subject of this presentation, namely, the role of affects within this central core, I would like to comment briefly on the concepts of identity and the self, so much referred to in current theoretical formulations as well as in clinical reconstructions. My goal is to place these into proper perspective in keeping with the main argument and interest of this essay (for our purposes I will treat them as one, since the possible subtle theoretical differences between them are not particularly germane here).

The avidity with which the concept of identity, for example, is embraced, not only by some analysts but especially and more impressively by the whole spectrum of the allied psychological profession as well as the public, is as deserving of an explanation by us as is the other generalized reaction of resistance or "vigilant interest" described above. These terms are used by many as definitive and specific explanations not only for individual psychopathological states, but for mass reactions as well, or even to explain such things as national character. The concept of identity, for example, has certainly encountered less resistance than has almost any other psychoanalytic formulation, especially those of a libidinal or other instinctual nature.

In my opinion, this is due to the fact that these concepts dynamically act like an inexact interpretation (Glover, 1955). This works, whether individually or en masse, by producing (possibly) beneficial but incomplete effects. I have pointed out that in the dynamic stream of intrapsychic events "identity" acts as an intermediate formation, i.e., it is as much a result of pre-existing intrapsychic conflicts and their derivatives and resolutions as a node from which further conflictful or adaptive constellations eventuate. Being part way between deeper unconscious conflicts and their external derivatives, explanations which center about them can act as screen memories or any other screen formations in: (a) attracting the observing and critical ego and thus resulting in partial insight, while simultaneously (b) warding off by the defensive segments of the ego the possibility of deeper levels of insight.

Incidentally, in the manner just described, the role of identity problems and even of identity disturbances is not at all limited to borderline cases or to severe character disturbances, but plays a prominent part along the entire spectrum of behavior from the benign and normal to the malignant and psychopathological. The following is an example of such an identity problem at the more normal end of the spectrum, a clinical instance which derives from the public domain. The story is told and has been written that Billy Rose, who suffered throughout his married life from the fact that he was known as "Fanny Brice's husband," finally felt that he had achieved a goal when he produced his first Broadway hit. During intermission on opening night, standing outside the theater, he observed the huge sign with flashing neon lights on which the name "Billy Rose" blinked on and off across Broadway. Mingling eagerly with the crowd he heard one lady ask another, "Who is that?" and heard the reply, "That's Fanny Brice's husband."

Problems of identity can be poignant ones. While their role should not be underestimated, they should be seen in their proper perspective and without replacing the more central background of intrapsychic conflicts that exist at the core. They can be of service en route to the latter, rather than either replacing them or serving as an obstacle to their access. A case in point which might illustrate this occurred when a patient described one day how he felt when chairing a rather large meeting for the first time during the course of his work. Contrary to his expectations, he reported that while up there he still felt "like a foolish little boy." By way of explanation he was reminded of a joke about a man who went horseback riding in the park. He rode proudly on a tall white horse, which he liked so well that on his next free day he returned and asked the stableman to give him "the same white stallion" he had had the day before. "Oh," came the reply, "you must mean the white mare—we have no white stallion." "No," said the man, "I mean the stallion. When I was riding the other day, some little boys looked up as I went by and remarked, 'Look at that big schmuck on the white horse.'" "That's how I felt yesterday on the podium," said the patient. Identity problems need further intrapsychic interpretations. The above opened the way to his phallic conflicts.

While the *sense* of identity or of the self, or what is usually referred to as the self representation, resides in the ego, the *contents* of the self, or of the identity, are broader in scope and comprise more than the whole or part of the structure "ego." Erikson (personal communication), for example, in describing how he conceives of the identity, considers it to be comprised of a combination of "instinctual drives, ego attitudes, superego characteristics, somatic factors, external relations, and object representations, etc." Actually, it is this composite self or identity, rather than just what we mean analytically by the ego as a structure, that is guarded and is the nodus to be preserved at the deepest anxiety layers described above. It is to this same effort to which Freud originally ascribed a whole class of instincts, i.e., the "*self*-preservative instincts," a concept he later modified.

In the manner described, identity conflicts are very much part of the central core and, as stated above, are present universally. But explanations on the basis of identity disturbances alone are similar to those based solely or centrally on the vicissitudes of self-esteem. These are not erroneous, but incomplete and unidimensional. For the full depth of psychoanalytic understanding in all its complexity, these must be seen within the nexus of their total intrapsychic impact, their roots and their derivatives, as participants in the hierarchy of conflicting and balancing forces, examined as all other psychic phenomena from the five or now perhaps six metapsychological points of view, which only together encompass a total psychoanalytic view (Rapaport and Gill, 1959).

III

I would like to proceed now with the one section of my chosen title of which I have not yet spoken and to lift out for special consideration another specific and, in my opinion, crucial component within this central orbit: I refer to the part played by the affects and their role and relationship to the other elements at the core. If we speak of a human core, does not being "human" commonly mean the ability to feel, and is not "inhuman" the reverse, i.e., to be cold and unfeeling?

From the historical point of view, I would briefly remind you that the earliest theories of Breuer and Freud (1893–1895) centered around the existence of "loculated affects" and, associated with this, the therapeutic method was *emotional* catharsis or abreaction. The successive historical developmental phases of our science in the epoch-making years that followed, perhaps best chronicled by Rapaport (1953a), moved from affects to instincts, from loculated pockets to intrapsychic conflicts, and from abreaction to interpretation. The latter underwent increasing elaboration and refinement paralleling our increasing knowledge of the nature of the internal conflicting forces.

I would like to submit the thesis that affects, the original center, in giving way to subsequent developments have become, wrongly, "the forgotten man." In spite of their ubiquity clinically, they have in a sense been bypassed, or at least minimized out of proportion, and receive a good deal less of systematic attention than they deserve in our total theoretical metapsychological system.

It is nevertheless the case that just as Freud (1926) in his theory of anxiety never completely discarded the original theory while superseding it with the second, the same, I believe, holds in the succession from affect to instinct theory. Actually, just as has been the case in the revised theory of anxiety, the role of affects should be reassessed to see how the old and the new interrelate, both in theory and in practice. Although Rapaport has shown how in all analytic theory the old phase is characteristically carried into the new and how the new is built upon the old, he notes in his last paper (1960) the "persistent confusion between affect and instinct, which . . . is embalmed in the ubiquitous term 'emotional disorder.' . . . [This] is also probably one of the factors contributing to the fact that to this day psychology has no accepted definition of emotions or affects."

In this instance the relations between the new and the old have obviously not been sharply established. And they need to be. An analogy can be made to the early cartographers. While the first map makers were subject to considerable correction in that huge unknown areas had to be subsequently filled in, the importance of these first maps has been shown to be unarguable (Kirsch, 1964).The same can be said for the original mapping out of the realm of the affects which, though much has been added, still remains vital empirically and which should remain prominent theoretically in the central explanations of human behavior.

To examine further the continuing role of affects, the following will include some observations of their role: (a) phenomenologically, within the clinical therapeutic process; (b) in the theory of therapy; and (c) in general psychoanalytic theory.

First, phenomenologically, within the psychoanalytic process itself, whether we deal with affect in its well-known role as a signal (such as anxiety, guilt, shame, etc.), as an end product in itself (such as within the normal spectrum of affects, as in moods, or as a major area gone wrong, such as in depression, elation, or pathological anxiety), or in its role as a means toward, or a cementer of, object relations, which is no small area of its applicability, it is not an occasional visitor to a psychoanalytic procedure or even to each individual analytic hour, but a constantly present factor to consider and deal with.

As such it is of interest, both as a datum of observation itself, and as a medium or vehicle toward obtaining all other information via a facilitation of communication. (Compare Karl Bühler [1934], who described language in its three phases of appeal, expression, and communication.) With regard to the first, it is a central characteristic of psychoanalysis that whereas most other disciplines regard emotions as contaminants which distort their data and must be eliminated, psychoanalysis sets out to deal with them and is alone capable of dealing with them as its data and subject matter, much as the Greek philosophers did for the science of knowledge.

In respect to its role in the communication of all other data, no analytic hour is complete or successful without an affective accompaniment, in one or the other senses named above, most often in combination. Ideational content without affect is significantly incomplete. The fantasy, conscious or unconscious, is insufficiently recovered and without therapeutic impact if lacking in its associated or contingent affect. The well-known cartoon of a woman patient on the couch diligently describing the ingredients of a menu or recipe, while the hapless analyst sits distraught and frustrated, is not an irrelevant joke but may be a perceptive observation of significant clinical applicability.

After all, what do we consider a good analytic hour? One which consists of content which has "meaning," i.e., is meaningful and about which the patient "cares." "Care" is in the neutralized part of the spectrum from greater to lesser libidinal cathexis, as is the case in friendship (see Chapter 30). Psychoanalysis centers on what the patient cares about, is concerned with, and by a short step away is in conflict about. To the extent that an analytic hour is about that, it is relevant. And conversely to the extent that it is not about anything about which the patient cares, it is shallow and ineffectual. A perceptive patient of mine had the habit of catching himself up short at such times with the self-observing remark, "Here I go, 'funffing' along again."

Nor is this to be judged by the manifest content, here any more than anywhere else in psychoanalysis. For example, a patient, pursuing the fact that he does not trust anyone because he is afraid to be hurt, makes the startling statement, "I don't know why that should be, because I never really cared for anyone." He goes on to say that as far as he can remember he never cared for his mother. "If anything, I was always ashamed of her. I might have felt some guilt about this, but hardly anything beyond that." As will surprise no analyst, the subsequent train of thought, stimulated by an occasional probing remark on the part of the analyst, led with no difficulty to a stream of associations charged with affects, which included not only "caring" but disappointed love. It was the latter, of course, that led to his pervasive mistrust, which grew in increments during his developmental history as a succession of five younger siblings came along to join him.

Unconscious affects, or at least, since this is a dubious and theoretically controversial concept, we can say with certainty unconscious potentials for affective discharge, are as much a part of human character and certainly as significant for the analytic process as are the overt emotional expressions. The so-called "menu hour" mentioned above, incidentally, applies not only to the reciting of recipes and other such mundane and unimportant trivialities, but can occur as much with the productions of a scientific genius. Analysts encounter similar hours and mechanisms from an engineer patient, or an atomic scientist, or a mathematician reciting formulae. Psychoanalysis is not for "pure" intellectual thinking.

As with all object relationships, a good hour has affective content, like a good speech. It is affects which bind the listener. The necessary empathy in the analytic attitude follows the presence of affects, not ideation or action. Empathic identification on the part of the analyst is, at least to some optimum extent, via affective identification. This holds not only for empathy but also for "interest." From the standpoint of the patient to be "interesting" and to project "interest" is to stimulate some degree of "caring." Interest on both sides of the analytic couch has an affective prerequisite. Not only is the transference neurosis an indispensable component in a viable psychoanalysis, but most vital is its affective center.

When during an hour, after some routine or dull minutes, a sudden compelling association commands interest, it is one which has an affective quality. I am not necessarily referring to associations in the nature of a dramatic bombshell, as when a patient recently related a memory of driving with his father and coming to a train accident where they both witnessed a dismembered body. I am referring more importantly to expressions or communications in the more ordinary course of associations which are felt as having a poignant or "touching" quality. In this vein, a patient, after expressing some concern about the analyst rustling or fidgeting about or, he thought, perhaps flipping a page, reassured himself with "I know that you are always on automatic pilot. When I say something, you're there." Some patients characteristically have a stream of such compelling and interest-provoking associations or ways of expressing their associations. Interest does not lag. I do not, of course, mean those patients who demand constant and unswerving attention and to achieve it even provide entertainment. I think rather of a patient who in trying to express his ever-present trait of indecisiveness—in this particular instance at the prospect of having to pick a surgeon for himself—stated in measured tones, "I just know I'll go into that obsessive-compulsive jig which I dance." The thought almost painted a picture in action, which was easy for both of us to follow. At the other end of the spectrum are other patients who hardly ever say anything even close to being interesting. It would not be accurate to say that there is a lack of affects in such cases, but rather that there are special constellations of affective combinations. These do not often include or enhance successful or compelling object rela- tionships or an ability to make friends and influence people. This, of course, can be expected to show itself in the analysis as well.

The same considerations also apply in the reverse direc- tion, that from the analyst to the patient in the service of the production of insight via interpretations. Communication both ways must have an affective component, although neutralized we hope at least in the one direction, and a certain basic minimum of the appeal component of language. From the analyst to the patient there is to flow not an academic stream of theoretical "psychoanalese" (Reik, 1948), but a "meaningful," i.e., affective (to be effective) flow. The analyst also cares for what he says and for whom he is saying it. This is not, of course, to be taken to condone the opposite extreme, i.e., of emotional "involvement" on the part of the analyst, with its opposite and even more disrupting stream of consequences. Kohut (1964) speaks of "that optimum mixture of emotional involvement and scientific detachment that allows for the correct assessment of . . . human emotional suffering and of the proper steps to relieve it." A good interpretation produces affective knowledge. It may result not only in laughter or even in tears (Tarachow, 1965), but more often in a moment of quiet solemnity during which affect in the patient changes into insight. The succession of analytic hours *in toto* should follow as well as possible the course of such a meaningful thread. I wonder how many incomplete, protracted, or interminable analyses are "menu" analyses, unsolved or even unrecognized as such.

The same is as true outside the treatment situation as within it. In life itself, it is also affects which bind object relations and are the vehicle on which the latter are conducted. Affective needs make object relationships and are in turn produced by them. The same is true on a mass scale as in a limited or in a diadic one. How much of humanity was drawn together, even if momentarily, as a result of the shared grief of November 22, 1963, upon the death of President John F. Kennedy. From the flood of newsprint which appeared the next day, the following captured my attention and I have selected it to quote. Commenting on the reactions of the diplomats of a hundred other countries watching with solemn wonder in their posts in the United Nations, one reporter observed:

> Americans, who often run away from real emotions, were caught in the depth of real sorrow and real shock that had nothing to do with political platforms or legislative policies. The nation of spectators was suddenly a participant in a shared tragedy. The hedonist veneer of the culture was torn off. Sorrow was not drunk away in a million bars. Theatre marquées were dark. The grind of rock and roll, the reverberations of singing commercials, the tranquilizer of superficial drama disappeared from every television and radio outlet; in their place came the buoyant themes of the masters, interpreted by great choruses and great orchestras [Fleming, 1963].

Also on a mass scale, the role of affects in communication is visible in the works of those timeless masters in all fields which continue to reach and touch us forever. The most recent example which left such an impact on me, and which I select to mention only because of its temporal immediacy, occurred when I visited the Rodin Museum in Paris a short time ago. Some of the random titles of the works of this intensely compelling artist, who, more than any other, continued into modern times the line from the Greek and Roman sculptors, through Michelangelo into our own generation, include *Le Désespoir, La Misère, La Tête de la Douleur, L'Amour qui passe, L'Adieu, La Pensée, La Pleureue, La Méditation, Exhortation, Le Rêve, La Dernière Vision,* all depicted with a power and in a manner which is forever human. And in all of these, the channels of communication are not only through the face, but through every other mode and channel of affective expression. I recall Rodin's hands of *La Cathédrale,* or those other timeless hands depicted by Dürer or Michelangelo.

At the Center of Advanced Study, Carl Rogers, with whom Erik Erikson and I, representing the psychoanalysts, debated about much else, kept correctly emphasizing the importance of what he called "gut experiences" (personal communication). About this we could agree. Conversely, the absence or loss of an affective bond heralds the paling if not the termination of an object relationship. A lack of sentiment or even of some degree of sentimentality (the two are not the same) often goes with a shallowness of object ties.

Turning now from phenomenology to theory, the emphasis on the centrality of affects which I have just been giving is by no means by way of recommending a shift back from instincts to affects as ultimate explanatory concepts. On the contrary, as I stated before, the task is now to integrate the two, and both of them with all other vital interacting components.

In a general and incomplete sense, affects, or at least one aspect of them, are derivatives and external representatives of instinctual drives, resulting, as Rapaport (1950, 1953a) has shown, from "instinctual discharges into the interior." (Ego components are not to be neglected and will be commented upon presently.) In fact, instincts are known by the affects which they produce. As Freud has pointed out, we do not see pure instincts but only their derivatives. The dual instincts express themselves as two basic and polar affects, that of love and hate. One suggested classification of affects divides them into positive and negative ones on this very basis.

While affects are prominent among the end products of instinctual drives in normal psychology, they are certainly among the most germane to neuroses and to the analytic process which undoes them. In neurogenesis itself, while clinical syndromes are customarily described primarily according to the vicissitudes of instinctual and ego interaction, the role played by affective factors can never be overlooked. This obtains not only for the frankly affective pathological states (such as in clinical depression or overt anxiety states) or for certain other syndromes in which the role of affects receives a central place, but as a background in *all* clinical pictures, even where other end results, somatic or ideational, emerge as the final presenting picture. An example which comes to mind is that of a patient whose complicated neurosis had as its first sign the fact that she had stopped laughing. It is this ubiquitous and central role played by affects which accounts for the observation by Rapaport (1960) that "many psychoanalysts, and even Freud, at times still spoke [i.e., after the advent of instinct theory] of affects and emotions as the intrapsychic factors which give rise to fantasies, wishes and symptoms."

But it is mainly in the theory of therapy that the role of the affective processes must be clearly understood in relation to subsequent present-day concepts. Ferenczi, in a series of historic papers which have had a considerable influence in shaping certain subsequent directions of analytic activity and developments (Ferenczi, 1920, 1930, 1931), returned to what he called "neocatharsis," to discover "new veins of gold in temporarily abandoned workings." While he and others later tended to use this as the *raison d'être* for certain heroic and dubious technical interventions, a refocusing on the affective experiences within the framework of our central analytic procedures cannot fail to be a felicitous reminder.

Nor does that mean that I speak now for a renewal of the centrality of abreaction, at least per se, in the therapeutic armamentarium. Just as I stated previously about identity and the self, so are affects also to be regarded as intermediate formations from which other processes must be gleaned. This is the case whether affects are basically discharge phenomena (Freud, 1900, 1915b; Rapaport, 1950, 1953a), or, in the opinion of some, tension phenomena (Brierley, 1937), or either or both (Glover, 1938; Jacobson, 1953a), while the other two, identity and the self, can be more static or stable in composition. Just as I (1959) have spoken for the separation of conversion from hysteria in the automatic phrase which links them together, so should affects and catharsis no longer be automatically linked. In fact it is precisely in psychoanalysis, in contrast to what occurs in life situations, that affects should no longer be discharged or dissipated *without* their ideational accompaniments and their associated unconscious meanings being made explicit. The special intent and opportunity in the analytic process is that the analysis of affects, just as stated above about identity and the self, are also en route to the analysis of the underlying intrapsychic conflicts. The goal is to continue the analysis of the latter through less and less distorted derivatives to the infantile neurosis, and not to bypass these in favor of concentration upon the affects alone. The latter would be a regressive return to the origins of psychoanalysis.

The affects as major derivatives of instinctual drives can also lead back to them. However, to state the situation more completely, the range and quality of affects are indicative of the nature and strength of ego activity as well. Not only instinctual impulses but also aspects of the ego reveal themselves to a great extent in the characteristics of the affective life. Affects themselves can be used by the ego for defensive purposes, such as those described by Valenstein (1962) in "affectualization," or by Greenson (1958) in the phenomena of screen affects. Rapaport (1953a) has described the hierarchy of affects depending on their closeness to instinctual or ego sources, or, in terms of Hartmann (1952), according to their degree of neutralization. The degree of "taming of the affects" (Fenichel, 1941a), their subtlety or modulation, is a measure of the success of neutralization and of the extent of ego mastery over instincts.

Affects thus provide the roadbed and are the rail to the understanding of *both* arms of the intrapsychic conflict, instinct and ego, both of which together and in their interrelationships comprise the rationale for the therapeutic march.

As dreams are the royal road, so affects are major roads, indeed indispensable ones, to the unconscious. They constitute a language in themselves, both preverbal and paraverbal. In frequency and from the point of view merely of statistics and ubiquity, dreams are in fact less constant than affects as analytic material. The analysis of affects goes a long way toward psychoanalysis. Dreams and free associations add the accompanying ideation. All are necessary for the total product.

I should point out here that while we have been concentrating on examining the role of affects, it should not be forgotten that the goal is not to understand them in isolation but to bring them under the supremacy of insight, of the ego's thought processes, as well as under the influence and control of other crucial ego faculties, such as the synthetic, the integrative, the differentiating, and the organizing functions. But unlike associations, affects are not characteristically connected with word representations nor even, as are dreams, with visual representations. They are not usually talked about, but as discharge phenomena are mainly demonstrated and experienced, in a sense "acted out." (Compare Rapaport's division into "affects felt" and "affects seen.") The goal then is to bring them under the dominance of the secondary process—of the processes of thought and of ego control.

The affect is frequently the crack in the wall toward widening the realm of understanding. A patient was describing having lunch with her sister while visiting the latter in a distant city. Describing the meeting as warm and friendly, her chin showed a perceptible quiver. It was this which was the analyst's cue and about which a gentle question elicited a flood of memories, ideas, and affects. Without going into detail here, the quiver was the final common motor pathway to a composite of pity, guilt, sadness, anger, and love. I have often thought it too bad that the analyst cannot regularly see the face of the patient, although of course we are all aware of the potent reasons as well as the historical development which brought this about. Without realizing it before, I must have been thinking of the physical side of the "human core" when, in my paper on the psychology of poise, I described the snout as the "window to the emotions" (Chapter 4). This concept seems to merge well with what we are considering today. An artist-patient who characteristically endeavors to portray the essence of his subjects, in describing his wife, speaks intensively of her "visage." As analysts we also note the hands, posture, gestures, etc., but the physical expressions of affect constitute another area which we cannot go into at this time.

Turning again to the last subdivision which I promised to talk about, that of a general theory of affects, I am surprised, considering their centrality, that "a psychoanalytic theory of affects" has been so lagging in relation to the other aspects of our theoretical structure. The closest to filling this gap has been Rapaport's meaty paper on "The Theory of Affects" (Panel, 1952). Besides attempting to organize the existing fragments into a systematic "psychoanalytic theory of affects," the paper also contributed a detailed picture of the historical development not only of affects but of many broader aspects of psychoanalytic theory. It provided a lucid and original description of the nature of progressive hierarchic ego development in all its aspects, including its influence on the hierarchy of motivational drives, the process of neutralization in general, and the taming and modulation of affects in particular. It is interesting and I do not believe that it detracts from the brilliance of Rapaport's paper that in the ensuing discussion Bertram Lewin remarked that we still did not have a theory of affects. With this Rapaport disagreed.

While we have been carried a long way toward "a psychoanalytic theory of affects," I believe we would be forced to agree that we do not yet have a full or complete theory of affects. "A secretory or motor instinctual discharge into the interior" does not sufficiently differentiate affects from other such internal discharges, nor does it separate one affect from another. Such a description perhaps brings affects under the proper generic heading, but not into the specific subgroup. The same applies here as to the subject of creativity or giftedness or talent. In *The Quest for the Father* (1963), Greenacre, commenting on creativity, writes: "The nucleus of creative ability may be in certain inborn qualities which are biologically given and are beyond the scope of psychoanalytic research. . . . [Psychoanalysis] does *not* attempt to fathom the ultimate source." Benjamin (1961a) expresses a similar view about our incomplete understanding of anxiety.

For a comprehensive theory of affects, just as for creativity, we will need combined insights from other fields probably not yet available—from biology, neurophysiology, neurochemistry, and genetics. Needles (1964), writing about the basic affects of pleasure and unpleasure, invokes a biological factor as an ultimate explanation. Probably the same can be said for our general theory of behavior as we are saying for the specific component of affects. Psychoanalysis encompasses one segment, the psychological one. Although indispensable for a total theory, we will also need a whole range of other facts, from a thorough knowledge of constitutional givens of all kinds, somatic and psychic, to a comparable knowledge of external reality. The latter can never be underestimated in assessing total behavior. Macroscopic as well as microscopic understanding is to be hoped for, and any whole answer will ultimately come only from combined efforts. Freud, as concurred later by Hartmann and others, never gave up the hope for an ultimate continuity between the psychological and the biological.

Finally, with regard to the subject of affects, I submit that while love, hate, anxiety, and guilt, i.e., the "major affects," are the hallmarks of psychoanalytic concern, less interest has been shown in the less intense or more "mixed" (Glover, 1938), or

"intermediate affects," the more subtle forms of human emotional experience. There is no one in a better position than the
analyst to study and understand the whole range of human
affects: a chuckle as well as hilarity; discouragement as well as
depression; bitterness, irony, and sarcasm as well as rage; or
whimsy, pity, or wonder, a wistful or mellow mood, as much as
the more clear-cut, easily distinguishable, and more classical
emotional states.

To be sure, some of the subtle forms have been individually studied, such as, among others, the psychogenesis and
pathogenesis of jealousy in its connections with paranoia and
homosexuality by Freud (1922); shame and guilt, by Piers and
Singer (1953) and others; envy and gratitude, in her own way
by Melanie Klein (1957); awe, by Greenacre (1953, 1956);
smugness, by Arlow (1957); boredom, by Fenichel (1934) and
by Greenson (1953); enthusiasm, by Greenson (1962); and
various intermediate moods, by Edith Jacobson (1957). I have
dealt with certain "intermediate" affects in connection with the
state of poise (Chapter 4), and "friendly" feelings (Chapter 33).
One might hold that all of these are sufficiently subsumed
under the concept of the continuum or the hierarchic series. I
would submit, however, that there might well be specific factors
worth pursuing in various individual emotional states. Considering this range of affects from one particular point of view,
i.e., the economic one, Jacobson (1953a) postulates "various
combinations of high and low speed discharge processes which
result in complex affective experiences as some of our most
sublime pleasurable states."

IV

In summary, I have in this paper attempted to give at least
some of the characteristics which constitute the "human core"
with which psychoanalysis deals and from which man is driven.
With a root and a major footing here psychoanalysts can look to
the periphery and, in alliance with all other students of human
behavior, can aspire to contribute specific understanding to

each of the directions in which man's intelligence and spirit have led him, the social, noble, and creative, as well as the retrogressive, destructive, and suicidal.

The psychoanalytic body has recognized and responded to this challenge, even this responsibility, both organizationally and individually. In the former category, many committees, both national and local, today explore the linkages between psychoanalytic contributions and a multitude of wider social issues. Among individual efforts, while it is almost an injustice to single out a few from the plethora which we enjoy, I am still tempted to remind you of the works of Kurt Eissler (1961, 1963b) in the field of art and literature, and his sweeping and inspiring look through the eyes of a psychoanalyst at the course of history (1963a). As another proud example among us, I would mention the works of Phyllis Greenacre (1955, 1963) on creativity and the lives of the gifted and how these have been illuminated by her own creative psychoanalytic insights.

Franz Alexander, whom this lectureship honors, has pioneered in this trend toward the extension of psychoanalytic knowledge. An early historical figure in this direction, he threw particular light on how such insights can enrich the important fields of medicine and psychiatry (1950), as well as many if not all of the medical specialties. More recently he turned in a more global way to an attempt to shed equal light on the current world order and on the mind and collective problems of Western man (1960).

Toward all such efforts, I would stress again and caution that to the extent that we relinquish our source in the central spring which we have outlined, and operate *only* in these derivative levels (there are analysts who err in this direction), we would lose our source of originality and unique specificity from the deep unconscious. Without it we could no longer claim expertness or add a distinctive flavor and had better listen to others. Under such circumstances, I would tend to agree with the sober and self-critical mood expressed by Erik Erikson. Writing from Kashmir to Boston in reply to Roger Fisher, editor of a symposium on Alternatives to Armed Conflict, who had requested a psychoanalyst's participation in "policy or decision making," Erikson (1963) expressed the conviction that "political and psychoanalytic thinking can and must confront one another before long." However, he went on: "There is . . . an as yet uncharted area between the two fields. . . . Where the necessary conditions cannot be created . . . or wherever the individual psychoanalyst might . . . not feel congenial to such work, there I submit he does better to cure and enlighten in the service of ongoing life, and toward man's increasing capacity for maintaining—and indeed tolerating—peace, than to mix and fumble in the area of preventing war."

But with the proper stance, as suggested here, and indeed only with such a posture, which firmly preserves the central interest and identity of psychoanalysis, can we hope to enrich the relationship of psychoanalysis to the whole range of the behavioral sciences. From its side, psychoanalysis can help, in Hartmann's words (1950b), by "insisting on a [deeper and] more complex view" doing what it can to preclude what Bixenstine (1964) calls "a science of the trivial." But nature can come and indeed is needed from the opposite direction as well. For many among us who express concern for the future of psychoanalysis, it is well to bear in mind that a tree can wither not only from lack of nutriment at its roots but also from inclement weather in its atmosphere. Both are to be guarded against and rendered optimum. Fortunately, psychoanalysts have it within their power, at least to some extent, to influence their climate, both internal and external.

Undoubtedly, as Hartmann (1956a), says, "a synthesis of psychoanalytic thought with other fields of knowledge [has] so far been only partly realized," and for this work we will need "a sounder methodological foundation" (1944). It is also true, with Hartmann, that a mere exchange of findings between psychoanalysis and sociology will not suffice, nor will it be effective to merely "apply" the theories of one to the phenomena of the other. It is rather only "a mutual penetration," and "a dynamic process of mutual inspiration . . . which can prove fertile for both sides." But that such a combined effort is in order there can be little doubt, if we are to assure, in the words of Faulkner (1950), that "Man will not merely endure; he will prevail."

CHAPTER 4

The Psychology of Poise

With a Special Elaboration on the Psychic
Significance of the Snout or Perioral Region

I

It is the purpose of this communication to group together a certain set of clinical phenomena, the central theme of which has to do with that particular state of ease or well-being connoted by the term "poise." An attempt will be made to describe and clarify from the psychoanalytic point of view some of the psychological concomitants of this state, an attempt which seems indicated and which I hope may even prove fruitful inasmuch as this particular qualitative state of psychic equilibrium seems to rank high among the various pleasurable states striven for by man. I believe we shall find that a consideration of it will reveal it to possess specificity and to have delineable borders.

It might be well at this point, in anticipation of the material

Awarded the Clinical Essay Prize of the British Institute of Psychoanalysis for 1953. Published in *Internat. J. Psycho-Anal.*, 35:313–333, 1954.

to follow, and, I hope, without detracting from it, to make the following general introductory statement. Clinical observations lead me to advance the hypothesis that the feeling of poise may be in large part related to, and centered around, mouth and perioral sensations. The feeling of being at ease, comfortable, poised in a social situation or interpersonal relationship, or the opposite feeling, that of being shaky, insecure, ill-at-ease, is at least in many instances expressed and accompanied by the state of satisfaction or dissatisfaction of oral instinctual needs in the muscles and skin around the mouth. An absence of tension in these is associated with a feeling of ease and poise, while accumulated tension in this area goes with the feeling of being ill at ease. The sensations involved are proprioceptive ones. The development and elaboration of the function and psychic significance of this perioral zone may be considered a secondary theme and purpose of this communication. However, while this specific linkage is being singled out as a particularly focal one and perhaps as a basic point of origin and orientation, it will not surprise us to find that the state we are setting out to describe is a complex one, with many facets, and distinctly overdetermined.

It will be best to start with an excerpt from the treatment of a patient which was in fact the original stimulus for the accumulation of this material and which will serve as a fairly representative prototype of the type of feeling with which we are concerned.

This patient, during the course of her analysis, began to relate and describe her great concern about her increasing drinking. This need occurred when she was in company of any kind, at which time she would increasingly feel compelled to start drinking. This had gradually progressed so that now she had reached the point of filling one glass after another. She called tolerate liquor very well, and the intoxicating effects did not seem to play much of a part, although they contributed. What seemed more essential, however, was the security she gained in knowing that she had a full glass in her hand ready to be put to her lips at any tense or challenging moment. With this safeguard at hand, she could maintain her poise and security; she even became quite glib, very witty, and gave the observer the impression of being at the acme of poise and control. The same situation existed with regard to smoking, so that a like feeling of contentment and security was achieved when the cigarette was held between the lips, or in the hand ready to be raised to the lips.

The patient, as we might expect, was in general orally oriented and had many other oral manifestations in her history, symptoms, and behavior. She was basically a severe depressive and had made at least two serious attempts at suicide. She had periods of compulsive eating with great gain of weight, alternating with periods of strict dieting. She was a heavy coffee drinker, taking an average of four to five cups with breakfast. A number of these latter manifestations had run a favorable course during her analysis, but not as yet the alcoholism, which involved certain special features, i.e., (1) the feeling of trying to achieve poise and control in a social situation, and (2) the need which accompanied it of having something in readiness to place between the lips.

The significant past history was somewhat as follows. The chief memory of the patient's entire childhood was that of chronic loneliness. Her mother was a cold rejecting person, who was openly and completely frustrated in her marriage with the father, whom she violently hated and with whom she had virtually no sexual life. She left the patient to go to work when the latter was still an infant of less than a year, and constantly thereafter induced a sense of guilt and obligation in the patient by her martyrlike attitude. The parents were divorced when the patient was 9. Every early memory was of being alone, without friends or playmates. During her school career she would come home to an empty house and have to amuse herself until her mother returned from work. She never felt surrounded by a family as other children were. She would walk for hours and look into lighted windows, imagining congenial family settings around a fireplace. She felt ashamed of her own drab, colorless, and unloving environment, and then felt guilt about her shame. She was "broken in" early, and was considered a "proper little lady" at the age of 2 or 3. But even at that age orally determined symptoms would break through in the form of easy disgust and frequent vomiting. She had early been a feeding problem and a finicky eater.

To add to her burdens during her formative years, a wide and unbridgeable gap was created between her low self-esteem on the one hand, due to a restrictive and oppressive training, and a lofty and unattainable ego ideal on the other. Her mother, though kept by circumstances and her own inner conflicts on the "wrong side of the tracks," nevertheless maintained a haughty demeanor and filled her daughter with a sense of the aristocratic origins of their family tree. She took great pride in unceasingly recounting to the little girl the tracing of the maternal lineage to an English royal duke. There inevitably grew in the patient a sense of never belonging, so that even in adolescence she developed the feeling of being above those few playmates whom she finally did acquire and hopelessly below those to whom she aspired. A derivative of this was seen in her present life. She managed to reach and achieve "high society" in a certain social and cultural sense; but her situation was such that one month they could not pay the rent or grocery bill, while a week later they were weekend guests on a luxurious yacht. And it was in this setting that the symptoms flourished which were of interest to us, i.e., that the patient felt tense and ill at ease and unable to merge into any social setting except with the aid of the above-mentioned artificial props.

The type of early play with which she occupied herself as a child is relevant to our main theme. Her chief toy was a doll, but this doll did not live like other children's dolls, that is, have babies, act like a mother, and do ordinary daily things. Her doll, as long as she could remember, was sophisticated and smart, lived in a mansion, had a limousine call for her, was elegantly dressed, completely composed, and obviously the essence of poise. This doll really "belonged."

The patient had made almost a fetish in her life of being sophisticated and smart, admiring and envying such people.

She would spend many hours in smart shops, just sitting there and watching elegant people being waiting upon. She would identify with them, imitate them, and orally incorporate them. In college, she gravitated naturally toward dramatics where she "played" such parts. She avidly read the fashion magazines for smart ideas. To be sophisticated was the opposite of being clumsy and gauche and ashamed. Her mother always accused her of being awkward, of slumping, and of having a bad posture. To be sophisticated was to be completely poised, to belong, to merge with the environment, and not to stick out as an object of ridicule. In real life, the patient alternated between looking "like a horror" and looking elegant and suave. She had often been told that she could at times look worse and at other times look better than almost anyone else.

From this brief clinical description, we can extract the following as being on the line of interest. The patient has, as she has always had, a feeling of not belonging when she is with other people, and at these times feels the need of something to bolster her up and reassure her. Her feeling is that of having no poise, of being as it were grotesque, dumpy, laughable, ridiculous, of sticking out clumsily, of being suspended in mid-air with no anchor and no support under her. Under these conditions, the specific antidote which can serve to change or bolster up her inner feelings and make her feel "on the in" and accepted, is to have something between her lips and grasped by them, or ready to be placed there for this purpose. In this connection, we see that poise, as we use the term, is a factor which comes into play only in a social interrelationship. It is not an issue when one is alone. This does not mean that one is then calm or free of tension or anxiety, but rather that there is no social threat, no danger from without, no fear of ridicule; one is not at the moment being observed and judged. When one is alone, one can let oneself go, assume a posture of which one is not proud, examine in the mirror a skin blemish of which one might be ashamed, let one's stomach stick out, grimace at oneself, or squeeze a blackhead; unless, that is, one fantasies other persons as still present; in the absence of this, even the most unpoised and vulnerable person can achieve a relaxed state when alone. In company and in a social setting such is not the case; a stiffening-up takes place and a certain armor, no matter how subtle, is assumed. These comparisons can be caught and demonstrated by the candid camera.

II

Let us at this point leave our patient for the time being in order to try to define and to clarify in some greater detail the subject under investigation. What exactly is connoted by the term "poise," and what, if any, are the distinguishing features which separate it from certain other allied and contiguous states of well-being, such as the feeling of security or that of satisfaction and the like? While there are a number of states or psychoeconomic conditions which the human organism seeks which are experienced as desirable or pleasurable, these states on closer investigation are seen to have subtle differences between them and to be individually specific.

Among these various goals, for example, is that of achieving the Nirvana state, or the state of homeostatic equilibrium, to keep the level of excitation equalized and constant. Although this equilibrium, in all living forms, is undergoing constant interruption, the successive disruptions are being brought back uniformly and successfully by the organism to its particular baseline level (Fenichel, 1945). Instinctual impulses as well as stimuli from all other sources are being managed or handled, as by discharge through action, thought, or affect (Rapaport, 1951a), or by being bound or otherwise adequately defended against. The ego here is in command and is successfully holding at bay energy and pressure from every side, from the id, from the superego, and from the external world. Relaxing or weakening of its position results in various states of tension, which ensue when energy begins to crowd in on the ego from any one of the three agencies mentioned above. Such states of tensions are in themselves not necessarily unpleasurable and can indeed be states of pleasure, not only when the likelihood of mastery or satisfaction exists, but also, as pointed out recently by Edith Jacobson (1952), under other independent conditions, according to the speed and pace of their discharge processes.

Security, one might say, is the condition of knowledge or confidence based on past experience that anxiety can be staved off and that in general satisfaction and/or mastery is within the grasp of the ego at command. It is a guarantee or at least a reassurance against the traumatic state, against unmastered tension, but from any or every direction. Forces from within or assaults from without, as they are likely to occur, will be dealt with. Impulses will be satisfied, either in whole or in part, or at any rate sufficiently; or else adequate defense mechanisms or other solutions will be forthcoming. The healthy ego, cradled by such comforting experiences in the past, feels secure in its capability to meet the stimuli which are likely to occur. Being at ease is probably synonymous with or at least closely analogous to this state. Satisfaction is yet another condition, and follows in the time immediately subsequent to gratification of an impulse or need. Such a state, for example, follows eating or orgasm or expression of an aggressive impulse. Satisfaction may be complete (satiation) or partial. The most frequent cause of fixation, according to Fenichel (1945), is simultaneous satisfaction and security, i.e., satisfaction of drive and security or reassurance against anxiety. A mother, for example, who serves as such a fixating agent is one who provides excessive satisfaction of impulse while at the same time serving as an external bulwark for the child against the forces of his own instinctual demands as well as against threats or dangers from without. This is before the formation in the infant of his own internal agent, i.e., ego, to serve this function.

How does poise fit in to this general spectrum of pleasurable states, how is it separated from those described above, what are its borders and what are its distinguishing features? Much sought after and apparently high on the list of the ego's goals, poise is seen to relate specifically to the interpersonal situation, and to have at its core the interpersonal exchange. (The usage here is much more limited and literal than the wider and more all-inclusive meaning of "interpersonal relations" as used in the Harry Stack Sullivan school, where the interpersonal field of action is considered to be the matrix of all psychiatry.) I should like to suggest that security is the main heading, under which poise is a specific subdivision. Security applies to the entire spectrum of potential invading agents, to any possible disturbers of psychic equilibrium. It implies an armor of successful defenses against too great pressure from aggressive or sexual instincts, and against superego demands; in short, the whole gamut. Poise, on the other hand, is more limited and applies only to a specific type of assault, i.e., a social threat. Total security must include poise, but not necessarily the reverse, for poise or what looks like poise can exist without the state of psychological security. A quite disturbed patient, for example, with much free-floating anxiety as well as with many instances of localized, bound, phobic anxieties nevertheless looked and actually felt very poised in social situations, since her anxiety and phobic formations happened not to include the social scene. Poise is thus a special variant of security, a special form of social security.

A careful consideration of the essential nature of the state of feeling poised will reveal its basic dependence on the wish to be wanted and loved. The essential object is the human object. The potential dangers which become possible at the anticipation or actuality of an interpersonal encounter are generally several specific ones. The event feared from the human contact is most often the advent of critical appraisal from without, disapproval, and with it a closing off or absence of the desired and needed flow of narcissistic supplies. Of the two basic fears, castration and loss of love, security in general is concerned with both, while poise is thus related primarily to the latter. In a social situation which is uncertain, and there may be specific prerequisites for this in different people, a question is posed. At the moment of decision, when poise or unpoise is to follow, there hangs in balance the question, "How will I do? Will I be accepted? Will the supplies to my narcissism be provided, will I be loved, wanted, respected, noticed, listened to; or will I not?"

The question of poise is not an issue when the contact is with inanimate objects or with animals, though anxiety very well may be. Since the provider of narcissistic supplies is always the human, as genetically it was first the mother, it is only the human object who can likewise withdraw or withhold the flow of these narcissistic supplies. One never fears the loss or absence of love from an animal of an inanimate object (except insofar as these occasionally become symbols of or displacements from humans), but rather this fear is always in relation to the human object. Castration, on the other hand, and its derivatives, any damage or mutilation, while originally feared from the avenging or angry father, is later in reality also possible from the nonhuman or the inanimate object. It is this combination of factors which is responsible for the fact that phobia formation, for example, so frequently takes place by projection or displacement to nonhumans, animals, or things. The realistic role of the latter as possible physical threats, as by biting, hurting, injuring, etc., makes them eligible loci for choice by displacement in phobic symptom formation. In contrast, the fear of loss of love clinically remains attached to the human object. While the affect itself is subject to some distortion, the object, it seems, is not. As such, every interpersonal encounter is a potential challenge, reviving the original query: "Friend or foe, supplier or denier, critic or praiser?"

Some have ample resources against these possible dangers, and therefore no particular problem in maintaining poise. Those who are poorly armed are vulnerable. Some maintain very much of a counterphobic type of defense and seem incapable of embarrassment, attempting at all times aggressively to deny unpoise or susceptibility to it. Such a situation, for example, exists with many comedians, for whom wit so often serves the function of an aggressive denial of weakness. Their repertoires, however, as anyone who has analyzed a comedian, professional or otherwise, will readily attest, may serve to maintain poise, but by no means does it achieve security. A notorious bald man, for example, is said not to consider himself bald, but rather all other men as hairy. To some extent, the quality of fascination and charm enjoyed by many psychopaths is on such a counterphobic basis. People with excessive poise usually arouse suspicion or hostility in others, reminding them unwittingly of their own vulnerability.

The fear of criticism and the sensitivity to it point to the participation of the superego, either in the form of a reprojection of its appraising function to the outside world, or an incomplete internalization of it in the first place. This entire issue is more apt to occur with those who live for the opinions of others. Such deviation and pathology of superego structure again are usually tied up with oral fixation and orientation, where self-esteem remains too strongly dependent on external supplies.

Closely akin to social disapproval is the sense of shame, which again is a specific type of anxiety warded off and defended against in a social situation. Poise in this connection is a defense against being shamed, and unpoise a traumatic state of being shamed, of being despised, ridiculed, and laughed at. The connection of shame with the partial impulse of exhibitionism applies here as elsewhere. The assertion of an exhibitionistic partial impulse exposes one to the danger of social shame, which therefore serves as a motive for defense against this specific impulse. Poise, which is used in the service of this particular defense, attempts to combat and to ward off this shame. While thus used as a defense, it nevertheless allows the return of the repressed, for in poise can be detected the repressed exhibitionistic features themselves, since poise carries with it a certain exhibitionism. Blushing confirms the linkage between the two, for in poise blushing is avoided and eliminated while in unpoise it plays a prominent part. The frequent relation of the state of poise to the subjective state of the eyes also owes its existence to this connection with exhibitionism, since the feeling accompanying seeing is so intimately related to how one feels about *being* seen. The exhibitionistic-scoptophilic partial impulse as well as the related sense of shame are basically connected with both the castration complex and the need for oral narcissistic supplies. The human appraiser will see the weak spots in the armor, the flaws and lacunae in self-esteem, and will probe precisely into these openings. He will recognize the castrated state. What is vital here is not the danger of castration, for then the picture would be that of anxiety. Instead the danger is to be discovered as castrated, and on that score scorned, laughed at, ridiculed, and despised—meaning, in effect, a loss of a possible source of narcissistic supply and the substitution in its place of a depreciating, critical, rejecting observer. In the former, the subject fears he will be made inferior, while in the latter he feels that he already is.

This leads to the question of the relation between poise and anxiety; are they straightforwardly and directly inverse? Is poise simply the absence of anxiety, and unpoise the same as or an equivalent of anxiety? I do not feel that this is the case. Rather, just as poise is a subdivision of security, so unpoise or poiselessness, like shame, is a specific form of or a topically defined anxiety. It is a later developed and more localized expression of the earlier primary type of anxiety or unmastered tension. The relation or connection with anxiety proper ensues with the question as to whether or not the anxiety will become known to others, and varies with the sensitivity to this. Various combinations are possible.

Anxiety can be and usually is present with poiselessness as well. "I am not only upset and shaking all the time" the patient says, "but I can't face anyone because of it, and I'm ashamed for you to know it or see it." On the other hand, anxiety is known to occur without the accompanying sense of unpoise. This can take place where (1) the anxiety dominates the scene, but because of historical determinants the exhibitionistic component to it is minimal (it does not matter who know or sees); or (2) it does matter, in the usual sense, but the situation is such that anxiety does not stand out as different. This is the case when the external situation produces universal and "normal" anxiety, as in war combat; or as frequently seen aloft in an airplane. The acceptance of anxiety by others reduces or eliminates the lack of poise on its account; the anxiety remains, but interpersonal poise is possible; (3) there is still another possibility, where anxiety is present but the defenses against its visibility and communication to others are strong.

At this point we may note the dominant role played by the cultural component in regard to this state. For a special value, in our culture, seems to be attached to the demonstration of lack of dependence on others, and indeed to freedom from controlling emotions and affects. There is a great glorification of the salesman type, of the influencer of others, and a depreciation of those who are influenced *by* others. To show emotions or dependence is considered weak, and *vice versa.* Patients with anxiety are often less concerned and tortured by the anxiety itself than by the question "does it show?" Indeed, schools are set up where the ability to achieve these desired goals is taught and sold. One tries to learn how to *look* poised, free, independent, and masterful. "Charm" is taught, what to do with one's hands, posture, voice. Needless to say, these do not replace an inner psychological lack. This was recently brought out pointedly in a depressed suicidal young woman who still retained her outward learned manner while expressing the feeling that she felt like an empty shell.

To advance this description of the characteristics of the state of poise further, I turn to the *Merriam-Webster Unabridged Dictionary.* Under the term "poise," we find weight, balance, equilibrium, stability, carriage, rest, pose, suspension of motion. Translated into psychological economic terms, balance or equilibrium is achieved between the quantity of expected stimulus and the sum of the ego resources ready to meet it. The two are posed in equal balance, and between them there exists momentarily a suspension of motion. With poise there exists a confidence of mastery, of ability to neutralize the oncoming encounter; while in lack of poise, the person's resources are inadequate to the approaching situation and will be outweighed. Technically, the state of poise inherently implies the condition of expectation rather than of action. The opposing or complementary forces are not yet interlocked, but stand in readiness for action. It is as a runner poised in readiness to take off just before he hears the starting whistle. There is anticipation, readiness, and flexing and tension of the musculature.

This can be graphically illustrated if we apply it to Rapaport's (1951a) conceptual psychoanalytic model. His primitive model of conation consists of: restlessness ♦ appearance of breast and sucking ♦ subsidence of restlessness. The restless tension is accompanied by disequilibrium, while the breast and sucking are the means and activity whereby equilibrium is restored. The state of poise can be said to exist at the moment at which the breast appears and its availability and potentiality are known. The organism then pauses, as though in smug satisfaction in the knowledge of what is to come. This already implies a certain amount of ego development and functioning, for anticipation and judgment are already at work. Before this, there can be no delay, and poise cannot come about before the drive object is actually in contact.

The stream of stimuli proceeding toward the organism is not only inevitable but becomes desirable, and poise is a phase in the process of meeting them. It is a positive integrating function of the ego. Although the pleasure principle in general demands tension subsidence, and the constancy principle strives for an equalized level of tension, the reality principle makes it necessary to deal with and be ready for the inevitable stimuli which will follow. Moreover, there is a "hunger for stimuli" inherent in the object-seeking instinctual drives. In addition, the experience and memory of stimulus mastery, with the accompanying pleasure, make for the desire to repeat, thereby stimulating and increasing the hunger for stimuli and therefore again the need to master them. The process is thus a circular one, and poise to meet the stimuli is a necessary part of this repetitive armor.

III

I return to my original patient, who could achieve the state of poise, or the feeling of being anchored, by the specific maneuver of having the object (glass) ready to be applied to the

lips. Without it she felt unpoised and suspended. In the latter
condition, there seemed to be an imbalance. Something added
to the scales produced poise or balance. What was it which had
to be added?

The psychoanalytic reader will long since have come to the
conclusion borne out by the preceding theoretical considerations as well as by the further clinical material. Through a
series of less and less distorted derivatives, the path in this
patient, as in other orally fixated syndromes, led back to the
original oral situation, with fixation and a psychopathological
relationship to the mother's breast. A victim of pronounced and
early oral frustration at the hands of her embittered and
rejecting mother, she had reacted with oral fixation and the
defense of reaction formation. The greatest problem to her of
childbearing and motherhood was the prospect of being
obliged to breast-feed, which to both her children she had to
deny, though not without enormous guilt and self reproach.
The picture of a mother with a child at the breast was to her a
revolting sight or thought; and kept her from even wanting
another child. This was her way of denying her own insatiable
urge to suck, for she herself had been denied not only the
breast, but all that goes with it, warmth, cuddling, closeness,
and the feeling of "belonging." She had early become a feeding
problem and a vomiter. But her intense, repressed, oral wishes
broke through indirectly, in that symbolically she nurtured,
extracted, and suckled upon the entire external world, her
family, friends, and analyst. The chief conscious sexual problem, incidentally, was her husband's strong predilection for
fellatio-cunnilingus and her own revulsion against it.

The object which, when brought to the waiting lips, tipped
the scales and achieved the desired state of balance and poise,
represented in the deeper layers, the breast, originally so
denied and missing. The total oral process, however, as pointed
out by Lewin (1946), is a wide and composite activity. From the
standpoint of specific relevance to our subject, we can break it
down and extract a certain limited part of the whole complex as
being pertinent. We wish to focus attention here not on the oral

process in general, not on the taking in of the oral supplies, or the actual trickling inward of the warm milk, or the further gastrointestinal satisfaction, but rather on one momentary and transient phase in this continuum. That point is the moment of knowledge of the availability of the drive object. The breast becomes ready to give and is on its way. The supplies are to be forthcoming, and the action is about to be set off. It is like a moving picture stopped at an individual frame. The object and the recipient are "poised" for action. Both know their parts, and the subject is in a state of calm satisfaction, secure in his anticipation of the immediate future. (Perhaps one can recognize a derivative of this state of poise *en masse,* natural and sure in some, artificial and forced in others, if one pictures a cocktail party. Each stands with glass poised, with perioral muscles poised, and with the psyche momentarily and more or less in the same state of poise.)

This already presupposes the ego's ability to recognize the breast. Prior to this, only the actual external supply, and not any internal anticipation and therefore ability to delay, can provide the desired repose. This really first state of belonging is with the breast in the mouth. The fact is to be noted that at the center of this desideratum is the being anchored, the being attached (again) to a larger unit, more firm and immovable, and thereby not being suspended. My patient had to feel anchored, attached, and not hanging in space. The infant hangs on by the mouth. It is at the breast that the infant reestablishes the original biological unity and, just as previously *in utero,* is again at one with the environment and with the source of narcissistic supply. Acceptance here is utter and complete; ridicule and criticism are absent. The perioral muscles have their object and are holding on. Poise is a hope of reviving this blissful and omnipotent state. As such, it is not dissimilar to what one attempts to achieve nightly in sleep, which, as Lewin (1950b) has shown, also represents unconsciously a repetitive wish to return to the same original oral breast situation.

IV

This section will deal with a consideration of the executive apparatus through which these dynamic functions are mediated. There are several which stand out as of special importance, and which will therefore be selected for some detailed inspection. These are (a) the mouth, (b) the general musculoskeletal postural system, and (c) the hand. Clinical and theoretical considerations support and illustrate each instance.

In any social or interpersonal situation in which poise comes into question, the subject is being made to find a niche for himself, to relate himself to some larger challenging unit (person or group) in a way which will be comfortable and into which he will fit. He looks for a place to stand or sit and a way to be. It is much like a mountain climber who gropes out for the next excrescence or concavity around which or into which to arrange his body for support. Feelings and symptoms in certain areas point to special foci of sensitivity during this quest.

Let us turn our attention first to the oral zone, to which I have already alluded as regards its function of grasping or clinging to the first human object. The material to follow at this point represents what has been described above as the subtitle or secondary theme of this communication, and has relevance, I believe, not only specifically in relation to poise, but in a more general way to every interpersonal encounter.

With a more microscopic observation upon this oral region, further reflection and a consideration of additional data make it necessary to enlarge somewhat the anatomical area singled out in relation to the psychic feeling being described. Rather than solely the mouth, I would widen the circle to have it include what is commonly called the snout. The region would now correspond roughly to a circle with its center in the philtrum of the upper lip or at the center of the mouth. Its lateral margins would be the two nasolabial folds; its upper margin, the ventral surface of the nose; its lower margin, through the middle of the chin. On closer thought, it is this larger area, rather than the mouth alone, which is buried in and is contiguous to the surface of the maternal breast during the earliest interpersonal contact. Direct observation will bear out this point. And it is in the tissues of this area, its skin, fasciae, and muscles, through which the first proprioceptive sensations of being steadied and attached and anchored are mediated. Correspondingly, in later life this is a focal area which, when one feels unanchored in any more complex social or interpersonal situation, feels unsteady and shaky and has to be supported. The thumbsucking child is often seen to stimulate this wider area, for in addition to having the thumb in the mouth, it is not infrequent to see a forefinger describe a larger arc, playing on or rubbing the upper lip or the nose or a contiguous area. Hoffer (1949), describing an individualized type of finger sucking in a 16-week-old boy, in which he held the ring finger in the mouth while pressing the three remaining fingers like a scaffolding toward the lower lip, interprets this particular position as being a voluntary reproduction of an epidermic stimulation which he felt while sucking at the breast. This, he postulates, may have been aroused on his chin or lower lip by his mother's hand holding the nipple in his mouth. In later life, numerous derivative mannerisms can be observed, e.g., how, in any embarrassing or trying moment, one may unconsciously play his fingers around his mouth, or steady his chin, as by feigning to lean on it, or dig a finger into each angle of the mouth, or bite his lips, or just cover the snout area with the fingers or hand. These actions are designed to provide this region with an object to hang onto, to prevent it from hanging open or quivering, suspended in mid-air; or from being seen to do this. Among other related derivative activities one may mention the chewing of gum, the extensive use of lipstick and other cosmetics in this focal area, and the growing of moustaches. It should also be pointed out that the oral and narcissistic attributes of this area can receive reinforcement from other later determinants. Thus, for example, in one patient his face and nose picking has to do not only with his patting and putting at ease, this early oral snout, but also combines picking out and playing with nasal secretions, which in this case has distinctly anal derivatives. He also does the same with his ears and with other areas of his skin. In another patient, his face concentration is a combination of oral narcissistic needs with a strong phallic cathexis, there having occurred a marked genital displacement from below upward. All kinds of identifications can add to and complicate the picture, such as one patient identifying certain features of her face with undesirable traits of her mother's and another patient covering up and being ashamed of his "jowls," because to him they represented his aggressive, greedy father.

There area a number of different reasons which all converge in giving to this area such a focal role in this connection, in addition to the factor already mentioned of the primitive ontogenetic role played by the snout area in the earliest human contact. Among these is first an anatomic-embryologic consideration, namely, that this oral snout area is, both phylogenetically and from the standpoint of embryological development, the true rostral tip of the organism, a fact which in quadrupeds is still anatomically visible. As the most cephalad and forward point, this area psychologically and biologically is the pseudopod which projects furthest into the outer world and is therefore invested with the function of making the first tentative contacts with objects of the environment, to determine which to accept or reject. Quadrupeds meet each other directly with their most forward points, nose to nose. In the dog it is the nose which is used to sniff and test and sample the environment, deciding what to accept or to reject. The first exploration of objects by the human infant is by bringing them with the hand to the mouth, or smearing them around his snout. Primitive human adults retain this in certain forms—primitives still greet each other snout to snout. Universally, where there is complete acceptance between individuals, as in the sexual embrace, these areas also meet. In fact, the deeper and closer the kiss, the more these areas seek to merge and become one. It is by a similar mechanism that sometimes the entire skin is, by displacement, used in an oral sense. Thus one patient, during sexual experience, wants to roll up in a ball and get inside his partner, while

another, in the opposite direction, wants to surround, encompass, and introject his mate. The following clinical material will
illustrate this point quite graphically.

An asthmatic patient with a long history of oral deprivation
had the fantasy and attitude of the upper part of his body being
like an invaginated tube. In most of his contacts with other
people which were unsatisfactory and left him frustrated and
wanting, he pictured the opening of his tube as not meeting
head on the tube of the other person, so that there was only an
inadequate exchange of air between them. With a girlfriend
with whom he felt he had the most satisfactory relationship that
he had ever had, he pictured the two tubes as meeting and
fitting completely together so that the air from one passed into
the other. When his contacts with human beings failed, he
would resort to his adrenalin spray, which he would put to his
nose and mouth where *he* could control the position and dosage
of the interchange. As an aside which cannot be gone into at
any greater length here, I wonder whether or not this does not
play a primary role in the psychogenesis of asthmatic conditions, that emotional deprivation through this entire oral-nasal
area from birth onward might lead to a stilted and irregular
and inadequate passage of gases between the external world
and the respiratory tract. I might also comment on the frequency of colds and question whether this might not also be
explained as an attempt to deal with or eject unwelcome stimuli
from the rostral intake point of the organism, the mouth and
nose. This would be the same mechanism as a sneeze. The
asthmatic patient above considered his frequent colds to indicate, "I concentrate on myself. I tighten up and pull in toward
myself. There is a tremendous concentration of feeling in my
nose." Accompanying this material, the patient expressed many
oral receptive tendencies, a desire for the breast, and a dream
and associations about receiving injections from doctors. During such a cold he said, "I told myself to relax and my nostrils
immediately cleared up." At another time this same patient
thought of himself as a cyclostome, with gaping mouth, holding
on. In another instance, when recalling material that had to do

with his not being able to talk to his mother and to express to her how lonely and abandoned he felt, he thought of a balloon which is blown up and the mouth of which is pinched or tightened so that no air could pass in or out. The opening of the balloon corresponded to his mouth and throat, while the rest of the balloon was his chest. This patient, incidentally, had a frequent gesture of rubbing his snout with his hand during the analytic hour, as though he were trying to put this area at ease. In several other patients who showed this gesture frequently during analytic sessions, I also had the impression that the dynamic motivation was to give physical support to this region, to steady and anchor it.

A decisive part in giving to the snout area its vital role is its close relation to affects and to the mimetic expressive system, which is so much at the core of man's relation to man. For the area delineated is the window to the emotions. It is the small porthole through which can be observed from the outside the person's affective state, how he feels and reacts. While, to be sure, the entire organism participates to some degree in receiving effector impulses as the endpoint of the complicated emotional reflex arc, for example, by sweating or generalized muscular tension, nevertheless the perioral and snout region is the focus of greatest concentration of effector response to emotions, at least in relation to the external world. It is there that we watch for a reaction. It was partly to avoid that constant observation from patients that Freud and later other analysts employed the use of the couch. Within these relatively few inches of body surface, the tone, position in space, and direction of the skin and facial musculature denote how a person is at the moment. The remainder of the body surface is considerably more neutral. The cartoonist or artist makes use of this fact; with one line in this region, pointing either upward or downward, he can connote a mood, happy or sad. The Greek masks of tragedy and comedy bear out this same point. The predominance of this zone in mimetic expression is in accord with the findings of most experimental psychologists, such as the work of Dunlap (1927), who found that the muscles of the lower half of the face and especially the area around the mouth predominated over the eye muscles in the expression of emotions.

The relationship of this area to the system of mimetic expression has steady and progressive development beginning already in infancy. In earliest life the first sign of displeasure is a drooping of the lower lip; continuing unhappiness results in more lowering of the perioral and nasolabial lines and finally crying, with a more diffuse spread of the motor reaction. To quote Charles Darwin (1897), "I believe that the depressor muscles of the angles of the mouth are less under separate control of the will than the adjoining muscles, so that if a young child is only doubtfully inclined to cry, this muscle is generally the first to contract and is the last to cease contracting" (p. 150). During equilibrium or a neutral emotional state, the folds are at rest, placid, in their baseline static position. Pleasurable tension is made manifest by an upward deflection, and finally by a more complete upward turning of the skin folds and muscles, with laughter and again a diffusion of the response. These are the primitive, the universal, and the central responses. Though elaborations of these and individual variations do, to be sure, take place, nevertheless this area retains throughout life its central position in giving expression to affects and emotions. The region immediately peripheral to it may frequently participate quite strongly in the total response, as especially the eyes and the forehead; or there may be a particularly strong development of one small part of the response, or a peculiar qualitative differentiation which stamps one individual as different from another. But the most primitive affects call forth the most universal and the least differentiated reactions, localized in this central area for mimetic expression. The nostrils quiver in anxiety or anger, the lip curls up in a snarl, the lips tremble in highly charged states, or a smile "may play around the lips." A person is admonished to "keep his chin up" or to "keep a stiff upper lip." A sneer is a compromise expressional state in this snout region which combines elements of the impulses and affect being felt plus the attempt to cover them.

Activity in this area may be chronic. A person may be characteristically grim-lipped. Clenched teeth or bruxism may occur even during sleep. In one patient his constant and repetitive grasping and stroking of his chin during the analytic hour seemed to be a physical attempt to prevent a whimpering state. His entire demeanor, character, and stance emphasized independence and self-sufficiency, which often, however, turned out to be a thin covering for an underlying weakness, dependence, and potential sobbing disorganization. The day after the interpretation was made about the defensive nature of his chin-holding, the patient, while talking with another person, suddenly broke down and wept profusely, being consumed with long pent-up feelings of guilt and self-pity about certain specific events which he brought the next day to the analysis. This same gesture is not infrequently observed in other patients, in which they steady the chin with their hands, sometimes for many minutes, to hold back an otherwise uncontrollable state of whimpering with frustration, rage, or impotence.

A patient in analysis was reliving a series of traumatic incidents in his childhood when he was subjected to repeated cystoscopies. He recalled how he used to cover his face and suppress any sound in order to hide his feelings and his intense suffering from the operators. Another patient, whose conflicts centered around violent oral sadistic impulses and his defenses against these, remembered how his facial muscles used to twitch when he faced his teacher or any authority. Then, and even into his present life in similar situations, his emotions would well up and concentrate in his face. Under such circumstances he felt "as if my face would blow up." He volunteered that his method of avoiding embarrassment and exposure was to force laughter in the facial muscles. He also brought his arm to his face in order to cover it; and he became a chain smoker so that he could do this frequently, bring his hand to his face and occupy the muscles by smoking.

The process of maturation and growth is accompanied, during the course of ego development, by an increase in control over these primitive expressions paralleling the acquisition of the faculty of poise. For poise in this sense is symbolic of mastery over affects, and hence is centered in this focal area for mimetic expression. The organism learns to "bind" emotions or to tame them (Fenichel, 1945), or to alter, or postpone, or otherwise dispose of their expression. Again individual variations abound. A high development of this specific control results in the characteristic of the "poker face." Or a deliberate training or natural ability along this line may, as in the case of an actor, enable him to subordinate this apparatus to his conscious will, and to simulate and "put on" or mimic emotional expressions. Another might have a noteworthy underdevelopment of this control, resulting in emotional incontinence. A feeling tone automatically and involuntarily spills over and is translated into motor expression. "Everything immediately shows on my face," such people complain, or they "wear their emotions on their sleeves." In the "norm" or usual case, a certain amount of control (poise) is achieved, which may, however, be overbalanced by the pressure of emotions seeking discharge in special affect-laden moments.

This developmental and functional description of mimetic facial activity is paralleled by and derives confirmation from certain structural considerations. The neurological mechanisms for mimetic expression are mediated in pathways separate from those for voluntary facial activity. A voluntary or forced smile can be differentiated from a genuine and involuntary one. Organic lesions can affect one and spare the other. Voluntary facial paralysis can exist while mimetic expression is normal, and *vice versa*. In general it is believed that the neurological pathways for mimetic control originate in the thalamus and/or pallidum in contrast to the voluntary corticospinal supranuclear innervation. Thus we see that neurophysiological, mimetic emotional expression belongs with the older subcortical structures, while control of these is taken over by the newer developed cortex. Embryologically, the olfactory or snout area is connected with the archipallium, while controlling forces are vested in the neopallium. Edinger, the neuroanato-

mist, describing the anterior perforated substance, which corresponds to the tuberculum olfactorium of macrosmatic
mammals, states that "the different fibers to this area are
probably especially concerned with feeding reflexes of the
snout or muzzle, including smell, touch, taste, and muscular
sensibility, a physiologic complex which can be called collec-
tively the 'oral sense.'" These anatomical observations point too
to the archaic and primitive organs of the functions invested in
this perioral zone—lending confirmation to our clinical and
descriptive accounts derived from genetic considerations.[1]

This snout area, anatomically the most cephalad point of
the organism, and invested as it is with mimetic function,
undergoes a characteristic shift and displacement during the
course of development. In man, in both the neural and
mesodermal developments, this rostral tip during the course of
embryologic growth assumes a more and more subordinate
position and is overgrown by newer and probably protective
elements. In the neural system, the older olfactory cortex, or
rhinencephalon, or archipallium, which represents almost the
entire forebrain of lower vertebrates (Arey, 1934, pp. 414 and
417) in mammals gives way to and is surrounded by the more
highly developed nonolfactory cerebral cortex or neopallium.
Similarly, in the facial or visceral development (Arey, pp.
136–143), which is in intimate connection with the history and

[1]The following observations lend further confirmation to the above.
Grinker (1953) lays special emphasis on the role of olfaction in the refinement
of anxiety as a signal, for it is this "which enables the organism to project itself
in future time and anticipate far ahead the satisfaction of needs or the
presence of danger" (p. 178). He also points to the role of the rhinencephalon
and the visceral brain in standing between inner needs and outer symbols of
satisfaction.
    Davenport Hooker (1953) and Humphrey (1953), studying the behavior
of human embryos, find that the first response to exteroceptive stimulation,
occurring at 7 ½ weeks of menstrual age, is limited to the circumoral region
supplied by the maxillary and mandibular divisions of the trigeminal nerve.
This is the first evidence of adjustment of the embryo as a whole to its
external environment.
    Bender et al. (1953), in studies of double simultaneous stimulation in
children and adults, find the face to be dominant to all other areas in these
tests. See also Linn (1955).

fate of the branchial arches, the early stages of the ontogenetic development of the face are characterized by the prominence of the nasal cavities and the derivatives of the first branchial arch (maxillary and mandibular processes); just as phylogenetically the snout constitutes most of the face of lower vertebrates. Again the course of further development is accompanied by a recession in this supremacy in favor of the surrounding areas, in keeping with the progressive subordination of smell as a dominant sense in the phlogenetic scale. Probably in addition the anterior and ventral shift of the rostral point in man is related to his assumption of the erect posture.

Nature characteristically protects and encases its crucial but vulnerable parts. Thus the "vital centers" neurologically are buried deep in the medulla, where they are covered and protected by thick layers of more neutral and expendable tissue. The heart is protected deep within the bony thorax, and the sensitive solar plexus is well covered under the thick fatty layers of the abdomen, etc. It is probably by a similar mechanism that the vital area for emotional expression in man becomes shrunken down to such a small space, shifted ventrally, and surrounded by a more neutral protecting area. A small, well-guarded fortress can be more easily defended, and behind its walls the primary and more disturbing affects can be more safely locked. The acquisition of poise is in the same direction as these structural and functional developments and is a token of the amount of success achieved in the struggle to tame affects.

Still another reason why this oral snout zone, this rostral tip, becomes pinpointed as an area of special sensitivity and cathexis in interhuman contact is the fact that to a certain extent this area, or at least the face in general, often becomes identified with the total person himself, the part being substituted for the whole. It is as if this portion labels the person and gives away his identity. It becomes the person, becomes the ego. The masked robber, for example, covers himself up and hides who he is by covering up with a triangular handkerchief just these few inches, though the rest of him be exposed. With a facial plastic, a person tries to change who he is. A certain riding master calls all his young charges "Schnoozle," and they in turn identify him by the same name; "Schnozzola" is another, related, well-known identifying name. A patient, at the end of his analysis, left with the analyst a ceramic piece which he had made. It was a face, the chief feature of which was a pouting underlip. It left with the analyst a token and a most succinct, accurate description of the patient himself. The following clinical excerpt will provide a more elaborate illustration of this same point.

A patient, close to schizophrenia though not actually psychotic, e.g., in his regressive behavior, his complete maladjustment to external reality, his disorganization, his defiance of society, his extremely labile moods, his unconventional dress, and severe and unremitting insecurity, one day brought to the office a drawing he had make of himself. (He has no formal artistic bent and has never drawn.) He had looked at himself in the mirror and put down on paper how he appeared. The result was the following drawing. He was struck by the resemblance (which indeed existed), and, in a state of great agitation, stated, "Whether of not this looks like me actually, it is exactly the way I feel to myself inside. All the anguish—that's it exactly." Pointing to the self-portrait, he continued, "This is the part I mean. This is the main part," pointing to and outlining the snout. "This is me. This is what I really am. This mouth— this is the mouth of a baby." He then pointed to the square steel-like jaw. "This is what the world used me for. This is what they took me to be. It was because of this that they forced me to play football, to be a rough guy. But what I really craved to do, what I always wanted and never dared to do was what sissies do. I wanted to write on a paper. I wanted to be in the glee-club. I can't sing but I wanted to be in the glee-club." The patient is a physical specimen, a brutish-looking hulk of a man whose external life was physical, rough, and earthy to the extreme. Now an actor, he acts the parts of psychopath, killer, fighter. He tells the analyst at this point how "I never see the real world sharply outlined as it actually is. The sharp outlines have jagged edges which can cut and rip and make you bleed. Instead, I always see it with the margin blurred, diffuse, and round. The edges never really come into focus, but graduate out of themselves into space, leaving everything soft, and I want to hold it close." It was this, he explained, that enabled him to trudge along in the deep snow of a blizzard during the Battle of the Bulge completely oblivious to the physical hardships and in a sort of an entranced state which he later described as "one of the happiest times of my life." He was fantasying being in the warm sun of New Mexico, riding a horse peacefully on a big ranch (completely fantastic in relation to his previous real life) and "holding this round thing close to me within my arms." The analyst ventured at this point that what he held in his arms was

a breast. The patient became jubilant and agitated. "That's it, Doc, that's it. That's it. This mouth, this mouth in the picture is the mouth of a baby waiting to be fed. That's me, that's the way I feel on the inside." He had labeled the picture "child at thirty." The snout area in this case stuck out through the armor and the mask around it. It was his Achilles heel, visible to the surface and rendering him vulnerable. It was also "the true self" into which were concentrated the expression of his deepest impulses and needs and the nature of his efforts to achieve satisfaction and security. "It goes way back" the patient stated, "it goes way back to the beginning."

In these last two factors, i.e., the connection of the face with mimetic expression and the identity of the face with the total person, the relation to exhibitionism again becomes apparent, and symptomatology in reference to this area receives strong reinforcement when an exhibitionistic component also exists. Face, emotions, exhibitionism are connected. Blushing starts in this area and radiates outward. One patient with a strong conflict over exhibitionism remembered as his most happy and triumphant moments several occasions when he acted and clowned on a stage but with a mask over his face to hide his identity. A central feature in the exhibitionistic activity of acting is the display of simulated emotions. A prime example of poiselessness is in stage fright, and common accompaniments of this state are dry mouth or twitching of the mouth. Not knowing one's lines will leave the mouth hanging open, suspended, unoccupied. Sometimes the mouth feels big and exposed. Using the mouth, as by ad-libbing or a push of speech, is a maneuver to counteract this. The wish in stage fright is to cover, hide, or bury the face. In an insightful paper, Fenichel (1946) discusses and elaborates many of these related mechanisms as they occur in actors.

Through these activities we can trace the following sequence and line of development: (1) infant with his mouth and snout buried in the breast; (2) 1½-year-old in his mother's arms, when approached by a stranger, turning and burrowing into his mother's shoulder; (3) older child turning his face into a corner so as not to be seen; and (4) adult, unpoised, blushing, and wanting to cover or hide his face. In the first instance, the mother will always protect or appraise well.

Connected as it is with control over emotions, poise will therefore also be related to and make use of the structures contiguous to the face which share with it the function of mimetic expression. Among these are the respiratory apparatus and the voice. The close relationship between emotions and respiratory activity has already been alluded to and demonstrated in the case of the asthmatic patient described above. This relationship is further confirmed neurophysiologically by the faciorespiratory pathways which mediate emotional expression. There is an intimate tie-up between the facial muscles already mentioned and the effector organs of respiration. Afferent stimuli which result in either crying or laughing produce their effects by a complex reflex are with effector responses in respiration as well as in the facial musculature. Thus laughter is accompanied by prolonged inspirations followed by short broken expirations instead of the usual inspiratory-expiratory cycle. Weeping and sobbing, on the other hand, are manifested in addition to the typical facial movements, by short broken inspirations followed by prolonged expirations. The latter is similar to the respiratory changes in asthma. The throat, too, with its enclosed voice box, which anatomically links the mouth and nose with the deeper respiratory tree, shares strongly in the expression of emotional experience. One gulps with emotions, or chokes a sob. A patient with globus hystericus would describe his attacks as beginning in the back of his tongue and nasal passages and then progressing downward to the throat. It is well known how the voice can serve as a sensitive barometer of one's feelings. One patient loses his voice, another stutters, another has to clear his throat frequently, another speaks with a hoarse voice during emotional episodes. Suggesting that there might be an accompanying physicochemical change also at work here is an observation made by the patient above with globus hystericus, who noted that during anxiety spells or during an attack of globus any gum which he was chewing at the time became finely shredded in his mouth like shreds of cotton. This might relate to the work on the parotid secretory activity performed by Lourie et al. (1942), and by Strongin and Hinsie (1938), who found in general that parotid salivary secretion increased and reverted to the higher levels of infancy and childhood as behavior regressed to earlier levels. This they interpret as being due to the release of lower subcortical centers from higher cortical control. Discussing the schizophrenic patient, the latter authors state that as the patient returns "to primitive grasping and sucking reflexes, the parotid rate too goes back to infantile levels" (p. 715). However, in anxiety states in which there is a predominance of cortical control, there is a diminution in the secretory rate below normal (i.e., the dry mouth described above). Poise implies a certain degree of control or mastery over both the respiratory and vocal apparatus at least as they relate to mimetic expression. Relevant to this observation is the well-known way in which "small talk" is used to achieve or at least to give the appearance of poise. It is as if by this means one asserts his control over the line of human intercommunication, voice, and thought.

Various types of pathological alterations can occur and are seen in relation to the mimetic expressive system, with accompanying changes at least in the outward appearance of poise. These can be of either organic or psychogenic origin. Organic lesions, as mentioned above, can affect the effector pathways even though the inner affect and tone may remain unchanged. Thus a person will feel laughter or crying but be unable to show it either on one or both sides (usually owing to interruption of the supranuclear mimetic pathways connected with the thalamus). Forced laughter or crying is seen in pseudobulbar palsy, where interference with voluntary control results in overactivity of the subordinate involuntary control. Multiple sclerotics often show this symptom. The outward expression of laughter or crying may not necessarily be accompanied by a corresponding inner feeling; in fact, the feeling and the expression may be contradictory. Parkinsonism with bilateral pallidal involvement results in the typical frozen facies. Emotions are felt, but their outlet is curtailed so that these people seem to be impervious and not to react.

Psychogenic alterations of this expressive system are no less frequent than those mentioned above. There are adults in whom there persists the infantile characteristic of emotional incontinence so that their feelings flow over into action uncontrollably. In states of tension or of "readiness for discharge" minor stimuli can precipitate such reactions, which may be inappropriate not only quantitatively but qualitatively as well. The depressed states are more apt to show the frozen apathetic facies than other psychopathological conditions. Here the regression to oral level and the state of narcissism makes the individual less susceptible to external stimuli and therefore motorically unresponsive. The same can be seen in deeply regressed catatonia. In general those people with a more lively and open object relationship show a greater lability of facial expression and of the state of poise. Those with less show less lability but less outward response in general. They appear grim, or indrawn. Those with healthier or more positive object relations have a more steady state of poise, showing contact with control. Tension can show itself as a tic in the perioral region, revealing a conflict between wanting to discharge affect (often hostility) and the effort to inhibit it. This is similar to an irritative organic lesion such as might result from pressure on the supranuclear facial pathways. A tremor of the lips and chin is common. A common mannerism of tense people is to cover the snout with the hands as though thus hiding any possible giving away of the emotions. As often as not, this applies not to a visible tremor or tic but to cover a feeling of which only the subject is aware.

Just as this area is the first to make contact in an interpersonal relationship, i.e, in the beginning of life with the mother's breast, so it is also the last to withdraw from external reality in the downward regressive path of mental disorders. One of the final regressive symptoms in the most out-of-contact catatonic is to refuse food, to be mute, to become impassive and frozen.[2] Erik Erikson (1950) has pointed out that in an early infantile stage of ego development, the child, to avoid the shame of being looked at, would like to "sink, right then and there, into the ground" (p. 223). But in so doing the snout or rostral tip would be the last to hold on to the outside world. It is like the picture of a fish under water with its oral region protruding out above the surface. This part, in man, must in reality remain in contact with the world for life to persist. I remember a patient in whom the schizophrenic process could be seen *in statu nascendi*. She was just at that point where she was giving up her grasp on the real world and was already partially sunk into a narcissistic delusional state. Her symptomatology at this time consisted of sensations in the perioral zone with a feeling as if the muscles there were twitching and moving and insects were crawling around under the skin. She played her hands plaintively around this area, alternately covering and exposing it, with a pleading expression on her face. This was partly a restitutional symptom, representing her last hope that someone would stop her downward path by offering support to this clinging area so that with it she could grasp and be pulled back to reality. A similar mechanism can be noted in a case described by Greenson (personal communication, 1951), in which a patient with depersonalization finally felt that there was nothing left of her but her mouth. She now felt that she was all mouth, as if this was the last part with which to hold on.

Before leaving this subject of the role of the oral or perioral component, it might be well to say a word about its relation to the other levels of instinctual development, which seem by comparison to have been neglected in this study. A survey of the situation from a somewhat distant vantage point leads, I believe, to the following explanation of these apparent lacunae and what it is that I have covered in this aspect of my presentation. The unpoised person is reeling back from some

[2]The clinical phenomenon of *schnauzkrampf* is most illustrative in this connection.

difficult situation and is simultaneously groping for some island of safety. The poised person is already on this island and has been safely on it to begin with. My study has focused its sights on the problem of where the unpoised person wishes to go, and where the poised person already stands. The other side of the picture, which still needs further comment, is the question of what it is that makes him reel back. What is it which at this point makes it particularly imperative that he receive the approval or support of others? There is a chronic background need for this, and yet at times it becomes more acute than others. In summary I may say that these latter times coincide with periods of increased awareness of forbidden actions or impulses. And the nature of such crises, as I have come to know them, consists in the last analysis of the pressures of the instincts, sexual or aggressive. The precipitating causes may relate specifically to any level of instinctual development, oedipal, masturbatory, anal, dirty, aggressive, greedy, etc. One's susceptibility to these pressures requires that he be on good terms with both his own superego and the external world. And susceptibility to instinctual pressure certainly varies, not only from moment to moment, but also during certain special periods, for example, during adolescence, when special conditions exist. It is this lability of instinctual pressure, primarily in a social situation, which serves as a frequent precipitating factor in touching off the various vicissitudes in the state of poise.

V

I return to the main body, to continue the consideration of the executive apparatus through which poise is mediated. I have been engaged for some time now in a rather detailed description of the first of these, the perioral region, having been led into this detail by the primitive and focal role of this area and its relation to mimetic expression. The other organs which I thought would justify special attention were the general musculoskeletal postural system, and the hand in particular.

With regard to the first, the general musculoskeletal system, poise implies and carries with it a certain amount of muscle tone, and therefore a relation to body posture. When ready for approaching stimuli, the entire musculature is in a state of at least partial tonus, and therefore cathected. Its fate and its position in space are of moment to the organism; how it will fare, how it will be thought of, and how it will be received are of consequence. The aim here, as with the sucking muscles, is to grasp and hang on, to be attached, to be anchored and supported on all its surface. In the original psychological interpersonal situation, the infant at the breast, it is not only the oral zone which is securely attached to its object, but the entire body surface is surrounded, cradled, and supported. Perhaps it is the possible loss or absence of this physical support which is a basis for the archaic and probably congenital fear of falling, present from the very beginnings of life. A year or two later, we see a child, when confronted by the presence of a challenging stranger or a potential shaming object, make for a parent's leg and try to curl his whole body round it. Still later, we note how a grown person, in a similar psychological situation, tries in a more subtle and disguised way to lean against or on something, or, in the absence of this possibility, at least aims to have his posture and musculature as self-supporting and as independent and as protected as possible. He is aware, during this state, of any potential weak spots in the armor, and may endow certain special areas, according to his history, with special susceptibilities. The aim is to fit in, to be surrounded, and to "belong." The fear is to stick out, to be noticed, and to be ridiculed or rejected. Common feelings in point are, as in the first patient described, to feel gauche, awkward, clumsy *in toto*, or "like a klutz"—generally indicating maternal rejection, criticism, or scorn, though often covered with maternal reaction formation. Or a special sensitive part may serve as the concentrated focus for such feelings, such as a thick ankle or a hairy lip, a mole, a shape, or the gait in general. The role played by displacement from castration or genital shame is obvious, so that there usually is overdetermination for such feelings.

It is worthwhile to point out how divorced such feelings

may be and usually are from reality, depending instead on the state of self-esteem, the concept of the self and body image, and the strength and status of the superego, which determines, by projection, how much criticism is to be expected from the outside. A young woman, for example, feels gauche and clumsy and childish in her movements and stature and appearance, while in reality she gives the impression from any angle of complete suavity, poise, and assurance. Yet this same patient, with such a grossly inappropriate feeling with regard to her reality appearance, was completely unperturbed and unaffected and unself-conscious during a month or two in which she was afflicted with a Bell's palsy. For apparently with the latter the disfigurement could be plainly observed and would remain at its source. With regard to the inappropriate affective state, however, since the real source and origin of the unpleasurable feeling was not in the posture itself, but rather displaced from an inner psychic source, i.e., that of not feeling liked and accepted and wanted, and since this real source was impervious to observation and therefore to change, the irrational feeling was able to retain its strength.

Body posture may be smooth and flowing and accompanied by a corresponding inner feeling that this is so. Or it may be outwardly halting, broken, inhibited, and staccatolike, as an outward expression of an inner sensation of awkwardness or unpoise. However, there exists in many cases a discrepancy between the two, between the inner concept and the outer performance as it appears to the onlooker, so that, for example, in spite of external defective areas, inner assurance may be strong; and in reverse, there may be a successful postural exterior which covers up and belies an inner faltering and fragility.

Further examples of the relation between posture and poise are the following. A patient, a man of almost 50, came face to face quite suddenly with a woman acquaintance of some renown whom he had known from some slight distance in the past. He noticed later in retrospect that, while he had handled himself better than in the past, he had, in order to be and to appear casual, leaned his foot on a bench and his elbow on his knee. This position, he was aware, was designed to lend support, literally, to his crumbling figure. An extreme example of this crumbling of the posture is seen in fainting. In contrast, an attempt to deny any dependence on the outside is seen in the way in which an adolescent, or an adolescentlike adult, will lie sprawled out on the floor or on a chair in a position designed to give the impression of the utmost poise. This position, a kind of opposite of erectness or muscle tone, is as if to say, "I don't need any muscle tone, you affect me or threaten me so little— I am so self-sufficient." It is in reality just the reverse—and one patient used this action to cover up a state of quite considerable agitation. This same desire, to appear casual and poised and thus to deny any need for others, was expressed in another patient by a more complex piece of behavior. Her habitual lateness had behind it the wish that people should come to call for her and find her not ready. Her goal was then to be "caught" by them, i.e., she would fantasy coming out of a dressing room with hair uncombed and saying, very casually, "Oh, just a moment, I'll be with you at once." This was of course designed to deny her great need for and oral dependence on others, and to thwart her impulse to be ready and eagerly waiting hours before the appointed time. In another patient the use of her posture and gesture as a necessary defense was demonstrated by the fact that she would lose her poise when talking to certain people on the telephone. Voice alone was insufficient, and she needed these other measures to bolster her up. In localized body language, one patient expressed the feeling that a tic of his shoulder was meant to convey "nonchalant defiance."

Of special focal interest, and sharing with the mouth in specific importance in relation to the feeling of poise, is the role played by the hand. This organ, too, of such primary function in grasping, sticks out and constitutes an issue, the solution of which seems crucially associated with whether or not poise is achieved. In a successful or comfortable solution, the hand is satisfactorily integrated into the body unit. When there is a disequilibrium, a state of unpoise, the hand, as much as any other organ, seems suspended, or as if groping and looking for the object. "What to do with the hands?" is an uppermost question during states of discomfiture; and people are taught what to do with them in order to appear at ease.

The unity of mouth and hand is brought out here as it has been described by Willie Hoffer (1949) in relation to ego function. Hoffer points out that already in intrauterine life the hand becomes closely allied to the mouth for the sake of relieving tension and that within this alliance is the first achievement of the primitive ego. Owing to the posture of the foetus within the uterus, the hand or fist is nearest to the chin and mouth. Neurophysiological confirmation of this alliance is provided by the palmomental reflex which is accentuated when separated from the higher centers by pyramidal tract disease. Writing on this reflex, Blake and Kunkle (1951) comment: "The primitive meaning of the palmomental reflex suggests a fragmentary 'wince' reaction.—The chin muscles play a prom-inent role in the expression of discomfort. It seems particularly relevant that quivering of the chin precedes or replaces an outburst of weeping." In earliest life both mouth and hand seek to grasp the mother object. From the twelfth week the hand helps in the feeding process by being placed half open on the breast or bottle (Gesell and Ilg, 1937). In the absence of the latter, they also find and explore each other, leading to the first self-discovery, which is enlarged later into an oral-tactile con-cept of the body and the world around. In the infant it is thumb and finger sucking, while in later life there results an abun-dance of derivative activities, all types of mannerisms in which the hand or fingers "play around" the mouth or chin or nose or face. It is the hand, as well as the lips, which is steadied and re-assured by the poised cocktail glass. Of similar effect is the ciga-rette, which spends more time comforting the fingers than it does between the lips. Knitting owes its popularity to this same mech-anism. The handshake unites people. In the absence of such satisfactory activity, during states of unpoise various movements are seen to be engaged in by the hands. One patient wrings her hands constantly, or grasps each finger in succession; another keeps pulling pieces of wool out of the couch, while still another holds on to his belt. I wish to exclude from this description hand movements which are symbolic of other specifically meaningful activities, such as a woman who keeps taking her wedding ring off and on, or a man who expresses his aggressive impulses by clenched fists, or obvious masturbatory movements, etc. Ferenczi (1950) has emphasized this last point. The functions alluded to here are specifically those of holding on for support.

A case in point is the following. A patient, whose current and professional life is characterized by the very essence of poise, considers herself inwardly "a great hand-holder." She remembers, or was told, how at the age of 3 she was out for a walk with her mother when they were approached by a friend. The patient, it is said, told her mother to let go of her hand, she didn't need to hold on any longer. Accompanying her present state of confusing and unexpected poiselessness in the analytic situation is a constant motion of her hands, which seek out and wring each other or play with and grasp one object after another. Unconsciously these movements constitute a plea to have her hands held by the analyst.

VI

This brings us into another interesting and fruitful area where the phenomenon of poise can be observed almost as if in an experimentally induced and controlled situation, in all its various developmental phases and vicissitudes, i.e., the transference relationship. The transference, as it begins to emerge and to assert itself, in many ways reverses and recapitulates the process of maturation and breaks it up into its component parts. Fragments of the instinctual life as well as the manifold defensive maneuvers employed against them are displaced from the past to the current analytic situation and are thus brought up for inspection and notation. Among these, a prominent and I would think it valid to say a universally observable phenomenon in the transference is the profound alteration and breakdown of the patient's poise. This is not yet present in the earliest days and weeks of treatment, when the analyst is still reacted to as a reality figure, much as the patient would react to any passer-by in his stream of life. However, the emergence of transference in the narrowest technical sense brings with it certain very special accompaniments.

Either gradually or abruptly, the patient begins to feel and to demonstrate the psychological and somatic expressions of poiselessness. The characteristic armor, which heretofore has encountered the analyst and his words with all its customary thickness and polish intact, begins to revert to earlier phases and to become thin and vulnerable in spots. Heretofore accustomed to the usual flow of stimuli which will impinge on him from without, and also in fairly full knowledge of what reactions from the outside his own actions will provoke, the patient has until now been relatively in control, knowing what to expect and therefore roughly what to do. In the new experience of the analytic situation, it gradually becomes apparent to him that this is a totally new type of interpersonal relationship. He is no longer met by the usual attitudes, nor do his actions provoke the accustomed responses. The result is finally a disruption and a suspension of his usual methods, which, while they are *in statu nascendi* again, leave him in a temporarily unprotected state. The analyst's analytic attitude and repetitive neutrality carry the patient back to a period when he did not yet know what to expect, and when his armor and defenses were being built in order to meet the experiences which were forthcoming. Of course, in the transference relation he then reveals what these experiences were.

This general regressive path thus involves one's poise as well as other defenses, and affects patients with varying intensity, depending on the specific history of the development of this trait. In some, during the transition phase the inability to tolerate the resulting lack of mastery or control leads almost to a shattering of their poise. They may feel childish or awkward; the hands feel big, the posture gauche, the mouth unsteady, the eyes timid. In other cases this is seen in milder form, for example, when a patient rides up in the lift with his analyst, and this same mechanism produces a feeling of embarrassment or of being ill at ease. There is also in this a projection of the superego, for of the analyst it is felt, "You have looked into me and really know; therefore you will criticize."

These feelings occur with greater intensity, of course, in those in whom security has been maintained with greater strain, even though poise may have been conspicuously present previously. To elaborate further, as a case in point, from the patient described just above with reference to her hand-holding. This woman, whose professional and even personal life was characterized by her noteworthy poise and charm, was particularly perplexed and bewildered by this train of events. She could not understand and felt exposed and frustrated by the feeling which came over her in the presence of the analyst. Whereas in her work and daily activities she greeted all with a kiss, turned on a smile at will, and posed effectively for photographers wherever she went or wherever they appeared, when she came into the analytic room her eyes would seek the ground and she would hurry to the couch as if to escape into it. She would not know what to do with her hands throughout the hour, and would either wring them or steady her chin with them. Mastery had been undone and was again *in statu nascendi,* as in original development. It was as if the patient was reexperiencing her earliest interpersonal relationships when she was trying to achieve mastery and to assure herself of the availability and cooperation of the drive object. She was again poised *en route,* in uncertainty as to which way the path would turn, toward acceptance or rejection. Sometimes this takes place whenever, in the transference relationship, the relation of the patient to the analyst is passing from one transference figure to another. One patient described how he felt like this every time he met a new person. Through the transference and working through, mastery should be reachieved, hopefully with the removal of neurotic lacunae.

The reverse process is sometimes observable when we

consider the countertransference. With the analyst, the mastery while at work is often threatened when confronted by the patient in a social situation. Seen in an unaccustomed role, and in a glass bowl as it were, his own defensive ego poise, to the extent that countertransference exists, can likewise be felt to waver.

The issue becomes more intense and active under certain dynamic conditions. For example, one patient observed how she promptly lost all poise in her life whenever she was in the presence of someone she liked. She would suddenly feel as if her feet were big and prominent, and would be focused on and seen by the man in all their ugliness. Aside from the implications of castration and denial of the same, the fact existed that this was a dynamic condition in which there was an increased desire for stimuli. She became suddenly open for stimuli in the presence of a desired object while the ability to master the needed object was questionable. The result was imbalance, suspension, doubt, and the feeling of collapse. This was reenacted by this patient clearly in the transference. Developing early in the analysis and with quick intensity, the patient displayed this same readiness to collapse in the transference situation. It even extended outward from the analyst's office into the environs, so that, during this phase, the patient noted a change from poise to unpoise as soon as she emerged from her parked car on the way to the analytic hour.

Similar states of imbalance and therefore disruptions of poise occur at certain transitional stages of development such as puberty or menopause, when a realignment of forces, of instincts and defenses, takes place and therefore causes temporarily labile states. At puberty, for example, the increased surge of impulses exceeds the ability of the ego to master them or to produce sufficient drive objects, thus resulting in a state of imbalance and with it the common accompanying feelings of awkwardness and lack of poise. During these periods the forces between ego and external world are being weighed out again and are very much in transit.

VII

In summary, the state of poise has been described. It is in its essence an integrative and sometimes a defensive function of the ego, constituting a state of anticipation of and readiness for oncoming stimuli. It comes into play only in a social or interpersonal situation. The event feared and warded off is the cutting off of the stream of narcissistic supplies and the substitution for it of the state of shame; and unpoise is such a state of traumatic shame. The aim in poise is to hold on to and maintain the source of narcissistic supply, to belong, to be anchored to a larger and firm unit (person or group). The organs especially cathected for this holding on or contact function and through which these functions are mainly mediated are (1) the perioral or snout region, (2) the postural system, and (3) the hand. The extensive and primitive role played by the first of these, the snout area, is elaborated upon to the extent that it becomes a secondary theme of this communication. Finally, the special fate and vicissitudes of the state of poise in the transference situation and in certain transitional developmental states in life are described.

CHAPTER 5

Beyond and Between the *No* and the *Yes*

I am most pleased at the privilege of being a participant on this happy occasion. It brings me back simultaneously to two nodal points which for me are loaded with positive affect. One is René Spitz and the other is Denver, both of which have converged.

The paper I present on this occasion consists of three parts. The first is about René Spitz. The second is a group of ideas which will take us beyond the *No* and the *Yes* gestures, to the *No* and the *Yes* verbal symbols themselves. The third is on the world between the *No* and the *Yes*.

I

With regard to Denver first, which is not having a birthday, and then to come to the main event, the man within it, this geographical area, with its many Air Force installations, was a

Presented at the 75th Birthday Celebration for René A. Spitz, Denver, January 29, 1962. Published in *Counterpoint: Libidinal Object and Subject*, ed. H. S. Gaskill. New York: International Universities Press, 1963, pp. 29–74.

high point for a small group of analysts during our military professional careers quite some years ago, during the last World War. As some of you no doubt will remember, four or five of us, led by John Murray, constituted a small analytic nucleus who conducted an Air Force School of Aviation Psychiatry here at Fort Logan, in which we taught dynamic, analytically based psychiatry to flight surgeons and other Air Force medical personnel, with acute combat returnees as our interesting and instructive and productive patient population. Those were exciting years, and I believe we set down quite a stimulus for psychoanalytic thinking in this glorious geographical center. And it was then that I learned about, and briefly met, your John Benjamin, I believe the first psychoanalyst here, working in a hard and solitary way in the mountains near Golden, the nucleolus for the future nucleus. With another colleague, Lewis Robbins, I came close to staying here, but there was not enough of a "group" then, which we felt we needed. Subsequently, we all dispersed, to every corner of the country, the East Coast, Topeka, Los Angeles.

Now to come to the main subject, my first view of the man we come here to honor today was a little over 20 years ago. At that time, before the War, as a student at the New York Psychoanalytic Institute, I listened to a new faculty member, shortly after his arrival in this country. One of my first memories of him is seeing some now-famous movies, in which a man with a beret was making faces at small infants, grimacing at them, turning away from them, dropping them, and then talking to us about how they looked at him. I felt sure I had wandered into the wrong field. I was also brought to mind of an Einstein story, in which a small boy sees a group of people surrounding the man with the sweater and long hair and asks his father who the man is and what he does. The father explains and gives some example of things being relative, to which the son replies "And from this he makes a living?"

In the two decades which followed, René Spitz extended in this country his work begun in Vienna, Berlin, and Paris, to build it into the edifice which it is today and which is now his.

It is difficult to give an adequate summary of Spitz's work, nor should one really even try.[1]

In the totality of his contributions, we can say that Spitz did for the first year of life, and especially for the development of the ego, what Freud (1905b) did for the first five years in respect to the psychosexual development, and what Erikson (1950) has done for the various crises of ego identity throughout the life cycle. The first year, with Spitz's trained microscopic view, was seen in its manifold component aspects, both with the individual streams isolated and teased apart, and especially in their composite, unified, and continuous operation. In this work, Spitz epitomized the genetic point of view, taking it seriously, and as a consequence turning his complete attention and his abundant energies to the beginnings to which it led, although it might have looked, at first glance, as if such efforts could yield only barren rewards. Not only did these investigations parallel and go along with the efforts of the first child analysts, of Anna Freud and Melanie Klein, who were among the earliest to direct attention to the child clinically, but they also constituted pioneer activities in the field of direct child observation. They were significant for the many longitudinal studies which we see today and which hold out such promise, notable among them those going on in this very University by John Benjamin (1959) and his co-workers. These efforts also introduced the experimental method into psychoanalysis, as difficult as this is to do, by providing and withdrawing and shifting variables in the field of early human behavior.

One is struck by Spitz's wide scholarship and his true multidisciplinary knowledge and orientation, in its best sense. There is throughout a firm base on biology and physiology, on experimental embryology, on phylogeny and evolutionary processes. He is quick to respond as well as to stimulate, to see and grasp the essential in other fields and what is contributory and of use in them to our own. Thus, for example, he was among the first to respond to the basic and generalized implications of

[1]See Spitz's writings starting in 1945 to 1972.

Selye's theory of stress and how it might relate to our own formulations (1954a). I had the opportunity of being the discussant of a paper of Spitz's along these lines given in Los Angeles some years ago, in which he pointed to the parallels between our psychoanalytic models and the models of modern physiological, such as stress, research. "Advances in science," Spitz (1957b) pointed out in the opening of that paper, "are not only due to the productivity, to the imaginative mind of the creative geniuses in a given discipline, but often to ideas of seminal value borrowed from a completely different discipline or science." In similar vein, with regard to the fields of ethology and of animal research, Spitz was quick to recognize, to respond, and to amalgamate what was assimilable, while also avoiding excesses and pointing out the limitations and the dangers (1955a).

His excursions into and his analogies between modern embryological thinking and psychoanalytic theory, from which he derives his theory of the three "organizers of the psyche" in the first year of human life, serve brilliantly to enrich our own thinking in our field. Yet again he knows the pitfalls, and points simultaneously to "disanalogies" as well, quoting Oppenheimer's similar awareness of the need for both boldness and caution in our interdisciplinary and cross-cultural thinking (1959, p. 60).

In building as he did, whether in dipping into contiguous disciplines, or in his concentrated attention to the first year of life, it is much to Spitz's credit that he keeps his perspective and never loses sight of the main body, an error into which some other investigators slip not infrequently. Rather, while he bridges across and establishes connections, he maintains a firm hold on the already-established. His use, for example, in his *Genetic Field Theory of the Ego*, of Waddington's diagrammatic descriptions of early embryologic organizations and progression, is not to take us away from our main operational base. On the contrary, it is reminiscent to us and bridges across to such a description as that by Rapaport (1953a) of the increasingly complex hierarchic development of derivative motivational drives and defenses which occurs with increased structural development, or of Hartmann's description (1939a) of the complex continuum of psychic development from an integration of maturational and developmental factors, and of inner and outer interaction. The excursions enhance, but never get us lost.

If you will permit me now to become personal, and to indicate at how many points, from my own vantage point and development, I met and benefited from René Spitz and his work, perhaps this will illustrate how many others have equally done so. Besides the general enrichment which I shared with the many psychoanalytic readers of his succession of papers, it happens that in the second of the two decades which I am describing, there turned out to be, along the lines of my own developing interests, many specific points of confluence and of mutual interests in which I kept approaching and working alongside of different aspects of Spitz's fertile contributions. From none of these happy encounters did I fail to derive stimulation and support as well as some added blocks upon which to stand and from which to build.

Although we came always from opposite directions, he from the child, even the youngest of these, and I proceeding generally from the analyses of adults, we would on many occasions meet somewhere in between. I am sure that this same experience was inevitable for anyone who took a serious interest in the most common and nuclear clinical and theoretical problems in human behavior. To enumerate or give the highlights of just a few of these mutual meeting grounds, I have been interested in and written on anxiety (1955b), and before that on affects in general (1952), subjects with which Spitz has dealt so centrally in many places. Exploring and investigating as I have in the field of object relations (Panel, 1962), I could not work in that area without being enriched by René Spitz. In 1958, I was chairing a panel at the American Psychoanalytic Association on "Early Psychic Functioning," in which René was about to give the opening presentation of the afternoon session when he suddenly announced that he had lost his paper! I thought, and hoped that a long-cherished wish of a valuable impromptu session was about to be forced to come to pass, but unfortunately the paper turned up just too soon. That paper, however, furnished another building block, consisting of Spitz's detailed observations on sleep as a precursor of defense (1961). In my work, I was never without Spitz's challenge and help. In his *Genetic Field Theory*, in his *No and Yes*, and in other works (1951), there are numerous speculations and abstractions relevant to the somatopsychic border, to body motor and sensory patterns, to the mechanisms of fixation points, and to the relations of these to nosology and nosogenesis, as well as to many other of the mutual grounds referred to above. But while all of these are general and rather global interests which we shared in common, we met above all, in 1954, at the *snout* or the perioral region, or, a better expression for our purposes, as I will presently attempt to show, at the *snoot*! It was here that our interests really became bound.

In 1956, Spitz and Denver met, and in 1957 they were joined together. Here came the remarkably hospitable soil, to use his own words (1957a), prepared and offered by the generous hospitality of Herbert Gaskill, and with the ready and indispensable collaboration, to achieve completeness, of John Benjamin. Further nutriment and fertilization were in due time provided by the Chicago Psychoanalytic Institute. Others came shortly and joined this about-to-proliferate nucleus and Denver was off to a propitious start.[2]

II

The second part and main content of this communication has to do with the *no* and the *yes*, to which I should now like to direct our specific attention. During the most recent years two comprehensive and definitive works of Spitz have appeared which can be considered to be composite in nature, and as

[2]Just a few months following this anniversary celebration, on April 10, 1962, the Denver Psychoanalytic Society was organized, with René Spitz most fittingly as its first President!

bringing much of his previous studies under one roof. One of these, *A Genetic Field Theory of Ego Formation* (1959), has already been referred to. The other major contribution was the monograph *No and Yes* (1957a), which was the outgrowth of a much briefer version written by Spitz for the Freud centenary celebration a year before. Its subject, "On the Genesis of Human Communication," has to do, in Spitz's words, with "the inception of semantic and verbal communication, the beginning of thought processes, and concept formation."

It is this subject which I should like to join up with and develop further, and which I propose that we consider in more minute detail. For here again I find that a line of my own developing thoughts and interests, in fact one which derives from the aforementioned work on the "snout" (see Chapter 4), converges with a particular contribution of Spitz's. I should like to show how these two lines merge and coalesce, and then pursue them to some further advance in our knowledge and understanding. The area concerns a further contribution on the development of language, on the origin of human speech and communication, Spitz's crucial "third organizer of the psyche" (1959) (after the smile and the eight-months anxiety). Commenting upon the importance of "primal words" and an understanding of the origins and development of language Freud (1910b) writes, "We cannot dismiss the conjecture . . . that we should understand the language of dreams better . . . if we knew more about the development of language."

If I may digress for a paragraph or two, but along a branch still connected to the main body, I should like to illustrate, using this same area as an example, how close wit is to profundity in making valid observations and connections. Freud (1895a) pointed out that screaming is among the first communications, in that what is originally a mere internal discharge process comes to be a means by which the helpless child is able to relieve his internal tension by enlisting external help. Similarly, in a rather hilarious current pair of comic records about a "2000-

Year-Old Man,"[3] someone asks this 2000-year-old man what
was the original means of transportation way back then. "Fear,"
he replies. "When an animal would growl at you, you would run
two miles in a minute. Fear was the main propulsion! Fear is
also the origin of song," he explains. "Singing came about when
you had to communicate. When you were in trouble and had to
get somebody, you'd sing 'Heelllpp.' The first songs were help
songs. Like 'A-lion-is-eating-my-foot-off. Somebody-call-a-cop.'
That was an early song." In fact, fear was the origin of
everything. "A handshake was born to see if the other fellow
had a rock or a dagger in his hand. You'd grab his hand and
shake it to get it out. Even love was based on fear. We'd need
someone to look and see if an animal was behind us. We'd grab
a lady and say 'Look behind me for a while.' She'd ask 'How
long?' We'd say 'Forever. We're married.'"

Freud (1895a), writing on the role played by the original
internal screaming discharge, writes, "This path of discharge
thus acquires an extremely important secondary function—viz.
of bringing about an understanding with other people; and the
original helplessness of human beings is thus the primal source
of all moral motives." Writing on infantile anxiety, Freud (1926)
states, "This anxiety reaction is still an expedient one in the
child at the sucking stage, for, just as it activated the lungs of
the new-born baby to get rid of the internal stimuli, so now, in
being discharged into the respiratory and vocal muscular
apparatus, it calls the mother to the child's side."

Returning to *No and Yes*, I should like first to summarize in
briefest outline Spitz's line of argument in developing his thesis,
as a base from which we can proceed. Starting out, as is often
the case, from the pathological in order to understand the
normal, Spitz noted first the negative cephalogyric motions of
deprived infants suffering from the syndrome of hospitalism,
and then turned his attention from these to the rooting
behavior of the normal neonate. The latter, a congenital and
reflex motor pattern of approach behavior which can be seen

[3]Capitol Recordings W 1529 and W 1618.

immediately after birth, can be set off by a releasing stimulus anywhere in the perioral region, or what Spitz calls "the 'snout' for short" (p. 20). (I shall come back to this parenthetical remark below.) This behavior occurs reflexly in the very earliest objectless stage and has an affirmative rather than a negative quality. It is turning toward, an approach, and, occurring with the mouth half-open and ready, serves to discover the nipple, which is grasped when encountered, and the motion stops. This reflex behavior, which is not yet an intentional signal, nor a directed communication with a subjective purpose, recedes rapidly with maturation, continuing only until the aim is surer, and then gradually disappears.

This same motion, after a period of being absent from the inventory of the infant's behavior patterns, is seen to reappear again at 3 months, but this time with a "change of function" intervening. The same side-to-side motion is called forth again, but this time *to get rid of* the nipple when finished. It is now, according to Spitz, refusal behavior, "a volitional motor pattern."

Spitz then traces in a most ingenious way the various steps by which this same motor pattern continues in an unbroken line to become the head-shaking gesture which specifies the ideational concept of the negative. Object relations and identification with the mother play a special role in the concretization of this process. This negative *no* gesture has been central in the Gestalt endured by the infant in the myriad of prohibitions which he has experienced from the mother. The latter has, for her part, fortified these gestures within herself by unconsciously identifying with the genetically early gestures in her infant which have been described above and which were subliminally perceived by her. Thus a process of reciprocal identification has taken place. I have described (1955a) a similar reciprocity occurring at a later stage of development, which is no doubt a continuation of this same principle of mutually enhancing interaction, in pointing to the role played by the parents in the oedipal complex. Erikson (1950) has also emphasized this process of mutuality between mother and child.

The actual achievement of this meaningful, subjectively purposeful, and intentional head-shaking gesture does not occur until the middle of the second year, at about 15 to 18 months. Its attainment marks the first symbolic expression, and heralds what is, according to Spitz, " beyond doubt the most spectacular intellectual and semantic achievement in early childhood" (p. 99). With its integration has come the momentous acquisition of the use of symbols, and the functions of judgment, concept formation, and abstract thought.

Why is the gesture horizontal? Spitz adduces a number of engaging embryologic as well as phylogenetic explanations, among which are (1) that man, an altricial animal, as compared to a precocial one, is held in the horizontal position to nurse; (2) that the rooting behavior from which the gesture derives is a horizontal motion; and (3) that the neck muscles in altricial animals are not yet strong enough in the early stages of infancy for a vertical, up-and-down approach, nor is there a visual percept to serve as a releaser stimulus.

Spitz then traces and explains the vertical, head-nodding, *yes* gesture. After a similar search for origins, and in particular a more careful retrospective reexamination of his motion pictures on infant activity, Spitz again found the clue in the nursing situation. Forward and backward nodding motions were seen to occur *during* the process of nursing, with the head supported, as part of and following the same up-and-down rhythm of the actual sucking movements. Such motions are due to mechanical causes, the head being pulled forward during vigorous sucking, and falling backward when it stops. They thus start with and accompany the consummatory act of sucking. Repeating an experiment previously performed by Margaret Fries, he observed that later, at about 3 months, when an infant can already support his head, withdrawal of the nipple is followed by a continuation of these forward and backward movements, now as an approach attempt, repeating the previous movements which had served it so well.

The motions in this case are thus affirmative in quality from the beginning and consequently in this instance do not undergo a change in function as the negative gesture, except in the change from a consummatory to an approach function. Spitz again traces the continuous path of development in which "interaction between object relations and endopsychic energy displacements forces a specific change in the structure of the ego," and the head-nodding gesture becomes the symbolic ideational gesture of affirmation, the semantic *yes* gesture, at about the same time as the *no* develops similarly. Identification with the aggressor has played a crucial role as a mechanism in the ego which brings this about. Both gestures are seen to arise from the affirmative. Both derive from the appetitive, positive *yes* strivings of undifferentiated drives, for the unconscious does not have a *no*.

This brief summary does not do justice to Spitz's brilliant and detailed lines of argument, but is presented in order to draw a line with which I hope to converge. If we consider what I described in Chapter 4 concerning the snout area, we can see that the archaic and primitive origins of the functions invested in this perioral zone, lend confirmation to our clinical and theoretical descriptions based on genetic psychoanalytic considerations.

I have accumulated a number of derivative streams of observations and thoughts in various divergent directions. It is one of these particular streams which is relevant here and which I should like now to pursue. This path has to do with a certain group of derivative words, which have been accumulating with me and coalescing in relation to the above study and focus of interest. This direction should not be surprising, since this area is after all, among its many functions, the executive organ for speech. However, it is not speech in general which I have in mind, but something more specific. My attention has been directed to certain sounds and words more directly connected with the actual anatomy and physiological mechanics of this particular area.

I will now embark therefore on a short excursion into

etymology, with the same due apologies and fearful look at the professional linguists which every psychoanalyst feels compelled to acknowledge when he ventures into this unfamiliar territory.[4]

Let us start with the actual perioral region or the *snout* or better still, for our purposes, the *snoot*. It is not, as Spitz said (1957a), "the 'snout' for short." For short, it would be *peri* or something of that nature. It is *snout*, or *snoot*, not for short, but because these particular words seem to be anatomically related to the area which is making the sound, and because they seem to bear an appropriate emotional charge, more rooted in primary process and the id than is the colder, more detached, more secondary-process-oriented and ego-derived word *perioral*.

If we start with the *snoot* and drop one "o," we get a word *(snot)* with a derisive and leering quality, which denotes not only an out-of-control mucus discharge, but also a character who lets it happen. It begins to border on the obscene. Proceeding along into a derivative and closely related (in sound) chain of words, we find: *snort—snore—snorkel*. A patient expressed an aggressive and negative transference fantasy toward his analyst, and yet with a note of pity and remorse, when he said, "I feel as if my words are coming out so fast and continuously that you don't have a chance to answer or to say anything. I picture it as if my words are drowning you and that you are being pushed higher and higher into a corner of the room, and that soon you will need a snorkel to breathe." A *snorer* is not particularly admired, nor is he thought of as being considerate to other people. One who is said to *snort* is also not exactly a social success.

Or, continuing along this line, we get to *sneer*, which is equivalent to something like, "Oh, yeah? Well, no!" With a slight twist, we have a *schmo*, or in another closely related tongue

[4]Compare similar words of caution to the philologists expressed by Bunker and Lewin (1951), writing on the roots Gn, Kn, and Cn and Stone (1954b) in his scholarly treatise on "The Principal Obscene Word of the English Language."

(Yiddish), a *shmendrick*. I recently listened to a case history being presented in which this word and concept was the central description given by the patient himself as the core of his self-image. Another closely related word, if you can call it that, and in the same almost colloquial tongue, is *schmegege*, which is probably a synonym for the expression just given.

In a recent lecture the political analyst William Winter, commenting on international tensions and the modes of international relationships and communications, observed astutely, "We have *snarl* words and we have *purr* words, and one can frequently judge what motivations and intentions are at work by which words are being used."

If we come back to the same (borderline) language referred to above, there is the word, or perhaps just the expression *schnorrer*, with a special and unflattering meaning and connotation. Or, in a perhaps more universal language, there is a *schnook*, defined for me recently as "someone who is neither here nor there. When he comes into a room you think he just left." Somewhat more proud, but also not very nice, is *snooty*, whose nose is up in the air, meaning "You're not good enough for me to take in." In close relation are *snub, snob,* or a *snip,* etc. The most epic and what Alexander Woollcott calls "the most enchanting nonsense in the English language" was written by Lewis Carroll about the *Snark*.

What are all these? Once having started to collect them, many more came to my attention, and I could add an impressive list. However, to stop before this becomes a hobby, and keeping this a scientific inquiry, I believe these might be sufficient upon which to make the following observations and further points. All of these expressions are derisive, and carry a negative quality, a *nn-nn*, or a *no-no. No* is in the *nose* itself (or even in the *nostril*), both in the word and in the organ. They all have in common the *no*, or the *nah*, the *nasty*, the *snide*, the *nagging*. (I am aware of the interchange of *m* for *n* in a few of the words above, but it is the dominant sound with which I am here concerned. I will comment later upon the overlap in function and the occasional interchangeability of the two sounds.)

Taken all together, they point to this quality which they had in common. They led me to keep in the background for some future investigation this matter of the *no*. I was convinced that *no* was in the *nose*, that it was a nasal word, and that it had something to do with the *snoot*. But what? What were its origins and its meanings and its genetic development? I put all this aside for some future occasion.

This was all before Spitz's *No and Yes*, between my *snout* paper and the appearance of Spitz's publication in 1957. When the latter came along, you won't be surprised that I turned to it with prepared, and excited, interest. Before getting too serious about doing any follow-up of my own, I turned to this book with expectant eagerness for the answers. Again I found myself on common ground with Spitz and looked to him for the origin of these words.

However, as I read with consuming interest his detailed exposition I found at the end that he had stopped short at the semantic *gestures*, and never really concerned himself with the semantic *words no and yes* themselves. "The genetic predisposition to the 'No' *gesture*," he writes at the conclusion, "is now substantially documented" (my italics). But this is not the case with the *no word* symbol itself.

I cannot say that I was unhappy at this discovery, for this left something for me to do. I still, however, left it for the future. There was something a little unsavory or inhibiting about following through with this, and I gave priority to other pressing subjects. This anniversary celebration, however, being one for René Spitz himself, wipes away my last pause, and gives me a welcome opportunity to continue to pursue this.

Paul Moses (1954), an otorhinolaryngologist, impressed by the influence of emotional factors on the voice, especially as he saw this clinically in singers, wrote an interesting book on *The Voice of Neurosis*. Spitz, in the works referred to above, elaborated on the *gestures* of early communication. Carrying this along further, from the voice, through the gestures, I now come, as part of a continuous spectrum, to the early *words* themselves.

Spitz has commented how few and isolated are the number of psychoanalytic papers on communication, both verbal and nonverbal. The gestures themselves are, however, after all, still body language, although it is certainly true that they indicate the achievement of abstract signal, of the symbolic function, and of the communication by symbol which Kubie (1953) describes as distinctively human. But, although Spitz (1957a) refers to the gestures as "semantic," they are not yet in themselves the true, fully semantic *verbal* symbols of which their achievement is either the accompaniment or the forerunner. Spitz in fact notes these gestures as "the first step on the road to the much vaster symbolic function in the verbal field which begins in the 2nd half of the second year." As gestural symbols, they are actually intermediate points en route in the progression from communication by direct volitional motor action to true verbal symbols.

To continue the path started by Spitz, our task and direction will be to follow from or alongside of the *no* and *yes* symbolic *gestures* to the acquisition of the *no* and *yes words* themselves.

To know where to turn first to serve our purposes further, we can take our clue from Spitz again, who, in looking for the origins of the *gestures*, both the *no* and the *yes*, turned to examine the nursing situation. The connections between orality as experienced by the infant during nursing, and the later use of the same organs for the performance of speech and language, in the service of communication, have also attracted the attention of many who have worked in the field of linguistics with other than the psychoanalytic frame of reference. Such, for example, was the case with Latif, or with Lewis, who pointed out that "in discussing the nature of language, we cannot evade the fact that the organs of utterance are also the organs of sucking." In similar vein, Spielrein holds that in speaking the child reproduces the nursing act with the movements of his mouth and therefore somehow reactivates the sensations experienced during nursing (quoted in Spitz, 1957a). It is no accident indeed that we should look not only to the mouth for the function of early word formation, but rather to the entire snout area to which we have already drawn attention. It is after all this latter apparatus which houses the organs which convert sound into speech, and through which the voice passes as it is transformed into language. Bonnard (1960) has described the vital role of the tongue as a first organ in exploring both the self and the outer world, and has discovered the role played by this organ in certain very regressive pathological conditions.

Let us, therefore, for further clues, look into the very mouth of the babe during the act of nursing, and into the mouths of others during the act of saying *no*, and turn the high power in both of those places for comparable observations. We will keep in mind in the latter case the mechanics of forming the sound *nn*, and later the word *no*, and in the former case, whatever parallels might exist in the nursing situation. What do we see?

In the word *no*, the *nn* ejects. The very performance of the *nn* sound ejects a column of air from the nose, much as one would blow nasal air out, or "blow his nose," in the same direction and manner as the nasal cilia would eject a foreign or unwelcome substance. To perform the act requires (a) that the mouth be open, and (b) that the tongue be flat (horizontal) against the hard palate. In this position, not only is there egress of air, but ingress to the oral passage is blocked, and nothing can get in. Within the mouth of the nursling, in the parallel situation, the same positioning of the tongue and mouth and the same forcing outward also ejects, while blocking ingress, but in this instance it is milk (or water), rather than air. At the beginning, it comes out from all over, from the mouth and the nose, over the entire snout and soon the chin. (My children worried about me as I sat in my study and tried these movements while writing this!)

In contrast to the intraoral positionings described above, the sound *mm*, Greenson (1954a) observes, "is the only sound one can make and still keep something safely within the mouth." It is made "with the lips closed and continuously so throughout the utterance," and with the tongue resting at the floor of the mouth. Whatever is inside is retained, and the way to the throat is open. Both sounds, *mm* and *nn*, according to Greenson, are made in discomfort, particularly in hunger, at 2 months, and "are later produced only in states of comfort from the age of six months." We see here a change in function again, as Spitz observed, but here in an opposite direction from what Spitz described in the change from the positive rooting to the negative refusal; the progression in Greenson's description is from the negative to the positive.

I would amend the above to state that while *mm* does become characteristically the positive, the *nn* remains basically the means of expressing and effecting the negative. I point again for confirmation of this to the many verbal and motor examples given above. This is not, by the way, to say that the sound is always connected with aggression or even unpleasure. There are many other developmental vicissitudes to be considered, and the negative itself comes to have many diverse functions, upon which I will comment further below. But basically, in accordance with the events just described, the *nn* is the channel for refusal.

Another fact upon which to build our next step is the observation of Lewis, who systematically recorded the development of speech in infants, that the first utterances of the infant occur in discomfort and are expressed in vowels. I would have us keep in mind, to exemplify his statement, the cry, in its variations.

I would like to propose the following thesis: if we put together the *nn* sound, whose ontogenetic and mechanical development we have traced above, and these unpleasant vowels (*ah, ow, o, eh, aw*), we have : *nah, now, no, neh, naw—nein.* Here you have the *no* and some of its equivalents.

I have proceeded from primary archaic discharges, through global, need-satisfying sounds, to words (another example of such a progression at this stage is from *mm to mama*). While, in Karl Bühler's terms, the acquisition of gesture has

carried the infant from the phase of expression to the phase of
appeal, as Spitz concludes with the *no* and *yes gestures*, the
attainment of the *words* carries communication to Bühler's next
step, that of description. This acquisition of primitive *words*
occurs at about the same time or perhaps slightly after the age
which Spitz gives for the meaningful *gestures*, i.e., after about 15
months, in the second quarter or middle of the second year.
The acquisition of the *no* verbal signal thus corresponds with
the onset of the anal phase, where we have always placed the
concept of *no* on clinical and developmental grounds. The ego
has now acquired a semantic *verbal* ideational signal, which
represents a further momentous step in the achievement of
symbolization, concept formation, and abstract thinking, and in
the increasing armamentarium of the self.

As another interesting and additional answer to Spitz's
search for an explanation of "Why horizontal" (for the gesture)
we may note, as another determinant, the horizontal position
here of the tongue, which lies flat against the roof of the mouth.
This horizontal position, during the utterance of the verbal *no*,
is confluent and synchronous with the simultaneous horizontal
direction of the negative gesture. It is all one, the sound and the
motion, each reinforcing the nature and direction of the other.

I now proceed to a parallel exploration of the origins of the
word *yes*. Performing the same steps as we did with *no*, I will
consider first the initial *y* sound, looking again for the mechanics of its composition within the oral cavity. In doing so I first
note the position of the tongue, which, in performing the
sound, forms a cradle, a trough, or receptacle, between the
tongue and the palate. In frontal section it would take a *u*-shape
very much in fact like the top part of the actual letter *y*. The
tongue is arched forward and downward at the tip, the mouth
is open, and the motion, in contrast to that in the *nn*, is a
milking one, rather than an ejecting one. The motion here, like
the position of the tongue, is an up and down one, a vertical
one. The column of air is literally milked, moved up and in.
And the way to the throat is open.

Comparing this, as we did before, to the anatomical and

mechanical conditions which obtain during the act of nursing, we see that this is exactly what takes place with the teat *in situ* when the milking process is on. Just such a trough is made by the tongue, the teat is in it, the motion is affirmative, and the way is open, all of it saying, "Yes, go in," this time not to the air, but to the milk. And what is taking place inside with the tongue can be seen on the outside with the neck and chin, which are simultaneously performing the same vertical movements. All in unison spell a lapping motion, directing the stream inward. It is an anterior swallowing, just like the posterior one, which it precedes and with which it alternates, with the way clear. (There is one difference between the *y* sound and the nursing: the air is not actually swallowed, while the milk is. But the preliminary movements are identical.)

While in altricials, as compared to precocials, head-nodding cannot take place early (as Spitz has pointed out, and therefore rooting is horizontal), tongue-nodding can, and so can lip- and (anterior) neck-nodding. Strong muscles of the back of the neck are not required for the latter. Indeed, it was the observance of this anterior perioral nodding which put Spitz on the road toward understanding the up and down *yes* gesture. We note in all these motions the vertical, the same as in the latter gesture. Even the letter *y* is vertical.

While the *mm* retains, and the *nn* ejects, the *y* milks in, especially when performed rhythmically. Add to this the vowel, as we did with *no*, and we have the *yah*, *yeh*, and the word *yes*. Perhaps, also, the vowel chosen here is at the pleasurable and soft end of the spectrum of vowel sounds, at least less discordant or harsh than the *aw*, *ow*, or *o*.

When the infant has had enough, the tongue flattens, the horizontal takes over, he pushes with his tongue, blows with his nose, shakes his head, and ejects. "No, that's it, no more, out."

With this further development and the explanations I have adduced, I may now say that not only the semantic gestures, as Spitz has shown, but the verbal symbols themselves rest equally on a biologic and genetic predisposition, and are in fact related to specific organs. In a way I might say that *no* is in the nose, and *yes* is the mouth. The infant approaches the environment with both, in the snout. Is the nose, with its longer reach, the guardian of the mouth?

Coming back to the anatomical considerations within this area with which I started, I recall, from the observations recorded above, that while anatomically the forward tip, or the snout, consists of the nose and the mouth together, functionally the nose extends further out, in that the sniff extends further than the taste. This relationship, which has been demonstrated in phylogenetic references, where the anatomical as well as the functional dominance of olfaction is still much in evidence, was seen to exist also in the ontogenetic development. Olfaction anticipates, a function which can well be an important precursor of the later crucial function of anxiety as an anticipatory signal. It is not uncommon that an infant will reject poison, such as boric acid solution offered by mistake instead of water, or perhaps also bad milk, on the basis of smell.

Is smell thus a first signal, a physiological precursor of later signal anxiety? Between the two there would be the occurrence of the first mnemic signal, which in the psychoanalytic model is of the first need-satisfying object, the mother or mother substitute.

As another odd example of a surviving residue of the primacy of this original archaic olfactory function, we sometimes see the following interesting occurrence clinically or in life. An otherwise very articulate person, confronted with unbearable frustration in an encounter which leads to a loss of all his poise, blurts out to his adversary, in utter and impotent exasperation, what at the moment comes to him as the ultimate negative, "You stink!" This curious regression, under such circumstances, is to a derogation frequently resorted to by helpless children, inexperienced in debate, when confronted similarly with overwhelming odds.

While we have seen that the nose, and its contained function of olfaction, recedes as we go upward along the developmental scale, its use as described in negation maintains for it a permanently vital position. I noted above, however, that its connections by no means remain limited to the negative, or to aggression, or unpleasure, but that many other developmental vicissitudes take place as well.

The persistence of the primitive olfactory sense in the sexual sphere, where it retains its central role, is well known up and down the developmental scale, whether in the effects of odor from the female cat or dog in heat, or in the role assigned to this function in the sexual attractiveness of the human female. Barth (1962), a biologist, recently isolated an odoriferous chemical, pheromone, upon which a female cockroach depends in order to attract a courting male, and the presence of which is dependent upon the intactness of the corpora allata, a pair of glands at the base of the brain. While this hormone of the cockroach acts only on nearby males, a similar substance produced by female moths is found to attract males for hundreds of yards around.

Greenson has referred to the pleasurable aspect of the sound *nn* which occurs in the infant, and this certainly continues phenomenologically during the course of further development. The negative aspect which I have described, which is centrally related to the ontogenesis of this sound, is only one aspect of an expression which becomes multifaceted in later life. The nose, as all other orifices, comes to be used for opposite purposes as well as in the service of ambivalence. Pleasure and gratification thus come to be among its achievements in addition to their opposites, displeasure and denial.

Thus, for example, the very act of ejection as described during nursing occurs mostly following satiation, thus associating it also with the contented state. Ejection connotes mastery, which in itself brings pleasure. The libidinization of the function of smell, mediated by the same organ, and its use in the service of the pleasure of sexuality has been referred to above. Pleasure in aggression or in the act of successful mastery is a means by which *n* and *no* also come to acquire pleasurable aspects over and above their initial functions as heralding displeasure, negation and rejection. We are aware, in fact, of how the entire negative world, of denial, stubbornness, and rebellion, can become even the dominant mode of pleasure during the anal phase of development.

It is on the basis of such determinants that other *n* sounds and words appear with opposite affective meanings than the chain of negative words originally referred to above. The *nn* and the *mm* become somewhat interchangeable, just as they did in some of the negative words above. Thus *snow* and *smart* and *snug* and *snuggle* begin to lead in an opposite direction from the path with which I started, i.e., toward the clean and the good and the comfortable, in fact even to the *noble* and the *notable*, rather than only to the critical and the unpleasant. Each orifice, each erogenous zone, comes to serve both the positive and the negative, and to consist of components from each.

I will forego any attempt to enter upon a similar investigation of other sounds, such as the sounds *ss* or *sh*, to which my attention has already been slightly drawn, on the basis of considerations similar to those which I have employed with *no* and *yes*. Besides the role of the tongue, there are obviously different complex combinations in the use and configurations of the lips, teeth, palate, etc., in performing each sound which might well turn out to be of special interest. While *mm* and *nn* seem to be the sounds most studied in this way, I would venture that similar considerations might shed light over a wider area of linguistics. Thus, careful studies of many other sounds might demonstrate interesting connections based on or influenced by inborn ontogenetic and phylogenetic motor and reflex patterns and their developmental vicissitudes.

I should like to submit the further hypothesis that the differentiation which has been described between the original *nn* and *y* motions and sounds follows a previously undifferentiated stage. I would venture that at the very beginning the motor patterns behind the *y* and *nn* probably take place together, with movements which are global, combined, and undifferentiated. These are the original, tentative, experimental, and preliminary oral-nasal movements, prior even to the successful establishment of effective sucking and swallowing motions. These global and undifferentiated movements probably last the very briefest time before the inborn reflex sucking patterns become effective, at which time the sucking y becomes gradually effectively separated from the "pushing-out" nn. During this early preliminary phase, before such effective separation, the offered milk goes both in and out, some in and swallowed, some just staying in without being swallowed, and some coming out, although wanted by the infant. And it comes out all over, through mouth and nose, over the whole snout, although such ineffectiveness lasts only for an extraordinarily brief time. Very soon it goes in alone. This spitting out, with the clumsy movements of the tongue, is involitional, and occurs of course long before the head-shaking, volitional refusal which comes about with the "change of function" described by Spitz (1957a) at 3 months.

The above facts fit with the findings of Greenson (1954) and of Lewis that the hungry infant makes both the m and n sounds in discomfort up to about the age of 2 months. Actually, at this stage even comfort and discomfort are not clearly differentiated. Spitz notes the same about the motor prototypes of the gestures, which arise in the period of nondifferentiation, and both of which arise from one common root, "an appetitive, assenting, affirmative endeavor" (1957a, p. 146). The infant about to feed is both uncomfortable and about-to-be comfortable almost simultaneously. At this stage, Spitz points out, even crying is confused with laughing by the observer. The period corresponds to what Hartmann et al. (1946) have also described, from a more general standpoint of psychic energy and structure, as a period of undifferentiation.

The above hypothesis with regard to the movements behind the sounds corresponds with Freud's idea (1910b) on the origin of antithetical words, that in most such primitive pairs of words, a first stage existed of both occurring together, before being later separated. Freud points to the double meaning of such "oldest roots," and to the fact that in the subsequent developmental differentiation one has no meaning unless related to the other. I suggest that a similar historical development took place with the above preverbal motor patterns, which were the forerunners of the later derivative words *no* and *yes*.

There are semantic instances and affective states in which regressively this borderland of undifferentiation or of precarious differentiations is approached again. These labile states are seen both in the semantic expressions as well as in the affective states which they connote. Thus a *smile* may become a *smirk* or fade into a *snicker*, or the reverse direction may obtain, thus indicating a thin line between opposite affective constellations. Or *snug* may become *smug*, or the two dangerously indistinguishable. Is *smooch or snooze or schmooze* a positive or negative word description, or are they on the line between the two?

Another example of a later derivative of this nondifferentiated state, expressed in a significant mechanical colloquialism, is one who speaks "with tongue in cheek." Does he mean it or doesn't he? Is it *yes* or *no*? Which way will the tongue go? One never knows.

III

This brings us to the area between *no* and *yes*. This is in a sense the psychological terrain which still binds them together, as well as keeps them apart, and which is perhaps the derivative of the time just referred to when they, or at least their roots, were actually bound.

Spitz has pointed out that the acquisition of *no* and *yes* gestures (and I add "words") marks a momentous achievement and "initiates a new dimension" in psychic development. In fact, "the volitional use of the ideational content of the negative . . . [is the] most spectacular intellectual and semantic achievement of early childhood." Among the many functions which it heralds, "the dignity of the *No* gesture," writes Spitz, marks the beginning of abstract thinking, converts passivity to activity, provides an avenue for the discharge of aggression, and goes along with the beginnings of ego autonomy and of judgment.

The above is true. I would like, however, in this final

section to extend these insights into the following additional observations. While the ability to think and to symbolize, and finally to utter and thus to communicate the affirmative and the negative are nodal points in the early establishment of second-ary process and abstract thinking, it is worthwhile also to describe how tenuous and shadowy these new acquisitions are, and what a long way they have yet to go. For there is a wide and important world *between no* and *yes* in which much consolidation has to take place and which will play an important part in the destiny of the individual. The ego has now learned the *how*, has acquired the first dim ideas which are to serve it so well, but it is not yet experienced with its two new possessions, nor are they firmly rooted. They are indeed only tentatively acquired modes which are by no means stabilized or autonomous as yet in the service of the ego. A world of mastery is required at each one of these now-separate poles as well as in the area between the two.

For between *no* and *yes* is the world of *nyeh*, meaning either "I don't know," or "I do know, it is maybe," or "Well, Yes *and* No," or "Who cares?"

While the above in-between state, or state of indecision, or perhaps just state of unfamiliarity with the crisp use of its newly won ideational opposites, certainly exists at the beginning, and undergoes a normal involution with experience and develop-ment, there are people who get stuck in this nether-nether and in-between land for life. There are of course the obsessional neurotics, who may be in such states for limited periods of time, and rather pained by them, and the obsessional characters, more diffuse in time but with considerably less pain on its account. There is also the phenomenon of ambivalence, which combines the two alternatives in variable combinations, and which is not particularly limited to obsessionals, but is even more widespread. One such patient swings constantly from one side of every question to the other, with, "Well, yes, and then again no; on the one hand . . . but on the other. . . . " An important determinant of this split-down-the-middle ego could be gleaned from the fact that in the transference, during the first year of the analysis, he regarded the analyst's steady consistent behavior, and seeing him every day, as smothering and overprotective, like his mother who used to cover him with too many blankets at night; while in the second year, he regarded the same behavior on the analyst's part as cold, detached, and inflexible, like his distant and reserved father, who never would tell him anything about himself and whom he never could reach.

But aside from the obsessionals, who are a numerous enough group in this dilemma between *no* and *yes*, I wish to mention a brand of characters who are not so much in any dilemma, nor in any painful affect at all between the two alternatives, but who are in what can be described as an amorphous state between the two, not leaning toward either side, and, most typically and most importantly, not caring. They are in the "Who cares?" group mentioned above, or, put in terms of another favorite expression and attitude of theirs, "I couldn't care less." Inaction, rather than obsessive action, is the rule, and lack of affects, rather than pained or alternating affects, is most characteristic. Anxiety is not prominent. I should like to cite the following example:

A patient had as his most visible character trait this attitude of "Nyeh. Who cares? What difference does it (or anything) make." This *nyeh*—the tongue changes its position *during* the word, in transit, from that described in *no* to the position described in *yes*, accompanied by a rapid shrug of the shoulder—this *nyeh* was very prominent and indeed pervaded most of what he had to do. In his early 30s the patient was a bachelor, having never been tempted to marry. Toward every girl he had met, his feeling was *nyeh*. When a girl he went out with talked long or animatedly to a girlfriend, or to anyone else, on the telephone or in person, his impatient attitude was "Nyeh. What's she talking so much for? What's worth talking about?" Any enthusiasm or even lively interest on anyone's part in politics, for example, elicited the same attitude or response, "Nyeh. What difference does it make?" Toward McCarthy, who was at his height politically at about this time, and whose activities had most of the patient's friends stirred up with strong affect, his expressed reaction was "Nyeh. What's everybody so excited about? He'll hang himself sooner or later, and that's that." Toward psychoanalysis, too, his attitude was "Nyeh, So what?" Fortunately, he had certain phobias, and fainting spells, and specific medical and psychosomatic worries which kept him faithfully attentive to the analytic process.

During the course of his long analysis, the patient gradually began to take sides on many issues, to care about things, fell in love, married, and became a father. With this last step he was really and finally moved, and said one day, beaming about his baby, and in a revelation of strong feelings, "You know, there's really something to all this!"

In these last pages I know I have come very close to a word widely known today which must have occurred to many of you by now in terms of how it might relate to our theme. I am referring to the Russian *nyet*, which, although so close to our ambivalent *nyeh*, nevertheless means *no*. There are probably other challenging and perplexing exceptions as well.

I would say the same about many of these exceptions as Spitz says for some deviant gestures, namely, that what I have described are universal processes resting on a biological base, in which early phonation proceeds directly from a universal physiological function. Although the processes described are universal, there may be variations in the resultants which do not thereby vitiate the main theme. Just as there are later head movements which seem to be contradictory to those described by Spitz, the same occurs with the words as well, as a result of variations in specific cultural institutions, in many other historical determinants, and in purely linguistic considerations from entirely other sources. Thus, in Greece, gesturally, it is an upward and sideward head-nod confusing to us, which means *yes*. Verbally, the processes which we have described for the negative and affirmative apply to the many widespread resultants which have these sounds or roots in common, such as the English, Spanish or Italian *no*, the French or Latin *non*, the German *nein*; and the English *yes*, the German *yah*, the French *oui*, while other determinants fashion the Russian *da* or the Spanish *si*. In the Hindi language, the negative is *nahi*, and the affirmative is *hâ*. While *oui* and *hâ* are certainly not the same as the *y*, some experimentation with the sounds will show that they might be interesting variations of the same theme. Coming back to *nyet*, there is within it the Russian "palatalization," an alphabetical and phonetic process which is used to "soften" any hard consonant which precedes it. One gets the impression that in practice, the expression has come to mean, "No, but try me . . . "

Regardless of subsequent cultural variations which lead to developmental changes, or to the many complex linguistic determinants with entirely other bases which are responsible for all subsequent language formation, I believe that what I have described for our basic words is a process which universally underlies the beginnings of language. As Spitz (1957a, p. 68) comments about the expression of "pouting," there are primitive symbols of expression which have "acquired a rather universal semantic meaning transcending national and racial boundaries." And, in accordance with what Spielrein, Latif, Lewis and others have noted about the relationship between language and nursing, probably even *da* and other seemingly different primitive words have an origin deriving from intraoral playfulness and experimentation during the earliest oral activity.

The area between *no* and *yes* is and remains a large segment of human life, in fact, in many ways the *raison d'être* of the psychoanalyst. The ego, buffeted between *yes* of the id, and *no* or the *wait* of the superego or of the external world, produces, among other things, the dream, or the symptom, or, in many cases, the ambivalent or the undecided.

The neurotic is poised between *no* and *yes* in his love and hate. As a result, to oversimplify it, he vacillates in his marriage, is indecisive in his work (to emphasize the two major spheres pointed to by Freud as decisive regarding the state of one's mental health), and up and down in his moods. One of my patients described herself in the initial interview as "a monument to indecision," and stated that "Indecision" was her middle name. A song by Jimmy Durante which remains timeless concerns having "a feeling that you wanted to go, and also a feeling that you wanted to stay." As a national phenomenon, the outcomes of elections in our country are often thought of as depending on "the great undecided vote." This might be auspicious if the road to ultimate decision depended on a clarification and comprehension of issues more than it does on the effects of the created "public image." Even our great scientists, whose accomplishments represent the triumph of intellect, abstract thought, and secondary process, are often caught up in this dilemma of doubt when the fruits of their efforts bring them to the social milieu and confront them with questions of applicability.

The full and ego-syntonic achievement of an unequivocal *no* and an equally unequivocal *yes*, to appropriate stimuli, as well as a comfortable ability to blend them, also appropriately, is a highly developed and complex postambivalent ego attainment. With it goes a maximum achievement of mastery, of dominance of secondary over primary process, of abstract thought, and of action in the service of the ego. The ability to produce a *no* and a *yes* gesture and then the corresponding words are of course a monumental beginning, but a mere beginning, and foreshadow all that is yet to come. The road ahead requires a continual and increasing neutralization of both libidinal and aggressive drives, and a continuous widening of the spheres of secondary ego autonomy, as described by Hartmann (1950a); an increasingly effective development of the complex hierarchy of defenses and of derivative motivational drives, as described by Rapaport (1953a); and a network of successful channels for sublimation (Hartmann, 1955). But especially, with all this there should come a satisfactory outcome of the affective development. Replacing the impulsive and explosive affect discharges of infantile psychic life, there must supervene, in the adult, as Jacobson (1952, 1953a) has described, the "various combinations of high- and low-speed discharge processes which result in the complex affective experiences as some of our most sublime pleasurable states." Fenichel (1941a) has described this process as the "taming of affects." Rapaport has pictured for us its metapsychological development (1953a). Spitz has shown us its earliest origins.

Much of what I have said is as much for future development as it is for anything definitive in the present. What Spitz did for the Freud centenary, i.e., prepare a brief draft of his "No and Yes" on that occasion, only to develop it more fully later, I ask the privilege of doing for this Spitz three-quarter centenary. In the same spirit, this contribution consists of as many preliminary as completed remarks, to lay down paths which need further thinking and exploration. Hopefully, these will be extended or completed by others as well as myself.

CHAPTER 6

Structure, Somatic and Psychic

The Biopsychological Base of Infancy

While this Congress is deliberately multidisciplined, I speak from the discipline that is multidisciplined in its basic theoretical orientation. Psychoanalysis, in its essence and principles, reciprocally fertilizes and is fertilized by the findings of Piaget, Watson, primatology, ethology, and neurophysiology, all of which have been mentioned at various times by previous speakers. With structure as the bridge, I continue and extend this multilogue to the progression from somatic to psychic structure with the goal of examining the fused functioning of both.

The term *structure*, as in "psychic structure," which was already implicit in "psychic apparatus," came with the development of psychoanalytic theory. Structures, as Freud applied the term to psychological elements, were defined by Rapaport and

Presented at the Second World Congress on Infant Psychiatry, Cannes, France, March 31, 1983. Published in *Frontiers of Infant Psychiatry*, ed. J. D. Call, E. Galenson, and R. L. Tyson. New York: Basic Books, 1984, vol. 2, pp. 70–81.

Gill (1959, p. 803) as "configurations of a slow rate of change." In this respect, psychic structures are not qualitatively different from somatic structures. Although psychic and somatic structures do not overlap, as Freud concluded when he moved from the "Project" to a more purely psychologically centered science, both are resistant to change, and neither is irreversible. Somatic structures also undergo less volatile changes than organic processes. And somatic structures are also subject to slow rates of change, toward atrophy or hypertrophy, growth or deterioration.

Psychic structure in early development results in the acquisition and retention of psychic elements which achieve the status of a gradually increasing psychic reality. These come with experience to be on a par with, if different qualitatively from, external reality, or the reality of the internal visceral body cavity or sensorimotor body space. This is in keeping with Freud's (1923a) description of the two surfaces of the ego, one directed toward the external world and the other toward the border of the internal environment. In changing from his original seduction theory to the role of fantasy, Freud (1950) did not abandon the former but added the latter. He did not, as some think, eliminate reality but expanded it; internal psychic reality took its place alongside of the external. The early phase-related fantasy of castration develops a reality of its own, with as profound an etiologic effect as a threat from without.

By serendipity or design, this gathering represents a bridging of three pairs of polar opposites.

The first such pair are infant observers and analysts of adults. One looks progressively forward, the other retrospectively toward early life, each toward the other to establish continuity. I am speaking today as an analyst of adult life whose view is toward the life lived in the past as far back as we can see. Can we see back to infancy? This is a theoretical question to discuss. We certainly think about and aim toward that time.

The second polarity is between body and mind. It is accepted as a truism that at the origin of life, more than at any other time, the two are closest—if not one. If I could have chosen my place on this program, which I did not, it would have been in this psychosomatic section, to discuss psychobiologic origins.

Third, this period of the beginnings of life is also prior to the divergent paths brought about by language and culture. From the moment the infant is born, the language around him immediately sets large groups and clusters apart, not only the words but the affects, the culture, the communicative styles. Infants who were the same—not completely of course as there are evolutionary built-in differences as well—become French, Spanish, or American children.

How far back toward infancy do we reach in the clinical situation? To age 5? Usually. To age 3? Commonly. To 2? Occasionally. Below that? Atypically, and rarely with surety. I think of a patient's dream which was quite clearly dated at age 2 because of the house he lived in. The dream occurred around the time his grandfather died. The patient dreamed of having two mothers, one in a loose nightgown with her hair down, the other in curlers, stiff, with her hair up. He had just lost his grandfather, who had served as his warmest maternal figure, much as the patient is at present to his own grandson.

In addition to looking backward as far as we can clinically, I will extrapolate to the period of infancy on the basis of data derived from both directions, filtered in each case through the understanding derived from total psychoanalytic theory.

Before doing so, as a comment on methodology, I wish to counter a commonly held fallacy that the unscientific approach of clinical psychiatry or psychoanalysis is made more scientific by direct observational studies, whether in young children or, as in the subject of this Congress, in our studies with infants. The fact is that, while both methods complement each other and are cumulative in their effects, one is neither more nor less scientific than the other. The method of direct observation actually operates in both instances—of infants in action and adult patients in words—as well as in the intermediate form of play therapy in child analysis or psychotherapy. At neither end does the observer have the controlled situations or quantitative or other hard criteria of the physical sciences. Both poles of human observation are equally within the soft and humanistic modes of science, subjective and contemplative rather than measured in their methods of understanding and in the means of their conclusions.

The data in each case are interpreted after having been filtered through the same theory of understanding, which is itself subject to change in accordance with observed and available data. Direct observations of psychological phenomena *in statu nascendi* do not make retrospective analysis a harder or more proven science. At each point, horizontally and vertically, there are synapses of understanding between data and explanations over which both the observer and analyst need similarly to provide bridges, which one of my patients hopefully described as constituting "the creative leap."

EXTRAPOLATIONS FROM THE THEORY OF ANXIETY

To advance the theoretical problems involved at the point in life we are gathered here to study, I would like to turn to the phenomenon most centrally involved in clinical psychoanalysis: the role of anxiety. Just as Freud (1926) considered anxiety "the fundamental phenomenon and main problem of neurosis," so do I feel that a challenging and indispensable subject in which to achieve clarity is the tracing of its origins and course from birth. And just as it has been traditional in analysis that understanding the pathological sheds light on the normal, so can this tracing of the origins of anxiety cast light on adaptive as well as maladaptive behavior, both in earliest life and its subsequent course.

To start with a dynamic condition that will have psychological relevance for the remainder of life, the initial psychoeconomic state at birth is the traumatic state. I do not yet say the traumatic experience, but the existence of the traumatic state. At first there can only be, as Greenacre (1945) says, automatic reactions, reflex actions, and involuntary responses without psychological awareness or experience. It requires a rudimentary and nascent beginning of what will become an ego structure to register what can at this stage be called an "experience." I would note that this original condition is generically not unlike the state of actual neurosis postulated by Freud (1926) as consisting of physicochemical processes reactive to an influx of stimuli without accompanying psychological content.

Approaching the subject of anxiety from the point of view of adult neuroses, Freud (1895) first described this state as occurring in a discrete type of anxiety neurosis "detached from" the psychoneuroses in etiology. In a unitary theory of anxiety in which I combined Freud's first and second theories of anxiety (Chapters 9 and 10), I said that this psychoeconomic state of actual neurosis occurs routinely during the intrapsychic sequences of conflict formation in the formative stages of every neurosis, a formulation in agreement with the views of Fenichel (1945).

At some very early point in neonatal life, probably in advance of the 6-month (or earlier) stranger anxiety identified by Spitz (1950) and Benjamin (1961a), psychological "experience," still not anxiety, enters life, a momentous achievement prior to those named by Spitz (1959) as the early "organizers" of psychic development in infancy. An organism heretofore serving as the locus of a state becomes a young, very young, "person" who suffers it. Such an awareness, probably preconscious, at first dimly, then more surely, becomes at some point the first actual psychological "experience." With it, a mental structure has been added to a somatic neuronal one, initiating what Mahler et al. (1975) called "the psychological birth of the human infant."

Does trauma thus become the first human experience? Or is the state of satiation—bliss, as it is called from an adultomorphic position—"felt" first? Does trauma become "known" because it interrupts contentment? Or is relief sensed only after trauma has been experienced? Such questions will remain subjects of debate in the realm of philosophers, or prove a fertile area for those who project their fantasies or preferences onto childhood.

Empirically we can say that, at least chronologically, the state of trauma comes first. The conditions of the first neonatal minute—Greenacre (1941) states that intrauterine stress can already predispose to the onset of this state—produce the helplessness of the traumatic state without the accompanying affect of unpleasure, which is still to come. The condition of helplessness is followed immediately by events which result in the cessation of this state as the neonate is warmed, covered, and allowed to sleep. The state of helplessness continues, but is inoperative for some minutes or hours, until mounting need repeats the process of birth, with somatic stimuli pressing again, this time from within, and the conditions which will soon bring on unpleasure reappearing. The cycle repeats: traumatic help-lessness interrupted by external manipulation that brings sati-ation and contentment.

At moments of development which can only be subjectively identified, affects of unpleasure and pleasure make themselves "felt," and from then on accompany these alternating states. While ontogenetically trauma antedates the state of homeosta-sis, the accompanying affects, in whatever sequence they begin, will alternate from that time on. Some might believe that a difference can already be laid down here for future character formation toward optimism or pessimism, in accordance with which affect comes first or at least comes to predominate: unpleasure or pleasure.

Grossman (personal communication, 1983) speculates that for Freud, the deepest abstract nature of the repetition com-pulsion results from "the imprint on the child of prestructural traumata damaging the child in the preverbal stages." Pine (1982) speaks of the opposite effect, of the potential resulting from gratifying experience for a future good self-awareness in the second year of life. Both observations relate to Emde's (1984) description of an affective core of the developing self. For completeness and clarity, I would add that the same applies to the future self representation and sense of self.

The first affective experience of unpleasure might well be the cornerstone prestructure of mental life (perhaps I have here stumbled upon the theoretical justification for Kohut's [1977] description of "tragic man"). From the moment of onset of the mental in human life, psychic "structures" are superimposed upon somatic ones. Psychoanalysts, psychologists, and neurologists have described the subsequent interdependence between the now rapid growth of the central nervous system and the psychological aspects of life. Just as the central nervous system takes time to mature and develop, so does the growth and development of the psychic apparatus. It is precisely this slow development and relatively long period of dependence of the human species that were given special importance by Freud (1905b) as leading to the most advanced neuropsychological evolutionary outcome among living forms. These observations about psychic maturation relate to Anders's (1984) chronobiological timetable with its innate temporal rhythms and organization and add to it a chronobiopsychological sequence.

Both psychic and somatic structures develop simultaneously from lesser to higher forms of organization. Among early built-in constitutional prestructures in the ontogenesis of affect described by Rapaport (1953a) are discharge channels—psychological pathways connoting direction—and stimulus thresholds—obstacles limiting rates of discharge, analogous to neurological reflex pathways with their facilitators or resistances to neural discharge. Both become parts of a later developed ego. The id-ego matrix present at birth (Hartmann, 1939a, 1950a) gradually differentiates into separate id and ego structures.

Psychic structures undergo a gradual unfolding, from *anlagen* to forerunners or precursors to prestructures to more formed and cohesive structures, and from these to systems of unified and functionally cooperating structures. Maturational expectations and timetables are built into the constitutional givens, with psychic expansion inherent within the growth potential and expectable forward thrust of originally somatic structures. Sensory apparatuses contain within them the functional capacity for perception, which will lead to the perceptual images of mental life. Motor organs possess the potential and

expectation for providing a function that will mentally fulfill
Hendrick's (1942) "instinct for mastery." Proprioceptive and
kinesthetic functions, mediated by the central nervous system,
provide the *sense* of balance and orientation that is an intrinsic
part of original and subsequent affect, of basic pleasure or
unpleasure, and the rudimentary beginnings of an awareness
of a self. Visceral and enteroceptive stimuli contribute, even
disproportionately at first, to the mental and bodily states of
well-being or disharmony. Early perceptions, the first experiences of pleasure and unpleasure, the mnemic images of these
original affects, and dimly perceived or felt external objects or
conditions constitute original mental impressions en route to
becoming more formed mental representations.

From unpleasure and pleasure, the first diffuse "experiences" of affect and the first affective prestructures to be laid
down, a next major psychological organizer of development is
the differentiation and experience of anxiety. Traumatic helplessness is not unpleasure but leads to it. Unpleasure is not
anxiety but leads to it. Anxiety awaits the ability to anticipate.
Necessary are the functions of memory and recall and, with
these, the capacity to imagine the recurrence of unpleasure.
Anxiety is the anticipation of the unpleasure of traumatic
helplessness. At the point at which it is achieved by the human
infant, anxiety brings with it the human capability to survive
and to suffer.

The deprived children Brazelton (1984) treated, in whom
he observed "a worried look," were already advanced to the
degree that they could anticipate danger. They were thus at a
higher developmental level than the marasmic children studied
by Spitz (1945), in whom apathy, rather than anxiety, was in
evidence. The hospitalized children described by Spitz were in
a chronic undefended traumatic state, while the infants Brazelton treated in his office or in their homes with their mothers
present could already anticipate that state, as well as the
condition that would ward it off (the presence of the mother).

The gradually evolving maturational process combines
both integration and differentiation. At every stage the

achieved position maintains the original bond between soma and psyche, a continuous union often overlooked, as well as resulting in a differentiation between the two. An intellectual oscillation throughout man's history has led to an alternating overvaluation of one or the other, either to a Cartesian duality of body and mind, in a philosophic and psychiatric-psychoanalytic sense, or to an undue fusion, leading, for example, to the attempt to explain both by the material and somatic. The result has been either an emphasis of mind over matter or an exaggerated organic bias. In actuality both psyche and soma evolve together and separately, with unity and differentiation, with independence and a separate course for each, as well as with an interdependence between man's corporeal being and his thinking and feeling.

The relations between functions and structures evolve gradually. Pathological defensive behavior can exist in infants without being continuous with pre-ego modes of defense, as Fraiberg (1982) pointed out on the basis of careful direct observations of a deprived infant population. Precursors and prestructures are more malleable, changeable, and fluid than psychic elements that have become structured and fixed. Perceptions and affects, before they enter into formed memories, are more subject to addition, replacement, obliteration, and modification than after they have achieved the status of structured fixity. Perhaps this is the basis for the clinically obtained understanding that the earliest influences, by which are usually meant the pregenital, have profound but still changeable effects, whereas by the oedipal period, which is quite synchronous with the formation of tripartite structures, a good deal of character formation and predictability of behavior have been laid down. New inputs, however, can still be continuously absorbed to affect the quality of the still-developing structures.

A psychopathological developmental variation is the phenomenon of premature structuralization, a defensive maladaptive event occurring in the presence of an abnormal degree of trauma. This can result from either overstimulation or deprivation. With the young child having automatically to sacrifice the long and beneficial dependency period and to develop defensively a premature independence for survival purposes, early pathology can result from prematurely developing structures encapsulating insufficiently developed ego or superego nuclei. Variations of such processes result in developmental arrests, ego deficits, or pathological fixations, which will exert a backward pull for future regression.

Freud's (1923a) observations of the early ego as being originally a body ego can be properly expanded or altered to refer instead to a body self, as Mahler and McDevitt (1982) have recently called it. While the self is a composite of somatic and mental, the ego is a mental structure. The self representation contained within it, however, in early stages of development of the psychic structure "ego," does consist of confluent images of the body, affective and cognitive, sensory and motor, surface-exteroceptive and enteroceptive-visceral.

Infancy is connected to adult life within the psychoanalytic theory of anxiety. The traumatic state of helplessness of birth and beyond, until the point at which a beginning ego embarks upon the process of stemming the tide from within, is the feared state behind all anxiety. Rank's (1952) birth trauma is not the model of anxiety but the model of the state that anxiety is dedicated to avoid. It is for this reason that Freud was ambivalent to his own first theory of anxiety, neither willing to retain it nor able to discard it. Freud's actual neurosis was the traumatic state (Chapter 20), as a stage in the intrapsychic process en route to symptom formation or, in favorable situations, to a more adaptive solution. It is also helpful and necessary to distinguish the traumatic state from a traumatic neurosis. A state of trauma appropriate to the stimulus is not a neurosis. The latter obtains only to a reaction inappropriate to the current stimulus, stemming from a latent, cumulative readiness to react.

Anxiety is never without psychological content, as Freud felt in his first theory, but is always the sign of such content, the cognitive-affective anticipation of danger. "The biological factor . . . establishes the earliest situations of danger," Freud

(1926, p. 155) stated, but a psychological factor is required to recognize and react to it. Arising at the point of development when danger can be foreseen, the capacity for anxiety, one of the organizing milestones described by Spitz (1959), along with the smile, which is its opposite and bespeaks safety, is called forth in every repetition of the sensing of danger from then on. Anxiety undergoes a complex developmental line, with both phase-specific and individual experiences throughout life. Developmental stages passed through ontogenetically and sequential phases passed through in rapid succession during the unconscious intrapsychic process, from the original impulse or perception to the final psychic outcome, are typically visible in derivative forms as the material in analysis unfolds during the psychoanalytic process.

DERIVATIVES IN ANALYSIS AND IN LIFE

Switching again rapidly from infancy to adult life, I would like next to point to certain clinically observable phenomena seen in adult psychoanalytic patients, which, to my way of understanding, derive directly from the tension state of the intrapsychic arc and genetically recapitulate ontogenetic development. In accordance with a formulation I suggest (see Chapter 26), that anxiety results from an unconscious recapitulation of the traumatic states of life, the dangers behind the unconscious anxiety in the clinical instances to be cited represent a series of defended against and increasingly distorted derivatives of the individual life history of traumatic states. Extrapolating back to our interest in the period of infancy, these traverse, in reverse order, states of trauma experienced in infancy and beyond, and either repetitions or derivatives of these remembered preconsciously in childhood, fantasied consciously and unconsciously later, and feared unconsciously throughout life.

Data in themselves do not typically prove or confirm theories employed to explain them. The same data can be explained by structural theory, object relations theory, self theory, and, not as close to the center of psychoanalytic theory

today, theories of environmental conflict or interpersonal relationships. Nevertheless, in the view I am presenting here, the
most convincing, enduring, experience-related, and time-
resisting explanations for not some but all clinical and life
observations rest upon total basic psychoanalytic theory, which
includes psychic structure, anxiety, conflict, and the explanations that derive from these for symptom formation and all
other human behavior. In specific clinical cases, there are
universal substrates upon which individual experiences of
traumatic threats have been superimposed. The closer the
danger situations approach the original states of infantile
trauma, the more does clinical phenomenology rest on common experiential ground.

I would now like to describe some clinical observations of
certain adult behavioral patterns which I have been accumulating in the past few years and which, I believe, trace their origins
to the earliest period of life. These include myriad postures,
mannerisms, and automatic actions occurring in a variety of
analytic phases and moods, which came to be understood as
they were interwoven with the surrounding accompanying
material and dynamics.

These actions can be divided into two groups: one serving
tension reduction, almost somatic, neurophysiologic, and similar to Freud's original clinical observations along the same line;
and another in which these same functions were admixed with
superimposed or parallel symbolic and hermeneutic significance. These activities, which typically involve the neuromuscular system or the skin or its hair, nails, or other appendages,
traverse a complementary series of phenomena from what I
regard as reflex psychosomatic transmission at one pole to
increasingly symbolic meaning at the other.

Whereas the significance of these traits and actions can
become known to the analyst, it may or may not be useful to
bring them to the attention of the patient in the interpretive
process. When and if pointed out, they are usually thought of
consciously as "little habits," typically fused with the character
and rarely egodystonic. Not only has learning "abiding change

wrought by experience," brought about structure formation (Rapaport, 1960, p. 99), but effects that can be "environmentally syntonic" as well. To the extent that these have accrued symbolic meanings during the course of development, they are rendered accessible to the interpretive process and to analysis. Just as preoedipal conflicts become embedded in the oedipal, and can be carried along analytically by analysis of the later more available experiences, so can these more primitive and direct mental processes be included in later symbolic acts and actions, and in the capacity of the analytic ego of the patient to understand and master them. Such automatic and seemingly reflex psychomotor acts may in this manner turn out in practice not to be outside the reach of analysis.

As evidence of the type of behavior I have in mind, in some patients a periodic or at times more continuous restlessness on the couch becomes prominent during the analytic hour. This is not so much at times of verbal communication or during the revelation of the concrete contents of psychic conflicts as in between these times. Although it is difficult to convey the clinical "feel" that is the background for my theoretical understanding of its meaning and dynamics, I have come to regard such motor activity as direct unconscious or preconscious expression of psychophysical tension, which is a discrete segment of mental activity upon which the bursts of verbal activity are superimposed. This type of behavior, freely available to analysts generally, in my view, represents an attempt to dispel tension occurring when psychic conflict mounts toward a relative traumatic state which would strain the capacity of the ego. There is, to be sure, psychic conflict operative at the same time and indeed at all times, but the motor innervations during these periods of visible activity are, in my opinion, attempts to discharge not the psychic content but its somatic accompaniments.

One patient would alternately flex his knees and then straighten his legs, move his head from one position to another, lie on one side and then the other, or rhythmically clench and unclench his fists. From the same dynamic background, another patient at certain times would energetically crack his knuckles and then rest. One could of course say that these movements expressed aggression, even if this was not in the psychic content at the time. But with or without this added, I came to understand these activities regularly and typically as attempts to produce physical, along with mental, homeostasis.

To be sure, such complex psychomotor actions are multi-determined, as is all final outward behavior, and consist of inputs from all levels of development. One patient stretched and yawned whenever a crucial interpretation was about to be conveyed, usually closer and closer to the castration anxiety. He also exhibited and noted a shiver, which he stated he did not understand. Here tension reduction was also operative as the specific anxiety was being approached, but the generalized movements were then joined by and utilized for an acute increment of defense, this psychological meaning being added to the baseline physiological process. The syndrome of "restless legs," known to physicians, and usually attributed to vascular insufficiency, is probably seen here in a more generalized form as a restless body, due not to vascular pathology but to a chronic psychosomatic malfunctioning in conflict resolution. This is probably related to Freud's "discharge of drive tension into the soma," cited by Rapaport (1950, p. 315) as a stage in the development of affective behavior.

Actions and behavior at the sensorimotor periphery of the body are complex, overdetermined, and serve multiple functions (Waelder, 1930). One patient rhythmically clasps his fingers and presses his hands tightly together, doing and undoing this repetitive action. In this case the patient is holding on to himself as a substitute for holding another, psychologically reassuring himself by seeking support, superimposed upon physical muscular tension reduction. Progressing in this series, another patient, in whom hand-seeking was more solely psychological, hermeneutic, and meaning-oriented, would put her arms and hands behind her head toward the analyst, looking to hold on, but no pressing or muscular movements were in evidence. Here the movements served a wish. There was no tension discharge. Still another patient clearly added masturbatory impulses from a later stage of psychosexual development. This patient kneaded the muscles and patted the skin on the inside of his thighs, first gently, then increasingly forcefully. At times when he came to his sessions in shorts after jogging, a not uncommon custom in Southern California, these actions could be seen more directly and undisguisedly.

Behavior in this category can be varied and changeable. In one patient, bursts of muscular activity accompanied irregular verbal outbursts, with silence as well as muscular inactivity simultaneously evident in between. One had the feeling of witnessing complex verbal and muscular tics, reminiscent of and not unlike sudden spikes on an electroencephalogram. Or the behavior is more stereotyped and ritualistic. A patient entered analysis with the main complaint of hair-pulling which he engaged in to such an extent that his wife was afraid he would cause himself to become bald. During the course of analysis, this patient came to display in the analytic position, along with constant and distracting gross twisting and turning of his body, a continued series of unconscious "habits," moving from one to another with rarely a quiescent period in between. He would habitually tear his fingernails or produce hangnails on the skin, pick these off, and then engage in a slow ritual of playing with the remnants. He would roll the nail fragments and dead skin into a ball with his fingers, hold and rub them for a while, and eventually drop them, after some hesitation about which side—whether to his left on the couch or to his right on the carpet.

The total action here was composed of complex psychological components and meanings, sexual and aggressive, from all levels of libidinal and ego development—oral, anal, and phallic. In this patient, there was a combination of chronic general tension reduction, along with a complex masturbatory and self-stimulating ritual. With nails and skin, as also with his hair-pulling, he could be seen to produce excessive stimulation, even pain, which was erotized and used as a displaced focus for sexual and aggressive motivational drives. This patient could never be alone or without bodily stimulation or reassurance. In spite of a successful, storybook marriage, he carried on a promiscuous extramarital sexual life, which was compulsive, automatic, and shallow. He had more total satisfaction, physical as well as mental, with his wife, but needed the constant reassurance of an available reservoir of stimulus satisfaction as a back-up system should he be left and need some one or some place to go to. Mainly, he wanted to snuggle into and feel attached to these partners and would go further toward sexual intercourse only because he felt it was expected.

Felix Deutsch (1952) has written about such analytic posturology, and Feldman (1959) described mannerisms and gestures of speech and action in everyday life. Both of these authors wove such observations well and convincingly into the total conflictual fabrics of their patients. What I am adding, however, is another component behind this aspect of behavior, a somatic substrate upon which the psychological motivations are superimposed and with which they are fused. This link, which ties psychic content together, a psychophysical ground upon which conflicts and their derivatives become the figures, is confluent with what Pontalis (1977) writes in his emphasis on the "in-between," the spaces and absences and nonverbal links between or behind concrete groups of psychic content. Pontalis, coming from another direction, interestingly notes a similar renewed interest in Freud's original concept of actual neurosis by modern French psychoanalytic theorists.

The recent emphasis on early deficit states converging from many modern psychoanalytic directions are not centered on the same phenomena I have been describing. Kohut's (1971, 1977) theory of ego deficits resulting from deficient early mothering, and also Kernberg's (1975) more widely based theories of preoedipal pathology, relate specifically to more regressed and disturbed psychopathology. What I am pointing to, in reviving Freud's original observations and theory about the genesis of anxiety, involves a more universal mechanism and set of intrapsychic dynamics.

This does not concern abnormalities of psychic structure

resulting from phase-specific traumas at later psychosexual stages of development, pregenital or oedipal. Nor am I speaking of cases of earlier traumatic events involving localized musculature or any other somatic structures, resulting later in derivative syndromes. Such a case was reported by Anthi (1983): an operation on an infant at a few months of age for a right neck muscle injured during birth, with subsequent physiotherapy to the age of 3, resulted in sequelae which were detected in the analysis of the patient as an adult. I am describing a more generalized failure, at an early prestructural stage of development, from the same events described by Anna Freud (1969) as affecting the transition from the early chaotic undifferentiated state to the first cornerstone of psychic structure. The result is an influence on future structural development with a specific but generalized later effect, a hyperalertness to anxiety and sensitivity to trauma. The traumatic state feared and avoided is the state of helplessness common to mankind, rather than specific traumas that come from individual experiences of later life. Frustration tolerance is low, and the stimulus barrier fragile, vulnerable, and carefully guarded.

Since such pathological effects have occurred before structure formation takes place, they are subject to compensation and amelioration until structure with greater stability and fixity ensues. Such early pathology is therefore not incompatible with subsequent more normal development, including future object relations, or with the formation of any more circumscribed pathological syndrome, borderline or neurotic. The effects I am describing may constitute a general background prior to the differentiation of later specific symptoms, including in infancy any of the attachment syndromes listed by Call (1980) or the general or psychosomatic afflictions of infancy categorized in the nosology of Kreisler (1984).

THE PSYCHOBIOLOGICAL UNITY

The main theoretical consideration I wish to point to, in an overall view of the clinical material cited, is the regression in common to the psychobiological unity from which we started. Anxiety itself, a center of this presentation, is a psychobiological phenomenon, a unity of opposites not routinely kept in mind or appreciated when being understood or treated from one side only, that is, either by the psychoanalyst from the point of view of conflict or by the pharmacologist who puts aside the psychological aspects. The fact is that, while the treatment may be legitimately limited to one side or the other, with theoretical complications resulting from combining the two, the complete understanding of the phenomenon of anxiety, encompassing in theory the total self which harbors it, can only be achieved by a unified psychobiological view.

It is consonant with this total theoretical approach that I have combined Freud's two theories of anxiety, the first, which purported to be physiological, without the effects of psychological conflicts, and the second, which centered on psychological content, eliminating its organic base. Traumatic helplessness, feared and already partially present in the experience of anxiety, is a psychophysical or equally somatopsychic state threatening a physical as well as mental dissolution of the self.

Jones's (1929b) aphanisis, Glover's (1938) fear of bursting from within, Kohut's (1971, 1977) fragmentation of the self, Winnicott's (1952) fragmentation of the ego, Waelder's (1930) fear of the ego being destroyed or overrun, and Anna Freud's (1936) "dread of the strength of the instincts," as well as Freud's (1920, 1926, 1937a) ultimate "resistances of the id," all refer to the same primitively feared states of physical and psychological disintegration. Fraiberg (1982) sensitively described a group of babies from 3 months of age, whose mothers were chronically not "good-enough," in whom hunger, solitude, or a sudden noise set off a state of helplessness and disintegration, with screaming and flailing about, which in effect was an already present traumatic state. But disintegrative states, as Fraiberg also pointed out, "are an extreme danger in themselves." Anxiety is a fear of the traumatic state; the traumatic state begets anxiety. Brazelton's frail and worried little patients demonstrated the ongoing mutuality and reciprocity of these contiguous clinical states.

Approaching the infantile state from the view point of adult psychopathology (see Chapter 4), I described the fear in stage fright, which can be applied to universal social anxiety, in which there is a fantasy, both a wish and a fear, of disappearing into the ground, with only the nose and mouth remaining above it. When the wish turns to pure fear, the remaining few inches of corpus will also submerge. All anxiety, in my clinical experience with pathological anxiety states, is ultimately a fear of claustrum, a respiratory panic of the unavailability of air to breathe.

The clinical phenomenology to which I pointed in these studies, proceeding from adult manifestations to their infantile origins, of skin and neuromuscular facial mechanisms involving the lips, tongue, chin, and the snout or perioral region generally, correlate well with the direct and experimental observations of affect attunement reported by Stern (1983). These same areas of affective facial expression were involved in his direct observations of the reciprocal communicative responses between infants and mothers.

Regression in the panic state, which Schur (1953) refers to as maximum anxiety, the feared state behind milder and more-defended-against anxiety states, is associatively and etiologically linked by a series of decreasingly distorted derivatives to the original preverbal traumatic state. One patient's ultimate anxiety, manifesting her fear of loss of ego control, was of losing bodily control of every orifice—that she would fall in a faint after sweating, vomiting, defecating, menstruating, and choking. In another patient, who, behind a very successful social and professional façade, had what he referred to as a "jelly center," his vulnerable state traced back to the birth of his sister when the patient was 2. Historically his life changed abruptly at that time from being his parents' Leonardo da Vinci, the only son, grandson, and grandchild of a large and doting family to what should have been realistically a normal state of sharing, but which to him became an intolerable state of deprivation. He remembered a period in his early childhood when he did not speak to his mother for two years. When, during his analysis, he inquired of his mother about this, she was incredulous, remembering nothing of it, and repeated her antagonism to his analysis and his analyst. In groping for the reasons for his chronic, depressed, and angry state at that time (after coming up with a number of trite and unconvincing explanations), the best he could lamely offer was, "I think she just wasn't nice to me."

Derivatives of anxiety throughout life fall on a continuum with respect to bodily or psychological effects. As with all continua or complementary series, most instances are in the midrange and combine polar attributes, with a lesser number of pure examples at either end. Thus most symptoms or other final common pathways of behavior combine psychic and somatic manifestations. Affects, so much stressed in these studies of infants, are themselves on the boundary between soma and psyche, as Freud (1915a) said about instincts, and utilize aspects of each in their composition and expressions.

Outcomes generally regarded as psychosomatic and non-symbolic, such as ulcer, asthma, or hypertension, can express ideational contents as well, aggressive or libidinal motivations and intentions from various phases of development. And presumably solely hermeneutic and conflict-expressing symptoms, such as conversion, can and do utilize bodily organs as well, with direct relief of tension or other nonsymbolic purposes admixed. Delusions or hallucinations are generally thought of as on the cognitive and ideational side of the continuum, and asthma, ulcer, or tics as more on the somatic. Yet there can be somatic delusions, and hallucinations involve auditory or visual perceptual pathways. Asthma or ulcer can express distorted oral longings. A tic can be a pregenital conversion (Fenichel, 1945; Rangell, 1959). Gilles de la Tourette's disease, a syndrome Mahler and I (1943) described from a combined psychoanalytic and neurological standpoint, is a complex combination of automatic, kinetic, muscular involvement with pathological, indirect symbolic expressions of aggressive drives and destructive intentions.

Anxiety expresses the psychological content of danger, yet its physical accompaniments are themselves direct bodily derivatives of the tension segment of the intrapsychic arc of conflict I have described. The shiver, so commonly regarded as intrinsic to anxiety and which I noted earlier as prominent in a patient whenever an interpretation close to castration either came or was expected, is not a fortuitous occurrence but might also have meaning. Its meaning, however, is not necessarily ideational but can be physiological. It can routinely signify an attempt to diminish the tension of anxiety, which comes about from an unsuccessful attempt of the defenses to stave off mounting instinctual or external pressure. The anxiety reaction is both a suffering of trauma, limited and experimental, and preparedness for restitution. While anxiety is properly regarded as a psychological reaction, in the last analysis it is a mental plan for total—that is, physical and mental—survival. The other side of the fear of disappearing is the wish to disappear for protective purposes, leaving, as I said earlier, the snout exposed for air.

The perioral region is the "window to the emotions." It is both protected and kept exposed. It is also the area of the body through which attachment is achieved, from the time of the infant's first perioral grasping and holding of the maternal breast. Every experimental thought that tests for anxiety is both to achieve separateness and to be assured of the possibility of return to the source of security. The combined search for independence and attachment, noted by Mahler and McDevitt (1982) as already present in the neonate, is continued in derivative form throughout life. Anxiety, from the time that it appears, is a practicing separation as much as the practicing subphase of a year or more later. And the "niche" sought by the reflex action of the infant is repeated throughout life in what I have called (1955b) "the quest for ground," manifested as a permanent need to belong, whether to a person, group, institution, or idea.

Section II

The Etiological Sequence

Introduction

This section consists of a group of papers which I think of as comprising the sequence of intrapsychic events which precedes and then is followed by any or all final psychic outcomes. Basically, these papers took up and expanded upon the psychoanalytic theories of anxiety, conflict, and trauma. As it happened, these were all assigned subjects, i.e., they followed invitations to participate in panels or symposia on these subjects. This was an interesting relationship, between subjects I became immersed in through initiation by others, and those which arose and were initiated electively. Empirically, there was always a reciprocal relationship between the two.

Although these papers center on conflict and anxiety, my developing concept of the psychic "core" changes from the area of unconscious intrapsychic conflict to the wider unconscious intrapsychic process. In addition to the "microdynamic" sequence described, a "macroscopic point of view" is also always to be kept in mind. Clinically, the microscopic and macroscopic views and orientations alternate in theoretical understanding throughout the therapeutic procedure.

The final papers in this section are on the theory of affects and psychic trauma. Affects and trauma are among the variable outcomes which appear during the intrapsychic sequence. These papers attend separately to their occurrence, nature, and composition.

CHAPTER 7

The Scope of Intrapsychic Conflict

Microscopic and Macroscopic Considerations

The theory of psychoanalysis has from the beginning been a conflict theory. In broad strokes, the sequence of Freud's thinking went through a number of crucial stages with regard to the nature of the basic etiological conflict (Panel, 1963b). The earliest phase, as reviewed by Rapaport (1960), was conceived as occurring "between the memory of the traumatic event and the dominant ideational mass of the person, or as the conflict of the ideas and affects present in the traumatic situation with the moral standards of society." When the latter were internalized and taken over by the patient as his own, the conflict was seen at once as an intrapsychic one, although a step removed from having been inner vs. outer. It was early conceived in topographic terms, i.e., between unconscious memories, ideas, and affects, and the essentially conscious inner dictates of morality.

This and the next paper were presented together in condensed form at the Panel on "The Significance of Intrapsychic Conflict," American Psychoanalytic Association, New York, December 8, 1962. This paper was published in *The Psychoanalytic Study of the Child*, 18:75–102, 1963.

181

The dynamic and economic points of view were implicit in the assumptions made, and were soon made manifest.

The intrapsychic locus of the conflict thus existed long before the structural point of view. In the next development, the conflict was seen as between "the wishful impulse" and the endopsychic censorship, or as between the primary and the secondary processes (Freud, 1900). Later, the intrapsychic components opposing each other consisted of libidinal vs. ego-preservative instincts, both forces residing within the instinctual drives (Freud, 1911a, 1914a). We know that with the elaboration of the structural point of view (Freud, 1920, 1923a), as well as with both the revised theory of anxiety (Freud, 1926) and the dual-instinct theory (Freud, 1920, 1923a), the intrapsychic conflict took its final and present form as an intersystemic one, a structural conflict between the instinctual drives of the id and the defensive forces, the anticathexes of the ego. The struggle had long before this already been conceived of as taking place mainly at the unconscious level. Jones (1953–1957) refers in a broader way to a striking and characteristic dualism in Freud's basic thinking, a fact which has been noted by Hartmann and many others.

Theory always brought with it, sometimes too rapidly, its results. The various phases described were accompanied by a series of pendular shifts with regard to the applicability of the new points of view and of the insights gained, not only by nonanalysts, such as parents and teachers eager with each new phase for its help, but also as reflected in the goals and techniques used by analysts in treatment as well. Anna Freud (1956) has outlined the phases of such applications and expectations. Since it was the pathogenic nature of intrapsychic conflicts which was the first to be exposed, the desideratum was considered to be to avoid or at least to minimize all conflict. The means of bringing this about prophylactically progressed, with the successive conceptual stages, from sexual enlightenment, to complete tolerance of sexual and derivative autoerotic activity, to abandoning all discipline so that there could be no difficult superego to be internalized, to permitting and even encouraging all aggressive behavior. In the face of the resulting chaos and the failure to achieve the desired goal, Anna Freud concluded by recommending that the mother can lend her own resources and ego strength to the child only until the time when he has matured enough to have incorporated these into himself. In this way the child's ego equipment could be optimally developed to deal in as rational a manner as possible with the inevitable developmental anxieties and conflicts of human life. The latter were not to be avoided.

Subsequently, with the recognition of the role played by such conflicts as a spur to maturational processes and to the entire line of developmental progression, the existence of conflict came to be seen as a necessary and even as the most desirable of psychological phenomena to assure the course of effective development. Anxiety, conflicts, and the need to resolve them were seen as the motive force and the *sine qua non* of all progression, without which satiety, stagnation, and emotional arrest would be the inevitable results.

Actually, as is usually the case with such pendular swings, the truth lies somewhere between the two extremes. The classic causes of fixation, as Fenichel (1945) has pointed out, occur with either excessive satisfaction or with excessive deprivation. Provence and Ritvo (1961), testing a hypothesis advanced by Ernst Kris that in the infant comfort serves to build object relationships while discomfort stimulates differentiation and structure formation, studied a group of institutionalized infants deprived of normal maternal care. These authors found that it was discomfort-comfort contrast of a certain degree which was important for stimulating differentiation and the formation of psychic structure. The "ordinary devoted mother," to borrow Winnicott's term (1945), ministered to her child in close proximity to the peak intensity of the discomfort, which was followed by an experience of fuller gratification and a greater degree of comfort than was the case in the institutionalized infant. In the latter case, protracted discomfort occurring over a long period of time and without relief resulted in disorganization and disruption of the infant's capacity for ego functioning. While the ego apparatuses and repertories for action appeared on time in the maturational timetable, they were clumsily used, poor in adaptation, and lacking in richness or subtlety. The crucial role of early object relationships in providing such favorable attention to the needs of the infant was stressed. Rubinfine (1962), elaborating on observations made by Escalona (1953), described mothers who were overzealous in anticipating and preventing frustration on the parts of their infants, thus permitting no buildup of tension to take place, and interfering particularly thereby with the discharge of aggression. In both sets of subjects quoted, those with a steady diet of excessive tension and those without the chance of developing a sufficient amount, the results were affects which were muted, shallow, and hollow, and an incomplete and stilted register of emotions.

A nodal contribution, which resulted in a major change in our viewpoint toward conflict, was Hartmann's classic monograph (1939a) in which he described and gave due place to the conflict-free ego apparatuses and their roles and destinies in psychic functioning. Present from the beginning as part of the constitutional endowment, they contain a potential for meeting the "average expectable environment" and are to serve an indispensable role in adaptation. While "the ego certainly does grow on conflicts," Hartmann writes, "these are not the only roots of ego development" (p. 8). In order to fulfill its role as a *general* developmental psychology, psychoanalysis must encompass and explore thoroughly that prolific "ensemble of functions" which develop and exert their effects outside the realm of mental conflicts, the "peacetime traffic" within the ego borders as well as the history of its conflicts. One of our major tasks is "to investigate how mental conflict and peaceful internal development mutually facilitate and hamper each other" (p. 11). Of course, Freud's interest in the phenomena of a "general psychology," such as in dreams (1900), wit (1905a), and everyday life (1901), had long antedated this, although, it is true, at first largely from the point of view of conflict-solving behavior.

In a series of illuminating articles which followed (Hartmann, 1950a, 1952, 1955; and with Kris and Loewenstein, 1946), this entire area was amplified in many necessary derivative directions. We learned subsequently of the differentiation between primary and secondary ego autonomy, and how in the latter large portions of the ego previously in the service of defense and conflict may acquire secondary conflict-free autonomy following "a change in function." Rapaport (1951c, 1958) later elaborated on the nature of autonomous structures; and Spitz (1957) on the phenomenon of "change of function," drawing parallels between such occurrences on the psychological and on the embryological and physiological levels.

With these contributions, and with the entire literature which they triggered, there came an enormous expansion in our understanding of the life of the ego, which was thus to catch up with the previous emphasis given to the role of instinctual drives. Ego action was now seen in fresh perspective, not only with respect to these newly appreciated conflict-free regions, but also, in conjunction with the impetus given concurrently by Anna Freud's detailed investigations into the mechanisms of defense (1936), with a more intensive understanding of its role within the conflict situation itself. With these, the processes of adaptation received new dimensions of understanding.

Hartmann (1939a) decisively pointed out, and it bears repetition here, that "It would be an error to assume that the contrast of conflict situation and peaceful development corresponds directly to the antithesis of pathological and normal" (p. 12). Such is of course by no means the case, nor is the dichotomy conflict-free vs. conflictful, by similar error, to be equated with congenital vs. experiential. Rather, all three divisions are scrambled together, in mutual and complementary fashion. For example, conflict or conflict-free activity can be associated with either the normal or the pathological. "Conflicts are part of the human condition" and absence of conflicts can be associated with failure (Hartmann, 1939a, p. 12). Ontogenetically, apparatuses destined for each sphere are included within the congenital givens, as well as being subject to the facilitations or the deterrences which are to come from subsequent environmental fates. There are inborn defense thresholds (Rapaport, 1951c, 1953a), as well as the innate conflict-free apparatuses, all with their own "primary ego energy" to provide their own motive power.

There are spectra in all of these, as we come to see in discussions of most of our psychological phenomena (such as sublimation, conversion, nosology) so that we may extricate ourselves at once, for example, from the fruitless nature-nurture controversy, or the other similar dichotomies, in all of which Freud's original description of the complementary series is to be applied.

The same spectrum and mutuality applies in the reciprocal interaction and overlap which take place continuously between the conflict-laden and the conflict-free spheres of activity themselves. Conflict-free apparatuses may attract to themselves, or else have thrust upon them, conflicting forces, such as in somatic compliance. Similarly, areas of conflict may become conflict-free or secondarily autonomous. Yet, as with all spectra, there are components which belong and operate in a polar fashion at each end. While some functions or organs are in the central band, there are nevertheless some which are prone to be free of conflict throughout their developmental histories, while others are more destined to operate within areas of conflict and of mounting tension.

I

I would now like to turn to the nature of the intrapsychic conflict itself, approaching it from two different positions. We might regard the first as a microscopic view; it examines the intricate components which make up the interior of the phenomenon and their sequential relationships, in a manner which I have described (1959) as micropsychophysiology. The second would be a macroscopic view, of how we are confronted with the ingredients and the consequences of conflict in a global way in the clinical and the therapeutic situation, and of what our task consists in that setting.

When applying the microscopic interior view, we should consider the following. Because of the tendency for fusion and synthesis among psychic products, it is necessary, for clarity, to distinguish the various components which take place within the entire arc which comprises the conflict situation and to separate the events which occur prior to, during, and following what can be called the actual period of conflict itself. This would entail delineating as separate entities, for example, frustration, the buildup of tension, the occurrence of anxiety, and what relation these bear to actual conflict situation, and then the defense cathexes, inhibitions, symptom formations, or hierarchy of symptom formations which may result. It is my contention that too often such statements as "the patient is overwhelmed by tension—or by anxiety—or by conflict" are loosely interchanged, without clarity. I take it as an opportunity, if not an assignment, to attempt to clarify such issues.

Hartmann (1939a) points out that "It would be meaningless to call every disruption of equilibrium a conflict. This would rob the concept of all precision. Every stimulus disrupts the equilibrium, but not every stimulus causes conflict" (p. 38). Hartmann then reminds us of four different mental states of equilibrium which concern psychoanalysts in relation to our regulation principles. There is the equilibrium between the individual and his environment, the equilibrium of instinctual drives (vital equilibrium), the equilibrium of mental institutions (structural equilibrium), and the equilibrium between the synthetic function and the rest of the ego (p. 39). To my mind, not all of these are of equal and central weight when we come to examine the question of intrapsychic conflict. It is the third of these, the structural equilibrium, which is most regularly involved and of most universal interest by the time a state of intrapsychic conflict is attained; I will comment in further detail below, however, on the important aspects of the equilibrium within the ego itself, as well as on the question of the equilibrium between the instinctual drives.

Freud has given us the model for separating contiguous and closely related events, and for the establishment of the proper sequential relationships between them, in his classic study on anxiety (1926), when he separated and clearly demonstrated the relationship between inhibitions, symptoms, and anxiety. Any further elaboration in this area has had to be built upon this base.

The chain of events which leads to, includes, and stems from the significant intrapsychic conflict situation comprises the following sequence:

1. Since we must arbitrarily select a starting point, let us start with a hypothetical state of psychic equilibrium, with a person at ease, content, at rest, not particularly "bothered" by anything. He is well *defended* and averagely satisfied with how *adapted* he is at that moment. (Such states are, to be sure, most often transitional and not too long-lasting in daily waking life.) You will also remember that in accordance with our constancy and nirvana principles, it is not called for that such a state be tension-free; rather a condition of optimum tension exists, indeed one "characteristic for the organism," (Fenichel, 1945). Actually, all four of Hartmann's specific equilibria enumerated above are in a relative state of quiescence to achieve this dynamic-economic state, although it is the intrapsychic reverberations (Hartmann includes the environment) which are decisive and which, from my point of view, we will be especially compelled to watch.

2. This existing equilibrium, between the psychic structures as well as at the other levels, is impinged upon by a precipitating factor. This may be either from an external stimulus (influx) or from within, somatic or psychic. The latter may come from any one of various possible directions, for example, from an increase in intrasystemic instinctual tension, or a relaxation of a defensive ego anticathexis. While a common instance is that of an increase in instinctual pressure, either libidinal or aggressive, it is possible, in accordance with Hartmann's principle of autonomy, that an increase in intrasystemic tension can originate *ab initio* from other than the instinctual

drive organization, for example, from the exercise of an ego judgment, or the arousal of a superego attitude toward a specific existing instinctual urge. Writing on hierarchy and autonomy, Rapaport (1960) states: "these more neutralized derivative motivations will be autonomous from—i.e., can be activated without being triggered by—the underlying less neutralized motivations. For instance, they may discharge when their autonomously accumulated energy reaches threshold intensity."

3. When such a stimulus encroaches, a new imbalance is created, and a new economic condition prevails. From whatever source it originates, when it reaches a sufficient magnitude, it is the ego which is confronted with this new situation.

4. There are a great variety of possibilities from this point on, some of trivial psychoeconomic import, not going many steps beyond this. For the sake of pursuing, however, what follows in the case of an appreciable and significant disturbance of the psychoeconomic condition, I will select one of the possibilities, in fact, one of the quite typical outcomes, and pursue this along its possible course. It should be borne in mind that this is selective and of course extremely schematic, as is inevitable in any such stripping process which attempts to arrive at "model" activities.

The "typical" situation I have chosen is one in which, from whatever source it originates, whether activated directly or by stimulation from any of the other sources mentioned, an instinctual temptation is aroused. This may be a new instinctual pressure, or a necessary recontemplation of an old one. At once, however, the ego is now confronted with this instinctual demand, while facing a superego and possible external figures ready to pass judgment. (The superego is a *sine qua non* in this intrapsychic process, the external figure may be an added burden.) Between these and after it judges the nature of these forces, the ego will have to make a decision.

5. In our literature it is frequently stated, quite summarily, that at this point the ego uses anxiety as a signal. While this is certainly true, we must interpose first a few vital steps, indis-

pensable links in the sequential chain, which take place at this
juncture as preparatory stages before the anxiety signal can
ensue—steps which it is my impression are usually glided over
in our descriptions of this process.

The ego is now subjected, automatically, to the experience
of this new balance of intersystemic forces and to their mutual
interaction. Not automatic, however, is the dosage. The ego, in
control, permits only a slight amount of discharge of the
instinctual tension, sampling the gratification which ensues,
and ready for the consequences thereof. The latter is forthcoming immediately, and again automatically, but again in
controlled dosage, in proportion to the cautious instinctual
pleasure which had been permitted. This is not yet *the* intrapsychic conflict but a miniature controlled sample of the
conflict which might ensue if the entire dose were to be
permitted. We might call it a minor preliminary phase. Hartmann and Loewenstein (1962) have called a similar process
"tentative temptation," but one which they refer to in a more
limited and special way. "Here the ego allows itself a small dose
of gratification which then serves to set in motion the forces of
the superego."

6. The ego samples all of these. The analogy which Freud
(1926) made between signal *anxiety* and inoculation comes to
mind and applies to this phase as well. This is like a skin test, a
preliminary small dose of the antigen, to test the reactions of
the host. Just as thought is experimental action, so this entire
interaction is experienced, in controlled amount, in an experimental way and in a signal manner. The experience, which was
an experimental conflict, is to conflict what thought, which is
experimental action, is to action. Neither is yet the end result.

The concept of the signal can, it seems to me, be extended
forward to explain, with profit, this phase as well. The experimental action, the controlled gratification, is a signal action, as
is the return signal of the superego's reaction. The ego receives,
judges, and reacts to this series of preliminary signals.

7. The reaction is crucial; it is the estimate of the danger.
The ego is the recipient of either an automatic reaction of

anxiety or else of a sense of safety. On the basis of this, the ego judges that there either is or is not a danger situation, and if so whether it is mild or severe.

8. If the latter is deemed mild or nonexistent, the ego can act accordingly toward the instinctual demands, and allow lenient gratification. During the course of everyday life such an outcome occurs frequently, with action or other behavioral discharge taking place without even the production of a significant intrapsychic conflict. Up to this point the latter cannot yet be said to have occurred. The scanning, judging, and filtering functions of the ego, which constitute a continuous action during the process of waking life, have performed their tasks without too much challenge. We might say, in Hartmann's sense, that the equilibria have been disturbed, but a conflict did not ensue.

9. However, the result may not be the above, but instead the ego may judge that there is indeed an appreciable danger involved if the instinct in question were to be yielded to, danger from the superego or from the external world (castration or loss of love), or from the strength of the instincts themselves. This is now the true stage of the anxiety signal. As a result of having experienced a small sample of a significant danger, and of being able to judge and anticipate what its full impact would be, signal anxiety is automatically experienced, a new level of signal, and the crucial one in this train of events. This may range in intensity from mild and easily controlled, to severe and barely controlled, or may presage the imminence of panic or of the traumatic state, as in Schur's (1953) series of controlled to uncontrolled anxiety. Incidentally, lest this point be overlooked, it should be made explicit that the outcome here depends not only on the particular current stimulus in question, either its quantitative or qualitative aspects, but more importantly on the extent to which this has access to and arouses a traumatic chain of memory traces, i.e., the pull from the repressed, as well as the push from above. It is, as always, the situation in depth, based on the ontogenetic history, which is crucial.

10. Only now does a significant increment of conflict ensue. I say "increment" to differentiate it from the quiescent conflict which existed as a baseline even before the present stimulus appeared. This increase is that specifically related to the new disturber (and its ability to arouse latent ones).

This present spurt of conflict is only one phase of the conflict's total later history, and can be designated as "major phase one" of the conflict (there has been previously the "minor" phase referred to above, i.e., the experimental, controlled, signal phase). It is anxiety—or more correctly, the danger which this anxiety heralds—which caused this new and major increment in conflict, just as this same anxiety will be the motive for defense. The motive must precede (this phase of) the conflict, and the conflict must precede the later defense. At this stage, and as a result of the estimate of danger occasioned by the degree of signal anxiety, the ego is "in conflict" as to what to do next.

It might at this point occur to you to intercede, as it did indeed to several discussants on first hearing this material, with the question, "But doesn't conflict *cause* anxiety, rather than the other way around?"[1] It might thus be thought, for example, that it is the perceived or experienced conflict between the superego and the id which causes the ego to feel the anxiety. To this I would say first that the superego's demonstrated opposition to the instincts has so far mostly been kept in check. At best it can be argued that only a minor and experimental conflict has ensued, with a more major one perceived as potential *if* certain things were allowed to happen (i.e., instinctual gratification). For this reason I said that the (i.e., significant) intrapsychic conflict has not yet taken place. However, speaking more strictly, I might say that even in the controlled minor and experimental interchange, what has been demonstrated and experienced so far has not been an existing *conflict* but a series consisting of act and punishment (in small doses). The potential

[1]Arlow and Schur both posed this question in discussing this point (see Panel, 1963b).

doer and the reactive punisher have been defined, but they have not yet locked grips, i.e., there is not yet a *conflict* between them, with forces deployed one to the other. Moreover, it is even a question whether the superego is in conflict with the id in the usual instance at all, or whether it is not rather in conflict only with the ego, in response to a certain attitude of the latter toward the id. In this sense, it might properly be said that the ego has by now suffered a small amount of experimental intersystemic conflict, felt by it from the direction of the superego as a result of its already slight gratification of the id. In this sense the anxiety can be said to be a *result* of this already-discovered conflict. What *actually* caused the anxiety was not the conflict but the *danger* which was revealed as lurking in the superego.

So, at the most, a small experimental and only minor conflict has revealed the danger, which provoked the signal anxiety. As a result of the latter, and depending on its extent, a major increment now occurs, what we may call a first phase of the major conflict. The ego is now "in conflict" as to what it should do next.

This is a good point at which to consider another issue which makes for confusion and which needs clarification at once. The term "conflict" has two different meanings which need to be distinguished. One is, according to Webster, "competition or opposing action of incompatibles—antagonism, as of divergent interests." Another is "a battle, a fight, struggle, hostile encounter." What I have just outlined about the ego's conflict applies to it in the first of these meanings, in the sense of competing alternatives, and the obligation to effect a choice. It is in fact this meaning which occurred to me first as the usual one, which an analyst thinks of when he speaks of the ego as being in conflict. However, the second has of course just as much validity and even a longer historical tradition in our field.

This differentiation has not been pointed out or at least is usually neglected or insufficiently kept in mind in the psychoanalytic literature on intrapsychic conflict. Historically, it was the opposition-of-forces type which first held exclusive sway in our early theoretical formulations. While the participants in the struggle changed a number of times, the form of it endured. However, the alternative competition or decision type of conflict described above entered the scene with the tripartite structural model and the role assigned to the ego as mediator and integrator between the other two systems. Although such a function came into play at once, this new distinction in types of conflict was not made explicit. This division of meanings of our main term, however, is indispensable and must clearly be borne in mind when we follow the changing interrelationships which take place.

I should like to make a number of other relevant observations. It may be noted, for example, that the severity of the conflict, at least this segment and form of it, is not necessarily proportional to the severity of the anxiety. I believe it would be accurate to say that the decision-conflict at this point is most intense, not with the most intense anxiety, but rather in the middle of the spectrum of intensity of the latter. Such a conflict-dilemma is at its height when the forces comprising it are most nearly balanced, while the issue is more easily decided in one direction or the other when the balance is uneven. In mild signal anxiety, this conflict is minimal, in favor of instincts. But similarly when the anxiety is severe or there is even the verge of panic, it is not the conflict which reaches a high peak but rather the ego's doubts with regard to its own resources. In other words, in the face of the severity or imminence of the threat, the ego's concern is not which way to go, but whether it is able to go in the direction it knows it must, i.e., repress, or otherwise defend. The ego is now not so much in a state of conflict as in a state of impending impotence, or at least of relative insufficiency. Can it stave off the threatening pressures? It is faced now with the possibility of the signal becoming an actual danger, to the point of psychic helplessness.

The severity of the (ultimate) outcome also is not necessarily proportional either to the severity of the anxiety or to the intensity of the conflict. There may be the most anxiety in a phobic, the worst conflict in an obsessional, and the most severe total pathology in a psychotic. The determining factor is the relative strength and resourcefulness of the ego in the face of the particular balance of threats.

Thus, an example of this most intense and raging conflict of this (dilemma) nature is that behind a severely obsessional state, rather than in more severe psychopathological conditions. Ambivalence, indecision, an almost precise and devastating balance are the rule, sometimes with simultaneous and at times with alternating opposing actions, representing in turn each arm of the conflicting forces. Indeed, the ego must be strong to contend with such formidable adversaries, and this is often the case in the obsessional neurotic, who may appear in many ways as if made of iron. In more regressed and malignant states, however, as in schizophrenic or other psychotic episodes, while the pressures may be more severe and the threats more overwhelming, it is the disorganization of the ego and its relative insufficiency in the face of these primitive archaic and violent forces, at the level to which regressions have taken place, which form the core of the psychopathology at this phase, rather than a greater intensity of the conflictual state.

11. We have seen until now how signal anxiety brings on conflict, which then behooves the ego to act, to choose, to look for a solution—of course, at the least price. What follows are the sequelae of this phase of conflict, the attempts at its resolution.

In a favorable situation, with the threat the least, the forces impinging not too great, and the sufficiency of the ego resources quite equal to the task, mastery is achieved with the least sacrifice and the most satisfactory and simple solution. Anna Freud (1962) quotes, as a good prognostic sign, the child who, when frustrated, can simply say, "Okay." (I add: In a way which we do not have to worry about!) In contrast to the situation described above in which signal anxiety was not forthcoming at all, as a consequence of which the ego was able to permit lenient discharge, the present situation generally calls, even in a most favorable instance, for at least a certain amount of defense, of denial, repression, or other. This is seen to institute the next phase of conflict, although here in a benign and adequate way, either an increment or at least a reaffirmation of the existing *inter*systemic conflict between the ego and the instincts. Now the form of the conflict changes to the opposition type, with countercathectic ego energy being called for and sacrificed at the ego-id border. We can call this the "second major phase" of the conflict emanating from the original traumatic stimulus which I hypothesized. It supersedes and outlasts the first "decision" phase, and will continue, after the latter may have come to rest, until a final point of relative stability is achieved.

12. Under less favorable circumstances, however, things continue to happen, and the instincts will not be so easily put off. I would like to single out, en route to symptom formation, a next intermediate phase which the ego undergoes in its successive and continuing steps toward an attempt at resolution. This is a phase, quite regular in its occurrence, which is often passed over quickly, and which I feel deserves the dignity of separate attention commensurate with its clinical importance. It is the state of dammed-up tension, occasioned by the fact that, while the blockage of discharge is exerted, the instinctual pressures will not abate. The intersystemic, opposition type of conflict continues in an unstable form. The resulting tension state, from a continuing increase and a damming up of this instinctual pressure, plays a regularly significant part in the ensemble of derivative sequelae which follow the suffering of conflict.

Intersystemic conflict thus results in increasing intrasystemic tension, which in turn exerts intersystemic effects. Tension continues to harass the ego, which, depending on its intensity and the relative strength of the ego to absorb or resist or otherwise handle it, may remain as an enduring state, or may be transitory, to be superseded by more definitive symptoms, or else may, in more favorable situations, recede.

This tension state has its own derivative effects, which stem directly from the dynamic and economic situation rather than from any other part of the total complex arc, or the composite collection of them all. Certain subjective experiences of the patient, which may be part of his final total symptom complex, may derive from these intrasystemic instinctual pressures themselves. They may come out in such expressions as "I feel like busting out all over," or "I'm going to burst out of my skin," or even by another derivative step of incipient somatization, "I just feel itchy and tense all over." One patient put it, "I feel like a Cadillac engine in a Ford body." Such feelings, sometimes spoken and most often not, may be quite universally behind all the more varied symptoms of severe and more definitive neurotic disorder, due precisely to an insufficiency of the ego in the face of continuously pressing instinctual demands. Fenichel (1945) is of the same opinion when he states that "actual neurotic symptoms form the nucleus of all psychoneuroses" (p. 192). Fenichel divides the symptoms attributable directly to this tension state into negative and positive ones (p. 168ff.). The negative symptoms, which consist of general inhibitions of ego functions, are due to a decrease of available energy as a result of the energy consumed in the service of defense. The positive symptoms are traceable to the instinctual pressures themselves, and consist of "painful feelings of tension, of emergency discharges, including spells of anxiety and rage, and producing sleep disturbances due to the impossibility of relaxation." I would say that the latter are already indirect effects.

13. The above phase, although I have belabored it to give it its due place, is most often a transitional one, to be followed by further attempts at a more stable and a more livable-with resolution of the unstable and continuing conflict state. I cannot discuss in equal detail all the possible succeeding steps toward conflict resolution, but will have to pass over the rest by merely stating them. This is due not only to limits of space, for such an undertaking would necessitate the space of a book, but also because these next moves involve the traditional center of psychoanalytic exploration, have been the phases most copiously studied in the past, and are not the center of our interest at this time. They involve the well-known methods of symptom formation, including regression (to previous points of fixation),

and the entire range of compromise formations which arise as end products. In a wider sense and over a more sustained view they also lead in the direction of character formation. Although these more stable resolutions are still along the line of conflict solving, in the interest of selectivity I have here enlarged only upon those relatively earlier phases which have usually not been highlighted and on the several dynamic details which to my mind have not been spelled out clearly before—see, e.g., Nemiah's review in (Panel, 1963b).

II

It should be noted that the process of conflict formation itself continues alongside of and subsequent to the various sequelae which its presence has initiated. The tension state itself may become a source of anxiety, with a new layering of conflict resulting and demanding solution on its own account. Similarly, there may be defenses against defenses, or a symptom may be defended against, or an entire neurosis may represent a new threat to the ego. These may be for reasons related to the original etiological conflict, or the motives and the anticipated dangers may be of quite a different caliber, but in either case they then trigger off a repetition of the entire process, which may then again be repeated, either in whole or in part.

The above process, however, is not limited to psychopathological events, but may similarly be responsible for the achievement of highly effective psychic formations. Rapaport (1953a) has eloquently described such a process of increasingly complex hierarchic development in the formation of derivative motivational drives and of increasingly complex ego defenses. The same layering process is at the root of the "taming of affects" described by Fenichel (1941a) and of the increasingly subtle shadings of affect discharge which become possible with the attainment of maturity (Jacobson, 1952, 1953a; Rapaport, 1953a). This continuous process of conflict solution, derivative conflict, and derivative solution results in the increasing neutralization and modulation which accompany the course of psychic development. Along with neutralization, increasing ego autonomy, and the use of increasingly effective sublimatory discharge channels, these processes, to quote Jacobson (1952), "change the quality of drives, bind mobile energy, and by producing various combinations of high- and low-speed discharge processes result in the complex affect experiences of some of our most sublime pleasurable states."

Rapaport (1960), writing on motivations, states "clinical evidence shows that the defense motives are themselves subject to defense formation, and indeed whole hierarchies of such defense and derivative motivations layered one over the other must be postulated to explain even common clinical phenomena. Knight and Gill have demonstrated this for the relationships of aggression, homosexuality, and paranoia. This hierarchic layering of structures is conceived to be the means by which the neutralization of instinctual drive cathexes is brought about. These multiple structural obstacles transform the peremptory instinctual drives into delayable motivations by setting the structural conditions under which the pleasure principle must operate."

The process of decomposing, which demonstrates the stratification in the developed state, can further be compared and viewed with profit against the background of the ontogenetic development. It will be remembered that the earliest months of life, in gross description, are characterized psychically by the experiencing of frustration, tension, unpleasure and pleasure, but not yet anxiety or conflict. The psychic apparatus, such as it is, is directed toward a unified purpose, that of discharge, under the complete sway of the pleasure principle. With the advent of anxiety—and it does not matter for our purposes whose timetable we adhere to as to when this supervenes—there is added the capacity to anticipate and to delay, resulting in the acquisition of conflict, but at this stage between inner (needs) and outer (sources of supply).

Perhaps we can say that the true intrapsychic conflict arises only with what Spitz (1957a) calls the third organizer of the psyche, the achievement of the ideational concept of the negative and the affirmative. Although there were barriers to discharge long before this, such as the inborn defense thresholds, or the stimulus barrier, these can by no means be said to have constituted the nature of a true conflict. "The tacit assumption that the stimulus barrier represents such an opposing force is misleading. . . .The stimulus barrier is neither an obstacle, nor does it express refusal. It is a manifestation of a maturational state, namely, that at birth the sensorium is not yet cathected. . . .The stimulus barrier does not belong in the same conceptual category as negation and affirmation" (Spitz, 1957a, p. 105). With the acquisition of apparatus for the latter, "beyond doubt the most spectacular intellectual and semantic achievement in early childhood" (p. 99), a new level of ego integration is reached which heralds the advent of symbolization, abstract thinking, and concept formation, and converts passivity to activity. While this new state brings with it the triumphant ability to refuse, deny, and oppose the environment, it also means, concomitantly, the same ability to oppose and countermand inner forces; indeed it brings with it an increased necessity to do so. The entire scope is enlarged, and with the increased range of ego functioning comes also greater exposure to danger, and hence a greater need, and with it a greater ability, to defend. Now there is possible, and exists, a true intrapsychic conflict.

This ontogenetic acquisition, in stages, of frustration, tension, anxiety, and conflict, has its counterparts and is recapitulated in the stratification which exists in the end result of psychic development. In regression, or in states of slow-motion psychopathology, they can be seen again in their separate states.

There are a good many further problems in relation to intrapsychic conflicts which center on the structural composition of such conflicts and the various possibilities which exist. These are of a sufficient order of magnitude and are sufficiently cohesive so that I have decided to deal with them separately (see Chapter 8).

III

The above presents the complexity of the procession of intrapsychic events in which conflict plays a part. It helps the accuracy of our understanding clearly to elucidate and to bear in mind that conflict itself is only a part of the process; that it comprises crucial links in the chain, but is not the entire process. We are apt, in the grosser clinical setting, to speak loosely of a patient being "overwhelmed by conflict," when we might more properly mean "by the unbearable tension from instinctual pressure, or by severe anxiety at the prospect of impending danger, or by an unconscious premonition of a hopelessly ineffective ego in the face of forces against which it will wither." These are all close together, to be sure, and intermingle, but it would benefit us conceptually to separate the successive components. Conflict plays an important part in all, but it is sometimes at the center, and sometimes at the periphery of the presenting segments from this etiological chain.

The above events, although they have been teased apart and presented as a discreet succession of psychic phenomena, can and usually are compressed in time so that they may take but a moment to exert their effects. As befits the variability of human behavior, however, the temporal characteristics of this process may range from almost instantaneous action at one end to prolonged, stabilized, and almost static behavioral processes at the other. Thus, for example, we all know how in daily waking life the entire gamut from initiating stimulus to a final end point of one kind or another can take place rapidly and repeatedly, most often entirely subliminally, but at times with such telltale surface derivatives that an analyst, or sometimes even the subject, can be aware of the process. The rapidity with which such psychic processes operate are familiar to us in dream formation, where we know how a seemingly long and complex dream can occur in but a moment following the application of an experimental waking stimulus. Or the same can be attested by C. Fisher's experiments (1954, 1956) in which the tachistoscopic signal is incorporated instantaneously into a ready and complicated psychic functioning. Or it is known to us in reports, such as I have heard from a patient, of how, in a moment during which death is expected, the crucial events in almost an entire life history can flash before a person. My patient was lying in a trench during the Battle of the Bulge and caught sight of an enemy soldier with a bayonet in full view above him. He lived to tell me later what went on in his mind during but a moment.

When I thought of what examples I might present to illustrate some of the theoretical sequences outlined here, I chose two instances at opposite ends of the temporal spectrum. One was at the short-lived end just talked about, and consisted of an episode in which a patient, talking comfortably to a few friends, had a question, or really just a remark, directed at him, which almost instantly caused him to feel a flush. Although so brief—and I chose it because of its benignity and universality—an analysis of the intervening phases into which the resulting process could be broken down, which took place in the moment between stimulus and response, would show some 15 to 20 separable components along the lines outlined above.

At the other end of the spectrum, both in time as well as in severity of outcome, I thought of a woman patient who had been living for the last 8 or 10 years between the horns of an interminable dilemma, caught in the gripping throes of an illicit love affair. Since her nature and her history did not make her particularly facile at such an activity, the dilemma was correspondingly more meaningful and rocked her very foundations. The forces of the commanding and all-embracing intrapsychic conflict were strong on each side and fairly evenly balanced, which accounted for its tenacity and long duration. As I knew this patient I could observe many of the phases which I have described, this time not all telescoped together, but living out their filtered effects in discreetly visible segments of time. One could observe either in the one hour or over a period of days or weeks how the patient would be dominated at one time by the victory and excitement of the instinctual drives, at another by the ascendancy of the nagging, tormenting, and threatening superego, and at still another overtaken by the state of some-times controllable and sometimes uncontrollable anxiety. Some of these states were quite transitory, others lasted longer, and some were fused in various combinations.

In opposite vein from the interior view of the discreet components of intrapsychic conflict, I would like to balance these by pointing out that at the other end of the spectrum, as in the final clinical state, we see a tendency not to dissect and to separate, but to fuse and to combine, so that the clinical picture is more likely to be a composite behavioral mass. This is what I meant at the start as a macroscopic as contrasted to a micro-scopic view of the ingredients and products of the conflict state.

The presenting picture might by this time be expressed by a nondescript cover-all, "I don't know, I just feel nervous," or "I just feel terrible," or "all in"—characterizations which are not necessarily evasive but are indicative of this agglutinization process. In Chapter 10 I describe the multiplicity of back-ground factors which lay behind the façade in a patient who could only say that he felt "weird." This was again seen to be a composite compounded out of many separate ingredients. The free associations of any analytic hour demonstrate this.

In keeping with the ego's synthetic function, what we are confronted with clinically is not only the symptom, which is already a compromise of impulse and defense, but a total clinical picture which might contain within it pressing instinc-tual tensions, derivatives and equivalents of anxiety itself, evidences of superego actions, and intricate secondary elabo-rations. The clinical picture is much like the dream, kaleido-scopic in its contents and distorted in its syntax. Besides the secondary gain of symptoms, I have described (1954b) a tertiary gain, relating to changes in body image and the concept of the self. There are probably other elaborations, as complex and as hierarchic as is the development of the psychic appara-tus itself.

All this is what the patient does, with and around and on top of his conflicts. Our task as analysts is to reverse the direction, to separate, to decompose, and thus to be able to analyze. In spite of his resistance, the patient welcomes this, at least with that part of his ego which is in therapeutic alliance with us. To get at the intrapsychic conflicts, and the succession of events around them, aimed eventually at the infantile neurosis, comprises the center of our task. The uncovering of the successive events, the accurate reconstruction not only of their subtle contents, but of their syntactical interrelationships, is what our *modus operandi* consists of and what we offer to the patient, "with which to build a better life." With every degree to which we accomplish this reordering, the patient receives added hope of eventual complete understanding and mastery.

This brings me to a final point of interest. It often happens that constructs arise, valuable and informative ones in themselves, which are in a sense midway and intermediate formations in this psychic unfolding, whether one thinks of it in terms of the direction from origins toward the final presenting picture, or in the reverse, the direction from the presenting clinical façade working backward, as we do therapeutically, toward origins. Such constructs, which usually have abundant validity as empirical phenomena as well as widespread theoretical significance, may then be used misleadingly as a central *explanatory* concept, presumably of irreducible import. As examples, I would mention the very useful concepts of the self, the self (and object) representations, ego identity, and other closely related phenomena, which have received a great deal of attention in our recent literature. Broad and lucid investigations of these psychic formations, in particular by Jacobson (1954, 1964) and by Erikson (1950), have enriched our understanding of many aspects of human behavior. However, there is also a tendency on the parts of many to use such concepts without proper perspective.

Both the concept of the self and that of ego identity are in themselves complex psychic achievements, each culminating from a combination of maturational factors, conflict solutions, and conflict-free experiences and activities. Each then in turn can serve as a nub which contributes further either to conflictful or conflict-free activities, and from which emanate either bland or charged affective experiences. They thus result from as well as contribute to complex psychic derivatives.

I can demonstrate, however, as an example of the misuse of these concepts, the use of "disturbances in ego identity" as an ultimate explanatory concept for a multiplicity of clinical states. While the recognition of this type of disturbance was a valuable addition which enriched our knowledge of psychopathology, this concept has been used excessively and inappropriately to *explain* the origins of many symptoms, character defects, and conflict states. Thus, not only did I recently hear a well-known psychoanalytically influenced author in a public interview diagnose the troubles of the modern American character as due to deficiencies in their ego identity, so that "they do not know who or what they are or what they want to be," but many analysts also offer similar explanations as the basis for many of our present-day "borderline" or character problems. At times this is done, as Waelder (1961b) points out, as a defense against, or at least at the expense of, libidinal conflicts.

I would contend that such ego disturbances are as much the results as they are the causes of psychopathology. A disturbance in identity, just as a disturbance in the concept of the self, or of the body image, evolves first as an *outcome* of intrapsychic conflict rather than being a satisfactory explanation of the cause of it. It is then likely to serve as a further stimulus to maladaptive functioning. An age-specific "crisis" of ego identity is an intrapsychic conflict (or combination of conflicts) composed of elements specific to the instinctual and ego problems of that particular age, such as occurs notably at adolescence. Erikson (1950) frequently refers to such identity *conflicts,* and Jacobson (1964) has stressed at length such interaction.

Of greater cogency are explanations whose scope encompass the broad range of the relevant intrapsychic conflicts and which take into account the nature of the forces and the structures of which these are composed. Explanations for many of the stubborn and frustrating cases on today's scene might include, among other elements, specific new types of crippling suffered by the psychic systems of persons brought up in a particular segment of today's cultural soil. I would also predict such findings as that they may not know whom to love or hate, so that instinctual object is only hesitantly attached to instinctual aim. The identifications of which the ego is a precipitate may have been spotty, shifting, and unreliable, leaving these characteristics behind in the patient's ego itself. But above all, the motives for defense are often not clear, so that such a patient is apt to ask clingingly, "Should I be afraid? Am I supposed to feel guilty, or to be ashamed?" Such stamps cannot fail to have a profound effect upon and to bring about new qualities of intrapsychic conflict. These certainly leave their mark on the identity and the self, but secondarily, and these then further influence the course of events.

As a general formulation, however, it can be said that the etiological core of a piece of psychopathology lies in an otherwise insoluble intrapsychic conflict, or group of conflicts, associatively linked through a series of less and less distorted derivatives to the infantile neurosis.

The goal of treatment is not the removal of all conflict or even of the potential for conflict, which is part of the human condition, but rather of the pathogenic conflicts and their derivatives, and of the entire sequential processes of which they are in the center. "Conflict-free," Erikson (1962) writes, "is a miserly way of characterizing our access . . . to the world of deeds." It is rather "an ego state of active tension" for which one strives. This, according to Jones (1942), results in the "gusto" of the healthy individual. Civilization, Freud (1930) has pointed out, owes its advances largely to the price of frustration, conflict, and neurosis. All students of the normal mind, as Jones (1942), Hartmann (1939b), Reider (1950), and Anna Freud (1959), concur in the fallacy of equating normality with the conflict-free. Gill (1963), discussing whether defenses can disappear after an analysis, writes, "In a hierarchical conception, the defenses are as much the woof of personality functioning as the drives and drive derivatives are its warp." Anna Freud (1962) emphasized the valuable and widespread use of regression, not only in the service of the creative and noble in human accomplishment, but in the daily lives of "little people."

Actually, the goal is to achieve optimum conditions for both the conflictful and the conflict-free spheres of operation, and the possibility for a mutually enhancing relationship between them. The ego should be free to benefit from the advantages accruing from each, which Kris described as stemming from peaks of comfort and discomfort in the developing infant. By various combinations of such experiences, as well as the "low-grade discharges with lower peaks, but more steady and sustained" which Jacobson describes, there can result the "sublime pleasurable states" of the adult which have been described by Jacobson, Rapaport, Fenichel and other psychoanalytic students of affect.

CHAPTER 8

Structural Problems in Intrapsychic Conflict

In Chapter 7, I attempted to assess the scope of intrapsychic conflict in human psychology, tracing briefly the historical changes and leading up to our present thinking. I then attempted to have us observe the course of an intrapsychic conflict, in somewhat stripped and "model" form, in what I called a microscopic view of the processes which take place from the time of the advent of the precipitating stimulus to its final resolution in one form or another. This was contrasted with a macroscopic view of what we see clinically and in the therapeutic situation in the manifest surface derivatives of this composite process.

This was a broad approach which traversed a long psychogenetic arc. While certain sections of this arc were selected for more detailed examination, other areas were dealt with only tangentially. Among the latter was the question of the structural characteristics of intrapsychic conflict. The present paper rep-

Published in *The Psychoanalytic Study of the Child,* 18:103–138, 1963.

resents an amplification, extension, and a more detailed exposition on this particular segment of the problem. It is accorded
separate treatment in the hope that the ambiguities inherent in
excessive condensation can thus be avoided.

Such a more extensive treatment is also indicated to take
into sufficient account the valuable new views put forth on this
specific aspect by Hartmann and by Hartmann and Loewenstein. The former, in his detailed inquiry into the structure and
functions of the ego (1950a), and the latter, in their similar
investigation more recently on the superego (1962), have
pointed to the possibilities of intrasystemic conflicts within
these respective agencies. The need for a proper perspective
and orientation toward such conflicts came up for extensive
discussion in the course of the panel on intrapsychic conflict
(Panel, 1963b). Hartmann, Loewenstein, and Schur stressed
that such intrasystemic conflicts may play a significant role and
be rather widespread, whereas I, supported by Arlow, suggested certain restrictions and qualifications of this concept.
This discussion was ended by the time curfew, without, in my
opinion, the opportunity for proper clarification. In addition, it
was agreed that further clarification was needed of such terms
as "competition" vs. "conflict" which had been introduced into
the discussion.

For these reasons, it appeared to me that a more extensive
and detailed consideration of this range of problems was in
order. The present paper is a result of my own continued
thoughts on this subject, enriched by the above discussion, and
after the luxury of a more leisurely consideration of the
relevant data, the theoretical problems, and the issues involved.

I

Before embarking on my main arguments, I would like to
begin with a clarification of the terms and recapitulate a
distinction between two different types and meanings of conflict. These are (1) an opposition type, of forces battling against
each other, in hostile encounter; and (2) a dilemma type, the

need for a choice between competing alternatives. Traditionally, before the advent of the structural point of view, intrapsychic conflict referred always to the first of these meanings, that of the opposition between forces. Although the forces which opposed each other underwent a number of changes in our theoretical formulations, the form had persisted. Although the second type of conflict came into play with the advent of the tripartite structural model, with the role of the ego as a mediator and integrator between the other two systems, this differentiation in forms of conflict was not explicitly spelled out. Actually even before the structural point of view, a choice conflict had confronted the ego, or its historical precursors in our theory, in its position between the instincts, or originally the wish impulse, and the external world, but this was also far from clearly stated. Incidentally, while generally overlooked in psychoanalytic formulations, this type of "choice behavior" is what is meant routinely by the experimental psychologists in their studies of conflict, in which the experimental animal, for example , is confronted by food together with shock or another noxious stimulus. At any rate this added variation in the form of intrapsychic conflict is to be noted as a specific addition to psychoanalytic theory which came with the structural theory, and the concurrent modifications of anxiety and instinct theories. This division of meanings of the term "conflict" must be borne in mind and is indispensable for a clear understanding of the various relationships and vicissitudes of conflict which I will trace and discuss.

I will now focus my attention on the structural problem in relation to intrapsychic conflict, the question of the locus of the conflict, and what is in conflict with what. I begin with Fenichel's (1945) summary statements—he was writing, it should be remembered, about the neuroses—to the effect that "The general formulation [is that] the neurotic conflict takes place between the ego and the id." Later he added: "The superego may participate on either side in the neurotic conflict, but the formulation [still] remains valid," i.e., the conflict takes place between the ego and the id. Fenichel then arrived at the two possible formulae, of (1) the ego and the superego vs. the id; and (2) the ego vs. the id plus the superego. The latter, which he sees as occurring especially "in compulsion neuroses, and, to an extreme degree, in depressions," is clearly meant by Fenichel not as an "indecision type of conflict"—the distinction between the two types of conflict which I have described above is, as far as I can see, not made—but as a "two-front" opposition conflict. He said, "All the defense mechanisms usually employed in the fight against instincts may also become directed against the 'anti-instincts' originating in the superego. In such cases, the ego develops a double countercathexis, one against the instincts and another one against the superego."

A few years after Fenichel's summary formulations of the intersystemic conflicts, which were the only types he considered, Hartmann (1950a), in detailed investigation of the development and functions of the ego, was the first to postulate and to lay special emphasis on the possibility of intrasystemic conflicts within that agency. Pointing out that "ego interests" and many partly independent ego functions have been neglected in analysis because of their unessential role in the etiology of neurosis, Hartmann felt that such factors became more relevant when we turned to general psychology. Many ego functions oppose each other, he observes, and there are many contrasts within the ego. "Because these contests are clinically not of the same relevance as those between the ego and the id, or the ego and reality, etc., we are not used to thinking of them in terms of conflict. However, we may well describe them as intrasystemic conflicts and thus distinguish them from those other, better-known conflicts that we may designate as intersystemic." As examples of such contrasts, Hartmann listed the ego's tendency to oppose drives, while also having as a main function to help them toward gratification; its role in arriving at insight, but also in rationalizing; its promotion of objective knowledge, coupled with its participation in the conventional prejudices of the environment; and its pursuit of independent aims, while also considering the demands of other structures. Hartmann then stated that "we have not yet trained ourselves to consider the ego from an intrasystemic point of view. On another occasion, Hartmann gave as a further example the conflict within the ego in the analytic situation between the wish to maintain its defenses intact and also to form a therapeutic alliance which would oppose this (Panel, 1963b).

Hartmann and Loewenstein (1962) made similar observations in a parallel study in depth of the superego. Pointing out that "a state of peaceful coexistence between the various aspects of the superego" did not often exist, they stated, "Contradictions between conscious and unconscious morality, between the demands of the ego ideal and the moral taboos, and between various parts of the individual value systems are frequent, and may be the rule. Contrasting tendencies in the superego do exist and can be compared to the intrasystemic conflicts in the ego. Still another analogy with the ego suggests itself . . . [Just as there are ego distortions, there can be superego distortions, etc.]."

II

With these nodal formulations as general background, I should now like to proceed to a detailed examination of the intersystemic relationships. Beginning with Fenichel's formulations, and extending our investigation of the structural conditions over a wider area to include not only the neuroses but all other types of functioning, normal and abnormal, I would make the following additional observations. First, it is well known that the formula given by Fenichel above as the significant one (i.e., "the general formulation," that between the ego and the id) is crucial not only in pathology but over the wider normal spectrum as well. The continuity between normal and pathological with regard to such basic mechanisms has been demonstrated from the beginning and is one of our basic propositions, shown by Freud in many works. The ego has a certain amount of defensive anticathectic energy deployed against a low level of instinctual pressure at all times, even in a state of quiescence, resulting in a certain optimum tension, or in fact in an amount of tension "characteristic for the organism" (Fenichel, 1945).

The same, however, is also true for the "double-front" conflict, which exists in both senses I have described, the "opposition" as well as the "either-or" or alternative type of conflict. Such a two-front concern, and in both senses, though it is present in a more acute and severe form in the pathological states mentioned by Fenichel, such as obsessional ones where the superego is especially highly charged, is also present to a much lesser degree in more benign and quiescent conditions. Thus, just as there is a certain constant tension from the ego to id, the same is also true in the direction toward the superego. This baseline state of vigilant alertness toward the superego is due, first, to the fact that the ego never gives in completely to the dictates of the prohibitive agencies, so that it must at all times remain wary of their reactions (this includes the external world as well as the superego). Secondly, there always exists the danger of a change in the latter's rules, which might make the ego's presently acceptable relationship to the instincts no longer to their liking. Thus, while one of the ego's fronts is directed toward the instincts, the other is cathected *at all times* toward the superego (and the external world), this being a derivative and residual of the original inner-outer conflict. It is only under unfavorable conditions, e.g., when the tension between them becomes heightened or especially changeable, that there may then exist what Hartmann and Loewenstein (1962) call "a kind of ataxia—between the two systems."

This constant and baseline double-front cathexis applies in both senses of conflict which must always be considered and taken into account. Thus, there is a need for the ego not only to oppose and ward off real or potential guilt feelings which may emanate from the superego, but to be ready to make a choice between instincts and prohibitions, and to change the existing balance or status between them. During periods of increasing activation of the latter, there is an exacerbation not only of the vigilance and of the *defensive* activity at this border toward the superego, but of the "competition-conflict" state within the ego, which must concern itself again more acutely with the comparative relationships between the *two* opposing forces which press it.

To add to the two formulae given by Fenichel, it is also necessary to include certain other intersystemic possibilities which can occur when we consider a more extensive range of data and a wider arc of possible actions. Thus, for example, a third possible formula would be the superego vs. the ego and the id, in instances in which the ego elects to grant the id its wishes, taking its chances as to whether or not it may have to pay for this later, for example, by guilt feelings. Hartmann and Loewenstein (1962) refer to a similar ego action as a mechanism of "tentative temptation."

To complete the gamut, as another possible intersystemic type of conflict some authors speak of the superego being at times directly in conflict with the id. Hartmann (1955) mentions that there are certain instances in which "the gates between id and superego are wide open." I would rather say, however, if we take the ego's assigned function as mediator seriously, that in the great preponderance of cases, the ego is sufficiently in control to stand effectively between these two systems. The ego's functions being what they are, the ego stands squarely in the midst of the conflict and can never really be left out of it, so that the conflict becomes one between the ego and the id or the superego or both. Through various changes and expansions in theory, the id and the superego continue to act generally upon and through the ego, rather than upon each other or directly upon external reality.

There are, however, certain exceptional states in which the pathways between id and superego do open into more direct contact. Such might be the case in certain states of ego exhaustion, for either psychological or even organic reasons, or of the ego being overwhelmed and rendered temporarily impotent, as in certain severe psychotic states. Perhaps then the energies do merge and intermingle, with the total organism being engulfed, flooded either simultaneously or else alternately with a voluminous surge of instinctual cathexis, both libidinal and aggressive, and counteraggressive and destructive thrusts by a punitive superego. The hapless ego, unable to stem the tide or to introduce any order into the chaos, is inundated with all the rest. Strictly speaking, there is really no conflict present in the true sense of the word during this period. There is no choice involved; and without an ego to exercise some control, there is really no combat conflict present either. It is rather an orgy followed by a punishment, or the two together, both having full access and full sway. It is true that pure cases of this are hard to observe. A mania followed by a depression may be a close and related example, but this is a special form with other characteristic economic conditions and really does not quite fulfill the above requirements. Here the ego, though battered and disorganized, is nevertheless holding on, and the conflict takes the form of opposing and giving in to both, but alternately and exclusively over longer periods of time. When each has had enough, or both id and superego have been spent, the ego, if it still survives, may begin to "restitute" itself. For a while, though, it is like a country which has been occupied beginning to get on its own feet again.

Thus the intersystemic oppositional encounters can occur in a variety of combinations. It can be illuminating to make some quantitative and comparative observations as well as qualitative ones. While the superego can typically, as described above, be in opposition to the ego, and in certain instances which have been mentioned can possibly be in more direct opposition to the id as well, the ego, in accordance with our major insights into the nature of intrapsychic conflict, can be classically locked in intersystemic conflict with either or both of its other two structural partners. Probably the most common dynamic and structural interplay, however, both in the psychopathological spectrum and in the normally maintained intersystemic balance, is the state of conflict between the ego and the id. For this reason Fenichel accords it the major role in his summary formulation in reviewing the psychoanalytic theory of neurosis. I do not think that this emphasis is due basically to the historical sequence of the development of our science, starting as it did with the neuroses, but that this view is confirmed and maintained by our subsequently wider orientation and experience, over a broader clinical front as well as after the inclusion of normal psychology. Such economic relationships derive ultimately from the nature of the forces involved, the unitary forward urge of the instinctual id and the central role of the ego in judging, guarding, and guiding this force. In a quantitative sense a dominant function of the ego is its permanent management of instinctual pressure. There is of course a more active, volatile, and "hotter" conflict going on at this border in the case of pathology, and a "colder" war, more quiescent and composed, operating with more neutralized instinctual as well as ego energies, in the "normal" intersystemic balance.

To make a further quantitative comparison, I would say that the ego-id opposition is the more usual and constant one, while the intersystemic ego-superego tension is, comparatively speaking, more likely to be one of vigilant alertness rather than of constant interim interaction. The typical situation for the ego would probably be, under usual circumstances, to have a small but steady detachment of countercathectic energy deployed at the border of the id, but relatively speaking only a watchful eye perched toward the superego, ready but not equally in *action* as is the case toward the id. Even in the case of pathology, where there is more activity on both of these fronts than there is in the relatively quiescent normal states, Fenichel has pointed out how much less frequently an ego-superego conflict endures than is the case between ego and id. It would thus appear that the superego is more apt to do its work and then rest than is the more constantly and easily arousable instinctual reservoir of the id. It is, however, as Schafer (1960) correctly points out, "ever on duty." There are nevertheless unusual cases in which this economic ratio and mode of action is reversed.

Fenichel's observation, that there is a general optimum tension "characteristic for the organism," can no doubt be further broken down with regard to the more specific internal components. It is likely that this includes a characteristic amount and quality of intersystemic tension among all three of the psychic structures, as well as optimum and characteristic intrasystemic tensions within each of them. Hartmann and Loewenstein point out specifically, for example, for the super-ego that "the scope of these [ego-superego] tensions tend to become a characteristic of the individual," and that "what matters above all is the degree to which the two agencies can collaborate, while at the same time preserving the optimum tension between them." Such a characteristic and optimum balance exists between each pair of the three corners of the structural interplay. Internal and external impingements that are there in copious and ever-changing combinations result in the various fluctuations and vicissitudes of these optimal inter-systemic balances, which are then translated into adaptive or maladaptive responses.

III

I would like to turn now from the intersystemic relation-ships to consider the situation of the possible intrasystemic conflicts which have been introduced and referred to above. While Hartmann and Loewenstein contributed these new sug-gestions as part of broader studies centering on the contents and functions of the ego and superego, I will focus more centrally on these specific observations concerning types of conflict, and try to follow in detail the resulting implications. In doing so, we will find, I believe, that while leading to new discoveries, these valuable new insights also bring with them certain problems which need to be considered and which call for a number of concomitant clarifications and decisions.

I would like to approach the relationships between intra-systemic components from several different directions. As a first observation, I would point out that the description of the "decision-making" type of conflict, which I have spelled out, is in harmony with the concept of intrasystemic conflict, in that its locus of action is certainly entirely intrasystemic. Although the factors which have brought about the need for decision have impinged from intersystemic directions, the resulting dynamic change following ego absorption of these stimuli is an intrasystemic one within the confines of the ego system itself. In fact, as stated above, it has not been sufficiently appreciated that such an intrasystemic state of being "in conflict" came into being at once with Freud's description of the tripartite structural model, with the role of mediator being assigned to the ego. This intrasystemic role existed despite the fact, as Hartmann (1950a) states, that "the intrasystemic correlations and conflicts in the ego have hardly ever been consistently studied." Moreover, the frequent description of clinical states as "a split in the ego" attests further to the recognition of such an intra-ego condition.

Considering first the situation of the ego, it will be seen to be different in crucial respects from what prevails in the other two systems. Although the concept of multiple functions of the ego has been considerably stressed (Waelder, 1930), and the fact that these diverse functions operate in different and not entirely harmonious directions has been increasingly known, Hartmann is correct that an appreciation that these internal component functions, or contents, can be in conflict has been lagging. In point of fact, the ego, being the recipient of messages from its two flanking systems, demands from one and warnings or prohibitions (if not permission) from the other, and having taken into itself these requests and dictates, now has a problem or conflict within, and may, in instances where no easy decision or solution is forthcoming, become, at least for a time, a house divided within itself. In this sense there is, to be sure, with great unbiquitousness, an intrasystemic conflict within the ego. As a result of a choice, and concomitant with its decided course of action, there may then ensue an intersystemic conflict as well, now one of the opposition type, against the id, or against the superego, or against both. In many instances, courses are mapped out through which the ego manages deftly to be in conflict with neither, having chosen actions or attitudes which can satisfy both contending parties.

To consider further the intrasystemic state within the ego,

it is certainly possible that, just as the ego is divided within itself between elements representing the id and others representing the superego (or external reality), so there may be similar intrasystemic ego conflicts about other contrasting or conflicting pairs within it. Thus the critical ego may be called upon to decide between internal, conflicting, and contradictory self-interests, or between interests of security and dependence vs. the tendency toward independence, or between opposing and contradictory ego value factors. In all such cases, we know that there are specific and indeed major ego functions, or rather a series of functions, which have to do with scanning, judging, and then deciding whether the objects or contents which are thus put to the test are external to it, in other systems, or other functions or contents within the borders of its own system. Or perhaps we may think that it is the matrix of the ego, the interstitial connecting portions which remain after all of its multiple other specific functions are accounted for and taken away, which is charged with this final function of deciding. (I wish to make it clear that I do not have in mind any physical or organic matrix here, lest it be thought that the language used suggests this.) Or perhaps we think of it as part of the organizing, or integrating, or synthesizing function of the ego to render such a final decision. Whether we think of it as a separate function, or as a global and integrating one connecting all the others, it is plainly our common usage and intent to assign such a "deciding" and coordinating function within the ego—and I might add, only within the ego.

This leads to the following thoughts. If we accept this to be the case, how does this reflect on the concept of possible intrasystemic "conflicts" within either of the other two systems? Hartmann and Loewenstein quite correctly point to contrasting and contradictory elements, or even pairs, existing within the superego, or within the ego ideal, or between the ego ideal and the superego (considering these both within the same system). Examples of these have been quoted above. Such contrasting tendencies, these authors suggest, "can be compared to the intrasystemic conflicts in the ego."

But to pursue this idea further, if we consider the only two possible modes of conflict as described above, we might well ask the following. With regard first to the "alternative" type of conflict formation, to which I am momentarily limiting my discussion, does the superego include within its scope a specific function of choosing or deciding (whether such a function resides in a special segment or in the matrix of the superego, as described above for the ego)? Would not such an activity or a responsibility be a prerequisite for the ability to "be in conflict"? Hartmann and Loewenstein ask a similar question about whether the function or capacity of "knowing" can reside in any other system but the ego, a question which, I might indicate in advance, they answer in the negative. Is this the same with regard to "deciding," and is this too a function left squarely and exclusively to the much overworked ego? Clearly an answer to the question of possible superego conflicts hinges to a large measure on how the first issue is resolved.

Thus, when contrasting or contradictory views exist, either between the ego ideal and superego, or from opposite values within the superego itself, is it the superego, within which an intrasystemic conflict resides, or are all the contents presented to the ego, to add only to the complexity of *its* ultimate problem of synthesis and choice? There are many ways in which one can look at this. Can it perhaps be that there is first an intrasystemic conflict within the superego, which is either solved there or *else* transferred *in toto* to the ego, for it to have the problem and to decide? Or is it solved in steps, partially in one, and then finished in the other? Or does the superego always first "decide" and then present only its decision, the final choice, to the ego? Certainly I do not feel that the latter corresponds with clinical evidence.

Many of these questions are difficult to answer, and depend on the definitions and the historical usages with which these concepts must be consistent. Indeed, it may be felt, and with some justification, that it does not matter much and that all emerging phenomena can be explained either way. Nevertheless, if one wants theoretical rigor and consistency, one has no choice but to pursue even what may become a thin line as far as it will go. I cannot offer unequivocal answers but merely wish to confront the questions which arise and which need to be followed through. Our increasing knowledge leads to further probing which brings with it these perplexities. I would like at this point to try not to give a definitive answer to the basic question I have posed but to approach the solution in another way, namely, to describe in succession two alternative ways of looking at this situation. We could then see with each possible answer what falls into place as evidence for the view, what elements, if any, are solved by it, whether any new or secondary problems arise, and whether any inconsistencies come into play with any established viewpoints. We might then be in a better position to arrive at a consensus.

IV

As a first alternative, I propose that we consider what would appear to be, from a total view, an entirely logical position: that the function of choice or consistency is left squarely and exclusively to the domain of the ego. In favor of this easily defended view, I believe that it is consistent with our historical as well as our present attitudes toward the various structural divisions and the functions comprising them to reserve the most definitive, and by this way of thinking the only, function of "deciding," as Hartmann and Loewenstein say about "knowing," to the ego. This then would make *ego*, and only the ego, the psychic structure which can be undecided, or "in conflict," in the sense which we are now speaking. It would follow from this view that the superego would offer whichever of its elements are sufficiently cathected to the ego, for the *ego's* use and consideration and choice. If such elements of the superego and the ego ideal are all of one persuasion, the task of the ego is relatively simple. It at least knows what the terms are, from the side of the moralizing and directing agency. If, however, the latter presents to the ego a composite of incompatibilities, it is the ego which faces the additional burden, having to amalgamate these with the further values and interests existing within its own borders.

With this view, one could also say, indeed one would have to say, that there can be contrasting or even contradictory elements within the superego without their being in conflict with each other. They neither oppose each other nor does the system have to make a choice, for they can exist, side by side, with each demanding its due, and both can come out. In accordance with a generally held proposition, the superego in this respect would be said to share a specific characteristic with the id, just as it has many other qualities in common with it: if there are no contradictions within the id, there are none within the superego. It could further be reasoned that contrasting and even contradictory elements not only exist but make up the very essence of the total system superego, and are responsible for the variability and flexibility and even unpredictability of its responses. Thus ambivalence could occur not only from instinctual contradictions but also from opposite superego attitudes, existing side by side in a nonexclusive relationship. If such contradictions are passed on to the ego, whether from the id or the superego, it would be the work of the ego to decide, to choose, or to synthesize, either eliminating one or the other of the contradictory elements, or to fuse, amalgamate, or compromise in some way. We have indeed in the past not assigned such a task, or such a function, to either the id or the superego.

This is in harmony with the view expressed by Hartmann (1960) that the *scrutiny* of moral values, or what "we might designate as *value testing*," in the service of the integration and organization of action, "is, very likely, a function of the ego" (p. 51). As further "evidence" and substantiating reasoning for this point of view, one would adduce the other known areas in common between the superego and the id. Thus the superego is known to operate with and to have at its disposal aggressive instinctual energy as well as libidinal energy (albeit it can and does operate also with neutralized energy). There is, moreover, the statement by Freud, in a passage which emphasizes the developmental continuity between the superego and the id:

"Whereas the ego is essentially the representative of the external world, of reality, the super-ego stands in contrast to it as the representative of the internal world, of the id" (1923a, p. 36). Thus it could be argued that the superego would share essential characteristics with the id, including in this connection its basic tolerance for contradictions.

At this point I would like to interject in a descriptive way that we can visualize the following as taking place during superego functioning. The superego can be thought of as enduring in a relatively passive way the cathexis of its "opinion" function. The latter, I submit, occurs automatically, and certain ingredients of its opinion repertoire are awakened and charged, in accordance with the meanings to it of the current act, or intention, of the instinctual push, or the reality event, or the ego decision. This repertoire consists of a spectrum of attitudes, or value judgments, which exist side by side, but any one of which, or more usually any complex combination, may be cathected at any one time or by any one event. The automatic nature of this arousal mechanism is similar in quality to the automatic occurrence of signal anxiety in the ego. These "opinions" are in fact to the superego what signal anxiety is to the ego. The nature and content of this automatic choice, as to which component or combination of superego opinions will be cathected, depend, of course, on the entire ontogenetic history and on the state of associative readiness of the various components in the same way as the previous history and former sensitizations will determine whether and which stimuli can elicit signal anxiety in the ego. Schafer (1960), in his excellent review of the characteristics of the superego, makes similar reference to the use of the signal concept in superego functioning and that the superego "can discriminate degrees of evil and react accordingly."

To be sure, then, the direction-giving, or the prohibiting, or above all the enforcing functions of the superego require the greatest degree of activity on its part, for which an appropriate amount of aggressive energy, either neutralized or unneutralized, lies at its disposal. The controversial nub which enters the picture here is whether, in addition to these active functions just named, there is also the activity of choosing one out of a number of possibly contradictory opinions or values, or of effecting a mean between them. According to the point of view being expounded at this juncture, such a function is *not* included in this repertoire, so that the subsequent activity response is stimulated by the entire range of the value spectrum which has been aroused and activated. The nature and amount of such subsequent activity can be extremely variable, both from a total point of view and selectively for each of the functions named—directing, prohibiting, enforcing, etc.

In general, in this view, the process of superego activation is such that its opinions are passively aroused, without its further shaping them, after which it does what it can actively with them, which may be much or little. This process would not include or allow for its "being in conflict," although its contents may be such as to turn out to be mighty confusing to the ego.

V

Thus far the point of view whose tenets and implications I have been tracing and following through and which seems to be restricting intrasystemic conflict to the ego applies only to the dilemma or choice sense of the meaning of conflict. We should now include, within the scope of this purview, conflict in the more traditional sense, that of opposition. Just as intersystemic conflicts have been traditionally composed of the mutual opposition of forces, so, as a corollary, opposition conflicts have always been thought of as intersystemic—until the recent suggestions of the intrasystemic locus. Let us therefore extend our scope and see how our alternative views fare in covering this possibility as well.

I therefore turn now to the interesting and significant question whether the "opposition" type of conflicts can occur intrasystemically. I have developed the theme and offered the proposition that the intrasystemic "alternative-choice" type of conflict does exist very definitely and even characteristically within the ego, while for the time being I have regarded its existence in the superego or the id as more dubious. We are nevertheless faced with the question whether the original opposition type of conflict does not in fact exist intra-systemically—in any of the systems, or in all of them, or selectively, as the first type, in one or more. Or is the possibility of intrasystemic conflict limited to the dilemma or choice type? It is indeed the direct-contact opposition type of conflict which I believe Hartmann, Loewenstein, Jacobson (1964), and other writers have had in mind exclusively in proposing and giving examples of intrasystemic conflicts. These authors speak uniformly of such conflicts as being *between* the contrasting pairs rather than in the superego, or ego, *about* them. Hartmann (1950a), in fact, states the matter quite explicitly, as "ego functions opposing *each other*" (my italics). In the absence of any statements of qualifying or contrary nature, we can only assume that the *form* of the conflict was carried over from the intersystemic model as one between opposing forces. Thus when Hartmann or Jacobson speaks of contradictory self-interests or of conflicting values within the system ego, or when Hartmann and Loewenstein list ego ideals which conflict with each other, or superego values or judgments which are in direct contrast and therefore in mutual opposition, they mean, I believe, that the energic forces of one of each pair are directly pitted against the force of the other, each one tending thus to negate or obliterate the other. Either the stronger of the two, or in some cases a compromise and resultant of both, emerges as the force which will then be presented in the intersystemic confrontation. This is in fact, I submit, what has routinely been meant by most authors who write about intrapsychic conflict, not having had in mind the distinction which I have been making here.

Do such intrasystemic confrontations and oppositions actually take place? In considering first the case of the id, while some authors refer quite commonly to instinctual conflicts, for example, between the libidinal and the aggressive drives, or between many other possible pairs of polar opposites, (Alexander, 1933; Anna Freud, 1936), it is the more general conception, it seems to me, as stated most explicitly by Fenichel, that instinctual drives exist side by side and are directed only toward discharge, rather than in any way toward each other. "Instincts contradictory in aim, without . . . reinforcement by the defending ego, would not conflict with each other. Within the realm of the id there is no conception of contradiction, logical order is here nonexistent. Instincts contradictory in aim can be satisfied one after the other, sometimes even simultaneously." This is Fenichel's rejoinder (1945), with which I agree, to the idea advanced by some that heterosexuality can oppose homosexuality, or sadism be in conflict with masochism, or passivity with activity, etc. (Alexander, 1933). "An instinctual conflict . . . is always a structural conflict as well; one of the conflicting instincts represents the ego . . . [or is] strengthened for purposes of ego defense" (Fenichel, 1945, p. 130). Note here that the ego, another system, chooses one instinctual stream, and opposes another, *which keeps pressing*. It is the latter force, continuing against the ego, which makes for the conflict.

Alexander (1933) has given the most explicit description of what he calls instinctual as contrasted to structural conflicts. He cites, in addition to the dichotomies named above, many other pairs of instinctual opposites, such as expulsive-receptive, masculine-feminine, exhibitionistic-voyeuristic, etc. But his subsequent descriptions patently indicate the structural participation when, in each instance, he speaks of "[one] striving [being] rejected because it is incompatible with another, *ego-acceptable* one which determines the *ego's* actual attitude" (my italics). It is the ego which is clearly one of the contending arms in the conflict. Similarly, while Anna Freud (1936) also gives a place, as does Alexander, to "conflicts between opposite [instinctual] tendencies," she attributes these to "the *ego's* need for synthesis," includes these under a heading of "defense *against instinct*" (my italics), and points out that the ego wards off one or the other of the opposing impulses or else arrives at a compromise between them.

In this context, however, we must consider the concept of drive fusion, which does visualize a coming together and thereby a mutual influencing of one drive by the other. But fusion is a complementary and harmonious blending, rather than a conflict, or due to a conflict. "That this takes place regularly and very extensively is an assumption indispensable to our conception" (Freud, 1923a). Correspondingly, in the regressive state of defusion, the two components again exist side by side, and press for independent and separate discharge, accounting for the strength and hence the danger emanating from each.

Hartmann, while describing such direct conflicts as occurring intrasystemically between contiguous tendencies within the ego and within the superego, has nevertheless given some support to the above view in the case of the id, stating that such a view about the relationship between contrasting instinctual tendencies can be argued with merit (Panel, 1963a). Thus, in summary, with regard to id components, I support the view which holds that neither a conflict of choice nor one of opposing forces can be held to exist within the id in accordance with our total prevalent concept of the psychological functioning of this agency.

I will now turn to the superego, which in this connection I propose to discuss separately from the ego, since it is likely that crucial differences might again exist between the two, and that different considerations might apply. We now face a slight variation of the question I asked before regarding the superego. Whereas previously I was concerned with whether the superego had the capacity to be in conflict over contrasting elements existing within it, I am now asking whether the *elements* can be in conflict *with each other*. With regard to the id, my answer has been that this cannot be so, i.e., that here the instinctual drives do not oppose *each other*. Can this be otherwise for superego elements? Can one value within the superego attack or defend against another? Does a function of defense, or of directional assertion, lie within the element itself? Or, for that matter, does a function of defense exist within the superego?

To answer these question in order, I would venture first

that there is no reason why we should assume or assign a more definitive function along these lines to *an element* of the super-ego than we feel to exist in an instinctual drive. There is not that much autonomy or complexity within the single value judgment or moral edict to direct itself against another, nor for that matter to defend itself against a force from another. This might be done by the entire system, or structure, or aggregate of functions, which can direct itself against, or oppose another system, and which has the energy and the functions with which to do so. But can this be done by one of its parts? It would stretch what we think to be the function of a part to assume that it can, and I believe that it would fit better with our way of thinking to answer in the negative. A certain amount of complexity, of differentiation, and of structural development is necessary for the capacity to engage in psychic conflict. Spitz (1959) points out that conflict in the human is "in terms of highly structured intrapsychic components" (p. 79).

An intrasystemic opposition conflict, however, is conceiv-able in still another way. If the parent structure is able to, or indeed must, choose between contrasting or contradictory elements within it, and the rejected element or elements *keep pressing* for discharge, or for attention cathexis, from the matrix of the system, or from its aggregate functions, there would then be the background for another opposition type of conflict—intrasystemic in locus—between the parent body and one of its parts. This would be a replica in miniature of what takes place intersystemically, when the ego, after *choosing* one between id and superego, then often finds itself in an *opposition* conflict with the other.

With regard to the superego I have for the time being proceeded on the assumption that order, and therefore choice, is not among its functions. The same reasoning could apply simultaneously with regard to defense. Can the superego employ a defense against an undesirable element within it? We come again to the same principle as before, whether the superego can perform a function ordinarily thought of as reserved for the ego—in this case the function of defense. I would suggest that whatever answer we pursue for one question, i.e., that of an organizing type of function within the superego, would apply similarly to the other, i.e., the question of defense. Thus pursuing my present line of argument, just as an organizing and synthesizing function is being reserved for the ego, and denied in the id and superego, so the function of defense would also be solely an ego function and activity. Hence, intrasystemic conflict of either type, of choice or of opposition, does not occur in either the id or the superego. This would follow from the assumptions made thus far, which I consider to be consonant with other parts of our present theoretical formulations.

On the other hand, with regard to the disputed and controversial functions which I have been examining in connection with id and superego, the entire concerted view of our literature converges much more uniformly about my views of these functions within the ego. Both the functions of deciding and of instituting defense reside squarely in the middle of the spectrum of the ego's activities, thus giving to it a central role in situations of conflict. Since we envisage unequivocally that the ego encompasses, and is centrally responsible for, the maintenance of order, logic, and consistency; of being the mediator between the various and frequently incompatible influences impinging upon it from all directions, not only from id and superego but continuously from the external world as well, and from multiple and variable components within each—the ego must and does have commensurate power and resources to deal with these. Since the power of defense and opposition is centrally and unbegrudgingly vested in it in order to achieve these functions, and the energy to carry these out is part of its armamentarium, it is easy to conceive, and makes for clarity and consistency, that the ego can apply such power and use such energy in all and any directions, wherever needed or wherever it can be of utility. This would apply, and would be possible in the case of the ego, in the case of intrasystemic divisions and oppositions, as well as in intersystemic ones.

Applying the same schema to the ego which I have just

used for the other systems to encompass all possible mechanisms for the formation of intrasystemic conflicts, I would say that the following obtains. The same reasoning would apply here as elsewhere with regard to the individual elements themselves, i.e., they can neither choose, nor oppose, nor defend, and hence can hardly in themselves be "in conflict." This would apply to the individual "ego interests" or specific ego functions or activities. Thus I cannot see, as Hartmann says, that ego components can "oppose each other." However, the ego itself can be "in conflict" about any contradictory or inconsistent parts within it just as about any incompatible forces outside of it. As a result of such conflict, it can and does make a choice or compromise. It may then encounter continued pressure from a rejected internal element, as it does from a denied or thwarted external one. Defensive energy can then conceivably be deployed against such pressure, setting up in this way an oppositional type of intrasystemic conflict.

Thus it is entirely logical and consistent with the roles and functions which we have assigned to the individual systems to consider that the ego can suffer as well as create conflicts within its borders as well as between itself and other parts. In this way, intrasystemic conflicts can come to abide within the ego involving any of its multiple functions or its varying contents or interests, with defensive anticathectic energy being employed at the borders toward any such incompatible elements, whenever such is necessary to bring about or maintain effective thinking, behavior, or even affects. The ego has the function, the responsibility, and the power to experience, create, and solve such multiple, varied, and widespread conflict situations. Such intra-ego processes complement parallel intersystemic ego activities in the service of achieving increasing neutralization, the advance and dominance of secondary process modes of thinking and action, and the achievement of order, logic, modulation, and subtlety, all of which are an expression of the firm dominance of an effective ego extending its influence and its power over a willing and cooperative and not-too-rebellious id and superego.

In the interest of greater precision and after more careful thought I would add the following about the ego's choice or decision-making function. While we have thus far not been quite exact in defining the relationship of this activity to its contiguous ego functions, I would have us now take a clearer stand and recognize that this function is actually separate from, although closely related to, the functions of organization or synthesis. Closer attention results frequently in our decomposing various functions or contents which on a grosser view we are apt to consider as one. Thus *to choose* is not the same as to organize, and neither is the same as to synthesize. Actually even to decide is somewhat different from choosing, although one may follow closely upon the heels of the other. Hartmann (1947) has asked for the same exactitude when he suggested that an organizing function be separated and delineated from the synthesizing function as Nunberg (1931) described it. Hartmann pointed out that organization may at one time consist of synthesis and integration, while it may at another emphasize primarily a differentiating process. The latter has recently been singled out and described in more elaborate detail by Hacker (1962) as a most important discriminatory function of the ego. While this process is characterized as almost synonymous and sometimes interchangeable with selection, deciding, and choosing, I would have us note that though contiguous and interdependent, these functions are still not the same. The ability to discriminate is a precondition for the capacity to choose, but the former may exist without the latter. Peto (1960, 1961) has suggested and described a closely related but still different function of the ego which he calls fragmentation. This function aims at splintering apart various complexes, also serves differentiation, and is postulated as a precondition for the operation of defenses.

The function of effecting a choice in the face of a dilemma, of making a decision in the case of competing alternatives, is an activity which I think should be spelled out on its own and given a central and prominent place in the multiple ensemble of ego functions. While such activity has certainly been implicit in general usage, it has heretofore been assumed in a rather nondescript and imprecise way as part either of the ego's mediating role or of its general organizing tendency. In keeping with our procedure of being ever more precise as we subject each specific item to closer and more individual inspection, I would suggest separation of this specific function and recognition of its importance as a crucial and indispensable link. The sequential chain in which it plays a part runs: filtering, scanning, judging, deciding, *choosing*—and then executing its choice and decision, via defense, or adaptation, motility, etc. All of these are subsidiary methods which aid and enhance the more global functions of coordination, synthesis, and organization. While these functions are all closely interwoven and part of one continuous action, we come to know their individuality by virtue of one or the other undergoing an exceptional development, either in a positive or in a negative direction. Thus any particular aspect of these sequential functions can become either especially highly developed or singularly deficient. Each separate ego function, as Hartmann has pointed out, can undergo its own selective development, both maturationally and experientially. Thus we see people who have good judgment but are slow or even paralyzed in decision-making, and others who can effect choices with dispatch but on the basis of incomplete appraisal or poorly conceived judgmental action.

It is to be noted that this function of choice is not limited to conflict situations; it is operative just as assiduously in furthering conflict-free interests and activities, such as any kind of coping, or most decisively in problem solving. The latter can operate with essentially neutralized energy—and may in the individual case be a highly developed and effective capacity quite independently of any involvement in intersystemic or intrasystemic conflict. In fact, the onset of the latter may blunt its effective operation in the former sphere. This special capacity of "decision-making" has of late come in for a great deal of attention in its many important and derivative aspects on the social front. Studies relative to its various manifestations are of active interest to experimental psychologists as well as to sociologists and political scientists. From the psychoanalytic orientation, we are concerned with the locus of its origins and its microscopic aspects, as a discreet and central and important ego function.

Following this digression, I would further summarize: by adhering to the propositions which I have chosen above, I come to the conclusion that intrasystemic conflicts of both the "opposition" and the "choice" types can and do exist within the ego, but it is not possible to support the existence of either of these within either of the other two systems.

Another line of thought leading in the same direction is that anxiety too, which is after all to the greatest degree responsible for conflict (and is—at least in the types of conflict to which I have hitherto paid the most attention—in reciprocal relationship with it) (Rangell, 1963), resides only in the ego, and neither in the id nor in the superego. The same is true for the related series of anxiety derivatives or equivalents, the other motives for defense, as guilt, shame, disgust, etc. The function of *being in* conflict—over contradictory forces—is furthermore so close to the function of *feeling* conflict that it is eminently logical that these both reside within the same agency. (Although we refer to the "feeling" of conflict, of course the whole process may be, and usually is, unconscious.) Thus the agency which experiences anxiety, and which is the seat of the affects, and which has the functions of knowing and judgment and cognition in general, all of which are so much part of one close and continuous process[1] is by the same token the seat of conflict, whether the latter is entirely encompassed within its borders, or extends from it to other parts. For such conflict to be able to reside similarly within another agency would presuppose that the latter would be similarly endowed with a motive, such as anxiety, or a need for synthesis or organization, all of which we consider as functions of the ego and not of either of the other structures.

It would follow from the pursuit of the present line of

---

[1] I have described this process in its "microscopic" aspects in Chapter 7.

reasoning that an intrapsychic conflict must involve the ego, although it may come from and emanate toward some other part as well (the exceptional instances in which the ego can be bypassed or at least its role diminished have been described previously). At least such conflict cannot be complete within another system.

VI

I have until now in one sense been taking the role of the devil's advocate. I have done so both because the position taken stood on a logical base, and because it led to a number of insights and conclusions which I think are incontrovertible and will stand. However, now that I have presented the logical sequelae of a strict and formalistic view, one which I believe stemmed from certain of our accepted and established propositions, I would like to show where I think we must bend and change our views to a certain degree. I have developed these thoughts thus far based on the assumption of a strict division between ego and superego in respect to certain crucial functions. Further thought, however, shows that the matter is not thereby put to rest—on the contrary, certain objections arise which make it necessary that we now consider an alternative view. These objections stem from two sources, one clinical-empirical and the other theoretical.

First, on a clinical and experiential basis, it does not seem that "there are no contradictions within the superego," as is true for the id. This does not seem to fit what we actually see. If we speak, in some cases of psychopathy, of a "corrupt superego," which can tolerate with ease mutual contradictions, and in other cases of psychosis of "an archaic superego" (Hoedemaker, 1955; Wexler, 1952), which also encompasses within it regressively defused and violently contrasting elements, and in still other instances, in certain character types, of "lacunae in the superego," do we not imply that in the "normal" development the superego does not tolerate such divisiveness within itself? I believe that clinically this is true. Rather than presenting to the ego a group of conflicting values, which we would expect and discern quite routinely from the assumptions we have made above, it appears more usual that the superego is more nearly "of one mind" in its value judgments. It does not seem to me that this can all be attributed to subsequent ego activity, but that an effort or striving toward uniformity and cohesiveness is more likely operative in both systems.

The same can be gleaned on certain theoretical grounds. Much evidence points to the fact that there is no such strict cleavage between ego and superego as I have here assumed, and that my formulations, although stemming from commonly accepted tenets, are predicated on a degree of purity which actually does not exist. The fact is that there is to a large degree a continuum in functioning between ego, ego ideal, and super-ego, as brought out by many writers (Freud, 1920, 1921, 1923a; Jacobson, 1964; Bing et al., 1959), so that the cleavage between ego and superego is not as sharp as that between the ego and the id. The functions of judging, value-giving, establishing directions, and others bridge across from one to the other. Thus, in spite of the developmental continuity between super-ego and id, the superego has more separateness from the id than it has in common with it. It is after all a superordinate structure, not only to the id but in many ways even to the ego. The superego is, moreover, in its basic origins the internalized morality of the external world, so that its relationship to reality can never be disregarded. Complete contrariness, a haven for contradictions, and an utter disregard for external reality can thus be said to exist with consistency only in the id, but neither in the ego nor in the superego.

I believe that these considerations are of sufficient cogency to necessitate a change in my position. It cannot be so clean-cut that all psychic elements are in a state of total haphazard disarray and in mutual contradictions until and only until they reach and are acted upon by the ego. I believe that such an economic and dynamic state can be said to be characteristic of the id, but I do not believe that it is either useful or correct to hold that a similar state is characteristic for the superego—after all man's most highly developed and civilized agency, his "higher nature" (Freud, 1923a), upon which his dignity, morality, and higher ethical values depend (Freud, 1920, 1923a).

I would therefore conclude the following: we must assume some concern with order and consistency to exist within the superego; from this it follows that there is, at least to a certain degree, an organizing and synthesizing function within the superego and the ability to exercise a choice in order to effect this; therefore the superego *can* suffer internal intrasystemic conflicts when such cohesiveness and uniformity are either disrupted or nonexistent. These assumptions would be consonant with many of the facts enumerated above and would resolve and clarify some inconsistent areas. The superego would carry some of these functions along in its development *out of* the ego (Freud, 1920, 1921, 1923a), including to some degree the functions of defense and of choice to carry on and resolve the above-named inner conflicts. Thus a sharp cleavage in its functions from the ego would be seen *not* to exist, which is consonant with Freud's descriptions of the superego as a differentiated grade "within the ego," and is in keeping with the efforts of some authors (Bing et al., 1959) actually to merge its functions, via the ego ideal, with the ego.

I would further vouchsafe, however, that we must now make some quantitative and economic comparisons of such activities within the superego as compared to the ego. Although there is this continuum and overlap in function, there is still a distinct difference in centrality and degree which makes for the differences between the two systems. While a synthetic and integrating function is a central activity within the ego, it is only secondary and peripheral to the superego, which is still basically concerned with its value and direction-giving functions. The former is subordinate to and only in the service of the latter in the superego. While the ego has the task of synthesizing elements from throughout the psychic apparatus, the superego does so only, if at all, to the extent that this is necessary within its own borders, and to perform its own central functions. When such intrasystemic incompatibilities or conflicts fail to be solved within the superego, it is most likely the case that they are then passed on to the ego for further and final action, in a manner which Hacker (1962) refers to as "a fluid division of labor between superego and ego." In this connection I would agree with Hartmann and Loewenstein and with Bak (1952), who, commenting on the pathology of schizophrenia, point out that "what is often called the 'disintegration' of the superego in schizophrenia—is at least partly traceable to the deficiencies in the ego." These authors attribute the central role in the pathology of schizophrenia "to the impairment of certain ego functions."

These conclusions bear out the suggestion of Hartmann and Loewenstein that intrasystemic conflicts can indeed exist within the superego. Unlike their formulation, however, such conflict would be envisaged as existing not between the contrasting elements but rather in two stages. First there is the conflict within the superego itself *about* such incompatible elements, due to a violation of its need for order and consistency, and second a conflict between the total superego and the internal element which it has decided to reject. The quantitative differences with respect to the degree and centrality of such activities which I have pointed out in superego as compared to ego functioning may correspond with Hartmann and Loewenstein's apparent reservations when they state that such contrasting tendencies in the superego *"can be compared to"* (my italics) the intrasystemic conflicts in the ego, in a paper in which they stress in another connection that analogies and precursors are not necessarily the same thing as the final product. Thus the processes may be similar in both systems, but different in efficiency and degree.

Other quantitative comparative variations and spectra also obtain. There are different degrees of the intrapsychic conflicts themselves, in conjunction with the different forms which I have been noting. Thus the intersystemic, opposition-type, anxiety-based conflicts which have heretofore been the cornerstone of our psychoanalytic interest are the most highly structured, the most definitive, and no doubt the most etiologically significant intrapsychic conflicts—certainly as far as psychopathology is concerned. But in the widest framework of our general psychoanalytic psychology, there is a spectrum of forms, of motives for, and degrees of, intrapsychic conflicts. Thus there are at the very start in the built-in apparatuses at least the potential for, if not actual, conflicts—the opposite instinctual tendencies, the instincts and the built-in defensive thresholds (Rapaport, 1953a), the constitutional id and ego apparatuses, or the primary enmity of the ego in relation to the drives (Anna Freud, 1936). In all of these the familiar problem of the differences between precursors and the final product, and of when the forerunners become the real thing, stalks here as elsewhere. By no means do any of the above as yet comprise conflict, as psychoanalysts think of the latter, any more than the early shadows of ego equipment are the ego, or the earliest internal prohibitions are yet the superego. Much more complex differentiation and structuralization have to take place to have the ingredients of true intrapsychic conflict. Hartmann (1939a) has pointed to the same principle and need for caution when he warns that not every disruption of equilibrium can be considered a conflict, without the latter term losing all precision of meaning. For conflict, one needs an opposing force, not just an obstacle. Spitz (1957a) inserts caution in a similar direction in noting that the early stimulus barrier likewise does not represent a true opposing force, rather "it is a manifestation of a maturational state, namely, that at birth the sensorium is not yet cathected."

As structures develop, and the forces line up in their ultimate relationships, there still exists a hierarchy of motives for and types of conflict. Thus I would say that an intrasystemic conflict, of any of the types which I have been describing, is not apt to have the same scope, or the same depth, or the same reverberations as does an intersystemic one of our more familiar and traditional variety. In general, I think the same would be true about the choice or competitive type of conflicts as compared with the opposition types; namely, the former do not have the force, tenacity, or serious implications of the latter.

That this is not *always* true, though, can be appreciated if one calls to mind certain cases of obsessional neurosis, or even perhaps certain obsessive characters. With regard to a spectrum of motives, a conflict based on the need for synthesis, or on inevitable, innate, opposing tendencies, is not of the same caliber or magnitude as one based on anxiety, certainly not of the same neurosogenic quality. Conflicts based on the need for synthesis are less global and significant to the entire organism than the usually more disruptive conflicts based on danger and anxiety.

There is thus a hierarchy of motives and of conflicts and of results, just as there is of psychic development itself. The anxiety-provoked, intersystemic conflict situations, with the broad range of interstructural participation as we have known them, is still the ultimate destiny of the usual and typical psychic dilemmas to which man is heir. Indeed, with the development of the complex psychic apparatus which is man's distinctive stamp, it is not likely that a process which has already reached a conflict stage will remain confined to the simpler units without becoming enmeshed in the more complex interrelationships which lie ready and able to take over. Actually, there is a simultaneous and reciprocal interaction between them all. Intrasystemic tensions create intersystemic effects which in turn influence new intrasystemic conditions, etc.

Thus clinically and experientially it is difficult, if not well-nigh impossible, to furnish a satisfactory example of an intrasystemic conflict, without it being easy to show how each arm of the conflicting forces has become intertwined with intersystemic implications. This was conspicuously evident in the panel discussion on intrapsychic conflict, when one considered any of the interesting clinical vignettes which were offered (Panel, 1963b). In the same vein is Fenichel's statement (1945) that an apparent instinctual conflict is always a structural conflict as well. In an internal conflict within the ego it can almost always be shown that one of the contending elements is an ego representative of the instincts, or of the superego. This is the case, for example, in the formulation sometimes made in the Kleinian system, or by some who work with psychotics, of a conflict between incompatible introjects or contradictory identifications within the ego. To cite another striking example, in the very interesting clinical report of a case of strephosymbolia, which was ingeniously traced to an intrasystemic disturbance of the synthetic function in the ego (Rosen, 1955), it was abundantly evident that within the conflicting forces were intense oedipal instinctual wishes, prematurely aroused and with catastrophic potential consequences to the patient. From the complex genetic determinants, it was ascertained that the auditory and phonetic aspects of words were associated with and meant for this patient the mother, while the visual and idiographic elements involved stood for the father. The ultimate effect of the failure of the necessary synthesis of these by the ego, however, was the achievement of an *instinctual* wish, i.e., to keep the parents apart—and hence oedipal fulfillment for the patient.

I agree with Loewenstein (Panel, 1963b) when he says that one does not have to find "a pure case" of something in order to demonstrate its existence. Indeed, it is the unusual instance in psychic life to be able to do this. We see not "pure" instincts but only the most filtered derivatives, or pure defense without instinct showing through, etc. Thus empirical clinical statements made above are meant not to deny the existence of the simpler forms but to show that in the developed organism the achieved complexity can also not be denied from playing its inevitable part.

To overlook these comparative and quantitative considerations and the hierarchic and mutual interplay of forces which are at work can lead to erroneous and incomplete theoretical formulations. Thus Jacobson (1964), in an otherwise comprehensive and full-bodied work which takes notable cognizance of the intricate genetic interrelationships between all of the psychic structures in forming the workable concept of the self, makes the rather surprising generalization that shame, inferiority feelings, and identity problems are not induced by intersystemic but by intrasystemic conflicts—a formulation which I would energetically dispute on empirical-clinical as well as theoretical grounds. One would not have to look far to see the artificiality and the indefensibility of such a limitation. Jacobson's own subsequent clinical examples disprove its validity. Elsewhere Jacobson attributes castration fear to "an intrasystemic (ego) tension," in contrast to superego fear which "is expressive of an intersystemic tension" (Jacobson at times uses "tensions" and "conflicts" interchangeably and somewhat loosely). These generalizations are not at all clear and are difficult to understand. They fail to take into account, for example, in the case of castration anxiety, the indispensable contributions of instinctual pressures as well as the dangers which emanate not only from the superego but from the external world.

Such formulations tend to take a new piece of insight—in this case, that of intrasystemic conflicts—and to overdo its role. In this connection, Arlow points out, in agreement with me, that too great an extension of the role of intrasystemic conflicts would lead in the direction of minimizing the importance of drives and of other intersystemic contributions (Panel, 1963b). What we might conceive of as a trend from this would be the tendency to impart to each of the individual structures the functions of all the others. Thus, as our knowledge increases in scope, depth, and detail, and we see the greater intricacies and complexities within each structure or function, we might tend to ascribe to each the abilities of the whole. In such a way, the superego would come to acquire the capacity for unity and synthesis completely within itself, instead of depending largely upon the ego for these. Another such example is the idea of id inhibitions as existing within the id, instead of the inhibiting forces being thought of a being part of the ego or at least of what will become the ego. There thus grows with development a tendency to see a complete homunculus within each unit, as though each could almost tolerate being split off and still survive. I can visualize, for example, that carrying the above intrasystemic process further, as we know more and more about smaller and smaller units, one might postulate that there are conflicts not only within the system but within each specific smaller element. Thus, with regard to each value judgment of the superego, or each goal in the ego ideal, or each interest in the ego, it could be said that there can be a struggle between contiguous attitudes of varying shades of intensity, such as "this is good, vs. this is less good, not so good, neutral, a little bad, worse," etc. Perhaps I am carrying this argument too far to make a point. However, one may also say that only such a hierarchy and multilayering of conflicts can explain a system as complex as the psychic apparatus, and indeed this may be so. But at some point, I believe, we will benefit from insisting on some simplicity and limitations and on establishing the irreducible. The concept of conflict needs to fulfill certain definite criteria, and I have indicated what I consider some of these irreducible conditions to be.

Actually, what the above trend does is to carry the concept of autonomy much further than, and I am sure far beyond, what Hartmann (1939a) had in mind when he introduced this useful term. The autonomy of the ego from conflicts and from drive influence was a true and an extraordinarily useful discovery, but Hartmann and Loewenstein themselves point out that autonomy is only relative and never absolute. "There can be no question of 'absolute' independence in this or in the other forms of autonomy we know in psychoanalysis." While this is true even for the ego, which is in our way of thinking the most complex of the structural systems, with the widest and most all-inclusive range of functions, I would venture that it must be even more true of the superego, which is considerably more limited in its scope, function, and diversity. Thus, while autonomous action can properly be achieved on a wide front by the ego, with its complex ensemble of functions and its own store of energy, such is probably quantitatively less possible of achievement by the superego. The latter remains throughout too dependently interrelated with other activities, particularly with many of the ego functions, for the process of autonomy to develop far in this direction. Nor do the superego's functions warrant it. Values and ideals are not independently viable without actions or behavior, or at least intentions toward the latter, to go with them. On the other hand, perception, motility, security interests, etc., can be more sufficient unto themselves. This is in consonance with the conclusions of Hartmann and Loewenstein that while the superego can become reasonably autonomous from the original objects and from drives, "its normal functioning is constantly bound to certain actions of the ego," from whose influence it cannot, nor should it, be separated. Just as these authors feel that the superego does not, as the ego, have consitutional, inborn elements—"present knowledge does not provide us with any cogent reason to speak of inheritance in the case of the superego"—so I believe the superego has less chance than the ego to become as autonomous. But this is in accord also with the reasoning I have advanced with regard to conflict—that by the same token the superego, though to some degree it possesses the ingredients necessary to encompass conflict within its borders, is quantitatively less able to do so than is the ego.

I must pose one further question which may have occurred to many by this time. That is, are we carrying this division too far, and are we asking for a precision in concepts beyond the point of either its usefulness or our ability to make such fine distinctions? This is a legitimate question, and comes more into focus when one considers the conclusions and final assertions made by many of the writers in this area. Many of the nuclear concepts are characterized as much by overlap as they are by separateness. Thus, as Fenichel (1945) points out, "the concepts of instinct and defense are relative; the two are always interpenetrated" (p.130), or "It is not the case of one definite defensive attitude fighting against one definite impulse; there are always variations, an active struggle, and mutual interpenetration" (p. 475). The ego operates with energy derived from the id, deinstinctualized and neutralized energy, as well as primary energy of its own (Hartmann, 1955). The superego also utilizes instinctual energy, notably aggressive, but also libidinal. It also is, as conceptualized by Freud (1921) genetically, a "differentiated grade within the ego," or "a precipitate in the ego—[or a] modification of the ego [which] retains its special position" (Freud, 1923a, p. 34). Many writers have noted the similarity between functions of the ego ideal and the ego, as well as the intricate interrelationships and overlapping between the interests and activities of the ego, ego ideal, and superego. Both of the latter arise genetically from the ego, as well as from the external object relationships. Bing et al. (1959) actually regard the ego ideal as "'anatomically' a part of the ego," while Hartmann and Loewenstein prefer to consider it, as most do today, as part of the superego system. Hartmann et al. (1946) have pointed out the common origin of all of the subsequent structural divisions from a common unified and undifferentiated matrix. Thus one can see the fluidity of the borders, at least from genetic considerations.

It is true, therefore, that both genetically and functionally we should be aware of common origins, original unity, continuity, overlap, and interpenetration. However, this does not militate against the eventual existence of separate entities, with separate functions, of specialized and limited scope. I have pointed to this dilemma between continuity and separateness, this frequent problem of the continuous spectrum (Chapter 20). In each instance, it is necessary and helpful to be aware of both, of the common line which binds as well as the borders which separate. Thus Jacobson (1964), in explaining why we need to postulate a superego as separate from rather than as just another part of the ego, points out that "Freud's last systemic distinctions are based on significant inner experiences. . . . It is not accidental that in times of conflict we may hear the voice of temptation, the id, the voice of reason, the ego, and the voice of conscience, the superego."

VII

In summary, with regard to the various structural problems which come up in connection with intrapsychic conflict, I have surveyed the range of intersystemic possibilities, as well as the question of an intrasystemic locus for such conflicts. The latter was seen to occur quite regularly within the ego, in connection with the ego's function as mediator and decision-maker. In fact, it was suggested that the function of making a choice and effecting decisions between contending elements, both outside and inside its borders, be explicitly spelled out as a central and major ego function which is not the same as its organizing or synthetic function. Such activity operates over a spectrum from essentially conflictful spheres to more neutral-ized and relatively conflict-free problem-solving activity.

I further concluded that the superego is a locus for intrasystemic conflicts, but relatively less so and in only a secondary way as compared with the ego. An accompaniment of this conclusion was the proposition that the superego must therefore also have some choice and organizing functions, but again less centrally and less dominantly than the ego. These comparative relationships are to be stressed and recognized. While the ego can achieve quite some autonomy, from conflict, drives, and even from the superego, the superego can do so to a much lesser degree. On the other hand, while the superego as well as the id can initiate conflict, the ego largely suffers it. Although I have described certain variations and exceptions, in general from wherever conflict may come, it is largely fought in the ego's land. The id, the pressor, is usually objected to; the ego is the objector; the superego is the warner. Sometimes the objector objects to the warner. But always the objector also has a "dilemma conflict" in addition, having to decide whether and what to do. This part of the action is always within the ego's own, and only the ego's borders. The ego then has action at its flanks as well, at one or both borders facing its neighbor.

One thought keeps presenting itself to me as I come to the end of what I have to say about this subject, a thought which I fear may speak against the most basic points which I have made. That is, it may be, following Freud, that the basic and irreducible conflict is between life vs. death *instincts*! Maybe so—analysts seem divided on this point. But perhaps, as a last statement, I would say that if this is so—and I myself tend to give the general idea of this dichotomy much respect—these two relentless forces are, in relation to each other, partners, rather than in conflict! Each can, and will, have its say. And it is not the clash between *them* that results in the phenomena with which analysts spend their working days.

CHAPTER 9

On the Psychoanalytic Theory of Anxiety

A Statement of a Unitary Theory

To the psychiatric clinician, anxiety is the *raison d'être*. The total network of its tortuous course, its origins, direct manifestations, its equivalents, derivatives, and consequences (defenses, symptoms), constitute the major background, and indeed the foreground of the clinician's field of operation. This paper is thus focused on a central, albeit a diffuse phenomenon. It will have proven a justified effort, even without the expectation of any new development of theory, if it serves merely to refresh and recapitulate, and to bring a subject as nuclear as this periodically up to date.

The statement or warning that if one starts at any point of the psychoanalytic framework one can proceed to touch on every other part is particularly applicable to a study of anxiety.

Presented at Panel on "Anxiety," combined meeting of the American Psychoanalytic Association and the American Psychiatric Association, St. Louis, May 1954. Published in *J. Amer. Psychoanal. Assn.*, 3:389–414, 1955.

The challenge it poses, besides that of precise understanding, is clearly one of selection and condensation. This presentation will attempt to serve as a bridge between the historical developments of the past (Zetzel, 1955), and the experimental findings and paths for the future, which are to follow (Holmes and Ripley, 1954). The areas to be examined will include: (a) an appraisal of the present theoretical status of anxiety and its place in psychoanalytic metapsychology, the divergences of opinion which exist, and a synthesis of these into a unitary theory; (b) the integration of the concept of anxiety into the psychoanalytic theory of affects and into the most recent developments in ego psychology; (c) some remarks on the role of anxiety in the clinical therapeutic process.

I

The delineation of the anxiety experience as a nodal point in the dynamics of psychic life stands as one of the milestones in the evolution of the psychoanalytic framework. When, in the description of the pleasure-pain principle (Freud, 1911a), the avoidance of unpleasure (*Unlust*), of which anxiety (*Angst*) came to be the most significant representative, was marked out as a basic aim of the psychic apparatus, this forged another link (already established with the description of the unconscious) between psychopathology and everyday life. Freud (1915–1917, p. 341) wrote, "The problem of anxiety is a nodal point—a riddle of which the solution must cast a flood of light upon our whole mental life," and a few years later (1926, p. 119), anxiety is "the fundamental phenomenon and main problem of neurosis." Ernest Jones (1920) saw anxiety as "the Alpha and Omega of practical psychiatry," as well as the most frequent single symptom "perhaps *in all medicine*," while to Fenichel (1945, p. 132), "the problem of anxiety is the essence of any psychology of neurotic conflicts." Spitz (1950) declares, "The anxiety signal . . . becomes the most powerful motivating force in human life, the power which organizes the character, the defenses, the neuroses." Concurrence in these views courses through the entire psychoanalytic and allied literature.

The general sweep in our concepts of anxiety from the original idea of transformation of affect, or the toxic-dynamic-economic point of view (Freud, 1894, 1898) to the later and present definitive signal theory (1926) is quite familiar. The latter remained Freud's final formulation, given in his *Outline of Psychoanalysis* (1940). It can be considered today as the most generally accepted view, which is found not only to fit most logically into the other existing elements of the metapsychological framework but also to be the most useful in the understanding of the bulk of clinical phenomena. However, it should be emphatically noted that though Freud superseded the older idea with the newer signal theory, he never abandoned the former, but retained it as an explanation for certain existent clinical states. Thus Freud (1933, p. 130) consistently distinguished between two types of anxiety: anxiety as a signal, and anxiety brought about as the direct effect of a traumatic factor whenever the ego was overwhelmed by undischarged instinctual excitation. "The observations which I made at the time [i.e., of arriving at the idea of transformation] still hold good" (1926, p. 55); in these conditions "a situation analogous to the trauma of birth is established in the id and an automatic reaction of anxiety ensues" (p. 113). This mechanism is considered to be operative in the actual neuroses, while the signal anxiety remains typical for the psychoneuroses (p. 114). Two sources of anxiety are considered to exist, one involuntary, automatic, and experienced passively, and the other actively produced by the ego as a signal (p. 153). The former hypothesis "possesses less interest for us now than it did," but "we shall have to distinguish different cases" (p. 154). The relationship between these two states will be further amplified and make clearer in what is to follow.

The current signal concept needs to be stated in only the barest outline, for purposes of this discussion. Anxiety is seen as the reaction to a situation of danger, involving anticipation of a traumatic state. It leads to and mobilizes preparedness, whether in external action or in internal defense. Turning to the danger situations, the kaleidoscopic variations which these may come to take throughout life may be condensed, in accordance with the succinct formulation of Anna Freud (1936, pp. 58–64), to the essential basic dangers of (a) loss of love, with separation from the source of narcissistic supply; (b) castration; (c) alienation of the superego; and (d) instinctual flooding. The anxiety provoked by one or more of these dangers is the motive for defense, the ego then warding off forbidden id impulses. Furthermore, under special conditions, the anxiety itself can, as all other painful affects, become the object defended against, when, for example, the ego estimates that this affect would itself lead to a situation more traumatic than the event which it purports to foreshadow. The above elements describe a *modus operandi* which is the everyday fare of anyone working with the unconscious, and further documentation of this is superfluous.

Let us at this time examine the relationship of these several danger situations to one another, not only to pursue the question "What is it that we fear?" but also as preparation and orientation for the discussions which will follow. Freud (1926, pp. 163–165) emphasizes the mutually enhancing and reciprocal nature of internal and external dangers. Thus, an instinctual demand becomes an internal danger because its gratification would bring on an external one, while an external objective danger must have managed to become internalized to be significant for the ego, i.e., must have been recognized as related to some previously experienced situation of helplessness. External and internal dangers converge in the traumatic situation, where external pain which will not stop, or instinct cumulation which cannot be discharged, result in the same economic situation—that of motor and psychic helplessness. This latter is the feared state, where ego resources would be insufficient to master the quantity of excitation. When actually experienced, it is a "traumatic situation," and when expected in advance, a danger situation (1926, pp. 160–161). The latter is an estimate of impending helplessness, an anticipation of being overrun by stimuli. This is seen to merge with the state of instinctual flooding noted above. Kubie (1941), approaching the same problem from the physiological basis, also looks to the internal situation and correlates these psychic states with the condition of the excitatory and inhibitory processes of the central nervous system as described by Pavlov. The traumatic state corresponds to an explosive and diffuse irradiation of the excitatory processes, with production of the startled state, while anxiety is a tense expectation of the imminence of this startled state brought about by a mounting summation of excitatory processes. Zetzel (1949), without wishing to minimize the importance of external frustration or danger, also lays special stress on the crucial role of the internal danger situation. She points to differences of opinion about how far the instinctual frustration is related to external situations and to what degree the frustration is inevitable owing to the dangerous nature of the instincts themselves. In general the English school around Melanie Klein (1946) bases their work on the latter view, and feels that the ultimate source of anxiety is attributable to primary destructive impulses directed toward the ego. It is interesting that Anna Freud (1936), after having described in detail both the external and internal sources of anxiety and danger, turns to the question of whether the ego derives the form of its defenses primarily in the struggle against outside or against instinctual forces. She concludes that the infantile ego experiences the onslaught from both directions at once and must defend itself on both sides simultaneously.

From this outline as a base, let us now take a closer view, in accordance with our pursuit of present opinion, at areas which still remain unclear or controversial. A survey of the most recent analytic literature on the theoretical aspects of anxiety reveals that these concern (a) the question of "actual neurosis" and with it therefore a dual theory of anxiety, and (b) the situation as it exists in the earliest period of life.

With regard to the first of these, the question of actual neurosis and with it the automatic production of anxiety has remained to this date a source of much divergent opinion ever since its retention by Freud after the description of his later theory. Opinions on this point run a wide gamut, and the grounds upon which they are based vary considerably. Thus, on purely clinical observational grounds, Kris (quoted by Brenner, 1953) disputes the fact that sexual frustration per se in the adult produces neurotic anxiety. Brenner goes a good deal further and, on a number of clinical grounds, questions the existence of the nosological concept of actual neurosis and of the clinical entity of the dammed-up state in general. He points, for example, to the lack of clinical evidence for the anxiety neurosis as defined by Freud, and to much evidence that traumatic neurosis is produced not by breaking of the stimulus barrier so much as by the mobilization of deeper unconscious conflicts. This conclusion is supported by the work of Sperling (1950) and Simmel (1944) on traumatic neuroses, the latter concluding that soldiers fall ill in the combat situation because of the mobilization of their castration anxiety. Schur (1953), on the other hand, apart from the question of the clinical validity of the actual-neurotic state, questions the existence of automatic anxiety on quite other grounds. Do we know of any metabolites of which we can be sure that they produce anxiety automatically, to the exclusion of its origin in the ego? Such has been claimed, for example, with regard to adrenalin, which hormone has even been equated on the physiological level to the experience of anxiety. Yet Schur quotes a case of pheochromocytoma in which attacks of severe paroxysmal hypertension and therefore of increased adrenalin output occurred without any undue anxiety. When anxiety results after an injection of adrenalin, this occurs, in Schur's opinion, not automatically but rather as a reaction to the various sensations which are perceived. Thus on these various grounds, the above authors would contest the existence of actual neurosis or of the automatic type of anxiety and therefore of a dual theory of anxiety.

In contrast, however, Blau (1955) not only confirms the existence of Freud's actual anxiety neurosis, but considers this entity "a significant and frequent psychiatric syndrome which merits a prime and equal generic place alongside the psychoneuroses and psychoses." The existence of a clinical syndrome is a matter of observation and not of debate, and should not be influenced by differences concerning its etiology. Blau would differentiate between "neurosis," a functional physiological disturbance, and "psychoneurosis," a functional psychological disturbance. The signs and symptoms of the former are phys-iological in nature, are not psychological distortions of, or defenses against, anxiety, and are either direct equivalents or incomplete manifestations of anxiety itself. Clinical instances of this, Blau feels, are abundant, and he cites a multitude of clinical conditions which he considers supportive of this view. While his cases are variously described as demonstrating "anxious expressions of conflict" or "visceral equivalents of anxiety," it is difficult to distinguish them clearly from psycho-neuroses or at least from admixtures between the two. The treatment of the anxiety neuroses, Blau feels, requires more immediate measures to strengthen the ego or relieve outside pressures, while treatment of the psychoneuroses is a long-term project requiring psychoanalysis. Fenichel (1945, p. 168) also includes actual neurotic symptoms in his diagnostic classifica-tion. These occur in the state of psychic conflict, in which there is a damming-up of tension without psychoneurotic symptom formation. Both negative and positive symptoms result, the former due to a decrease of available energy and the latter stemming from painful feelings of tension and their derivatives (pp. 185–192).

Before attempting a resolution of these divergent views, I want to look into the other area in which unclarity prevails. This concerns a more precise investigation of the period of earliest infancy in relation to the origins of anxiety and its relation to the first pleasure-unpleasure sensations. Does anx-iety indeed span the continuum from the first shock of birth, through to other later danger and traumatic situations as originally supposed? While taking a number of critical excep-tions to Rank's concept of the role of birth trauma in the development of subsequent neurosis, Freud (1923a, pp. 106, 132) concurred with Rank in the genetic sequence connecting birth with the subsequent first separations from the mother. Thus these very earliest separations engender in the infant, in the face of an excessive instinctual need, the state of psychological helplessness, the prototype for which was the act of birth, and in such states anxiety is seen to be automatically reproduced. However, a number of critical exceptions to this view have recently been taken. Thus Spitz (1950), in his observational study of anxiety in early infancy, finds that the first unmistakable manifestations of anxiety proper do not occur until the third quarter of the first year. This corresponds with the period of development of true object relations and also of differentiation of the ego. Lacking an ego, tension states can be dealt with only by diffuse neuromuscular discharge, characterized by the phenomenon of overflow. Similarly, Greenacre (1945) states that "Anxiety as such cannot exist until there is some dawning ego sense and therefore some individual psychic content." Kubie's (1941) conclusions are in this same direction when he points out that the ability to form conditioned reflexes is a prerequisite for the experience of anxiety, since it is the former which introduces to the organism the idea of a warning signal of something to follow, and a gap between stimulus and response. Brenner (1953) would also regard the earliest feelings of the infant as consisting only of diffuse pleasure or unpleasure and would limit the specific emotion of anxiety to the time when the ego learns to anticipate danger in advance. From the diffuse unpleasure of the earliest months, there would then be other genetic possibilities of affect development parallel to that of anxiety. In connection with this is a recent work on depression by Edward Bibring (1953) in which he describes four parallel basic ego states, on the same plane, all of them being basic ego reactions to the common state of psychic helplessness. These parallel states are: (a) balanced narcissism (normal self-esteem); (b) exhilarated self-esteem (elation); (c) threatened narcissism, this resulting in the anxious ego; and (d) broken-down self-regard, the nucleus of a depressed ego. Schur (1953) would bypass this problem of when anxiety starts to be experienced in infancy and would remove its emphasis on theoretical formulations by adding to the definition "anxiety is a reaction of the ego" the words, "and of its predecessor." However, the basic question would still remain about whether anxiety as such does indeed exist in the precursors of the ego. We have pointed to authors who think not. Traumatic situations, Schur states, start with birth or even earlier, but the way the organism experiences them changes with growth and maturation.

With regard to the above issues and the divergent views described, I would like to present the following framework and set of propositions, which I believe to have both clinical validity and theoretical consistency: (a) The nosology of actual neurosis, or the state of being dammed up, or state of psychic conflict, is a valid and demonstrable entity. (b) The production of automatic anxiety, i.e., in the sense of being without psychic (more specifically ego) participation, *does not* follow from this. (c) It is not necessary to retain a dual theory of anxiety. A unitary theory, in consonance with the signal function, is applicable to all demonstrable instances of anxiety reactions, including those in the dammed-up state. An explanation of these points follows.

The actual neurotic state, described by Freud originally in connection with sexual frustration, was, after its historical dissociation from the latter, retained by Freud and others not for sentimental reasons or reasons of loyalty, but solely because of the fact that its dynamics were found to be applicable to a definitive and significant series of clinical events. This situation obtains whenever, as Fenichel (1945, pp. 185–188) describes, either from a heightened influx of stimuli (traumatic neurosis), or from a blockage of discharge (increase in defensive forces), there results a relative insufficiency of the ego. Such a state represents a minimal and abortive experience of psychic helplessness, which indeed one might say is experienced during the transitional stage of development even of every psychoneurotic symptom. Thus Fenichel (p. 192) believes that "actual neurotic symptoms form the nucleus of all psychoneuroses." Indeed, in the course of the organism's encounters with the environment throughout life, the ego is constantly busy meeting and taking care of stimuli, from within (id and superego) and from without. In control, it binds, allows discharge, or otherwise takes care of them, but even without the formation of actual neurosis, it is confronted with periods in which its resources are taxed, if not overrun. I have investigated such states in a study on the psychology of poise (see Chapter 4). Thus reference might be made, as a patent and uncomplicated example, to the state of being flustered. Here the suddenness of confrontation by a challenging situation catches the ego unaware, and the condition which ensues is a mild and transitory state of help-lessness. It is not long, in most instances, before the ego catches up and the helplessness is then superseded, ideally, by mastery and re-equilibrium. Where, however, the ego encounters diffi-culty in "taking care of the matter," anxiety may then occur or be admixed.

This leads to the second point. Does it follow that in these states of mild or more severe damming up, the production of anxiety is automatic, i.e., in a manner essentially different from its occurrences as a signal of danger? I think the answer must be given in the negative. What takes place automatically is the affect of unpleasure (although this too does not imply without psychic participation). When anxiety is added or admixed, it is here, as always, a reaction to danger. The danger of what? The danger that (a) the helpless state will get worse, and/or (b) it will continue and never stop. The still bearable state of inner tension will become unbearable. This matter of the quantitative factor and of the magnitude of excitation is referred to also by Freud (1933, p. 130): " It is only the magnitude of the excitation which turns an impression into a traumatic factor, which paralyzes the operation of the pleasure-pain principle and gives significance to the danger situation." Anna Freud (1936, p. 63) has given due place to the "dread of the strength of the instincts." This traumatic state, which corresponds to Rapa-port's primary model of passivity (1953b), is one in which the apparatus can neither defend nor discharge, but is overrun and can only passively endure. It may signify being abandoned to one's fate (Fenichel, 1945, p. 123) or presage annihilation. What the ego fears in states of heightened inner tension is, according to Freud (1923a, p. 85), in the nature of "an overthrow or of extinction" or, to Waelder (1930), that the ego's whole organization may be destroyed or submerged. To Melanie Klein (1946), the danger is destruction of the ego by the force of instinctual aggression. Thus the formula that anxiety is always a reaction to danger holds here as well, a formulation which concurs with the views I have quoted of Kubie (1941), Spitz (1950), Brenner (1953), Schur (1953), Greenacre (1941), and others.

The term "automatic," which has been used repeatedly in the literature in connection with this subject, has, I believe, been used loosely and deserves clarification. In the original description of the toxic transformation theory, and in its derivative residual theory today, automatic is meant to imply direct, passive, involuntary, and without psychic participation. "The anxiety . . . is not derived from any psychical source . . . [but] in the deflection of somatic sexual excitation from the psychical field, and in an abnormal use of it" (Freud 1894b, pp. 96–97). In contrast, signal anxiety is repeatedly described and referred to by Freud as being produced and used actively by the ego in accordance with its needs (1926, p. 153) and with psychological content. Blau (1952) expresses this difference most forcefully in differentiating the physiological symptoms of anxiety neurosis from the psychological symptoms of psychoneurosis. I would like to suggest that on closer inspection these views are subject to amendment. Automatic in the sense of being without psychological meaning can be applied neither to the diffuse unpleasure of the traumatic state nor to the anxiety which heralds danger. For without psychological content there can be physiological tension or discharge processes, irritable responsiveness, and automatic reflex patterns but neither the affect of unpleasure nor anxiety. Conversely, automatic in the sense of occurring involuntarily and passively applies both to the traumatic state and to signal anxiety. For in neither case does the unwelcome affect occur by choice. Just as diffuse unpleasure is an automatic accompaniment of the uncontrollable psychic tension and diffuse discharge of the traumatic state, so, when the ego perceives danger, is the anxiety an inevitable and automatic psychobiological accompaniment. The anxiety is then, to be sure, used and responded to actively as a signal, but it is not produced by the ego in the first instance. This point of view has been expressed by Fenichel (1945, p. 134), and was elaborated upon by Schur (1953). A motorman sees the red light and responds to the signal appropriately, but the red light is produced automatically by the dangerous proximity of another train. Similarly the ego's estimate of danger automatically lights up the anxiety which is then taken as a signal and responded to accordingly. This amounts to a slight restatement and modification of the signal theory itself, which heretofore has given a teleologic explanation, that anxiety is produced rather than suffered. Thus the existence of automatic mechanisms really fails to stand up as a distinguishing feature between Freud's two theories of anxiety.

These various considerations resolve the existence of the actual neurotic state with a unitary theory of anxiety, and make the two compatible. Damming up of instinctual energy is an economic dynamic condition of unpleasure, and anxiety a specific reaction to the danger which this (or any other condition of danger) entails. I submit that this formulation not only has clinical and theoretical validity but also fuses what have hitherto remained as two immiscible propositions. These were the basis for Freud's famous "non liquet" statement which he never did resolve.[1]

[1] I wish to refer here to two recently appearing papers. Since this was written, Blau (1955) extended his observations to the broader field of emotions and affects in general. While purporting to describe a unitary framework into which the various specific affects can be fitted, Blau in effect retains the same duality. Emotions and emotional symptoms are differentiated from "psychogenic" symptoms, as in his earlier formulation "neurosis" was differentiated from "psychoneurosis." The emotional component per se of affective disorders is considered to be grouped with the actual anxiety neuroses, and to consist in essence of "straightforward physiological reac-

II

To be firmly anchored into the totality of psychoanalytic metapsychology, it is necessary that anxiety be integrated into instinct theory, and also that we look in the following other directions. Keeping in mind anxiety as an affect and its seat in the ego, I may rightfully expect to advance our understanding and to obtain further definition of the concept of anxiety by integrating it into the most recent developments in the psychoanalytic theory of affects and the newest insights in ego psychology. The latter two will be taken up first.

As an affect, and indeed the main affect with which Freud dealt, anxiety belongs with a psychoanalytic theory of affects, the most definitive statement of which was recently set down by Rapaport (1953a). In the description given by the latter of the developmental phases in the psychoanalytic conceptions of affect, one can see parallel stages to those which occurred in the development of anxiety theory itself. Thus, whereas affect was first seen as equated to drive itself, "like an electric charge over the memory traces of an idea," it came to be seen later as resulting from a discharge process dependent upon and related to complex defensive structures of the ego. What takes place essentially, in Rapaport's formulation, is that, in the absence of available drive object, one of the fates of drive impulse or derivative drives (motivations) is a discharge into the interior of the organism resulting in the experience of affect. With the increase and elaboration of defensive thresholds by the developing ego, there results an increased damming up of

---

tions," upon which psychological features may be superimposed. This differentiation is at variance with the unitary concept formulated in which the psychological component of anxiety, or for that matter of any affect, either conscious or repressed, is a *sine qua non*. Blau's thesis does indeed come close to overlapping with my point of view when he separates affect, the inner subjective experience, from the outer manifestations of emotion.

In another related paper, Szasz (1961), investigating the phenomenon of pain, regards pain as an affect analogous to anxiety in its function, the one warning the ego of possible injury or loss to the body, and the other of the danger of object loss. In the genetic formulations described by this author, both these affective experiences, pain and anxiety, coincide, in their universally signal functions, with the formulations described above.

drive energy and with it an increasingly varied use of affect discharge channels. Yet, as Gitelson remarks, "Affects depend on the state of organization of the ego, from primitive to highly elaborate states. At any stage all levels may be found, and there is no need to discard earlier mechanisms of affect formation in favor of later ones" (Panel, 1952).

These considerations are directly applicable to the subject of this investigation. In the traumatic state, either before an ego has developed, or as a result of the passive overrunning of the ego even after it has taken form, there is a complete or relative inadequacy of outward discharge channels and a consequent prompt and massive, diffuse, peremptory discharge into the interior of the organism. The accompanying affect is the sensation and experience of helplessness. The development and structuralization of affect-discharge thresholds and the gradual attainment of ego control, with establishment of the ability to delay, are necessary forerunners or accompaniments in the shift to anxiety as an anticipatory signal. Further, with general maturation and with the increasing growth of psychic structure, anxiety, as other affects, changes from being attack-like to being more modulated, controlled, and effective. Fenichel (1941a, 1945, pp. 43 and 133) has described this general process as "the taming of affects." Its progression parallels the growing dominance of the reality principle and the development and ascendancy of the secondary process. When for any reason there is again weakening of ego control, for example, by sudden influx of stimuli, there can occur a reversal of this process and a regression to earlier modes. Thus either anxiety itself can become more primitive and diffuse and less controlled (the series from controlled anxiety to panic) or, in extreme instances, the anxiety can once again give way to the traumatic state, with complete loss of effective action or defense. Schur emphasizes the factor of ego regression in every anxiety experience. Jacobson (1952) delineates the importance of factors of speed and rhythm of psychic discharge processes and the role these play in affect experiences. Sudden dramatic and rapid high-tension discharges are associated with primitive affect explosions, while the mature ego is able to achieve greater tension tolerance and more low-speed controlled discharges, which go with more controlled and effective use of anxiety signals. The molding and integration of the signal anxiety pattern, Jacobson (1953a) feels, are a characteristic expression of the influence of the reality principle and of ego formation on affective development in general.

It is readily seen how the above considerations dovetail into modern concepts of ego development and structure, with which they have been seen to converge repeatedly. For signal anxiety to be the dominant mode, in controlled and regulated intensity and leading to effective counteractivity, presupposes the existence and development of a complex and effective hierarchy of defenses, a process which goes hand in hand with the binding of mobile cathexes and the progressive neutralization of drives described by Hartmann et al. (1949). In massive inundation of this complicated and sensitive apparatus by diffuse drive or affect discharge, the secondary process is threatened or overthrown, and signal anxiety is converted into the traumatic state. The same discharge channels are traversed, but the intermediate regulatory mechanisms, ego controls, give way.

This is a juncture at which we may inquire again into the long-perplexing question of the economics or source of the energy of the anxiety reaction, a question for which one should expect some explanation from any theory of anxiety which is presumed to be comprehensive. This problem, which had an unequivocal answer in the old transformation theory, where the source was considered to be directly converted libido, became more ambiguous in the later signal theory. Indeed, Freud (1926, p. 24) now felt that the causal relation between anxiety and repression "should not be explained from an economic point of view," and later (p. 112) that "my present conception of anxiety as a signal . . . does away with the necessity of considering the economic factor . . . it is no longer of any importance which portion of the general energy is employed for this purpose." However, it must certainly be the

case that anxiety as a response to danger is also always econom-
ically justified. The intensity of the anxiety reaction is in
proportion to the extent of the danger which is apprehended.
To Schur (1953) it is proportionate to the degree of ego
regression, which restores archaic situations and thus re-creates
economic conditions. Jacobson (1953a) describes the anxiety
signal as an outstanding example of temporary suspension of
the pleasure principle for superior economic purposes.

Returning to the question of the energy source, I emphasize that in the present state of our knowledge the answer to this
remains obscure and speculative. Indeed, the source of origin
of this affective defensive reaction lies in the same state of
uncertainty as the parallel question in relation to the origin of
the defense mechanisms of the ego (Anna Freud, 1936, p. 191;
Hartmann, 1950a). Nevertheless, certain possibilities do
present themselves and should be noted. Much evidence and
much thinking on this subject point to the idea of an innate,
phylogenetically determined pool of such defensive affective
energy, instinctive in contrast to instinctual, a historical precipitate of the alertness or vigilance of lower forms. Freud (1926,
p. 24) speaks of affective states in general as having "become
incorporated in the mind as precipitates of primaeval traumatic
experiences," and likens them to "the more recent and individually acquired hysterical attack." Freud also alludes to early
childhood phobias (e.g., of small animals and thunderstorms)
as being due to "vestigial traces of the congenital preparedness
to meet objective dangers which is so strongly developed in
other animals" (p. 165). These views received fresh impetus and
confirmation in the writings of Hartmann et al. (1946) in which
self-preservative activities are regarded as instinctive and pre-
formed, and both ego and id are assumed to become differentiated from the undifferentiated matrix of animal instinct. The
organism is born with the apparatus for adapting to the
"average expectable environment," and this must include, besides the sensory apparatus and other aspects of the autonomous ego, the preparedness for anxiety. Rapaport (1953a)
commenting further on these inborn affect discharge channels

and thresholds, points as evidence for these to various psycho-somatic disturbances in the first days of life, certain archaic features of childhood phobias, and again the fact that affects have been looked upon as "inherited hysterical attacks." The following quotations are also in point. Greenacre (1941) states that "the anxiety response, which is genetically determined, probably manifests itself first in an irritable responsiveness of the organism at a reflex level." And Schur (1953): "The matrix of anxiety consists of reflexes, instincts, regulatory mechanisms of our biological ancestry and the discharge phenomena of early infancy." Grinker and Robbins (1954, pp. 49–50) describe anxiety as "a direct derivative of protoplasmic irritability and animal vigilance," and also say, "Irritability is the property of all protoplasm, but the capacity of the organism to project itself into the future is only acquired late in the phylogenetic series and hence is found only in the more highly evolved animals. Anxiety in the human being is a capacity which accompanies delayed action, self-awareness, and choice among several of appropriate future responses." This corresponds in all essen-tials to the view expressed in this paper, differentiating the earliest response to trauma of diffuse irritability from the later one of anxiety, and shows that the ontogenetic development recapitulates the phylogenetic one.

The energy source of the traumatic state, of the state of diffuse uncontrolled unpleasure, is again, as stated above, the massive instinctual discharge into the interior, reverting to the original direct transformation idea. In the state of helplessness, one of the fates, and indeed the main one, of the uncontrollable rise in instinctual tension is its direct conversion, by internal discharge, into affect. When this is accompanied, as in the more differentiated state it usually is, by anxiety, it is now the ego's perception and judgment added to the uncontrolled affect which gives it its additional flavor. This is what takes place in general in anxiety as a signal. The ego's sampling of the danger situation releases the instinctive defensive reaction of tension and discharge, which, admixed with the ego's judgment of it, yields the anxiety experience. The discharge as well as the tension quality of anxiety is attested to by Jacobson (1953a), who shows that the signs and symptoms of anxiety give direct evidence that it is expressive of both. Thus, in the last analysis, anxiety in the human is the resultant of internal tension and discharge phenomena, instinctive and/or instinctual, filtering through ego faculties of perception, judgment, anticipation, and response.

The question of individual differences, of predispositions to anxiety, and of the effects of traumatic prenatal or natal influences form another and fascinating chapter which cannot be gone into here, and which has been well described, among others, by Greenacre (1941, 1945), Bergman and Escalona (1949), and Bender (1950).

Finally, to complete the orientation of anxiety into psycho-analytic theory from all possible directions, I should take notice of its relation to the theory of instincts, into which it must of necessity be centrally integrated. This relationship has already been alluded to in passing in a number of previous references, particularly in the previous discussion of the internal danger situation. Thus, the first massive inundation by stimuli at birth, which constituted the original traumatic situation, consisted of instinctual flooding from within as well as massive impingement from without. When anxiety sets in subsequently at the recognition of loss or absence of the mother, it is precisely the repetition of this economic state which is the "danger" to be avoided. The absence of the object needed for discharge will result in nongratification, and with it an increase in inner tension to an unpleasant height without the possibility of mastery or discharge (Freud, 1926, pp. 106–107). Still later, the same state of nongratification can be brought about not by the absence of apparatus to effect discharge, but by external prohibition which forces instinctual demands to be opposed. When these external oppressors are internalized later into the superego, there is then a new and constant potential deterrent and source for anxiety.

Instinctual gratification per se is not dangerous but only pleasurable; but the expression of aggressive or sexual impulses, when it conflicts with the environment, becomes an invitation to external danger, i.e., loss of love and/or castration. It is well known how an increase in the force of instincts increases the danger, either objectively or by projective animistic misunderstanding (Fenichel, 1945, pp. 63, 68, 81), so that anxiety perforce increases with increased intensity of drives. Thus an increase in aggressive impulse will effect an increased possibility of retaliation, both from external agents as well as from an aroused superego, resulting in an increased fear of these dangers. The more direct views of Melanie Klein (1946) in this connection have already been alluded to, in which the danger is considered to arise not from external retaliatory sources but from the primary destructive nature of the aggressive impulses themselves. Anna Freud has noted the primitive nature and special force of the "dread of the strength of the instincts" (1936, p. 63). Freud (1926, p. 26) points out that "the protective barrier only exists in regard to external stimuli, not in regard to internal instinctual demands." And on this same point, Schur (1953), commenting on how much better the ego is equipped to withstand outer than inner stimulation, observes: "The maturing ego has learned to meet outer danger with secondary thought processes, the use of the motor system, and that fabulous extension of our muscles—the machine. But how can we meet internal danger? We cannot shoot at low blood sugar or run away from a high pH."

With modifications of the instinct theory, the role of anxiety and with it of the theory of neurosis may undergo concomitant alterations. Thus, in a proposed revision of the theory of instincts, Brunswick (1954) would include both anxiety and defense within the instincts rather than as ego activities. Basing his classification on the biological division into sympathetic and parasympathetic nervous systems, Brunswick would divide instincts into (a) erotic or vital libidinal instincts, related to he parasympathetic nervous systems; and (b) defensive-aggressive instincts, related to the sympathetic nervous system. Under the latter, anxiety and defense are considered as much instinctual as rage and aggression, both serving the same function, i.e., protective. In a somewhat different vein, Bose (1952) considers anxiety and sexual tension identical and mutually convertible states. Anxiety is seen as a masochistic wish fulfillment, providing id gratification. The neurotic conflict always consists of a castration fear opposed to a castration wish, i.e., between the male and female components within the individual. Anxiety is the libido of the unconscious component of this contrasting pair, thus going back to Freud's original transformation theory. Waelder (1953) divides neurotic anxiety into (a) fear due to a threat to the self-preservation, and (b) anxiety resulting from a threat to the level of narcissistic satisfaction, a formulation which incidentally tends to revert to Freud's (1894, 1905b, 1915a) first division of instincts into libidinal and self-preservative ones.

A number of these modifications must bring with them a revised concept of the structure of conflict and one to which certain objections must be raised. For the conflict now comes to be between instincts, a situation which does not conform with our view of instincts as always striving for discharge nor with our knowledge that contradictions do not exist within the id. What then is the opposing force and especially what is now the motive for defense? An answer might be pointed to by Anna Freud (1936, p. 73) in her suggestion that "the mere struggle of conflicting impulses suffices to set the defense mechanisms in motion." Or might a sufficient motive be the adult ego's need for synthesis between opposing impulses, as described and documented by Alexander (in Anna Freud, 1936)? Or can it be simply the operation of the reality principle? But the need for synthesis is a relatively late development. And closer inspection will show that the reality principle is adhered to only to avoid secondary pain or anxiety (Anna Freud, 1936, p. 65), so that the latter is seen again to emerge as the true motive for defense.

In one sense, these various modifications, when they link anxiety to self-preservative and other instinctual forces, are seen to be not too distant from a number of the observations referred to above, such as those relating to the existence of inborn defenses, the primitive and instinctive origins of the anxiety reaction, and the concept of the undifferentiated ego-id matrix, from which both ego and id functions derive. To the extent, however, that these modifications alter the structure of neurotic conflict in the direction described above, and for the reasons given, these revisions in my opinion tend to weaken rather than enhance our ability to understand or explain the multiplicity of clinical phenomena. This point of view concurs with that of Fenichel's (1945, pp. 129–130) on the structure of neurotic conflict. This remains, however, an area of unsettled problems.

III

I have so far considered, with a rather microscopic view, the theoretical base, and in particular, in accordance with the genetic point of view, the question of origins. For the remaining observations I turn to the opposite end of the spectrum and reflect on the role of anxiety in the clinical situation, as the patient is before us. Here the subtle differences regarding origins become distant and the operations against anxiety assume the center of the stage. While anxiety and its surrounding phenomena constitute the objects observed, it is also the presence, or potential appearance, of anxiety which produces an ally for the therapist within the ego of the patient. For within limits, it is the presence of, or susceptibility to, anxiety which urges the patient on in the hope and direction of therapeutic progress, and serves as the track on which or alongside of which therapist and patient proceed into the areas of diffuse or loculated conflict spheres. Of course, as is so often the case, it is optimum rather than maximum or minimum intensity which is the desideratum. For a sudden overwhelming unleashing of anxiety can be a trauma causing regression and increased pathology, while its complete absence or unavailability can lead to clinical stagnation and maintenance of the status quo. Optimum and controlled amounts have the possibility of leading to insight into the mechanisms of its production, the neurotic operations against it, and hopefully the institution of more effective means. These considerations apply not only to the movement within a therapeutic process, but to the initial selection of patients as well.

At this end of the spectrum we see, not isolated or easily distinguishable phenomena, but more typically a global composite behavioral mass. The quality and quantity of the individual components, their relative proportions, and the resultant pictures vary, giving to each its characteristic stamp. What often confronts us in a clinical picture is a mixture, of anxieties, instinct derivatives, defenses, other affects, symptoms, reactions to these, and secondary elaborations. This is in keeping with the ego's need and striving for synthesis. Freud (1926, p. 167), discussing the occurrence of anxiety, pain, and mourning, points out that in the infant "certain things seem to be confused in him which will later on be separated out." We are here, however, taking note of the reverse process. Psychic products grow together. Solitary instincts become fused, single affects become compound ones and moods, mobile energies become bound, and there is the increasing hierarchy of defenses and affects described previously. Symptoms, at first sharply delineated, are pulled back into the ego and the latter bends every effort to bind them, incorporate them, and to blur the boundaries between them (Freud, 1926, pp. 33–35). The taming of primitive and infantile expressions, and the opening up of new and more complex discharge channels by the maturational process go on side by side, and result in more fused, more modulated, and more enduring states (Jacobson, 1953a).

The therapeutic process involves a destratification of this mass. In one of the earlier clinical studies, Breuer and Freud (1893–1895, p. 109) employed a descriptive account analogous to this concept. Regarding the pathogenic material as stratified in layers of different resistance potential, with the pathogenic nucleus at the core, they state that the analyst "should himself undertake the opening of the inner strata and the advancement in the radial direction, while the patient should take care of the peripheral extension." An advance radially, inwardly, takes place when a quantity of anxiety is exposed and overcome. Between such occurrences the patient moves in a concentric layer, equidistant from the center. In Chapter 2, I used a similar structural analogy, that of a wheel, in the analysis of a doll phobia; it proved an effective device for orientation both as to the psychopathological streams and the therapeutic movements.

The following brief glance into several clinical sessions will illustrate, I believe, both the factors selected above for discussion, i.e., the composite nature of the clinical picture and a therapeutic advance in the radial direction. With regard to the first of these, a patient came to an hour and described that he felt "weird." Since the evening before, he had been feeling badly, tense, anxious, sort of peculiar, heavy and upset, and yet excited and tingly, a feeling of vague hopelessness and futility, depressed, and yet, "I got up in the morning with a feeling like ecstasy—but I felt I shouldn't let myself feel it." In all, "I don't quite know how I feel," except that he felt "weird." The background associations included: a child's tale of her dog going to dog heaven; a discussion the night before of war atrocities, and of Americans shot inadvertently by their own airmen; a dream with veiled sexual content; depression and futility about certain current decisions to be made. "Weird" was seen to be compounded of: rumblings of his own aggressive hostile wishes with the accompanying affect of rage, the satisfaction accompanying the fantasied discharge of these urges, anxiety as to the consequences thereof, guilt feelings, the turning of the aggression inward (killed by our own airmen), with revival of fears of death (dog heaven), one of his prominent symptoms; also sexual excitement, anxiety again, and the struggle to keep this down, and in the background, depression and incipient symptoms of dizziness, nausea, and transient pains. The last-mentioned had been previous precursors of fainting episodes. To all these there were differing degrees of insight in this hysterical patient in the early stages of treatment.

The therapeutic task is to uncover and separate the elements, destratify, and proceed toward the pathogenic (infantile) nucleus, to establish logical syntactic connections and to reassemble the contents in a more cohesive and structurally more compatible edifice, with elimination, of course, of the neurotic components. Zetzel (1949) agrees with the above-mentioned role of anxiety in making such a therapeutically progressive direction possible. She has emphasized the importance of the capacity to achieve and tolerate anxiety in the ability to face and resolve unconscious conflicts. "With respect to the analysis of neurotic patients, this capacity of achieving and tolerating the anxiety associated with insight is of decisive importance."

Another excerpt from the same patient will serve to illustrate a perceptible movement in this therapeutic direction, perhaps from one layer of resistance potential to another, which occurs when a certain quantity and quality of anxiety are overcome. This was demonstrated by a visible expression of surprise, laughter, and relief. The father was a tyrant of severe degree, for which the patient gave continued evidence without being able to verbalize the conclusions. "Right or wrong, your father is always right" was the family motto, and the patient not only had to shake hands with him and kiss him good night each evening, but had to look as if he liked doing it. This came out when the patient insisted on shaking hands with the analyst after each hour. Unconscious death wishes against the father, converted into the patient's own fear of death, had been patently visible for some time and from many directions. On the particular occasion being described, the anxiety about this had been overcome, and the hostility toward the father had spilled over in a torrent of recognition, as well as in some direct acts. It was in the hour following this that the patient was gay, laughing, almost euphoric. Now he volunteered, "You know, there are many things I see and think about my father which I don't want to see, like—you'll think I'm a nut—but I think he has designs on my mother-in-law." (This again with a gush, with laughter, relief, and the expectation of being ridiculed.) He went on to tell of his father's "cute" ways, of his antics with the mother-in-law under the dinner table, and of how the patient, incredulous, waited to see what the father-in-law would do. The patient was now speaking on a new level. The overcoming of a quantum of anxiety had led the way.

As a final clinical observation, I should like to point to how the ego fluctuates in anxiety, poised between the primary and secondary process, between regression and attempts at restoration of control. Schur (1953) cites as examples of this the period of awakening from anxiety dreams, when the ego works to establish the domination of reality testing and secondary process. As a converse to this, two of my patients recently described that their only periods free of anxiety are for a few moments immediately upon awakening, after which they "remember" and then anxiety takes over. One of these patients wakes up normal, but in a matter of seconds he remembers that he is anxious, and feels "the butterflies" from then on. Perhaps this is a crucial moment in determining which agencies or principles are to gain ascendancy in mental life for the day. On a recent television quiz program, a 102-year-oldster came forth. Asked the recipe for his longevity, he replied, "Every morning when I get up I can either feel good or bad for the day. I decide, 'Oh, what the hell' and I decide to feel good. That's how I live long."

I would like to conclude by noting what was and was not selected for consideration out of the wide totality of this subject. The emphasis was on the present status of the theory of anxiety within the psychoanalytic framework, the divergences which exist, and an attempted synthesis of these into a unitary concept. Genetic considerations led to a special focus on the period of origins. A few general remarks were made on the role of anxiety in the clinical setting. Not considered, though by no means therefore to be taken as less vital (for each is a subject for larger investigation), were such subjects as: (a) the sequelae and derivatives of anxiety, i.e., defenses and/or symptoms; (b) physiological concomitants of anxiety, and the links into psychosomatic medicine; (c) the differentiation of other topically defined forms of anxiety, also motives of defense, as shame, guilt, and disgust; and (d) the elaborations of danger situations with the multitude of later environmental contributions.

It is hoped that this presentation, though wide, will have provided some boundaries and cohesiveness to an otherwise all-embracing subject.

CHAPTER 10

A Further Attempt to Resolve the "Problem of Anxiety"

It was no accident or matter of semantic choice that one of the translations of Freud's classic *Inhibitions, Symptoms and Anxiety* bore quite another title, *The Problem of Anxiety*. This translation, authorized by Freud, pointed to the heart and center of the work. For although Freud dealt with a wide range of crucial and central issues, with resistances, repressions, and defense, with pain and mourning as well as anxiety, with differences between realistic and neurotic anxiety, and with inhibitions and symptom formation, his central theme and preoccupation throughout were the theoretical problems involved in the genesis of anxiety itself.

Although the question of anxiety was a major concern of Freud's and appeared prominently in his writings from the beginning to the end of his work, the nature of his thinking on the subject was relatively steady, and clustered around only two major nodal, theoretical points during the whole history of its development.

Presidential address, American Psychoanalytic Association, New York, December 17, 1967. Published in *J. Amer. Psychoanal. Assn.*, 16:371–404, 1968.

The first idea appeared early, around 1894–1895. Freud's attention was first directed toward anxiety in a group of cases which he saw fit to "detach" from other cases of psychopathology and symptom formation, characterized by massive undischarged sexual tension in which anxiety was also a prominent feature (1895b). It was in these clinical cases that Freud felt he saw a source and origin and from which he ventured his first theory of anxiety. Still attached to his neurological thinking and under the influence of Fechner's biological "principle of constancy," Freud saw the cause of anxiety as due to a process of direct, toxic transformation of the excitation of the repressed, dammed-up libido into the affect of anxiety. The anxiety was automatic, a substitute for libidinal discharge and an organic process, without psychic participation. From this mechanism and genesis of anxiety, which Freud felt he detected at its origin in these cases, he extended its applicability to include the psychoneuroses generally.

I would have us note that there are a separate and discrete number of elements intrinsic to this first understanding of anxiety by Freud, which is usually overlooked and which should be borne in mind as we set out to trace the history and to arrive at a present evaluation of this subject. These are (a) the first recognition of the clinical and phenomenological association between anxiety and what came to be known later as the traumatic state; (b) the postulation of a causal connection between the two; (c) the explanation is in terms of a somatic process—but, it is to be noted, *only* a somatic process; and (d) the specific mechanism described, the "how" of the transformation, i.e., a direct one-to-one change of the repressed libido into anxiety. It will be important for what follows to keep these individual insights and their separate vicissitudes clearly differentiated.

But it was the specific mechanism of direct transformation which gave this theory its central stamp and determined its future fate. A static and narrow concept, without a place for a psychological motive, it may have impeded more than it helped and failed to radiate any profound psychological meaning to other or wider areas. Nor did any technical precepts stem from it, except that it implicitly supported the technical emphasis on the search for instinctual discharge, catharsis, and abreaction. It is of historical interest that although this formulation lacked the luster as well as the ring of conviction of the other concomitant and dramatic discoveries of psychoanalysis, this explanation held away for some 30 years. It is also of interest that during this long nascent and developing period, no other of the growing number of analysts seriously challenged, advanced, or essentially altered this prevailing view. An exception was Ernest Jones (1953–1957), who stated "As early as 1910 I had criticized this unbiological view and maintained that anxiety must proceed from the ego itself, but Freud would not listen and only changed his opinion when he approached the subject in his own way sixteen years later" (vol. 3, p. 255). It would have been more appropriate, however, as it turned out later, to have quarreled not so much with its unbiological principles as with its unpsychological nature.

It was Freud himself who, in the fertile spurt of the late '20s and early '30s, contributed a major shift in the total theoretical position, resulting in new dimensions, broader vistas, and a new central orientation. Along with the shift from the topographic to the structural point of view, a significant addition to instinct theory, and a more meaningful separation of the ego from the id, came, in 1926, his new presentation of the genesis and psychological meaning of anxiety. To condense the essence of this classic contribution, instead of a result of the traumatic state, anxiety was now seen as a signal of its approach. The anxiety reaction was no longer automatic, a direct transformation of libido, or physical-toxic in origin. It now had psychological meaning, was a function of the ego, where it resided, and was produced and used by the latter in controlled amounts to serve as a signal of the approach of danger, which was an impending or potential traumatic state. I only mention here the corresponding new orientations in technique which followed in the wake of these theoretical changes, which have been abundantly written about and discussed on other occasions. This new orientation became the center of technical operations, with the analyst now in a neutral position vis-à-vis the three interacting psychic structures, analyzing the components of intrapsychic conflicts and the specific causes and outcomes of anxiety.

It is well known, however, that Freud did not make this shift easily, nor was he able to reconcile completely the two quite different theories and approaches. We have it from Strachey (1926) that he continued to be troubled and that he "found an unusual difficulty in unifying the work." Both theories, though they could not be easily fused, were somehow felt to be applicable and necessary. At the end of the fourth chapter, after having presented, reviewed, and compared the two theories side by side, and tried "to reduce the two sources of anxiety to a single one," he concluded, with one of the most famous of his typical succinct formulations, *"Non liquet"* (p. 110).

It is generally considered, however, that Freud, after a long devotion to his first theory, came to terms with the change and gave up the last vestiges of his former ideas. Thus, according to Strachey, "This last relic of the old theory was to be abandoned a few years later" (p. 80), while Jones states, "This belief, however, he also discarded seven years later" (vol. 3, p. 255). Both were referring to the same statement in the *New Introductory Lectures* (1933), when, writing again on the anxiety neurosis, Freud stated, "We shall no longer maintain that it is the libido itself that is turned into anxiety in such cases" (p. 94). In a footnote to this, Strachey similarly stated, "With the present sentence the last trace of the old theory is abandoned." I would point out, however, that this was by no means the case. In the sentence which follows, Freud (1933) goes on, "But I can see no objection to there being a twofold origin of anxiety—one as a direct consequence of the traumatic moment and the other as a signal threatening a repetition of such a moment" (p. 94f.). A conflicting central *mechanism* was withdrawn, but not Freud's continuing belief in a twofold *origin*. This opinion Freud neither withdrew nor did he ever solve to his own satisfaction.

Nor did he ever offer an alternative explanation to that which had been removed. Freud was to remain with this unsettled view for the remainder of his life and was never able to fuse the two lines of thinking in a way satisfactory to himself or others.

It is solely to this question and dilemma to which I wish to restrict the remainder of my remarks on this occasion. While this may seem like concentrating on a very minute psychic occurrence in the larger view of human behavior and one which has already received its share of attention for some 40 years, I feel that turning the high power onto this small area has a great deal of merit. In a theory in which great pride is taken in its elegance of concept, clarity, consistency, and parsimony, it would seem that an element at its very core should be its brightest star. Instead Jones characterizes this central work of Freud's as a "discursive book, with little of the incisiveness we expect from Freud" (vol. 3, p. 254), and Strachey comments on Freud's special difficulty, atypical for him, of "tidying it up." Benjamin (1963) characterizes this work "as among the most cautious, empirical, and uncertain of Freud's major theoretical writings" (p. 122), and Schur (1958) attributes the "confusion" to the "atmosphere of utmost urgency" and pressure under which it was written, Freud being then 70 and seriously ill.

While my point of emphasis may seem to be an overconcern about a minor kink, it appears to me to be comparable to an organic defect which, while only an inch or less long, nevertheless happens to be on the aortic or mitral valve, in the very heart of the organism. Moreover, as is always the case, we can anticipate that clarification of such a central theoretical consideration may well prove to have definite clinical relevance and usefulness. Certainly, if this central issue is to be laid to rest, it would be better, for practical and theoretical reasons, that it be put away in a settled rather than an unsettled condition. This presentation has as its goal the hope that this may be achieved.

In my previous paper on the subject (see Chapter 9), I described a "unitary theory of anxiety" based on retaining certain selected and valid elements of Freud's two overlapping theories and an attempted fusion of the two. In summary, the

state of actual or anxiety neurosis as observed and described by
Freud was seen clinically and phenomenologically as the traumatic state, the state of psychic helplessness or of being overrun
by stimuli. As such its presence was attested to not so much as
a separate entity, but in "a definitive and significant series of
clinical events," as a transitory occurrence during certain common situations in life, and during the transitional stages of
development of every psychoneurotic symptom. That anxiety
occurs and is universally produced under such conditions is a
relevant and valid observation. But Freud's second theory, of
anxiety as a signal of danger, was considered to cover the
situation here as well. The anxiety generated under these
conditions, however, is not a result of a direct transformation of
repressed libido, is not a toxic or organic process without
psychological meaning, or without ego participation, but is a
signal of danger just as in every other instance of its occurrence.
The dammed-up state, or state of psychic helplessness, when it
actually exists, is also a danger, the danger being that it will get
worse or never stop, and that relative insufficiency will proceed
to complete motor and psychic paralysis. Finally, the descriptions of "automatic" and "direct," which were applied by Freud
to the phenomena of the first theory in contradistinction to the
second, were more carefully defined and applied. "Automatic"
in the sense of being without psychic meaning or participation
applied neither to traumatic nor to signal anxiety, while "automatic" in the sense of passive, direct, and involuntary applied to
both. Thus anxiety as a signal of danger, just as in the first
theory, is suffered passively and automatically, although in a
mitigated form, rather than being *produced* actively by the ego.
To be sure, it is then *used* by the ego in an active sense, to be
followed either by instinctual discharge or by repression or
other defense.

   This, in brief, was my version of a fusion and integration of
the valid elements of both theories, rather than an elimination
of one in favor of the second. For the most part the insights of
the second theory were applied to cover the first as well, while

indelible aspects of the first were preserved and necessary modifications in both were suggested.

In a paper which unfortunately turned out to be his last, Robert Waelder (1967a) brings this important subject up to date, and gives us a retrospective view 40 years after he first reviewed Freud's work on anxiety on invitation for a small study group which met in Freud's home. In an assessment today of this central problem, which he touched upon among many others, Waelder acknowledged my formulation just given as "particularly interesting." While he went on, however, neither to confirm nor to discard these views, the extent to which he found them persuasive can be gleaned from his conclusion at the end of the paper: "The attempt to construct a unified theory of anxiety, encompassing both anxiety as a consequence of dammed-up libido and anxiety as a signal of danger, has not been successful, and most analysts do not feel a need for such a unified theory in the first place because they do not believe in the existence of the first type of anxiety."

Spurred by this view, and having been stimulated by many subsequent thoughts and new material in the course of the dozen years since my previous paper, I would like to use this occasion as an opportunity to bring my formulations up to date. Toward this end some of my previous thinking will be repeated, but hopefully strengthened and clarified, with new material and dimensions added. Mainly, however, while my former presentation concentrated chiefly on the influence and applicability of the second theory on the first, the other side of the coin will be to add now the effects and relevance of some of the formulations of the first theory to that of the second. Such an integration, I believe, can help round out the picture and fuse the whole into a unified theory. In doing this I shall also borrow from several relevant papers written during the interim.

To turn first to the question which I discussed in my previous paper, of the very existence of the clinical state upon which Freud based his first theory, I would like to add new aspects and thoughts to those already given. First, I would have us clearly differentiate Freud's observation of the state as a

clinical and phenomenological entity from his explanation of
the mechanism of the occurrence of anxiety within it, for in this
differentiation lies the avoidance of a repetition of traps and
dead ends. Regarding the existence of this dynamic economic
state, I argued in my previous paper for its undeniable existence phenomenologically within the observable clinical spectrum and the daily clinical experience of every practicing
analyst. This state, to which Freud attached the label of "actual
neurosis" (a semantic term which has contributed its share to
the confusion), is today, by common agreement, and from
Freud's repeated descriptions of it in other contexts, the
well-known traumatic state, dammed-up state, state of mounting psychic tension, of being overrun by stimuli, and affectively
accompanied by feelings of frustration, loss of control, and
psychic helplessness. In today's view, thanks to Hartmann
(1950a), we would describe these more definitively as states of
mounting intrasystemic as well as intersystemic tension. Strachey (1926) puts it explicitly: "The traumatic situation itself is
clearly the direct descendant of the state of accumulated and
undischarged tension in Freud's earliest writings on anxiety" (p.
81), and illustrates the continuity from 1894 to the day of
writing between Freud's description of the traumatic situation
at present and previously described states of accumulated
excitations, undischarged tensions, and psychic helplessness,
resulting from tensions of physical as well as psychological
(libidinal then) nature. From this point of view, and to
Waelder's assertion (1967a) that I am "one of the very few
analysts who actually believes in the existence of *Aktualneurose*,"
I would ask whether there is any analyst who does *not* believe in
the existence of this psychic traumatic state? It is this identity
which I aver and on the basis of which I would maintain that
Freud's clinical observations are to be maintained and concurred in. Freud's actual or anxiety neurosis, called today by
other names, is this presenting clinical picture, not the explanation of the genesis of anxiety which he drew from it.

   And is not the clinical association of anxiety with this state
of helplessness also a common and routine observation today?

The connection, along with his theoretical deduction of a causal relationship between the two, were both essential ingredients of Freud's first series of observations on anxiety. Far from being dropped, this clinical state is today attested to by everyday clinical experience. Fenichel (1945, p. 187) gives ample space to the existence of this "tension state," which he even refers to as anxiety or actual neurosis, either as an occurrence in and of itself, or during the course of symptom formation along the entire spectrum of psychoanalytic symptoms. "Actual neurotic symptoms form the nucleus of all psychoneuroses," he states (1945, p. 192), and describes the direct and indirect manifestations, and the positive and negative effects by which they make their clinical appearance. Schur (1963), noting the clinical importance of the state of sexual frustration in phobic patients, states: "this undeniable fact was the basis for Freud's concept of an actual neurosis," and "The clinical observation is pertinent, and the importance of the 'dammed-up state' should not be overlooked." He also notes the existence in phobic patients of "tension pleasure."

Waelder, in spite of disavowing the existence of actual neurosis, repeatedly gives evidence of his belief in the existence as well as the dangers of such a tension state. "The observation of the first and simplest situations which may be considered as dangerous, say a small child being left alone, gives us a penetrating insight into the essence of danger; it is the condition of non-gratification and with it the growth of tensions resulting from ungratified needs" (1967a, p. 5f.). Or, again uncertain about the very existence of this state, and partly along the lines which I have just described, Waelder states, "But whether or not *Aktualneurose* exists, it seems to me that there are *phenomenological* characteristics of neurotic anxiety—a kind of frustraneous excitement—which remind us of some sexual manifestations so that the possibility of relationship between anxiety and sexuality should not be so easily dismissed" (p. 24). In a paper which is extraordinarily fertile on all other broader aspects of anxiety, Waelder repeats the contradictory views and inconsistencies which have characterized this one central question since its inception. And here the error is made again, which is so regularly fallen into, of automatically combining the existence of the clinical state with the *explanation* of anxiety which came along with it. Similarly, in spite of Waelder's assertion about little belief in its existence, he and others have misgivings about allowing Freud's first theory to sink into oblivion. Anna Freud (1968) also expressed the thought that we should look again into the relationship between anxiety and repressed sexuality. But here again is the same trend, of moving automatically beyond the averred and valid phenomenology to the implicit assumption that with it must go the specific mechanism which Freud in his early thinking assigned to it, i.e., the theory of direct transformation of anxiety from repressed sexuality itself. Moreover, the connection is made specifically to sexual impulses even though the theory of instincts has since been changed and enlarged. Freud had at other times referred to physical tensions as well as libidinal ones (1950, p. 93), and later, in another connection, "what we have come to see about the sexual instincts applies equally . . . to the other ones, the aggressive instincts" (1933, p. 110). In this instance, however, it is as though Freud's original connection has been transmitted it its total form, as though only all or none of it is likely to be valid. Such will not turn out, in my opinion, to be the case. To look again into the connection between anxiety and instinctual flooding, I suggest, would have been a more accurate way of putting it and a more productive pointer.

I would state, therefore, that Freud's actual or anxiety neurosis, called today by other names, exists clinically, in spite of a widespread assumption of the opposite, and consists of the clinical combination of psychic helplessness and anxiety, without having to agree with Freud's original explanation of the anxiety which went with it. The neurosis is the clinical state and not its explanation. Freud himself, it will be remembered, also came to a separation between the two, retaining the clinical state and the origin of anxiety within it, but giving up his explanation of the specific mechanism of its genesis.

Before going into the matter of an alternative explanation,

I would like to make a few brief comments on another phenomenological aspect. While accepting the existence of this clinical dynamic state, I would disagree with Freud regarding it as a distinct clinical nosological entity and his "justification for detaching a particular syndrome: anxiety neurosis" (1895b) from the remainder of psychoneurotic psychopathology. It is rather a dynamic-economic state, with varying fates, during the course and vicissitudes of the evolving intrapsychic process. I have described how this state of mounting intrapsychic tension occurs as a transient psychoeconomic condition during the genesis of any other type of psychoneurotic symptom formation, as well as during the course of the normal intrapsychic process even when symptom formation is not to be an outcome. Jones means the same, although he uses somewhat different language, when, in discussing actual neuroses, he states that these are "conditions which are now generally regarded as syndromes rather than independent neurotic affections" (vol. 3, p. 255).

Fenichel (1945) also regards this tension state as a way station occurring in early stages during the formation of other definitive syndromes. Schur (1963) describes the direct and derivative effects of the dammed-up state in phobics as well as in other symptom outcomes. In more normal variations, I described the state of "being flustered" as a transient, relatively mild, and reversible psychoeconomic condition during the course of ordinary interpersonal relationships, based on a temporary inundation with uncontrollable stimuli with a resultant lack of mastery during the course of such social interchange. More severe effects of such sudden ego-dystonic psychic episodes can be felt subjectively as feeling shattered, broken up, crushed, humiliated, fragmented, or mortified under certain specific conditions. These can still be temporary and short-lived states, albeit severe ones, during the course of rapid and fluctuating intrapsychic events. There also are chronic conditions of such internal and traumatic undischarged and unmastered tensions, more akin to the cases described by Freud. Such patients are hypermotor, agitated, pace and feel like "bursting from within," over a sustained period of time. But rather than comprising a distinct and separate entity, these more chronic and pathological instances of damming up serve to alert us to the same dynamic mechanisms operating in milder and more transient instances across the patient spectrum.

To turn now to the specific theoretical explanation of anxiety itself as first given by Freud, its historic influence on the rest of the theory, and an evaluation of its current status, I would say that Freud's *general* insights into this segment of psychopathology, and the theoretical deductions from them which should be lasting ones, tended to be cast aside as a result of his early associated hunch, which proved to be a miscalculation, about the *specific* theory of the genesis of anxiety. It was this latter theory, of the direct one-to-one transformation of the repressed libidinal excitation into anxiety, which led to the persistent quandary on the part of Freud, apathy on the part of others, lack of progress, and finally was to be given up. In addition to its elimination of a psychological role, which led to complications in applying it to other psychopathological states, such as obsessions and phobias, Jones (1929b, p. 298) also referred to its being at "variance with the biological theory of instincts," and objected to "a radical transformation" on these grounds. Based on the physical principle of constancy of the time, it was the specific formulation of a direct equation between the repressed and undischarged sexual energy and the quantum of anxiety which emerged, which Freud unequivocally later renounced. His continued perplexity, however, and his continuing to advocate a twofold origin, stemmed from his failure to be convinced of the inapplicability of other aspects of his original thinking.

A new explanation had to be found for the old as well as new observations. A rider which had missed the mark, attached to an area of important discoveries, had tended to invalidate the latter. What Freud observed and discovered about psychic trauma and its relation to anxiety, which was not only valid but which, in my opinion, was a road toward his future discoveries, was negated by his subsequent misjudgment about the specific mechanism relating the two. I would have us reverse the trend to consider this as all one theory, and instead distinguish the separate ingredients, keep what is valuable, and alter what needs modification. Even the rider, I shall attempt to show, needs not a totally different but a clearer look.

Freud's signal theory was the flash of insight which changed the whole picture and gave it its new look. This was never received with apathy, never became controversial, was never opposed on any serious theoretical basis even by those most skeptical of psychoanalytic theory as a whole. It had more of the ring of conviction, and brought with it more of the "aha" phenomenon, more of the "of course" reaction, than perhaps any other theoretical construct or any single element of what Freud called the "witch metapsychology." His new, simple, but global explanation of anxiety fitted in equally with ordinary observations and common sense, as it did in explaining the most irrational products of uncommon sense, in understanding the concrete, and in fulfilling the criteria for the most abstract thinking. It applied and superimposed the logic of secondary process thinking to the illogic of the primary process and unified and integrated the two.

While Freud supplied a new answer for a wider scope of observations and data, he did not feel that it covered the old as well. Signal anxiety was immediately seen by him, and acknowledged by all, to cover the sequence of operations of the ego when in control, to apply to functioning of the ego when it was confronted by a threat which it could in general contain, whether this led eventually to adaptive behavior or to symptom formation. But the reservation which continued to bother Freud was, in his view, its failure to apply to those old formerly observed situations in which the ego had been overrun, where in some way the "traumatic moments [each time] . . . construct their anxiety afresh" (1933, p. 94), i.e., on a model different from a signal which stems from a memory of past events. Here, since anxiety certainly was present, another origin and expla-

nation seemed to Freud to be necessary. What this was, *in lieu* of
the old theory, Freud never came up with.

But Freud's persistent refusal to erase all of the old
formulations, far from being obstructionistic, preserved for us
what I now hope to show was a necessary part of the final work
without which the latter would be incomplete. The attempted
"solutions" to this dilemma have taken various forms. Mostly, as
Waelder attested and himself largely felt, there is considered to
be no problem, since Freud's *entire* original construct of the
actual or anxiety neurosis was deemed a false lead and as such
is seen as not to exist. This simple and reassuring view, as I said
before, violates continuing clinical facts and experience. This
view is fortified to some extent by a corresponding belief that
Freud himself recanted his entire theory. To these, a unitary
and exclusive theory of signal anxiety exists by default of the
other. To some few others, however, a continuing feeling is left
that something of the original formulation still needs explaining. Mostly this leads to a backward look toward Freud's entire
first theory, including specifically the linkage to sexuality itself,
which invariably leads to the same confrontation and dead end
as when Freud dropped his theory of direct transformation,
and again a feeling of truce, no solution, two sets of seemingly
contradictory factors existing at once, and again *"non liquet."*

I wish to present a suggested solution which I first advanced in Chapter 9 and which I would now like to carry
further. I believe, with these latter and with Freud's final view,
that two separate and distinct clinical dynamic states exist in
which there is a need for an explanation of the anxiety which
occurs. But I also believe, on a path different from that taken
by Freud and looked back to by Waelder (1967a), Anna Freud
(1968), and others, that there can be one consistent and unified
theoretical explanation which can satisfactorily and totally
explain the facts of both—and that this unified explanation
combines certain elements of both of Freud's two historical
theories of anxiety.

The link between the two comes from elucidating and
clarifying the connection between the traumatic state and

anxiety. Once having been recognized and established as caus-
ally linked in Freud's first theory, and having gone through
several vicissitudes of explanation since then, it remains to
explain this link satisfactorily and from all directions to encompass fully the mechanism of the formation of anxiety. To
complete this circle it will be necessary to see how insights from
each theory are necessary to clarify and explain obscure areas
of the other.

To start this line of reasoning, when Freud withdrew his
first explanation of anxiety in favor of his second theory, the
latter was conceived of not as explaining the first series of
observations but as a new and wider set, in which anxiety
anticipated dangers in the future rather that reacting to them
in the present. This left the former *observations* still in need of
an alternative explanation. It was on this basis that Freud
retained his thought of there still being a twofold origin,
although the alternative explanation was never forthcoming.
The second theory did not, in Freud's opinion, cover the
observations of the first, which was the reason for his "*non
liquet.*" While this new explanation erased the previous one, in
doing so it left the situation in states of *existing* trauma unac-
counted for.

Some solved this dilemma by denying or negating Freud's
first set of observations. Brenner (1953), in a tightly reasoned
argument on this central issue, questions the automatic connection between the dammed-up traumatic state and anxiety. He
concludes, on the basis of his own clinical experience as well as
a review of the literature by Freud and others, that there is "no
satisfactory evidence in favor of the existence of such a clinical
entity." It was to this point that my first paper on anxiety
concentrated its main theme, maintaining that the original
situation did exist, but that Freud's second theory of anxiety as
a signal of danger applied to and explained it as well. It was an
incorrect assumption, in my opinion, that Freud's new theory of
anxiety as a signal of danger eliminated the connection to the
presence of danger itself. It was as though Freud's insights into
the role of anxiety, and of the ego, in anticipating a traumatic

situation, were unconnected with, and indeed superseded and disposed of, his concern about what happens in the actual traumatic situation when it is here, either as in his original chronic cases or when it appears suddenly under other conditions.

To come now to what I propose as the alternative explanation, and one which will explain both sets of conditions, anxiety is *always* a signal of danger, and the explanation of the second theory extends and flows over the conditions of the first. Anxiety in the presence of a traumatic state is still automatic and direct, but is also in its essence a signal of danger. And why not? Is not an existing and "actual" (that word again) traumatic situation as much of a danger as a potential one? In fact, why not a greater danger? Is an automobile accident which *may* happen a danger, while one which is happening or has just happened is not? Is the ego, if it is still alive, no longer afraid? Does not the danger exist and continue in both? Why does the same logic which applies to the one not apply equally to the other? This seems to me to be an incontrovertible position. Indeed, my surprise is that this point of view seems to have been so overlooked and to need so much belaboring.

The danger in trauma is in its continuing, or getting worse, or never stopping, and, in its worst form, of its eventually overrunning the resources of the ego to the point of its extinction. Freud rightly distinguished a traumatic situation from a danger situation. The former is the latter come true. But the presence of a traumatic situation, whether anticipated or by surprise, also serves as the start of another danger situation, which continues until the trauma either disappears or is brought under control. In his final *Outline* (1940, p. 16), Freud states, "An increase in unpleasure which is expected and foreseen is met by a *signal of anxiety*." But such an increase, in fact an increasingly spiraling one, is expected, foreseen, and therefore feared *in the midst* of every traumatic situation, during which time the ego's defenses and resources are being overrun and are therefore in a fluid and uncertain state. This is why traumatic states are always associated with anxiety (as in Freud's first theory), which, however, here as always, signals, heralds, and warns against danger (from the second theory).

But the opposite is also true, and will help us round out and close this important circle. While traumatic states are always an origin of anxiety, anxiety is also always preceded by the experience of a traumatic state, either large and present, or small and potentially larger. Both are signals of worse to come. In the explanation given thus far, the insights of the second theory are seen to extend and apply to the observations of the first. Now an approach from the opposite direction, to show how an observation from the first can help explain an obscure area in the second, will be seen to converge and coalesce with the first. This has to do with a closer and more microscopic look at what takes place during the intrapsychic sequence of events in the course of bringing about the anxiety signal.

In Chapter 7, I pointed out that anxiety as a signal is preceded by and is a result of a wider preliminary signal process as follows. The ego, confronted with increasing instinctual tension pressing for discharge, by regulating defensive thresholds permits a small sample trial discharge to take place. It is based on the results of this that its subsequent actions depend. Either there will be the likelihood of mastery and therefore the possibility of further and adequate discharge or—and here comes the point of interest—a small traumatic state ensues, commensurate with the amount of discharge which had been permitted by the ego. This traumatic state, by eliciting a memory of previous trauma with which it is compared, results in the ego's judgment of its future potential if further discharge were to be permitted. This results in an awareness of danger on the part of the ego, which automatically brings on the anxiety signal.[1] The feared trauma, the antici-

---

[1] This cognitive function of the ego in anticipating the feared danger is not minimized by the importance of the affective experience being described and is at the center of this series of operations. The cognitive function is applied to the experimental affective experience. It is this which led Freud to compare signal anxiety with the function of thought as experimental action. Schur (1953, 1958) stresses this same cognitive function, this "thoughtlike awareness of danger," at the center of signal anxiety, and shows how this

pated unabsorbable excess of stimuli, will come either from disapproval by the external world, or from loss of love from the superego, and/or, as a result of either of the above, from an inability to cope further with the instinctual demands, resulting in the "dread of the strength of the instincts" (Anna Freud, 1936, p. 63). Any or all of these states, in their qualitative and quantitative aspects, are sampled and experienced by the testing ego and reacted to accordingly.

From the above sequence I would stress the following: the fact that a traumatic state precedes and brings on the signal anxiety is qualitatively the identical mechanism as in the instance of Freud's first described cases, in which anxiety also followed and accompanied a traumatic state. And here too, as in the first cases, the ego does not produce or create the actual occurrence of the anxiety, as Freud postulated in his second theory, but suffers and experiences it passively. The anxiety is as much automatic and involuntary here as it was in connection with Freud's first theory. Schur (1953, 1967), Fenichel (1945, p. 134), Benjamin (1961a), and others support this view against a teleological and anthropomorphic explanation. What the ego permits, produces, and controls actively is the quality and quantity of instinctual discharge. What follows later, either anxiety or the lack of it, the ego experiences and judges. It is actually only the instinctual discharge, not the trauma or the anxiety, which the ego experienced passively and uncontrollably in the past and now repeats actively in a weakened and regulated version. The trauma, and then the resultant anxiety, come about in their turn relentlessly, inexorably, and automatically, depending on the character and degree of the instinctual impulses which have been turned on, their capacity to elicit counterdangers (from superego or external world), and the resources of the ego to cope with the results. It is, as Schur (1953, p. 89) puts it, an "automatic ego response to a traumatic situation." The ego turns on the faucet and controls the

---

signal function can apply to other affective states as well. Zetzel (1965) has pointed to a similar mechanism operative in the depressive spectrum.

amount, but does not and cannot know whether the water will come out hot or cold. If the water comes out hot, it experiences it, and acts further according to what it finds out, judges, and anticipates.

Waelder (1967a), in also looking into the interior of the ego's reaction to danger, similarly tries to counteract the trend toward teleological explanations, to return to Freud's earlier and more satisfying modes of finding causal mechanisms of behavior, and to search for "ultimate, irreducible constructs." In this vein, not satisfied with the explanation given heretofore by Freud and others that "the ego *anticipates* future events," Waelder (p. 17) feels that a question still remains: "the implicit ability of the ego to anticipate still contains the whole secret: how does the ego do the anticipating?" The answer to this crucial question, I believe, at least with respect to the phasic *psychological* components, is the succession of intrapsychic events just described. The sequence which Freud gives (1926, p. 166), anxiety—danger—helplessness (trauma) is only half the story, i.e., the events which follow the perception of anxiety. The latter is preceded by a preliminary sequence, actually the reverse of the above, which tells its *origin*. The total sequence then can be described as follows: tentative instinctual discharge—mild helplessness (mild trauma)—perception of danger—anxiety—continued awareness of danger—fear of greater helplessness (greater trauma). This sequence then leads to the ego's operations of defense or selective discharge in accordance with the goal of the pleasure principle. This description answers Waelder's question as to how the ego does its anticipating, fits in with our view of the ego as a tester and censor, and moves from the teleological to a causal explanation in a manner more consonant with our concepts of the rest of psychic functioning.

Thus, proceeding from opposite directions, we have come to a unified view that anxiety, which is always a signal of the danger of psychic trauma, is also always a reaction to its presence. The latter varies from a small minimal token amount, brought on by the ego in a controlled and experimental way, to a moderate or larger degree of already-present helplessness, which has overrun the ego from outside of its control (from instinctual impulses or the external world). The anxiety experience is the same in both, and in both it is a signal of danger ahead, of a worse condition impending or potential. Freud's final verdict of a twofold origin thus has proven to hold. But no other than the one mechanism with which he was left is necessary or valid. The results of the two approaches converge into one: two origins, which can set off the one mechanism, explain all the observable facts.

Strangely, I must express a feeling both that none of this is new and yet that it has never been said before. In the rich, abundant, and thoughtful literature which exists on this subject, all of this and much more has been said in various pieces many times before. And yet I feel that it has never been unified, all put together, or satisfactorily concluded. Either essential parts of Freud's first series of thoughts are left out (I say "series" instead of "theory" deliberately), or, if included, have always become part of an unanswered puzzle. The formulation given here, I suggest, is inclusive and explanatory. Yet in certain respects, particularly in relation to elements of Freud's first theory, there are in most cases distinct differences. And in no other instance is the total integrated theory exactly the same.

Thus Freud, later Waelder and others, were repeatedly close to this formulation, but for reasons which I cannot understand, since they expressed inclinations and beliefs in this direction, were never quite on it. Freud (1933, p. 89) spoke of the ego sampling "an emerging instinctual demand" as a result of which "the automatism of the pleasure-unpleasure principle . . . now carries out the repression of the dangerous instinctual impulse" (p. 90). But the intervening step is not spelled out, which would have linked his two theories satisfactorily, i.e., that this sampling first causes the unpleasure of the helpless traumatic state, from which, as in his first theory, anxiety is again the result. It is the experience of this state which causes the ego to "conjure up one of the well-remembered situations of danger" (p. 89). Elsewhere, in a formulation even closer to the point, "The ego, which experienced the trauma passively, now repeats it actively in a weakened version, in the hope of being able itself to direct its course" (1926, p. 167). Here the trauma is explicitly recognized as an intervening phase, yet its implications for a unified theory are not extracted. Coming from the opposite direction, i.e., that of his first theory, Freud similarly fails to traverse the final step. Instead, when again on the verge of an explanation which would have merged his two theories: "It will not be easy to reduce the two sources of anxiety to a single one. We might attempt to do so by supposing that [in the case of undischarged sexual excitation] . . . the ego scents certain dangers to which it reacts with anxiety" (p. 110), he instead veers off with: "But this takes us nowhere"(!). It would, in my opinion, have taken him somewhere. It would have unified his two theories and solved the puzzle which was with him from then on. Schur notes this same point as one of closeness on the part of Freud to a coherent unitary theory, saying, in one paper (1953, p. 89), "The explanation was given—but not accepted by Freud himself—when he said: [and then gives the same quote as just given above]"; and in another paper (1958, p. 193), "Freud came quite close to a unitary theory of anxiety when he said: [same quote] . . . , but he rejected his own interpretation in the same paragraph by saying 'non liquet.' " There are other inconsistencies which make for the lack of "incisiveness" with which Jones characterizes this work. Anxiety is in some places "a reaction" of the ego, or "a response" of the ego, and yet elsewhere "is produced," or "reproduced," or "given by," "evoked," or "put into action" by the ego, etc. Here again the former formulations are closer to the point: a reaction or response to what? The answer must be: to the danger of a traumatic state, which has just been sensed, in a minimal way.

Waelder (1967a) demonstrates the same closeness to and yet shifting stands on this minute but crucial point. "The ego *anticipates* future events and samples the unpleasure of a future catastrophe in small doses—the anxiety signal" (p. 17). Here the anxiety is equated with the "unpleasure" of the trauma itself, contrary to a sequence come to by Freud and by Waelder many

other times, that the unpleasure is not the anxiety but leads to
it. It is no different here than in Freud's original anxiety
neurosis, where the unpleasure of the state of psychic helplessness then led to or resulted in the anxiety. "The ego . . .
samples the unpleasure," Waelder states in the quote just given,
but again, like Freud, instead of this unpleasure being explicitly
noted as a small traumatic state which then *produces* the anxiety,
it is referred to as the anxiety signal itself. The explicit
identification of this intervening step, the experiencing of a
small traumatic state prior to the onset of the anxiety signal, is
what answers remaining questions and introduces a sought-for
consistency. It is a traumatic state, here as in Freud's first
theory, which, by conjuring up danger, goes on to, produces, or
in some way is converted into anxiety.

    With regard to the fact that this point is so much there and
yet had remained so elusive, I recall a discussion which I believe
is relevant to this. This had to do with a difference of opinion
which developed as to the amount of trauma or helplessness
necessary to call it "trauma." It was interesting that here, too,
Waelder expressed a preference, at least at first, to limit trauma
to "real trauma," i.e., to big and catastrophic events, "in the
sense of the old days." A division seemed to shape up between
older analysts who held out for such "real" and big traumas and
the "younger" analysts who preferred a spectrum from such
overwhelming traumatic states at one end to states of relative
and milder helplessness at the other. The latter would include
"the minor traumas of everyday life" which explain and are
behind "the anxieties of everyday living." Trauma would then
range from feeling flustered, through being shattered, to the
frozen immobility in the face of extreme and catastrophic
events. And it was Waelder who, although giving voice to his
taste and preference, recalled and contributed Freud's own
examples, quoted earlier in this paper, of a child whose mother
left the room (1926, p. 136), or who missed someone he loved
(1905b, p. 224), as demonstrating the same basic principles
regarding trauma as occur in a more dramatic event. Perhaps,
however, it was just such a disinclination toward equating or

linking a small with a major trauma which prevented both Freud and Waelder from explicitly singling out the small traumatic state as a prelude to small "signal" anxiety—a formulation and insight which in my opinion would have helped unite the two theories, which both felt needed to be united.

The renewed emphasis given here on the role of the traumatic state in anxiety also makes room for the contribution of the id in the production of anxiety. Both the pressing instinctual impulses and the testing and anticipating functions of the ego play a part, and although the final reaction resides in the ego, id components are included in the final product. This fits in with Waelder's (1967a) pointing to Freud's preference for the concept of fluid boundaries between id and ego, with "constant traffic or migration back and forth." The traumatic state contributes the id effects of undischarged instinctual pressures, while the ego adds the cognitive components of judgment, awareness, and anticipation of the future. Brunswick (1954, 1967) has also pointed to the drive components in anxiety, but he includes the latter totally within the orbit of instinctual drives. Thus, in a suggested revised schema and classification, Brunswick would regard anxiety as belonging within a class of "defensive-aggressive instincts." Many of the functions of defense currently assigned to the ego are considered by him to be instinctual in nature and origin. Schur (1958) considers the discharge phenomena of anxiety, which are "manifestations of the affect charge," to be id contributions, whereas the affect of anxiety itself is an ego reaction. A statement by Freud in his final *Outline* (p. 108) expresses his view of the parts played by each: "The id knows no . . . anxiety; or it would perhaps be more correct to say that, though it can produce the sensory elements of anxiety, it cannot make use of them." And completing the thought of a few pages later (p. 111), "[the ego] makes use of sensations of anxiety as a signal to give a warning of dangers threatening its integrity."

In line with the above, I have pointed out (Chapters 7 and 8) that although the intrapsychic process can be dissected as above into a discrete succession of events, the final psychic product with which we are confronted clinically is always a composite picture. Partly due to the rapidity with which the intrapsychic sequence takes place, and partly a result of the synthetic function of the ego, the anxiety reaction, just as any presenting symptom or any other affective mood, consists of a number of psychically adjacent and actually fused components. Although anxiety itself is related specifically to the anticipated danger of the future, the entire reaction also includes elements of the presently experienced trauma upon which the latter expectation is based. Freud expresses this double composition when he states (1926, p. 166): "Anxiety is therefore on the one hand an expectation of a trauma, and on the other a repetition of it in a mitigated form [here Freud does explicitly acknowledge the presence of a small traumatic state in the anxiety sequence]. . . . Its connection with expectation belongs to the danger-situation, whereas its indefiniteness and lack of object belong to the traumatic situation of helplessness—the situation which is anticipated in the danger-situation." Lewin (1952) also recognizes more than the signal in signal anxiety and points especially to the revived traumatic memory: "For anxiety, though a signal, is not merely a signal. It has a content and it is a sort of 'memory'. That is, anxiety attacks not only serve as warnings; they also reproduce earlier life events" (p. 311). Actually the total discomfort of the clinical anxiety reaction consists of a fusion, or agglutination, of the presently experienced trauma, the past traumatic memory which it revives, and the future danger which it expects. Quoting Freud (1926, p. 150): "dangers are the common lot of humanity; they are the same for everyone." And later (p. 166): "A danger-situation is a recognized [present], remembered [past], expected [future] situation of helplessness."

Anxiety, then, is a traumatic reaction of helplessness, present and past, filtered through the perceiving, judging, reacting, and anticipating ego, which adds its estimate of the future. Each leaves its residuals and imprints. What ranges from "controlled to uncontrolled" in the series described by

Schur (1953) is not just the anxiety, the anticipation of the future trauma, but the actual traumatic state being contained and warded off. It is this aspect of the composite reaction which may be restricted to a degree which permits a "thoughtlike" signal experience, or may proceed through relative degrees of helplessness and loss of control to an uncontrollable and rampant traumatic panic. And I would modify the final definition arrived at by Schur (1958, p. 217): "*Anxiety is a reaction to a traumatic situation, or to danger, present or anticipated.*" It is *always* to a danger, which is *always* a traumatic situation, which is *always* present, *and* always anticipated. What is anticipated is always the worsening of a present lesser traumatic state. The total situation can again be best encompassed by reverting to the more succinct formula given by Freud in his second theory (1926, p. 150): "Anxiety is a [Strachey says "the"] reaction to danger."

There is one final piece of content to which I would like to attend. Having answered Waelder's question of "how does the ego do its anticipating?" by stating "by experiencing a mild and controlled traumatic state," I again come to the nitty gritty question of "how does the traumatic state lead to anxiety?" What is the mechanism by which instinctual flooding (from the id) leads to the experience of anxiety (by the ego?). This is now seen to be operative in all anxiety, whether mild and controlled (as in Freud's second theory) or more severe and less controlled (as in Freud's first instances).

Here is the same question which Freud confronted in 1894, and to which he gave his startling and provocative answer, which he did not withdraw for over 30 years. But even then he asked that we take a second look, that there might still be something in it, although different from what he had said at first. I would like us to do just that, 75 years later, and caution not to throw out the baby with the bath, but to consider whether in Freud's general rather than specific thinking to this question something viable and enduring might not have been encompassed. What I believe we will find is that while some parts do have to remain discarded, others still give productive leads and should be retained, modified, or added to.

What I believe we can discard, or at least what are probably the least defensible of Freud's earliest ventured opinions on this question are: (a) that there is a specific and exclusive relationship between anxiety and mounting *sexual* impulses; in spite of the desire of some to go back specifically to this point, this is one aspect for which I believe there is the least compelling clinical or theoretical argument; (b) that such a relationship is also a quantitative one, based on maintaining a constancy of energy level; and (c) the originally described exclusively physical nature of the transaction—it was probably this as much as any other feature which closed the doors to future expansion for many years. It was these specific, and direct, and exclusively somatic aspects which Freud discarded and which have become "a relic of the past."[2]

[2]Not everyone regards the connection between sexuality and anxiety as conclusively invalid. I have mentioned both Waelder and Anna Freud pointing up the possibility of a reopening of this specific issue. Schur points to the deep phylogenetic links between sex and violence and therefore danger, evident both in clinical work and in the findings of ethologists, and keeps open the possible validity of Freud's early linkage. He also points to the many connections between sexuality, tension, and neuroses, and still notes the frequency of coitus interruptus and sexual frustration in phobics, the same observation which was the basis for Freud's concept of actual neurosis. The similarities between the discharge phenomena of anxiety and sexual tension have been noted repeatedly. Marie Bonaparte (quoted by Schur, 1958, p. 212) emphasizes "the deep biological roots of anxiety and masochistic elements in female sexuality." Bose (1952), in a formulation very much like Freud's original one, considers anxiety and sexual tension identical and mutually convertible states. And finally, in an isolated passage written by Freud almost at the very end of his life (1938, p. 300), brought to my attention by Piers, Freud reflects again on the wide effects of sexual damming up due to early sexual inhibitions: "*August 3* [1938].—The ultimate ground of all intellectual inhibitions and all inhibitions of work seems to be the inhibition of masturbation in childhood. But perhaps it goes deeper; perhaps it is not just inhibition by external influences but its unsatisfying nature in itself. There is always something lacking for complete discharge and satisfaction—en attendant toujours quelquechose qui ne venait point ['Always waiting for something which never came']—and this missing part, the reaction of orgasm, manifests itself in equivalents in other spheres, in *absences*, outbreaks of laughing, weeping [Xy], and perhaps other ways.—Once again infantile sexuality has fixed a model in this."

Thus biological, early ontogenetic and phylogenetic linkages keep being

But can we say the same about the more general insight and orientation contained in this early view? If we broaden the original idea of sexuality (to which Freud was limited by his original instinct theory of the time) to the broader current view of sexual and aggressive instinctual impulses, do we see no relationship between the pressures of these and the quality and quantity of anxiety which emerges? When Freud said (1933, p. 94) "We shall no longer maintain that it is the libido itself that is turned into anxiety," did this apply to *all* instinctual pressures? In the next sentence he left open the possibility of "a direct consequence of the traumatic moment," a point which has been elaborated upon in this paper. On the contrary, I would say that it is entirely consonant with our present views and experience that anxiety bears a distinct relationship precisely to the force and fates of instinctual impulses. While this is no longer, however, in terms of a closed energy system, it is now in terms of the danger which the latter represent. And this depends on the relation of these pressures to the resources of the ego to deal with them in the face of the total psychic situation, i.e., to the degree of psychic helplessness present and expected. Thus, while the direct relationship between degree of repression and degree of anxiety in Freud's original postulation was never borne out, I would say that such a relationship between degree of anxiety and degree of expected helplessness would be consonant with clinical facts.

But beyond the fact of its existence, what even more precisely is the relationship between such pressing impulses and the anxiety which emerges? Here we find ourselves at the nodal point of a larger problem, at a core which is both an internal microscopic nucleus as well as one which reverberates outward to almost the totality of human behavior. I am referring to the problem of psychosomatic interrelationships in general, which is seen here in a nuclear instance and which can

---

adduced toward reconsidering a possible direct linkage between anxiety and sexuality. While there is no conclusive reason to close or discard this issue, I feel that further interest or revival of it must depend on new metabolic, chemical, and physiological findings.

perhaps serve as a model for other psychosomatic problems. This area, of anxiety in particular and affects in general, has always been, both inside and outside of psychoanalysis, a borderland between psyche and soma, between biology and behavior, where at best only large outlines can be seen but the ultimate core cannot yet be discerned. Putting aside the theory of direct transformation from sexual libido, is there any reason not to believe, or is there not still reason to entertain the fact, that there is *some* type of progression from undischarged psychic tension to anxiety, that *in some way* instinctual impulses are either converted into, or transformed into, or become part of, or lead to the reaction of anxiety—but that this now involves *both* psychic and somatic aspects (we remember that Freud, in his original formulation, eliminated the former)? This is notwithstanding the fact that a psychic structure ego intervenes to "recognize" the danger and to react with the psychic and somatic components of anxiety. Does it conflict with anything we feel at present that there can be *some kind* of conversion or transformation of pressing instinctual impulses, of their biological and psychic aspects—Freud (1915a, p. 122) sees instincts as "on the frontier between the mental and the somatic"—to the physiological and psychological components of anxiety? The actual phenomenological similarities between the two are so close that Freud and Waelder both occasionally interchange one for the other, indicating the unpleasure or helplessness of the traumatic state as the anxiety signal itself—and I have described the closeness and even fusion of the two clinically.

The mechanism of this transition, of this "leap" from the traumatic state to anxiety, from the psychological and somatic components of instincts to the psychobiological experience of anxiety, is one of the most challenging nuclear points in our entire theoretical framework, is unclear, and has never even been established. This much can be said: while Freud's first approach to answers was along somatic lines and his second added the psychological, to eliminate the former with the advent of the latter would again leave us with only half the story. On the psychological side, which was given its due role in the second theory, the present trauma elicits a memory of a past traumatic experience which results in anticipating a future one. But can we eliminate considering an accompanying somatic transmission from the unpleasure to the anxiety?[3] Benjamin (1952, 1958) has pointed to the equal danger of a biophobic and a psychophobic attitude in understanding the totality of human behavior.

Anxiety is a psychobiological organismic event, both in its origins and its response. Just as Waelder (1967a), in asking how the ego anticipates danger, asks similarly how does the pituitary recognize danger, so the answer to both questions suggests itself: that it is a psychophysical organismic response to the traumatic situation which encompasses the whole and which automatically results in the anxiety reaction. Both the traumatic state and the resultant anxiety have a combination of physical and psychological components, each of which feeds and feeds back into the other in a complex network. The mechanisms of this interchange constitute one of the central riddles of modern neuropsychophysiology.

It is in fact at this point that psychoanalysis and biology will probably one day meet in a common focus, as Freud always believed and as described since by Hartmann (1950a) and others. Nor is this a static field but one which has been burgeoning with significant research in recent years. From the old, well-known vegetative and autonomic accompaniments of anxiety, to psychosomatic states resulting from chronic and unremitting anxiety, to Selye's recent work (1950) on the psychophysiology of stress, and now to the newest and most sophisticated findings in neurophysiology, neurochemistry, psychopharmacology, genetics, and, with analysts among them, "the new biology of dreaming," there is increasing promise of a

---

[3]The sexual impulses would be included within the broader spectrum of instinctual pressures even if no longer considered as specifically or exclusively etiological in this connection. The transmission would be from nonspecific instinctual pressure, under the influence of various inhibiting and regulating forces, to anxiety. Whether there is also a specific transmission, from specific qualities of instincts, would be an additional problem to be considered.

hoped-for breakthrough at this very point to help understand the leap between psyche and soma, in both directions, and the combined psychology and biology of behavior. Thus even here, Freud's original bridge from cases of internal traumatic inundation with stimuli to the anxiety reaction, via some speculated physiological process, the part of his original theory most readily discarded, may yet turn out to have been, although with many modifications and subsequent discoveries, a harbinger of things to come.

Before making a final summary statement, I would like merely to list the following subjects which are related and important but upon which I cannot elaborate.

1. While we have been dealing here with the basic mechanisms and therefore universal and ultimate meanings of anxiety, the developmental life history will determine its outward forms. Thus the forms and content in which psychic helplessness is expressed become, with progressive development, fear of separation, castration, superego anxiety, etc., in the well-known genetic succession of life's events. None of what has been said here contradicts or minimizes the importance or the variety of these kaleidoscopic individual developmental determinants.

2. I indicated at the beginning the clinical usefulness of theoretical understanding, which is here no exception. Just as our theoretical knowledge of the universal Oedipus complex helps us watch for and interpret its individual forms in a particular life development, so our knowledge of the basic mechanism of anxiety formation, with its basic fear of helplessness and loss of control, can be a beacon in our clinical and technical conduct of an analysis throughout its various vicissitudes.

3. It would be instructive to trace the special differences with respect to trauma and anxiety, and their relationship to each other, which unfold during the course of the analytic process. Under the protection of the latter, special qualitative and quantitative alterations take place.

SUMMARY

A comprehensive psychoanalytic theory of anxiety, which applies to all instances of anxiety, combines elements of Freud's two historical theories of anxiety. The anxiety reaction is always set in motion by an existing traumatic state, either one which has invaded the ego involuntarily and from outside of its control (as in Freud's first theory); or one which has been brought about by the ego under its control in a minimal and experimental way (from Freud's second theory). This constitutes a twofold origin, in agreement with Freud's persistent idea. Both origins then converge in setting off a single common and unitary mechanism. The reaction is always a signal of the anticipation of danger (from the second theory). The danger is that of the traumatic state getting worse and out of control (first theory), or that the trauma which was sampled tentatively will come on in full force (second theory). The reaction always results automatically and involuntarily (as in the first theory), and is then *used* by the ego in an active way (from the second). The reaction, which is experienced by the ego (second theory), has both id (first theory) and ego (second theory) components. The reaction itself is both a psychological (from second theory) and a somatic one (from first theory).

While neither Freud's first nor his second theory alone is complete in itself, the combination given, in my opinion, retains the valid and indispensable elements of each and can explain all the observable clinical phenomena. With this combined, unitary, explanatory theory the small but definite kink at the heart of psychoanalytic theory may be smoothed out, and Freud's *"non liquet,"* I submit, can be changed to *"liquet."*

CHAPTER 11

The Psychoanalytic Theory of Affects

Affects are feelings. For practical purposes, affects, feelings, or emotions can be used interchangeably. Definitional differentiation between these terms has been attempted from time to time but has not led to any satisfactory or generally accepted formulation.

Affects have historically been a central focus of psychoanalytic theory as it has evolved from the beginning. Yet it has always been more possible and satisfactory to conceptualize affects in their relationships to associated and interactive phenomena than to arrive at a theoretical understanding of the nature of affects themselves. Thus the derivation of affects from instincts, their relations to ego and superego, their associations with ideas, and their connections with somatic expression have all been incorporated into general and specific aspects of psychoanalytic theory. The understanding of their own nature, however, has lagged behind and remains one of the most obscure areas, if not theoretical mysteries, of psychological, somatic, and psychosomatic theory.

Written for the *Compendium of Psychoanalytic Terms and Concepts*, Ed. B. Moore and B. D. Fine (in press).

Empirically, by serendipity or otherwise, the evolution of a psychoanalytic theory of affects has paralleled both the progress of general psychoanalytic theory and the ontogenetic development of the psychic apparatus. In the earliest phase of psychoanalytic theory, affects occupied a disproportionately large and central role, as the etiological theory of strangulated affects held sway, and with it the theory of therapy by catharsis and abreaction. With the development of the theory of instincts and drives, affects came to occupy a secondary position along-side of other instinctual derivatives, with the theory of therapy advancing to the analysis of conflict. With the ascendancy of the structural view, affects came to occupy a more limited and circumscribed place, resulting from an increasingly complex interaction between all three psychic structural systems. Both affect theory and general psychoanalytic theory, moreover, are seen to parallel, in a remarkable way, the ontogenetic development of the psychic apparatus, from the original id dominance, through the gradually increasing role of the ego, to the contribution of the superego as well as of reality and the external world.

Rapaport (1953a), presenting what has been considered the closest approximation to a definitive theory of affect, traced and documented the cumulative development of affect theory with the historical development of the theory of psychoanalysis. Rapaport dates the first period of the theory of affects from the beginning 1890s to *The Interpretation of Dreams* (1900). During this stage, when therapy was centered in catharsis and abreaction, Freud equated affect to a quantity of energy "like an electric charge over the memory traces of an idea." Drive, energy, and affect had not yet been effectively separated. Psychic tension of this still indeterminate nature was disposed of by action, affect, and binding through the work of thought.

The second period extended from 1900 to the publication of *The Ego and the Id* (1923a). During this time, along with Freud's developing metapsychological framework, which approached psychological phenomena from multiple points of view, affects were looked upon as discharges into the interior from their origins in the unconscious. According to Freud (1915b), "Affectivity manifests itself essentially in motor (secretary and vasomotor) discharge resulting in an (internal) alteration of the subject's own body without reference to the external world" (p. 179).

Affect discharge, according to Rapaport, results in affect expression and affect felt, referring to the unconscious and conscious experiences of affects. The existence of innate discharge thresholds, which change in characteristics with developmental events, ushers in conflict, experientially and in theory. The dynamic, economic, and genetic metapsychological points of view are prominent in theoretical understanding during this phase.

Rapaport's third stage spanned from the introduction of the structural view and Freud's signal theory of anxiety to the present time. With an expanding and varied use of affect discharge channels, continuous ego development results in an increasingly complex hierarchy of drives, motivations, and affects, coordinated with secondary process development and a constantly increasing neutralization of drives (Hartmann, 1939a; Hartmann et al., 1946). The structural view, with its emphasis on the role of the ego, adds to the understanding of the developing affects throughout life. In mature adult life, continuous interaction between the three psychic structures produces changing tensions and discharges which combine and blend into an integrated whole. Affects proceed from being peremptory, explosive, and attacklike to becoming more and more controlled, modulated, and "tamed" (Fenichel, 1941a; E. Kris, 1950). Along with the achievement of an effective anticipatory signal of anxiety, a rich and modulated affective life is associated with and equivalent to a strong ego.

Affects, ideas, and actions are derivative formations through which instincts are expressed and become known (Freud, 1900, 1915a; Nunberg, 1932; Brierley, 1937; Fenichel, 1945; Rapaport, 1951b, 1953a). Although affect is thus a derivative of instinct, it consists of more than its instinctual component. Just as external behavior is a composite of many preceding intrapsychic elements, consisting of compromises between instinctual drives, ego defenses, superego inputs, and other forms of ego activity which fuse the disparate elements into a cohesive whole, so are affects composed of ego and superego as well as instinctual components, and external along with internal determinants.

The resulting affects are in constant contiguous relationships with other mental and also somatic elements. The total phenomenon of subjective human experience, into which affect is embedded and of which it is one part, consists of feeling, an associated idea or set of ideas, and accompanying somatic changes. Although these three aspects of human experience are associated or even fused, they are not interchangeable and are definitionally separate. Affects and cognition are contiguous, connected, and reciprocal, but are not one. Every affect is associated with but is not thereby the same as the idea which evokes or accompanies it. Conversely, every idea evokes and is then associated with an accompanying affect, although in the case of some ideas or class of ideas the affect may be minimal to the point of approaching zero. And just as idea and affect are together but separate, the same holds for the affect and its accompanying somatic relationships. As the idea is not the affect, and vice versa, the physical experience is not the feeling, nor is the affect the somatic phenomena which accompany it.

A question unique to psychoanalysis is whether affects or feelings can be unconscious as well as conscious. Freud was inconsistent on this point. While at one point he stated, "It is surely of the essence of an emotion that we should be aware of it, i.e., that it should become known to consciousness" (1915b, p. 177), in other contexts, Freud spoke freely of affects as being unconscious. This occurred in the discussion of clinical cases, in specific theoretical discussions of anxiety or guilt, in referring to repressed affects in traumatic neurosis or psychoneurosis, or in describing repressed affects in the transference (Freud, 1937b).

Following extensive discussions of this point in the literature, analysts generally agree that unconscious affects are routine experience in clinical work and in life and that affects can be as unconscious as ideation. With regard to the criterion of "subjective awareness" as given in the definition of affects in the *Glossary* (Moore and Fine, 1968), to which this compendium is being added, both "subjective" and "awareness" psychoanalytically are to be acknowledged as not synonymous with conscious. There can be, and routinely is, unconscious awareness of feelings as well as ideas. This quality of awareness, with and without consciousness, is included within subjectivity.

While recognizing the dilemma Freud had on this subject, many authors have concluded that affects can be unconscious and preconscious as well as conscious. This has been described, with varying degrees of emphasis and conviction, by Eissler (1953a), Jacobson (1953a), Rapaport (1953a), Schafer (1964), Lewin (1965), Joffe and Sandler (1968), Schur (1969), Pulver (1971), Brenner (1974), Loewald (in Panel, 1974), Rangell (1974b), and Sandler (1983a).

Another distinction relevant to unconscious affects, described by Freud and elaborated upon by Fenichel (1945) and Pulver (1974), is that affects in the unconscious can exist either as fully formed but repressed mental contents, or as predispositions or potentials, i.e., a more-than-usual readiness to be formed into and operate as a particular affect. This distinction has a practical, clinical, and theoretical significance. The more structured and fully formed an affect is in the unconscious, the more it presses to be discharged, in either a direct or derivative form, or the more it operates to instigate defenses to keep it in repression. A less formed potential for affect is less pressing and further from requiring defense or action or psychic definition. Eissler (1953a) stresses similarly the clinical importance of distinguishing the different states and forms of the repressed impulses in the id and the affects within the ego. Of the same theoretical significance, Fenichel (1945) sees the hyperaffectivity which one encounters clinically or in life as a readiness for affective discharge.

Approaching the subject from the standpoint of individual affects, Freud (1895a, 1900) laid down a major initial building block early in the development of psychoanalytic theory when he delineated the dichotomy of pleasure and unpleasure in psychic life. This polarity was described not only as an initial understanding of the nature of affects, but as an enunciation of one of the basic regulatory principles of mental functioning. In accordance with this "pleasure-unpleasure principle", the human organism is motivated biologically or, as Freud came to enlarge it, biopsychologically, to the seeking of pleasure and avoidance of pain, unpleasure, or the traumatic state.

In its reference to affects, the pleasure-unpleasure principle is a more accurate description of the two major divisions of affects than pleasure-pain, with which is often loosely interchanged. Pain is generally conceived of as a somatic sensation which, as it increases, can lead to the psychological feeling of unpleasure or, more specifically, to the affect of anxiety. Diffuse unpleasure, which is undifferentiated in the earliest developmental periods, gradually becomes differentiated into more specific and delimited affective states, as anxiety, depression, guilt, shame, and a variety of subtle combinations and derivatives of these.

Relating this first delineation of the pleasure-unpleasure principle to the economic point of view, Freud first equated unpleasure with the build-up of psychic tension and pleasure with its discharge. With increasing experience, however, Freud (1905b) came to modify this oversimplified formulation, noting for example, in regard to erotic tension, that high tensions of pleasurable affect can be enjoyable, while low tensions of painful feeling can be intolerable. In one of his final works, Freud (1940) concluded that qualitative considerations as well as rhythms of tension and discharge processes also need to be considered. Jacobson (1953a) elaborated on the influence of factors of speed and rhythm on the pleasure-unpleasure qualities of feelings. Primitive affects are higher-peaked, and more sudden and explosive in their discharge processes. Low-speed discharge, Jacobson writes, can result in "pleasurable enduring feeling states," while combinations of high- and low-speed discharge processes may result in complex affect experiences as some of our most sublime pleasurable states.

A major affect delineated early and pursued intensively in Freud's emphasis on affective experience was the affect of anxiety. Freud (1926) considered anxiety not only "the nodal point of the neurosis" but a critical factor in normal behavior and psychic life in general. The history of the conceptualization of this central affect by Freud underwent a developmental process during the course of its understanding which paralleled and was crucial to the development of general psychoanalytic theory. The course of the understanding of this affect may also be considered a model for the understanding of affects in general.

The specific and ubiquitous role of anxiety in both the causation and resulting phenomenology of neurosis was recognized at once by Freud, although his views with regard to its origins and mode of operation underwent a metamorphosis during the course of his theory-building. In his first references to its clinical role, beginning in the draft of a paper contained in a letter to Fliess in 1893, Freud saw anxiety as a physical sequel to abnormal sexuality, such as compulsive masturbation. In this type of psychopathology, which he called "neurasthenia," Freud saw neurosis as being first the physical and then the psychological aftereffects or accompaniments of this anxiety. In a later variation, Freud (1895b) "detached" from this group a separate group of cases stemming from too little rather than too much sexual discharge, as in incomplete or inhibited sexuality or coitus interruptus. In this early concept, repression, which at that time meant inhibition, blocking, or defense as a general term, caused the anxiety from the state of being "dammed up," which then resulted in the physical and derivative, subjective, psychological symptoms. The syndrome resulting was called by Freud "anxiety neurosis." Another name for these cases, which has come to have historical meaning, was "actual neurosis," in the sense that the anxiety by this conception was real, physical, and current, i.e., an "actual" state, from which the clinical phenomenology resulting then became psychological in nature.

A simultaneous path toward the understanding of the affect of anxiety developed from the analyses of cases of hysteria and obsessional neurosis, which Freud (1894, 1895c, 1896b, 1898) called "psychoneuroses" in contrast to the anxiety or actual neuroses described above. A gradual evolution of psychoanalytic theory, shaped to explain continuing clinical observations, resulted in the mid-1920s (Freud, 1923a) in a major revision of theory, culminating in a new theory of anxiety as its central pivot. Along with a change from a unitary to a dual instinct theory (Freud, 1920), and a division of the psychic apparatus into the tripartite structures of id, ego, and superego, came the second or signal theory of anxiety (Freud, 1926). Where instinctual discharge of sexual or aggressive drives is judged by the ego to constitute a danger, anxiety now ensues as a signal of this impending danger. The danger, for example, of loss of love, castration, or punishment by the superego, leads, among other possible outcomes, to the institution of defense. Anxiety is now the cause of repression, not its result, and is the cause of all neuroses, not limited to those siphoned off as anxiety neuroses.

While analysts have universally accepted the signal theory of anxiety, there is a division of opinion regarding the fate of Freud's first theory. Although Freud himself defined the new concept of anxiety, he hesitated to abandon his first theory but retained the two together in some indeterminate manner. Most analysts such as Waelder (1960) and Brenner (1953), feel that Freud should have been willing to see his first theory discarded, and have done so in their own formulations and understanding. Others, as Fenichel (1945), Blau (1952), and Rangell (chapters 9 and 10), see both mechanisms of anxiety operating together, but in all neuroses, not separating one class of neuroses from another. The psychological and somatic aspects, stressed separately in Freud's two theories, exist together.

Traumatic neurosis is part of every psychoneurosis. The traumatic state, with its flooding by stimuli from the breaching of the stimulus barrier, from within or without, is close to the condition described by Freud in anxiety neurosis from the damming up of instinctual pressure. In my view, following the institution of defense brought about by the anxiety as the fear of danger, during the intrapsychic sequence leading to neurosis, continually pressing, undischarged drives result in mounting instinctual tension, which constitutes a biopsychological danger in itself. The background in common behind all psychological dangers is the fear of the traumatic state, which is the psychoeconomic condition of unpleasure behind the original feeling of traumatic helplessness. The prototype of this state occurs at birth, which is the aspect of Rank's (1952) theory of the birth trauma that Freud accepted in his own studies of anxiety. Anxiety thus occurs from a psychological origin, the fear of danger, which, following repression, leads to a somatic state, i.e., continuing instinctual pressure, which in turn results again in a psychological as well as somatic danger. Psychosomatic and somatopsychic sequences affect and reinforce each other in circular fashion.

Attempts to understand anxiety both as an affect and in its relation to a variety of clinical phenomena have been numerous and persistent. Anxiety can serve as a model for the understanding of all other affects, and all are equally connected to these general theoretical concepts. Signal anxiety can be widened to the concept of signal affect. When the ego permits a tentative instinctual discharge to test the reactions of the superego and external world, or engages in thought as experimental action, the result it receives is an affective signal. While the anxiety signal occupies a special place in the subsequent formation of neurosis, the affective signal in everyday life can be one of pleasure (G. Klein, 1976) as well as unpleasure, of safety (Sandler, 1960a) as of danger. Within the affect of unpleasure, while the scanning for anxiety, i.e., the presaging of danger, is a moment-by-moment ego function, the entire spectrum of unpleasurable affects can come into play, either in a general, nonspecific way or with a specific, highly differentiated affect.

The signal function of affect, in addition to operating intrapsychically, leading either toward defense or action, is also utilized externally, as a communicative signal in object relations. Affects come to have multiple functions (Rangell, 1974b), discharge in psychoeconomic terms, expression in terms of the individual or self, and appeal as a function in object relations. Affects as a signal serve to alert both one's own ego internally and those to whom one relates externally. The role of affects in object relations, in their appeal or communication to the external object, has been stressed by many analysts, including Riviere (1936), Brierley (1937), Moore (in Panel, 1968b), Lofgren (in Panel, 1968), and by direct observations by many observers of infants and children, such as Mahler and her co-workers (1963, 1975), Emde (1983) describing the affective self, Stern (1984) studying affect attunement, all following the pioneer work of Spitz (1965). Novey (1959) stresses the role of affects in communication via signaling both on an intrapsychic and interpersonal level, just as Sandler and Rosenblatt (1962) pointed out the role of affects in the representational world. Modell (1971) goes further in stating that a complete and systematic theory of affects needs to be based within the framework of object relations theory and of group as well as individual psychology.

The quality and differentiation of specific affects, as well as the quantitative variations which are possible, span a spectrum which is typically human, and which, on the evolutionary scale, differentiates man from other animals. Just as Schur (1953, 1958) describes a spectrum of anxiety from explosive and uncontrolled to signal and thoughtlike in quality, with increasing development there is an increasing variety and hierarchy of experienced affects. As all psychic elements, these undergo an increasing maturation and differentiation during the course of the developmental process.

From the diffuse pleasure and unpleasure of early infancy, affects become less explosive and undifferentiated, and more variegated, differentiated, modulated, and controlled. This is in keeping with Rapaport's (1953a) description of an increasing hierarchy of motivational drives, resulting in an increasing modulation of affects from diffuse to subtle. While in earlier stages affects can be said to be more id oriented, they gradually come under ego control during ontogenetic development.

A special variety of affects studied has been the more chronic, long-lasting, and low-key condition of moods. Mahler et al. (1975), studying basic moods in relation to the separation-individuation process, referred to mood as "the habitual mode of response to inner and outer stimulations with positive or negative affects" (p. 213). Along with "the taming of affects" (Fenichel, 1945; E. Kris, 1950) in more mature life, Jacobson (1957) and Weinshel (1970) have described moods as pervasive affects, diffusing discharge patterns throughout the ego. Moods thus provide a relative degree of stability (Weinshel, 1970), and "may be indeed called a barometer of the ego state" (Jacobson, 1957, p. 75). Jacobson (1953a) described this process in terms of the control of energic discharge, resulting in the capacity to experience more modulated "moods," i.e., sustained low-level affects, chronic over time, in contrast to shorter-lasting, more circumscribed affects, up to uncontrolled and explosive affect discharges.

The nature of affects, in their structure and composition and in the characteristics of their expression, undergoes a developmental progression synchronous with the course of development generally. Reider (Panel, 1952), for example, feels that rage is an earlier affect related to the id, specifically to the development of the expression of aggression; that anxiety comes later, with the specific achievement in ego development of the ability to anticipate; and guilt still later, after at least the beginnings of the formation of the superego. Similarly Mittel-mann regards pleasure and rage as predominantly id affects, while anxiety and feelings of safety belong to the ego, and qualms of conscience and depression are connected with the superego (Panel, 1952).

Classifications of affect have varied and have followed different criteria with different authors. An early qualitative classification, beginning with Freud, was according to whether an affect falls on the pleasurable or unpleasurable side of the pleasure-unpleasure duality. Another is based on the criteria of developmental progression, and the relation of evolving affects to the maturing and developing psychic structures. One division is according to the relationship of affects to the two instinctual drives, i.e., love or hate, derived from the sexual or aggressive instincts. Jacobson (1953a), basing her classification on the structural point of view, distinguishes affects deriving from intrasystemic tensions from those based on intersystemic conflicts. While analysts generally agree that the experience of affects resides in the ego, affects can originate from energic tensions anywhere within the psychic organization.

Affects have been divided into fixed and labile, simple and complex, single affects and those that are mixed or fused (Glover, 1938). There are positive and negative affects, primary and reactive affects, affects due to frustration as differentiated from those resulting form gratification. Both Glover and Jones (1929a) have described fear, guilt, and hate as primary derivatives of instinctual drives and other secondary affects as radiating from these. Affects due to the buildup of tension are separable from those brought about by the discharge of impulse. The specific affective and somatic state of laughter (Freud, 1905a; E. Kris, 1939) is related to the suddenness of the release of built-up tension.

Greenacre (1959a, 1960, and in Panel, 1952) differentiates two types of pleasure, active and passive, the pleasure of rest and that of activity. Pleasure arises from explorations into "the not-so-familiar," although this is not to be too intense to prevent anxiety or even trauma. Hendrick (1942) described pleasure in mastery. This is consonant with ego pleasure, effectance pleasure, pleasure centering mainly in ego satisfaction, as described by C. Bühler (1954), K. Bühler (1951), Harrison (1984), and others.

Jones (1929a), studying the complex and reciprocal interrelationships between fear, guilt, and hate, describes the layering of affective states one upon the other. I (1978) have utilized the concept of agglutinated or conglomerate affective states presenting themselves clinically, which then need to be destratified in the psychoanalytic process into their linear relationships. Among specific affects which have been subjected to separate study, Melanie Klein (1957) has elaborated on the prominent role of envy in psychic life. Riviere (1932) has analyzed the affect of jealousy as combining grief, anger, and fear.

Brenner (1975) considers depressive affect on a par with anxiety as a co-equal cause of defense. Guilt, shame, and all other affects, however, besides anxiety and depression, can similarly serve a signal function, and any affect of unpleasure can be a motive for defense. While any affect of unpleasure can be a motive for defense, anxiety occupies a supraordinate position since, in contrast to any of the other affects, anxiety is never absent in the intrapsychic sequence of events prior to the institution of the defensive activity (Rangell, 1978). The common etiology for this anxiety is over the possibility of the unpleasurable affect, whether depression, guilt, shame, or even anxiety itself, becoming out of control and leading to the traumatic state.

In addition to being motives for defense, affects can also themselves be defended against as derivatives of instinctual drives. They can serve as defenses as well as being defended against. Lewin (1950a) has described the use of screen affects as a defense against other repressed elements, and Greenson (1954b) has written about the defensive aspects of moods clinically and in life. Affects can also become ego-dystonic symptoms in their own right, coming about, as other symptoms, by compromise formations between the id and the ego. As symptom complexes they can be further repressed, so that a person can, for example, become aware only during analysis, following the undoing of defenses, of the existence of a chronic depression or anxiety state.

The most puzzling and elusive theoretical area in the psychoanalytic conceptualization of affect has to do with the relations between affect, ideation, and somatic phenomena. Affect, as pointed out by Schur (1969), is a response to cognition. Ideational or conceptual contents may arise from without or within, from perception and experience of external events, or from stimuli arising from either the psychic or somatic interior. Where affect is a response to an external event, perception and registration of the external condition have first produced a cognitive response, which may be conscious or unconscious, which then results in the associated affect. Either the affect or the idea or both may be defended against, repressed, and rendered unconscious. And either one can come about by primary or secondary repression, i.e., simultaneously with perception and registration, or as an "afterrepression," whether after an instant of conscious recognition or any length of time thereafter.

Brenner (1974), in what he terms a unified theory of affects, includes ideation within the concept of affects. Affects are classified in this system according to the ideational content associated with the "sensation" of pleasure or unpleasure. Affects consist of varying degrees of these "sensations" of pleasure and unpleasure, and of fantasies, conscious or unconscious, which determine the differentiation of one affect from another. Thus, it is the concept of anticipated danger which makes for and characterizes the affect of anxiety, the idea of loss which determines depressive affect, and the sense of deserving punishment which makes for guilt.

Since Brenner includes in his definition only phenomena which can be observed during the psychoanalytic process, the somatic accompaniments of affect are not included, whereas the accompanying ideation is considered part of the phenomenon. To most other theorists, however, ideational and somatic phenomena are both accompaniments of the affective experience but not definitionally part of affect itself. In keeping with the generally accepted formulation noted above, that thoughts, affects, and action are all separate derivatives of instincts, it would follow that however close all of these are clinically, they are conceptually separate phenomena with their own boundaries, contents, and definitions. Ideation and affect, for example, are considered separate derivatives of instinctual drives as modified and influenced by ego and superego activity.

A differently oriented unification of affect theory is exemplified by the unitary theory of anxiety (see chapters 9 and 10) which, as other instances relating anxiety to affects in general, can also serve as a model for other affects. In this unification, fusing Freud's first and second theories of anxiety, it is the psychic and somatic aspects of anxiety formation which are integrated into a continuous sequential whole, phenomenologically, experientially, and in theoretical understanding.

There are no longer two separate theories of anxiety, but two and actually more factors which are part of and associated with the unfolding of all anxiety. On the one hand, feeling or affect is recognized as associated with but nevertheless separable from ideation. On the other hand, this formulation also makes room not only for an association of affect and ideation, but of both of these with their accompanying somatic neurophysiologic phenomena. While ideation accompanies and even determines the qualitative differences between specific affects, the cognitive accompaniment is no more the affect per se than is its somatic expression. Nevertheless, the inevitable association of the three together allows for an operationally wider unification of affect, ideation, and somatic accompaniments.

Although affects, ideas, and related somatic phenomena typically occur together in a clinical situation, the need for separate conceptualization of each phenomenon is considered desirable and necessary by most analysts. Most authors, however, also consider the subject elusive and even inconclusive. Noting Freud's separation of affects from ideas and perceptions, Loewald (in Panel, 1974), referring to this as an ineffable subject, points out the unitary character of cognition and affect clinically, yet that in other respects, by which he apparently means theoretical considerations, they stand at opposite poles. Pulver (1971) sees complex clinical manifestations occurring together but feels that the narrow meaning of affect is necessary theoretically. For the broader context, Pulver prefers to use "affective phenomena." "Pure" affects, in the consideration of some, may be seen in epileptic rage or other ictal phenomena, in decerebrate or similar organic conditions, or perhaps in neonates or the earliest stages of infancy. That we do not see "pure" affects clinically, however, is no more reason against their being a separate theoretical entity than is the case with instincts, which we also see only in derivative form, and combined with other elements.

Following Rapaport's presentation of his most definitive paper, Lewin (1952), speaking from the floor, declared that we still do not have a psychoanalytic theory of affects. This opinion was repeated in the panel on affects in 1977. Sandler (1983a) feels that Rapaport failed to clarify the conceptual problems because of his adherence to a unitary theory of affect, which in Sandler's opinion encompassed "the physical, energic and experiential aspects within the same concept" (p. 82). Brenner feels that Rapaport's contribution is limited by his emphasis on theory while expressly avoiding references to subjective states (Panel, 1968b). Sandler, as Pulver and others, would reserve the term "affect" for the feeling state. "While physiological processes may be associated with feelings, it is important to distinguish between the two" (p. 88), Sandler states, making the same point about affects and somatic expression as others have made about affects and ideation.

Nevertheless, Greenacre (1960) has stated that the deepest substrate of affect lies in physiological processes. Specific organ systems have different patterns of tension or relief pleasure, and out of this matrix are formed the complex affects of adult life. However, to satisfy the requirements of a theory of affect, one faces the difficulty of needing to define the nature of explanation or causation, the question of whether a physical or psychological or only a combined theory offers an "explanation" of any complex behavioral phenomenon.

The fact is that "explanation" in a total sense of the behavioral phenomenon of affect does not belong entirely within psychoanalysis. Affect, as Freud said about instinct, is another phenomenon—feeling state or sensation?—which belongs on the frontier between psyche and soma. While the specific mechanisms, such as the psychophysiological synapses involved in the formation, evolution, and expression of affects, are not known or completely understood, the three closely associated phenomena, ideational, somatic, and affective, are linked together clinically and in theoretical contiguity. Interfaces between each respective pair unite the three into an integrated and harmonious experiential whole.

We cannot automatically equate the relationship between endorphins and impermeability to pain to a parallel relationship between any known chemical substance and susceptibility to or resistance against unpleasure. No comparable leap can be made from our understanding of the psychosomatic synapse in somatic pain to the same neurophysiological sequence in the production of affects. Knowledge of anxiolytic or antidepressant medication has not yet contributed significantly to an understanding of the psychology of anxiety states or the psychopathology of depression. And our increasing knowledge of neurotransmitters or of the chemical agents operative across neural synapses does not aid us in understanding the psychodynamics of the production or maintenance of affective states.

In the understanding of affects, psychoanalysis contributes an indispensable part, but not the whole. Psychoanalysis provides only data on the psychological side of the psychosomatic and somatopsychic reciprocal arcs. Between perception, external or internal, and affect is a neurophysiological bridge which it is the domain of somatic science to understand and expand. The role of neurophysiological processes in addition to psychological and metapsychological understanding has been stressed by Needles (1964), Moore (in Panel, 1968b, 1974), and others.

There is also much to be known about neurophysiological differences in specific affective states. In his first theory of anxiety, Freud did not show or know how the state of increasing instinctual flooding led neurophysiologically to tension and stress, and from these to the psychological experience of anxiety—but he pointed in this direction. While the precise mechanism remains unknown, Greenacre (1941), among others who support this exploratory view of Freud's, cites the view of Cannon which approaches the same phenomenon of dammed-up libido from a physiological angle. Describing how strong emotion and sympathetic and parasympathetic nervous system discharges reciprocally energize each other, Cannon writes, "Any high degree of excitement in the central nervous system—whether felt as anger, terror, pain, anxiety, joy, grief or deep disgust—etc." (p. 36). The mechanism, however, remains unknown.

For a complete and integrated theory of affects, open-ended interfaces are necessary to bridge between contiguous areas of human functioning. This is consonant with the view expressed by Freud (1920), and held by many psychoanalysts and neurophysiologists since then. It is for this reason that at a panel (1974) on affects, and in an article on the subject of affects (Emde, 1980), the title "Toward a Theory of Affects" was used. Psychoanalysis can only provide one path in a necessary cooperative and multidisciplined approach.

CHAPTER 12

The Metapsychology of Psychic Trauma

HISTORICAL BACKGROUND

Trauma, more especially external trauma, was a central tenet in Freud's early theories and was at the heart of his early explanations about neurosogenesis. Freud's first theory regarding external seduction, for example, was centrally a traumatic one. When in subsequent theoretical developments external seduction gave way to inner fantasy, external reality to psychic reality, and external pressures to the strength of inner instinctual drives, trauma did not necessarily recede in importance but merely changed its locus. There has been a continuous evolution and increasing understanding with our expanding knowledge as to what trauma is, what its varieties may be, where it can come from, and what it does. In the present state of psychoanalytic psychology, trauma has a more varied, subtle, and rich texture, both in our theoretical concepts and in our clinical confrontations with its manifestations.

Various explanations, or at least points of emphasis not

Presented at Symposium on Psychic Trauma, Psychoanalytic Research and Development Fund, New York, March 1967. Published in *Psychic Trauma*, ed. S. S. Furst. New York and London: Basic Books, 1967, pp. 51–84.

quite reaching the formal definition stage, have been given by
Freud in scattered references regarding the essence and nature
of trauma during the various phases of the development of
psychoanalytic theory. These have been extensively reviewed,
especially by Furst (1967) and Greenacre. I would like to single
out the following four major concepts, first because in my
opinion they represent the nuclear developing ideas of Freud
regarding the essence of trauma, and second because they all
will be included in the final integrated theory of trauma which
I will later construct. These ideas and the historical sequence in
which they appeared were as follows:

1. In 1893–1895 in *Studies on Hysteria,* Freud regarded
trauma as "any experience which calls up distressing affects
such as those of fright, anxiety, shame or physical pain."

2. In 1917, in the *Introductory Lectures,* the central idea was
"an excessive magnitude of stimuli too powerful to be . . .
worked off in a normal way."

3. In 1920 came the most important concept of the breakthrough of the stimulus barrier, "any excitations which are
powerful enough to break through the protective shield," a
disturbance connected with "a breach in an otherwise effica-
cious barrier against stimuli."

4. In 1926, in his definitive reformulation of the problem
of anxiety, Freud saw trauma as the state of psychic helplessness, a situation of helplessness that has been actually *experienced,* as differentiated from an *expectation* of danger.

Note that each of the above explanations has a different
center and a different point of emphasis. I will attempt to
integrate these various concepts and explanations into a composite whole, and I will try to show that they are not contradictory or mutually exclusive but rather that they interdigitate
with each other. This integration, however, will come only after
many more preliminary considerations.

PHENOMENOLOGICAL FACTORS

It is difficult to make adequate and sufficient generalizations to cover the great variety of factors that can set off the

traumatic sequence and the kaleidoscopic possibilities of what can thus come to constitute psychic trauma. (I am now speaking of the precipitating traumatic events, which are frequently loosely referred to as "the trauma" itself. The rigorous differentiation between the successive phases of the traumatic sequence of events or of what constitutes "trauma" will be elaborated upon in later sections and is in fact the goal of this paper. But here I am describing where trauma can come from and what constitutes its beginning phases. The resulting intrapsychic traumatic state—i.e., the state of psychic helplessness—is a more uniform psychoeconomic state.)

From without or from within, from bodily ill or from world event, the trauma can come from any direction, from any locus, and can be of any magnitude. To make an analogy with physical insult, trauma may be described as being constituted of the psychic equivalents of a series of pinpricks rather than a crushing blow; a gnawing from within rather than an oppression from without; or a process comparable to being teased apart as much as one of being pressed down upon. Although caution is necessary in making such physical comparisons, I believe that one can readily think of psychological counterparts for all of these physical pressures. A gradual and piecemeal teasing apart of self-esteem, for example, can be quite in contrast to, and yet can have an equally deleterious effect as, a crushing rejection or abandonment from without by a loved object. Such parallels between physical and psychological processes are not unknown or even untraditional among us. Freud (1895a) originally leaned heavily on neural and physical prototypes for his earliest psychological formulations. Greenacre (1941, 1945) has since elaborated in great detail on the earliest psychobiological unity existing in infancy and on the subsequent parallel development as well as the interdependence between psychological and physical growth. The derivation of psychological coldness or warmth from similar earlier physical sensations and the relationships between early psychological defenses and parallel and related physical precursors have been described by Greenacre (1958), Spitz (1961), and others.

CONSTITUTIONAL FACTORS

The biological limitations built into the organism are a source of future traumata. From the birth process onward the relative incapacity of the organism to deal independently with the overwhelming physical odds against it is a physical and inborn source of the traumatic state. This continues for a certain and prolonged period, even under the best of circumstances. (Indeed, the protracted period of dependence of the young is responsible not only for the prolonged period of helplessness but for man's achievements as well. The early structural differentiation into ego and id that results from this protracted helplessness is mainly responsible, Hartmann [1948] suggests, for the differences between the instinctual behavior of lower animals and the behavior of human beings.)

Innate differences exist both in the potentiality of the organism to provide psychic trauma and in its varying capacity to suffer or deal with it. In the former category belong the constitutional strength and tenacity of instinctual pressures, the relative strengths of aggressive versus libidinal drives, and the relation between instincts and the inborn capacities of the particular ego to perform its various functions vis-à-vis them. Differences exist in the intensities of symbolic needs, which bring with them different potentialities of exposure toward trauma by separation.

Instrumental in determining one's relationship to and fate toward traumas that do impinge are certain specific attributes of the inborn and inherited ego apparatuses (Hartmann, 1939a, 1950a) and the specific capacities of the latter to deal with the traumas of the average expectable environment. The nature and strength of the inborn defensive thresholds (Rapaport, 1953a) and the constitutional makeup of the stimulus barrier are among such variable factors crucial in determining the ego's resistance to trauma. Just as Bergman and Escalona have pointed out unusual sensitivities that exist from the beginning, so also are there those with unusual toughness and with an early and happy ability to withstand average traumatic intrusions. Such factors must be taken into consideration in a total evaluation of the role and fate of traumas. Anna Freud (1962) has remarked on the impressive and far-reaching adaptive implications of a young child's early ability to simply say "Okay," when confronted by a difficult and potentially traumatic external situation.

THE ECONOMIC POINT OF VIEW

There is no doubt that Freud's initial concept of trauma was clearly related to what was to become the economic principle of mental functioning—and with it was tied up early to the concepts of homeostasis, the nirvana and pleasure-pain principles. All these, as is always noted in reviews of the historical development of Freud's thinking, were based predominantly on quantitative considerations and on concepts of the interplay of quantities of psychic energy. In fact, it was precisely by way of these views on the nature and mechanisms of psychic trauma that the economic point of view became one of the first to develop in our evolving metapsychology.

"It is only the magnitude of the excitation," wrote Freud (1933), "which turns an impression into a traumatic factor, which paralyzes the operation of the pleasure-pain principle and gives significance to the danger situation." Similarly, the pleasure-pain dichotomy itself was also explained by Freud initially in economic terms, that is, whatever resulted in a decrease in tension led to pleasure and an increase eventually to pain. Schur (1962) quotes Schneirla's conclusions from his evolutionary experimental work with animals, i.e., there is "convincing evidence that stimuli of low intensity generally initiate approach responses, while stimuli of high intensity initiate withdrawal."

Increasing clinical experience and more sober theoretical reflection gave pause both to Freud and to many later students of the theory of affect about the validity and consistency of this appealing and insightful formulation. From his studies on masochism, Freud (1920, 1924) himself modified his original concept by recognizing that both pleasure and unpleasure can be connected with either increase or decrease of psychic excitation. I mention this here because of the relationship of the onset of unpleasure to the definition of what can become trauma. Freud, it will be remembered, restricted traumatic stimuli to those accompanied by the release of any distressing or unpleasurable affect (Breuer and Freud, 1893–1895).

Nevertheless, despite the problems which accrue, it must be remembered that the original connection between trauma and "the magnitude of excitation" cannot be omitted, although it has to be added to and refined; this is not the complete picture, however, and the factors involved are complex. It is common experience that certain stimuli, trivial in quantitative terms, can exert a powerful traumatic effect, and that other stimuli of quite formidable magnitude can often be easily tolerated. But quantitative and economic considerations of subtle and varied types do obtain in determining whether a particular stimulus will be pleasurable and stimulating on the one hand or traumatic on the other. Often the line between them is a thin one. In clinical instances eliciting awe, for example, as in awe of the penis (Greenacre, 1953) in both men and women, it is often uncertain whether the stimulus will go on to have a positive and pleasurable effect or a traumatic effect. But one factor among many does relate to the quantity of force impinging, the quantity of structure impinged upon, and the quantity of energy released or displaced *per unit of time*—in relation to the quantitative and qualitative capacities of the ego at that particular moment of its time-space orbit.

While a number of other points could be made about the role of economic factors in determining the occurrence and the nature of trauma, I mention only a few that I consider especially significant. One is that economic factors themselves are subject to the genetic developmental process and undergo phase-specific modifications with development and maturation. This prevails not only in the early formative preoedipal and oedipal periods but throughout the entire life cycle as described by Erikson (1950). Economic conditions that are traumatic early can be not only tolerable but sought for at a later stage. The same variations obtain here as apply to the changing conditions of pleasure-seeking, of object-seeking, and even of tension-seeking versus tension reduction during the course of life. The excitements of adolescence would be unbearably traumatic in old age, while the sought-for "calm" of middle life might constitute an intolerably traumatic boredom at certain stages of youth. Thus the magnitude of excitation, or indeed the degree of absence of excitation, is a significant factor only in relation to many other conditions of the host.

One other consideration in the area of quantitative factors that I consider of special significance in arriving at a precise concept of trauma is the question of the extent or the "bigness" of the trauma that is required to justify the use of the term. In my view, the intrapsychic chain of events leading to the state of traumatic psychic helplessness may range from partial to complete. Clinically one rarely sees—at least in adults or in older children—the complete form of psychic helplessness in which the ego is *completely* overrun, has lost every modicum of its available resources, and is a completely helpless and passive victim. When this does occur, one may see clinically either a wild, aimless, uncoordinated motor thrashing, or a state of paralysis or frozen immobility, or at other times a state of limpness and atonia which may precede a faint. (These are the phenomenological variations in the traumatic *state*.) The regressive ego disorganization would be to the state of psychic organization (or lack of it) characteristic of the neonate.

However, what is more frequently seen are either *partial* states of such helplessness and loss of control or, as Keiser (1965) has pointed out, the disorganization or impairment of certain selected ego functions, while others remain uninvolved. There must be, however, a sufficient or significant degree of such loss present, of such a "hurt" to the organism, before the occurrence can justify the label of "trauma" or "traumatic." While the required degree of such breakdown might vary somewhat among analysts in accordance with individual analytic experience, I believe we all can and should agree upon some reasonable common consensus as to the degree of disorganization or helplessness necessary to render the term meaningful. Otherwise, at the other end of the spectrum, a stretching of the term to include occurrences too mild in degree would invite semantic confusion and render our terminology useless. Just as Hartmann (1939a) pointed out that not every disturbance of psychic equilibrium constitutes intrapsychic conflict, similarly not every intruding stimulus is a traumatic one.

However, the same caution also needs to be applied at the opposite extreme—that is, just as the concept of trauma cannot be extended to include the trivial, so must it not be restricted to refer only to the catastrophic. There has been much discussion about the question of the degree or extent or "bigness" of trauma required. In the early period, the traumas that were mainly referred to, essentially by the older analysts, were "big ones," severe, cataclysmic, those spoken of as "real" traumas. In fact, there was concern that the term "traumatic" was being diluted too much, almost to the extent of losing its meaning. Dilution of terms is generally an American trait, some analysts have ventured, so that, for example, to a European the word "starving" means that someone is emaciated from having literally nothing to eat, while in America this same term might simply mean that one cannot easily afford a second glass of beer ("although in England," one analyst has remarked, "if a man is starving, we say he's going hungry"). Or in this country "to have power over" might simply mean " the ability to influence," while in Europe (at least the Europe of a few decades ago) it meant "who can arrest or shoot whom." Whatever truth exists in these observations reminds me of a patient in "Hollywood" who, when missing an appointment, would send a telegram to her analyst with a message like "Sorry. Will miss appointment today. Love."

Nevertheless I do feel that we see all variations of psychic trauma and traumatic effect from the most severe to relatively more mild. As the result of much discussion and exchange, the concept of trauma became more inclusive and it seemed necessary to encompass relatively less intense and more circumscribed events under it. Waelder,[*] for example, in close to a final statement, recalled that Freud himself had used trauma in two senses, one for events that could only be seen as cataclysmic, and one that would include the experience of a one-year-old boy whose mother leaves the room and who then plays peek-a-boo. This latter may not qualify, but it makes the point.

There is of course no reason to lament these trends, nor does it mean that we are getting soft. We have no choice but to recognize changing forms and changing patterns of neuroses, and these include patterns of traumas. They have become more subtle, more complex, more partial, and often much less discernible. Not only has the locus and emphasis shifted from external to internal, but various new forms, both quantitatively and qualitatively, have also come to be understood. Thus Ernst Kris (1956) has pointed to the differentiation between shock trauma and strain trauma. Much elaboration of these and other concepts has come from others; by Sandler[*] on strain trauma, Khan (1963, 1964) on cumulative trauma, and others on partial trauma, chronic trauma, screen trauma, retrospective trauma, and retroactive trauma. Greenacre[*] refers to trauma that acts like an erosion, and Waelder[*] to differences between revolutionary and evolutionary processes, although he would restrict trauma to the former. Waelder also correctly points out that a strain may not be a trauma but a prolonged state of tension without discharge. I would agree with this and have pointed to the same discrete state of tension in describing the sequential occurrences in intrapsychic conflict (Chapters 7 and 8). Only when the strain finally results in a break is there a trauma, but I would say that there can be many "little breaks." Solnit[*] suggests that trauma may need a definable end-point.

Keeping in mind the need to fulfill certain minimum prerequisites, we need not hesitate to recognize the existence of these diverse types of ubiquitous life experiences. I have described more acute although equally common instances of traumatic disequilibrium in situations of sudden and acutely

[*]Contributors to *Psychic Trauma* (1967).

painful loss of social poise (Chapter 4). As examples of the latter, one can think of the state of becoming flustered in certain social situations. This might occur, for example, in the simple act of entering a room and being suddenly confronted with certain people or situations which one cannot immediately absorb or master, resulting in a relative although usually temporary and limited loss of ego control. Marianne Kris* mentions a rent or crack in the stimulus barrier instead of a breakthrough, or the possibility of a slow breaking through rather than a sudden piercing. While the possibility of our losing the concept of trauma by widening it too much has been well taken and must be borne in mind, I would submit that expanding clinical experience requires us to admit such less-than-cataclysmic processes under the aegis of trauma, provided that we adhere carefully to the presence of the minimum requisite effects that I have described.

Finally there is one further point I would mention under economic considerations: that the timing of the intrapsychic sequence of traumatogenic events also varies considerably. The component segments may follow one another in immediate succession or the time lag may be considerable. With respect to the effect of the quantity of traumatic stimulus, not only is the magnitude of the excitation crucial, but its *suddenness* of occurrence is also a most significant element in determining its traumatogenic effect. Examples of "adjustment" to chronic external conditions that would be overwhelming if they were sudden are too well known to need documentation. Moreover, with respect to timing, an event occurring at one phase of development may acquire its traumatic quality at a subsequent maturational phase when susceptibility to the particular past event has been achieved. This accounts for the phenomenon of retroactive trauma. For example, being present in the midst of primal scenes may have little or no effect on a young infant in his or her first year or even later, but such repeated perceptual experiences may suddenly acquire a traumatic impact in the prephallic or phallic-oedipal phase, when a sensitivity to them has developed. Or, in another variation, a current environmental situation may in retrospect render an event previously experienced as traumatic, resulting again in a delayed appearance of a traumatic effect. Such occurrences are often dramatized in caricature form as the phenomenon of the "double-take."

THE GENETIC POINT OF VIEW

I have noted repeatedly, in some of the examples already given, references to the conditions of the host, the capacities of the ego, and factors of specific sensitivities and susceptibilities of the latter, developmentally induced. The "magnitude of the excitation," Freud (1933) said, is crucial, but not in any fixed quantitative way. Rather it is *relative to* the particular ego resources available, the ability of the particular ego to contain the types and degree of stimuli that threaten to invade. As stated before, it is common experience that certain stimuli, trivial in quantitative terms, can exert a powerful traumatic effect, while others of formidable magnitude can often be easily tolerated. And genetically speaking, what may be a trivial and innocuous stimulus to one can be an overwhelming trauma to another, to a point comparable to anaphylactic shock. Analogous to the latter, such variable effects depend on the genetic history of previous sensitizations. Moreover, again as in the physical analogy, exposure to the same noxiae can lead in one instance to sensitization and in another to resistance and immunity. This explains why, for example, the same upbringing (or as close as one can come to this in such difficult-to-control matters) can lead to two diverse and opposite outcomes.

The genetic point of view adds much to the consideration of constitution and of magnitude of excitation. It contributes the insight that, in general, for a particular precipitating event to possess traumatic qualities or potentialities, it must either be strong enough or else comply with the areas of previous sensitization in the individual. For what can become traumatic varies with the individual ontogenetic development and the history of previous sensitizations. What has been traumatic once will tend to be so again, along with anything associatively connected with the original traumatic situation. Thus separation will be an exquisite trauma only if it characteristically has been so before. In Chapter 29, I stress that while in one sense termination can be thought of as always bringing out separation problems, this is mainly and prominently the case only where such problems have been typical and dominant before. In other instances, the termination process can revive mainly castration problems, if sensitization and previous experiences have gone particularly in this direction. The equation of trauma of diverse origin and form to castration is the cross of those who have suffered this type of anxiety throughout life. Clinical examples abound to demonstrate this in phobics, perversions, and anxiety-ridden characters of many types. However, where the universal castration complex has been worked through and resolved with sufficient solidity in the original oedipal situation, this particular traumatic potential does not protrude as a vulnerable Achilles heel or an abnormally tender area from then on.

The same applies to all possible variations of specific individual traumatic experiences suffered in the historical and genetic past. Many complex factors and vectors of the genetic development determine the vulnerabilities as well as the strengths of the ego with respect to general and specific potentialities for trauma. Thus one person remains sensitive to being alone, another to being unwanted, and another to the trauma of frequent moves and changes of scene. Each is determined by individual genetic experiences that result in a specific vulnerable area of potential traumatic narcissistic injury.

THE TOPOGRAPHIC POINT OF VIEW

The traumatic elements are usually unconscious and exist in the latent meaning of external events rather than in their conscious, overt, or manifest appearances. Our point of view here is much the same as our persistent quest for the latent content behind the manifest dream. Always it is the latent and unconscious meaning of the psychic event that is most crucial in determining the course and outcome. Thus, for example, the overt and manifest event of leaving for the Army may mean to one the threat of separation, to another homosexual temptation, to still another the threat of uncontrolled aggression or again oedipal, phallic, or castrative conflicts. The varieties of potential trauma and their underlying individual meanings will vary respectively. Similarly, neurotic breakdown in combat has been maintained by Simmel (1944) to be due not so much to the immediately imminent physical threats in their readily apparent form as to a revival of unconscious and latent castration fear. Patently the analytic process is a constant search for such unconscious and latent meanings of traumas behind their external and distorted façades.

THE DYNAMIC POINT OF VIEW

The chain of intrapsychic events, of which trauma is merely one link and one possibility, must be broken down into its separate components with clarity and precision. This succession of dynamic, intrapsychic, sequential events comprises the essence of the psychoanalytic literature and is in a sense the center of the psychoanalytic contribution to the understanding of neuroses.

In this sequential chain, the concept of trauma is inextricably bound up with the theory of anxiety and with the nature of intrapsychic conflict. Without going into detail and repeating the entire series here, let me mention that there are fine but definite and necessary differentiations between tension, danger, anxiety, and trauma, and each must be clearly understood in its own role. Danger, for example, is not yet trauma but the possibility of trauma. Trauma is the danger come true. Anxiety is the awareness of its possibility. These are oversimplified, since more complex relationships also hold. Thus, for example, trauma may also be experienced without previous anticipation and hence without previously existing as a feared danger. The noxious precipitating stimulus may have struck unheralded and have produced its traumatic effects unsignaled and unprepared for. (This sequence is the rule in the earliest months of life, before the capacity for signal anxiety has been achieved. It probably takes place very rarely in later life. It takes but a flash for signal anxiety to intervene even before the most sudden impending disaster.) Or, despite the differentiation just given, anxiety of sufficient tenacity or degree can itself become traumatic, just as symptoms can produce anxiety.

The traumatic event, which is frequently and incorrectly used interchangeably with trauma, needs to be differentiated from the traumatic state that it produces. The traumatic state of helplessness, panic, or being overrun by stimuli can be the result, or at least is the feared result, of uncontrolled trauma, but it is not the same as the traumatic event or insult itself. The latter can be infinitely varied, while the traumatic state is a rather uniform psychoeconomic state, except in degree. The traumatic event, such as the primal scene, the rejection, the act (or thought) of being abandoned, or the physical insult, is the precipitating stimulus that sets off the noxious chain, while the traumatic state is the result that ensues in the absence of more or less successful intervening defenses. Of course in happy circumstances the threatened trauma may be warded off or otherwise dealt with in earlier phases and not result in a traumatic state. If this takes place with sufficient completeness, then the threat was averted and the dangerous stimulus turned out to be no trauma at all.

The traumatic state itself, however, may act as a further traumatic insult, as is the case with any disturbing affective state, such as anxiety or depression, or a state of continuing frustration and psychic helplessness. This in itself, in patients with heightened narcissism, easy vulnerability, high ego ideals and yet shaky self-esteem, may serve as a traumatic narcissistic injury that sets off a further trend of regressive decompensation to a still deeper and more severe traumatic state. Such a circular and hierarchic layering of psychopathology is not uncommon and is responsible for many typical cases of severe and widespread emotional disturbance. The mechanism of a symptom-producing anxiety going on to a traumatic effect and producing new or more symptoms has been described by Fenichel (1945) in his basic account of neurosogenesis, and in more detail in my own description of the "microscopic" processes that take place in intrapsychic conflict (see Chapters 7 and 8). Elizabeth Zetzel (1965) has shown how, in patients with shaky self-esteem and an inadequate achievement of separation and individuation, anxiety leads to depression by a mechanism similar to the above. Although such a hierarchy and stratification of events can and in clinical practice does typically occur, we should maintain clarity in our concepts of the separate components and their interaction.

This brings to mind the cases of several adult patients with massive rather than circumscribed states of depressive anxiety—that is, in which the latter has no particular beginning period and seems to be all-pervasive and omnipresent in the patient's time and space. I would not necessarily classify these cases as "borderline." The mood, the oppression, the burden is, as one of these patients puts it, "the story of my life." The reconstructed early life of this particular man—aside from what he refers to as his "pink period," when he was happily cradled and loved and fed in his mother's negligeed lap before his sister was born when he was 3—consisted only of darkness, despair, and hurt. It would not be possible in these few lines to document or give the flavor of the uniform atmosphere of trauma upon trauma, danger upon threat that he suffered or at least remembers or feels he suffered during all the subsequent years of his youth. The downward spiraling effect noted above was prominent, with each reversal serving as another blow in endless procession. The fact was also frequently brought out that there was no relief, no figure in the family or the surroundings, and no particular developmental period that could bring about a lift or a respite. It is only the early "pink period" of his past that gives us hope for his future. Fortunately the more that is known both about it and about the repressed details and significance of the years of trauma, the more mastery this patient acquires in his present adult life.

Just as Schur has described a stratification of anxieties (1953, 1958) and also of dangers (1964), so can we postulate a stratification of traumas that are phase-specific during the course of developmental progression. Thus the primal scene is not a trauma to the neonate or during the first year of life, but it may well become an overwhelming traumatic stimulus a few short years later. Separation is not as much of a trauma during the latency period or later as it is in the tender preoedipal years. Still later, in adolescence or beyond, it may be the *failure* to separate that serves as a traumatic neurosogenic stimulus. It is this fact of phase-specificity by which both cumulative trauma (Khan, 1963, 1964) and retrospective trauma can have their effects. An event or a succession of events, nontraumatic at one point, may achieve traumatic effects when (1) their magnitude has accumulated sufficiently so that they would have such effects in anyone, and (2) the sensitization and reaction point of the particular host have been reached.

It should be stated, although by now it must be clear, that the traumatic process is not synonymous with "pathogenic." As (normal) mourning is to be differentiated from (pathological) melancholia, so is the traumatic state different from a traumatic or any type of psychoneurosis. Just as conflict and resistances are part of the human condition, so is traumatic experience. It is as much a part of human life to suffer helplessness at certain critical points or inevitable crises as it is to taste the loss of a loved object. Part of a general psychology, trauma may be followed by complete recovery and successful adaptation as much as by a resort to pathogenic development and symptom formation.

One may indeed go further and speculate that traumas are not only inevitable but also, in a sense, to a large degree apparently needed. This might seem to be consonant with the love-hate dualism in instinctual life and the life-death dualism in nature, part of the dualistic approach so central in Freud's thinking, as Jones (vol. 2) quotes Hartmann. The very act of living is a first trauma to the organism, and the trauma of birth is a prototype to future ones (Freud, 1926). Just as there is object-hunger and stimulus-need, so might there be said to be a prevalent trauma-need. This could be the case not only because without pain one would not know pleasure, but also because of the many well-known behavioral phenomena beyond the pleasure principle (Freud 1920), such as masochism, guilt, and the need for punishment.

One might sense the quality of this need by considering the extreme opposite situation, that is, the phenomena that occur in conditions of isolation or sensory deprivation. The boredom, frustration, agitation, and at times the hallucinations that result (Shurley, 1960; Solomon et al., 1957) attest to the need for stimuli, which clinical and other experiences in various life situations indicate can reach the point of no less than noxious stimuli. Not only is there from *external* sources what I have referred to as "the wear and tear of everyday life" (Rangell, 1960a), but there is also the *inner* and built-in "crises of maturity"—i.e., the series of internal and inevitable crises, which can and do quite characteristically go on to the point of becoming traumas, which obtrude from within at certain nodal periods during the course of the entire life cycle.

Actually, in the last analysis, trauma can come from too little or too much with regard to stimuli, just as in early life traumatic fixation can ensue from either overdeprivation or overgratification. A short story by Somerset Maugham (1948) tells of two inmates of a tuberculosis hospital whose lives were dedicated to torturing each other and "to make life hell for one another." When one of them dies, the other becomes depressed. I have written of a "tertiary gain of symptoms" (1954b) whereby the disabling and ego-alien symptom becomes incorporated and integrated into the self and the body image and is tenaciously guarded with narcissistic libido and interest. The disease itself comes to serve multiple psychic functions and becomes a needed element in the total psychic life situation. A patient revealed this same peculiar search when shortly after surgery for an intestinal growth he observed: "I've just had what you can call cancer surgery. What greater sign is there that I've arrived? And yet I still don't feel that way." Not too long ago I watched a man proceed step by step to break up a satisfactory marriage and a thriving, successful business and home life as he relentlessly chose a path toward self-destruction. We analysts have of course annotated such a trend in human affairs for many years, e.g., Menninger (1938) in the phenomena of *Man against Himself*. Repetition compulsion, aggressive drive, death instinct, masochistic need, superego pressure, guilt, and the need for punishment are among the many explanations we have adduced for this seemingly self-imposed quest for traumas.

However, while I have in the interest of completeness described this speculative idea of a possible primary traumato-philia, a strong case can also be made against it. It can be argued, and with merit, that a need for stimuli, which is incontrovertible, is not the same and is indeed far from a need for trauma. And it could be shown, I believe, that in many of the examples given it is not a traumatic disequilibrium or a loss of ego control which results, but on the contrary in each case it is equilibrium and ego *mastery* which are achieved by these perverse and seemingly destructive trends. The tubercular patient could well have been depressed, not because he missed being tormented but because he missed the object for his aggression or even, to the surprise of no analyst, an object he unconsciously loved. Thus none of these instances would really qualify to be called traumas, and the latter, when they do occur, could be states that are endured rather than sought for. Or, in many instances of what seems to be a relentlessly masochistic path, lesser traumas could be shown to be accepted or even sought in order to avoid more major ones. Greenacre[*] has pointed out that in instances of severe early traumas such mechanisms are often ultimately in the service of the very preservation of life. I would subscribe to these latter points of view. However, the entire question of traumatophilia joins with the related and philosophically fertile but equally controversial area of the death instinct in merging from the realm of psychology to that of philosophy. And we will leave them both there.

THE STRUCTURAL POINT OF VIEW

It is mainly with the elaboration of the structural point of view that new dimensions of understanding accrue. With progressive structuralization and the increased breadth and complexity of psychic development attendant upon this, traumas can be more carefully defined and the role that they play can be understood in a more subtle, varied, complex, and multidimensional way.

Thus from the standpoint of locus of origin, a trauma, or rather the precipitating stimulus that will initiate the train of intrapsychic events that constitute trauma, may originate from an external stimulus (influx) or equally from within, from somatic or psychic sources. With respect to the last of these, if we consider the psychic apparatus in terms of psychic structure, such impingement can originate from the direction of any of the tripartite psychic structures. While a common instance is from the instinctual drive organization, as a result of an increase in either libidinal or aggressive instinctual pressure, it is possible, in accordance with Hartmann's (1939a, 1950a) principle of autonomy, that an increase in intrasystemic tension in any psychic structure can reach a point at which it can initiate traumatic psychic consequences. Thus in some instances such a stimulus can also occur *ab initio* from the direction of the ego, for example, by the exercise of a strong ego judgment or by a critical decrease in self-esteem. Or there can be a reduction in strength or capacity of the stimulus barrier or of a specific ego defense, such as denial, resulting, for example, in a sudden confrontation with a phobic object. Similarly pressure can stem from the side of the superego, by a rising momentum of superego criticism or disapproval that ultimately becomes more oppressive to the ego. The increasing intrasystemic tension results in increasing strain that, when its intensity reaches beyond a certain threshold, can become a traumatic stimulus.

Rapaport (1960) states: "These more neutralized derivative motivations will be autonomous from—i.e., can be activated without being triggered by—the underlying less neutralized motivations. For instance, they may discharge when their autonomously accumulated energy reaches threshold intensity."

The functions of memory, fantasy, and the thought processes in general are another important ego activity by which stimuli, traumatic ones among them, can emanate from within the psychic apparatus. Past traumatic events, fixed in memory, can be meted out at any time in fantasy, conscious or unconscious, thus enabling past experiences to retain current traumatic valence. Keiser (in Panel, 1965) has pointed out the special proclivity of the gifted to traumatic disturbance on the basis of their more highly developed memories. And Eissler (in Panel, 1965) adds that what seems like overreaction is really not so if understood in relation to the magnitude of the memory of the trauma. While by this means the dosage of trauma can be mitigated and controlled, the trauma is also at the same time converted from an acute to a chronic one. Traumatic neurosis owes its origin to this mechanism, although over a span of time psychoneurosis based on intrinsic instinctual impulses hardly ever fails to become admixed (Fenichel, 1945).

The capacity of the ego to bear or cope with the stimulus is of crucial importance in determining whether the latter reaches traumatic intensity. From whatever source the stimuli emanate, it is only the ego which suffers them and which can be traumatized. The instincts push for discharge, which is either granted or not, and the superego admonishes, which is either listened to or not. But it is only the ego which, besides having the responsibility of choice, also has the possibility of mortification, in keeping with its being the seat of the affects. Freud's (1933) statement that "all along we are dealing with questions of *relative* quantities" (my italics) now acquires more definitive meaning. The ultimate presence or absence of trauma is determined by the relationship of the excitation to the capacities of the ego to handle it, by binding, defending, discharging, or compromising, in one form or another, such as by symptom formation. The myriad of possibilities for ego action is beyond our concern and has been described in much other literature. The role of identification processes, in combination with other more autonomous growth factors in determining the ego's operations and capacities toward impinging stimuli, has also been annotated elsewhere.

For psychic trauma to be possible, it is necessary for a receptive ego to be present. Genetically, in the earliest pre-ego states, it has been shown repeatedly that while physical traumas and reflex activity may occur, there is not yet the intervening mental sequences that are the necessary accompaniments of psychic activity. At least what Greenacre (1945) has called a "dawning ego" is a prerequisite for the beginning of the latter. Soon there is a transitional phase of organic and early psychological admixture in which a borderland of psychobiological reactivity takes place. Gradually, in steplike gradations, from such an earliest nascent dawning existence a structured ego begins to evolve that becomes more or less constant, enduring, and time-abiding. Trauma too follows this line of development and itself progresses from an initial role that has purely physical and mechanistic consequences to a more complicated and multidimensional psychological significance. The period prior to self-object differentiation and before anxiety as a signal is achieved, when the affective possibilities are only satisfaction or diffuse undifferentiated unpleasure, is the period referred to previously when trauma and psychic helplessness can and do occur unprotected by previous anticipation. The advent of signal anxiety brings with it the capacity to expect—danger as well as pleasure—with the enormous impact this has on the history of future traumas. There follow, in gradual succession, the ability to delay and then to stave off, first crudely and then by increasingly more polished methods. The ontogenetic history of these methods and the accompanying vicissitudes of the fates and styles of his traumatic experiences is the history of the individual's ability to cope, which is a large segment of the history of his psychic development.

THE ADAPTIVE POINT OF VIEW

Any psychic situation which threatens a necessary and sought-for adaptation can of itself acquire a traumatic quality. Here too it is a major function of the ego, that of maintaining internal-external equilibrium in addition to ensuring internal homeostasis, which is subject to threat. It was the original overemphasis of this environmental aspect that caused the early view of trauma to be seen purely as external. Trauma can now be seen as coming from either direction and having disruptive consequences to both the internal and external equilibrium.

Finally, the adaptive value of traumas should be recognized and not overlooked. From the adaptive point of view (Rapaport and Gill, 1959), it should be noted that trauma may lead not only to pathogenesis but also to *higher* levels of adaptation. These latter, however, are not inherent in the traumatic occurrence itself, but when they do occur it is as a consequence of the "bounce" or reparative qualities in the ego and its ability to learn from experience. Anna Freud* pointed out that when, after an earthquake, a town is rebuilt better than it was before, it is not the earthquake that should get the credit but the people who did the rebuilding. Zetzel (1949) has emphasized the adaptive role of the ego's capacity to bear anxiety and, more recently, depression (1965) as a token of and a stimulus to ego growth, and has brought out the salutary effects of such adaptation on the development of ego autonomy and psychic maturity in general. Certainly the same is true in an even broader sense of the ego's capacity to deal in a resourceful and nonpathological manner with the entire broad spectrum of traumas to which it is subject. Of course the opposite occurrence is better known when regression of a temporary or even permanent nature takes place and when subsequent behavior is at a lower level of adaptation as a result of severe or repeated traumas. Ekstein (1963) talks of a "positive trauma" that enhances creativity and a "negative trauma" that leads to the experience of being overwhelmed. However, creativity brought about in this way, remarks Greenacre,* can contain a certain degree of "touchiness as well as responsiveness." Freud (1937c) points similarly to two opposite trends that follow trauma: a positive effect that stimulates efforts to confront and overcome it, and a negative effect that aims toward repression and avoidance. Sometimes one component, sometimes the other predominates, and both of these trends, especially following early traumas, leave their marks in the subsequent character.

The history and fate of an individual with regard to his traumatic experiences is of course a hallmark in the diagnosis and the offering of a prognosis of his psychic life. The ontogenetic developmental history in respect to whether traumas have in general had an eroding and deleterious influence or have been followed by reparation and advance is of crucial significance in determining the subsequent strength and stability of the ego. The interrelationships and the mutual interaction of such a history of conflict with the conflict-free and autonomous psychic elements together comprise much of the whole of an individual's psychic development.

RECAPITULATION, INTEGRATION, AND SUMMARY

I have now finished examining the various metapsychological points of view in my effort to encompass the subject of psychic trauma. Next I should recapitulate and to try to combine and integrate all of the above data and observations and the many seemingly diverse elements that I have accumulated—historical, empirical, and theoretical—into a complete and concise theory of trauma. Toward this end, let me now mention that of the many different views and points of emphasis which have been offered none is contradictory or mutually exclusive, but they are all components which need to be tied together into a continuous integrated unit in order to give the whole story of trauma. With all of them, even as with the seemingly different explanations given by Freud during the periods of historical evolution, it was merely that each piece of insight was discovered and reached one at a time; however, all

of them belong together. The traumatic occurrence, in my
opinion, is a dynamic sequence which needs to be broken up
into its various components as well as viewed as a composite
psychic experience. It includes a stimulus and mode of onset,
the occurrence of a specific intrapsychic process and a requisite
psychological result to encompass the complete experience. No
part alone is sufficient.

These sequential components can be considered to be
comprised of the following: (1) The precipitating stimulus,
which will set off the traumatic process, is the *traumatic event*
(the seduction, the rejection, the insult, the psychic invasion).
The event alone, however, without the ensuing specific process,
would not be traumatic and could in fact be entirely innocuous.
Its subsequent effects are *sine qua nons* for it to qualify as being
part of a traumatic disturbance. (2) The traumatic event goes
on to elicit an intrapsychic *traumatic process*. The essence of this
traumatic process consists of a breakthrough of a significant or
sufficient degree of the protective stimulus barrier. This is
accompanied by a loss of ego control or of the mediating power
of the ego, again to a certain minimum required degree (the
matter of the degree has been sufficiently discussed and should
conform to some generally accepted consensus of theoreticians-
clinicians). (3) The occurrence of this traumatic process is
followed by a *traumatic effect or result*, which is the state of
psychic helplessness, again of sufficient or significant degree.
(4) The latter results in and is accompanied by the release of
painful and unpleasurable affect.

This continuum of events constitutes trauma. It is seen to
include in its scope each of the four major components that
were stressed at different times and in different historical
contexts by Freud, as noted and reviewed at the beginning of
this chapter (in their original order, the distressing affects,
excessive stimuli, breakthrough of the stimulus barrier, and
psychic helplessness). While this is the presentation of a skeletal
or model occurrence and while clinically there is always a great
deal of superimposed complexity and variation, I believe that in

the essence of a traumatic occurrence the various elements in the above sequence take place.

I would like to conclude by offering this composite description—still not rigorously a definition—of trauma (containing what I consider the *sine qua nons* and yet conforming to the parsimony for which I indicated at the beginning that I would strive):

A traumatic occurrence is characterized by the intrusion into the psychic apparatus of a stimulus or series of stimuli (the *traumatic event*), varying in their qualitative manifest contents, in their quantitative characteristics, and in their time relationships, which set off an unconscious train of intrapsychic events (the *traumatic process*) beyond the capacity of the ego to master at that particular time. The dynamics of the traumatic intrapsychic process which ensue lead to the rupture, partial or complete, of the ego's barrier or defensive capacities against stimuli, without a corresponding subsequent ability of the ego adequately to repair the damage in sufficient time to maintain mastery and a state of security. The resulting state (the *traumatic state*) is a feeling of psychic helplessness, in a series of gradations from brief, transitory, and relative to more complete and long-lasting. As a result of insufficient resources on the part of the ego, there is a feeling of lack of control and a vulnerability to further stimuli, without the expectation of adequate containment, mastery, and adaptation. In relatively mild or transitory degree, this state is as much a part of the human condition as is anxiety or intrapsychic conflict, from both of which, though contiguous, it is different. In moderate or severe degree, either in quantity or in duration, it itself is a pathological state, comparable to an anxiety state that is substantial or long-lasting. The traumatic state can be followed by recovery or can go on to resolution or to a further elaboration into symptom formation. In itself it is characteristically an unstable and transient psychoeconomic condition, which in the course of mental functioning goes on to a state of greater stability, in the direction of either favorable adaptation or a more pathological psychic end product.

Section III
Choice and Responsibility

Introduction

This next section focuses on what I consider the most innovative contributions of this series of papers. These constitute not only an expansion of work which had been laid down before by Freud and others but the delineation of new ideas not hitherto recognized or at least focused upon. Anna Freud said that analysis does not create but discovers, that it uncovers what is already there. The evidence for an active unconscious ego, the activities of which I have called the "executive functions of the ego," has been there but undiscovered and unarticulated. An active decision-making role on the part of the ego has been overlooked in theoretical discourse, certainly in emphasis, but also in being specifically formulated.

This section deals with decision, autonomy, integrity, and will. Subjects brought up and studied have to do with the active ego, the unconscious decision-making function of the ego, ego autonomy, moral conflicts, the syndrome of the compromise of integrity, psychic determinism, and a psychoanalytic approach to the problem of "freedom" of will. These pose a new look at the question of responsibility and of accountability.

One paper deals with a special area and instance of decision-making—suicide, the unconscious aspects of the decision to terminate one's life.

CHAPTER 13

The Decision-Making Process

A Contribution from Psychoanalysis

In the past decade or so there has come to exist a vast body of literature on what is called "decision theory." Its borders are diffuse and ill defined, the number of titles overwhelming, and the areas of knowledge which contribute to it are many and scattered. Deriving its original impetus from a motivation of salesmanship, the theoretical literature on decision has remained intimately attached to hard questions of practical application in business, commercial, and military life. Until today it is more abundant in the journals of mathematics, economics, business, and applied statistics than in the behavioral sciences, and is part of game theory, but has also found its way into psychology, philosophy, and sociology.

Psychoanalysis, however, is conspicuously not represented. In the author index of a recent survey on decision-making

Fifth Annual Freud Anniversary Lecture of the Psychoanalytic Association of New York, May 18, 1970. Published in *The Psychoanalytic Study of the Child*, 26:425–452, 1971.

(Edwards and Tversky, 1967), of some 500 listed authors, Freud's name does not appear, nor, to my knowledge, does that of any other psychoanalyst. Although recently lip service has begun to be paid to the need for "a dynamic decision theory," such theory remains "static" and "ahistorical," and "decision theorists look to the current situation, rather than to the past experiences of the decider, for the variables that control decision" (Edwards and Tversky, 1967, p. 8).

This is not to say, however, that we are excluded from without. The same lacuna is curiously evident within the psychoanalytic literature. "Decision" does not appear in the subject indices of our journals, in any of the *Annual Surveys of Psychoanalysis* in the past 20 years, nor is it a familiar title or subject in our scientific panels or discussions. Close in the alphabet to "defense," the latter generally occupies a half page to a page of listings, with no listing of any contribution to "decision-making." Yet the institution of defense requires a decision.

It is obvious that a lag is in evidence and that decision-making has a deep root in the unconscious and the genetic past, which brings it into the center of the domain of psycho-analysis.[1] I would like in this presentation to begin to fill this lacuna and to add the psychoanalytic view to this crucial aspect of human psychic activity.

To bring the subject into focus, I shall start with a clinical situation. As is often the case in psychoanalysis, psychic functions come to be best understood if we study instances of their breakdown. To understand decision-making I shall therefore turn to a case which is mainly one of indecision. Problems of decision-making occur perhaps in all psychoanalytic cases, but in some they are the central issue. In the case to be presented, indecision raged as the central feature, both in the patient's life and during the psychoanalytic process.

---

[1]Mathematicians and engineers call what comes from here "noise" in the system! (Swets, 1967).

CASE ILLUSTRATION

Mr. A. came to analysis because his wife, to whom he had been married for 10 years, was pregnant, about which he was in a state of severe anxiety and panic. One of his conditions of the marriage had been an agreement not to have children. This was not merely a matter of preference or predilection, but his aversion to children had a phobic intensity. He took every precaution and watched every movement during the marriage to carry out this prerequisite. His wife, in contrast, used every guile and trick and many ingenious maneuvers to try to bring a pregnancy about. She had managed, in the most creative ways, to become pregnant three or four times, but each time had conveniently miscarried, probably deliberately and mainly to please him—not out of love and consideration, but out of awe, fear, and a deep respect for the intensity of his fear and determination. Now she was pregnant again, but on this occasion she seemed to be determined to keep it. By this time he was too guilty and ambivalent to stop it. The result was severe anxiety and his move to come into analysis to enable him to face what was to come.

Almost as soon as he started, his wife miscarried again. The patient's anxiety ceased at once, but his analysis continued and settled down to a natural and unhurried course. What gradually unfolded was a chronic, relentless, and paralyzing indecision, present virtually throughout his life, coupled with an incapacity to carry anything through to completion. The pervasiveness of these traits was evident centrally and alternately in the two major areas of psychic activity, the history of his love and work.

Mr. A. had married his wife after going with her for some time when she told him she was pregnant. He did not check or wait, just married her secretly out of town before a Justice of the Peace, because he knew that otherwise he would never decide to marry her or anyone else. He continued, however, to live with his parents for a year without telling them, trying to decide how to do so. He remembered finally telling his father, expecting him to break down at the news of the marriage. Instead, the father seemed happy and said, "We'll have to get you an apartment," at which the patient broke into tears. Similar episodes took place when he successively informed his mother and his brother.

There followed then all the years of his determination not to father a child, for which he gave a host of rationalizations and spurious reasons, all boiling down to a severe anxiety about becoming committed any further. Parenthood would make his choice irreversible. The effect of this attitude on the couple's sexual and object relatedness can easily be imagined. Bitterness, ambivalence, arguments, and chaos ensued, with each chasing and running away from the other. She would chase him and he would run, and then she would walk away and he would chase her. A chronic, mutually teasing and taunting, sadomasochistic relationship developed from which neither would go forward nor retreat. He repeatedly mistreated her, and she railed against him in return, and both were filled alternately with complaints and remorse. His attitudes toward her vacillated, over long periods of time as well as during each individual hour, between: "She's a bitch. She's impossible. She's horrible. She's a monster," to "Poor Joan. It's all my fault. She's a beautiful person. I've wasted the best years of her life. I see her growing old and wrinkled."

The quality and intensity of this marital dilemma were matched only by his occupational history. The patient was trained extensively not in one, but in two related, highly skilled professions, either one of which, or both in combination, or any one of the many specialties of each, provided a choice of many remunerative, rewarding, important, and prestigious ways of life. He could not, however, choose any one aspect of the many opportunities available, but vacillated endlessly between all the possibilities, and spent his time occupationally—presumably on a temporary basis, which, however, proved to be permanent— as a menial technician at the lowest rung of the ladder in the lesser of the two fields, ruminating about what he could and should do, finding interminable excuses not to proceed to any of them, and constantly bemoaning his fate. It became apparent, as his past history unfolded and his present behavior became understood, that the goal was always just to be accepted, wanted, chosen, and favored by a father figure—by the dean of the professional school, by the professor, by the president of the business, by the general in the army, by the analyst—to promise them all, and be accepted by and promised to them in return, and never to carry through.

Each opportunity was inexorably and in turn aborted. He never had a plan for what to do after finishing school or a piece of training, except to begin the cycle all over again. While working in one area, he would be full of fantasies concerned with completely alien fields and daydream about dramatic achievements in the stock market, advertising gimmicks, TV, promotion schemes of various sorts, financial deals, and certain spectacular and potentially important research ideas. There was always enough promise, substance, and beginning recognition in some wild, glamorous, exhibitionistic idea to stimulate him to persist and to keep those around him interested and hopeful, to prevent them from giving up on him. He talked his way into every office, never failed to interest a potential benefactor, and never followed through to fruition on any plan.

THEORETICAL CONSIDERATIONS

From this small thread of a complex case as a base, I turn next to a specific segment of psychoanalytic theory which I believe is relevant to the topic of this paper and which in the past has served as a track for my own interests. I came to delineate a microdynamic sequence of intrapsychic events which could serve as a model for what takes place in the unfolding of the intrapsychic process. Prior to the experience of signal anxiety, the ego, by permitting a small and controlled amount of instinctual discharge, and sampling the resulting and proportional reaction of the superego, brings about a preliminary, tentative, and experimental signal conflict. It is

following this reactive response of the superego, which depends on which of the store of traumatic memories have been
evoked, that signal anxiety, if it is to occur, takes place. The
next step, though often overlooked, is a crucial one, which I
feel illuminates a large segment of derivative external behavior.
I would have us stop the action, as it were, at this point, to
absorb fully an understanding of its theoretical implications.
The resulting anxiety, when it occurs, confronts the ego with a
dilemma between alternatives, with the necessity for a choice as
to what to do next, which of two competing psychic systems to
follow. This introduces into metapsychology a new concept of
the meaning of intrapsychic conflict, an intrapsychic choice
conflict of the ego, which is different from the oppositional
type of ego-id conflict usually meant in descriptions of intrapsychic conflict. In my earlier papers I have elaborated on the
relationships between this specific choice-dilemma type of
conflict and the more general concept of intrasystemic conflict
introduced by Hartmann (1950a).

What I have specifically added centers mainly on the initial
phases of the intrapsychic sequence: (a) I have extended
Freud's signal theory to include the preliminary experimental
signal conflict *before* signal anxiety takes place. In terms of
Freud's inoculation analogy, this in effect includes a description
of the injection phase of the inoculation prior to the reaction to
it, which is the signal anxiety. (b) From this I subsequently
attempted a clarification of the psychoanalytic theory of anxiety, and suggested a unification of Freud's two historical
theories. (c) Following the anxiety, I believe there occurs an
intrapsychic choice conflict within the ego, in addition to the
more usual oppositional type of intersystemic conflict between
ego and id (which may come later as one outcome). (d) Within
the inventory of ego functions I delineated a decision-making
function of the ego, specifically designed to resolve this intrapsychic choice or dilemma conflict.

It is this composite phase of the intrapsychic process with
its intrinsic ego sequence of anxiety-choice-decision-action
which, I submit, serves as the theoretical model for the psycho-

analytic contribution to decision theory. I do not believe that indecision stems from polar and opposite instinctual drives, or drive components, or qualities of drives. Such instinctual dichotomies result in ambivalence but not in indecision. Without an ego dilemma, both drive elements can be discharged and given expression, either simultaneously or successively. Where love and hate are in opposition, one of them, usually love, has made its claim upon the superego, which then succeeds in rendering the ego opposed to the opposite instinct of aggression. The dilemma and indecision follow.

The psychoanalytic process reverses this inner sequence and, starting from outward behavior, gives increasingly clear views of its origins within (see Chapter 21). The psychoanalytic process results in an evagination of the intrapsychic process. It is of central interest to this study to trace the connections between the core intrapsychic activity described and the variations and vacillations of decision-making as seen in external behavior—and thereby arrive at an understanding of the history, vicissitudes, and characteristics of the decision-making process itself. Having understood this in the analysis of individual patients, we may hope, as always, to transfer such knowledge to the decision-making process of man in general.

EARLY DEVELOPMENT

In order to pursue this early development, I return to the case of Mr. A. and cite the genetic factors that were associatively connected with his behavior. The patient's father was, we agreed, Willy Loman of *The Death of a Salesman*—full of schemes, promises, and failures. "They wanted me in Alaska" became a meaningful phrase in the analysis. When the father retired with a stroke after faithfully serving his firm for many years, he was presented with a gold watch inscribed "To Joe, a nice guy."

One of the patient's most vivid early memories was of sitting on a bannister, out of sight, watching his parents fighting, in terror that "daddy would kill mommy." There was one particular occasion when, after such a scene, the father sat the patient on his lap and said slowly and deliberately, "Danny, daddy is going away and is never coming back." The patient remembered breaking into inconsolable sobs, feeling shattered, helpless, as if his heart would break. His grief was so extreme that both parents became alarmed, tried desperately to console him, and repeatedly kissed each other, saying, "See, it's all right. Mommy loves daddy. Daddy loves mommy. It's going to be all right." He remembered feeling that somehow he had been bad and was responsible for all this.

The events surrounding this scene and his perception of them became a nodal traumatic memory. For years thereafter—in fact as long as he could remember—his one goal was "not to make waves," "don't do anything." He would "walk on eggs" not to antagonize one against the other, so that they would continue to be nice to each other, so that "mommy and daddy would love each other." He remembered anticipating his father's return home each night; he would check the dinner table to make sure that the knives, spoons, and forks were set exactly right, that the right dishes were used for each of them, so that neither of them would get mad at the other.

Another shattering experience, another determining traumatic incident in his life, occurred at age 11, when his father visited him at summer camp and informed him that his mother had given birth to a baby brother—but again saying, "It's all right, everything is okay. It's all going to be all right." He remembered getting sick in the pit of his stomach, feeling as if the world had come to an end, wandering off alone in the woods to compose himself, and suffering a crucial anxiety attack such as he was to know many more of later. This initial reaction was quickly submerged and replaced by a reactive love and devotion to his brother of exaggerated and maudlin degree. Another memory, recalled with horror and guilt, was of a year or so later: he inserted his penis into the mouth of his baby brother who was standing in the crib. This memory was part of another important line of development and played an equally crucial role in subsequent events.

During the course of years of analysis, many of the unconscious roots were exposed and linkages established between his present alternating anxiety and indecision and the early genetic backgrounds from which they developed. Forward movement in his marital life would both break his existing real oedipal attachments to which he was fixed and committed (his wife was an avowed enemy of his mother) and create new ones in disguised and displaced form. Each of these would result in an intolerable increase in anxiety. On the other hand, he would not sever the marriage and leave his wife, which would mean being wrenched away from the regressed pre-genital comfort he derived from his willing wife-mother. She, for her part, took care of his every need, fed him, gave up all her friends and activities to stay with him, coddled him, babied him, masturbated him—and also lost her temper with him, screamed, threatened, and beat at him in her exasperation. The latter only made up for his guilt and made him feel better. The stalemate and only the stalemate suited his every need. His father had died during the analysis, and the patient now had his mother (two of them), his brother and himself as a menage, all of whom depended on him. His brother now was his son. He need not and would not repeat the trauma of his birth by voluntarily having another.

The same gains were forthcoming from his frozen occupational status. His identification with his father in his present situation was clear and became evident. Going forward to a new and advanced position would both betray and dethrone his homosexually loved father and lead to further demands and expectations from his wife-mother, whom he was of no mind to treat better than his father did. "I am watching her being strangled to death," he complained, and continued.

The patient lived on a razor's edge between decisions—actually on two razors, one with regard to the marriage and one to work. And there was another razor between the two: whenever the discussions about either one began to lean him toward moving to one side or the other, he would turn to an endless to and fro concentration on the other issue. Any

associations leading in one direction were automatically balanced by bringing up some which pulled in another. This
mechanism was further fortified by somatic accompaniments.
He developed a head nod so that whenever he was associating
about potent reasons for one side of any dilemma, his head
would be rhythmically and desperately nodding "no." And
whenever he came up with strong reasons for staying with his
wife, his face would simultaneously assume an anxious grimace,
or he would bare his teeth, and automatically put on record a
few reserve associations about some bitchy and impossible
episode on her part.

FURTHER COMMENT

In the sequence of intention-anxiety-choice-decision, the
interrelationships between the elements are as complex and
varied as is human life itself. The fate of decision-making is not
necessarily parallel to the degree of anxiety experienced;
neither is it to the benignness or malignancy of the final psychic
outcome, but has a specific and individual background of its
own. There may be acute and severe anxiety with no faltering
of the decisions to be made and, conversely, less severe anxiety
may be associated with paralyzing indecision. As a general
statement, decision-making is most difficult when the greatest
evenness and the most exquisite balance exist between desired
gratification on the one hand, and expectant punishment and
disapproval on the other—and when a person's life history has
not resulted in experiences leading to an undeniable inner
advantage and therefore a clear-cut preference of one over the
other. This was the case with the patient just described.

At this point in my presentation, I would have wished to
describe, as a contrasting example, a patient in a chronic,
severe, unremitting anxiety state in whom the decision-making
function nevertheless remained intact and efficient. For reasons of space, I shall insert this here, so to speak, by title only,
to make the main point without the luxury of the details.

In the face of her severe anxiety which stemmed from a

different genetic development than those of Mr. A., Mrs. B. knew decisively, unconsciously what she wanted to do—to withdraw from and deny the noxious stimuli. This mechanism helped but did not suffice. The anxiety continued to rage due to the uncontrollable impulses, the continually pressing traumatic memories, and the relative incapacity of her ego to contain or deal with them. Her decisions were not in question, only her capacities. She displayed no indecisiveness in the small or large decisions of life. It was remarkable, for example, how, when a good husband prospect appeared, she came out of herself long enough to be courted fairly normally and to enter upon what turned out to be an enduring marriage.

PSYCHOANALYTIC DECISION THEORY

Leaving psychopathology, I turn to general theory. The delineation of a psychoanalytic decision theory serves as a link between motivation (Rapaport, 1960) and action, and is en route to a psychoanalytic theory of action, which, as Hartmann (1947) pointed out, we do not yet have. From this point on, in commenting on the normal decision-making process, I shall select only a few of what I consider the most salient and pressing considerations in a voluminous subject.

Decision and indecision, where psychoanalysis has given them direct and specific attention, have been linked historically, from the genetic point of view, with influences and residuals deriving from the anal stage (Freud, 1909b, 1918; Abraham, 1921a; Jones, 1918). As we look back at this connection, which by continuous usage has become quite automatic, we see a phenomenon that commonly occurs in the development of our science. A historical linkage which, at the time of its origin, was responsible for an important leap in understanding, turns out upon closer inspection to be true and important but somewhat too exclusively specific. To cite an analogous example: I have previously (1959) spoken for a severance of the automatic linkage between conversion and hysteria, and pointed out that conversion occurs over a wider range of etiological foci than in hysteria alone. The same, I submit, obtains with what by now has become an automatic association between doubting and pathological indecision on the one hand, and anal and obsessive psychopathology on the other. Further experience with this psychic phenomenon, as with many others, has repeatedly shown the existence of a more continuous etiological spectrum.

The capacity to decide, to choose among alternatives, and thereby to shape rather than only to suffer one's destiny, has a unique and individually determined ontogenetic history. As it arises out of the matrix of physiological reflexes, its precursors and the necessary equipment with which it will be exercised begin with the origins of psychic structure, the differentiation of the ego from the undifferentiated ego-id matrix (Hartmann, 1939a, 1948), and with the first awakenings of what Greenacre (1945) has aptly called "the dawning ego." Following up Spitz's (1957a) description of the origins of the "no" and "yes" gestures, I studied the backgrounds and origins of the "no" and "yes" verbal symbols themselves and showed how these were related to the physiological occurrences within the oral cavity in relation to the incoming supplies of milk (see Chapter 5). In the earliest physiological state, the newly born organism either can comply with this incoming flow and move it along its path, in which case the lip-tongue-palate-throat movements effect ingress and swallowing, or it can close the throat and push with the tongue toward the nose, in which case it ejects and spits out what the mother gives. In the first instance the lapping motion of these organs serving the "come-in" function is the same as that later used phonetically in the "yy," which linguistically develops into the "yes." On the other hand, the opposite motion, with the tongue upward toward the palate and nose, ejecting milk and air, is the same movement that is later used in the "nn" sound, which progresses gradually into the "no." If the infant "chooses" to do neither, i.e., remains truly passive and neither helps the milk in nor pushes it out, the milk of its own accord goes in all directions, down the throat, out the mouth, and out the nose as well.

The acquisition of the no and yes during the toilet-training phase—according to Spitz, "the most spectacular intellectual and semantic achievement in early childhood" (p. 99)—demonstrates in a very visible and concrete way the nodal choice between compliance or rejection achieved at this point. In addition to its definitive forerunners and neuromuscular channels, however, subsequent elaboration takes place in a gradual and continuous transition with every step in development. Child analysts have recently disputed the existence of a latency phase (Maenchen, 1970), of any lag or delay in maturation, in any aspect of instinctual or ego development.

Decision-making, as other psychic functions, increases steadily in complexity, importance, and scope. I shall again refer by title only at this point to a section which I can only allude to since to deal with it comprehensively would require another paper. I am referring to the problems and agonies of modern youth. One etiologic aspect is pointed to here which has to do with the fact that this period is the expected "time for decision," again in the two major areas of psychic life, love and work.

Just as decision-making can receive increments at any level of forward development, there may be fixation and regression in decision-making at each developmental phase. Each may variously affect the quality, the content, and the scope of this function. The etiologic connection between pathological indecision, doubting mania, and the doing and undoing of anal-sadistic impulses, established by the first major insights into such psychopathology by Freud, Abraham, Jones, and other psychoanalytic pioneers, turns out to be but one example—and by no means the only one—of the psychic background of such conditions. The same type and degree of ego alternation between id and superego as was originally shown to exist over anal impulses can rage with equal intensity at any other stage or level of development. The case of Mr. A. reported above centered mainly around oedipal, castration, and separation conflicts. The other patient alluded to, Mrs. B., exhibited a wider range of diffuse pregenital conflicts, but the decision-making function of the ego was not centrally involved.

A person's capacity to make decisions does not by itself speak for his adaptedness, since decisions can be as characteristically destructive as they can be constructive and psychically economical. There are also a myriad of decisions which are come to instantly, impulsively, in much the same way as a counterphobic attitude or action. These are often predicated basically upon an inability to tolerate intrapsychic tension, whether of delayed gratification or of the pain of an unconscious traumatic memory. As a result there is an aversion to expose the ego to the necessary intermediate steps in unconscious decision-making, the anxiety, the uncertainty, and the experimentally induced painful and traumatic tension states upon which more considered opinions and more appropriate decisions would be based.

It is also to be noted in this connection, however, that the secondary effects and sequelae of decisions are not always and automatically to be counted as their original motivations. Hartmann (1956b) has pointed out that reality is more than man's unconscious. Man's decisions can set off actions the effects of which from then on can well have an autonomy of their own. The migration to California in the 1940s or to Israel during recent history was motivated on the parts of hundreds of thousands by a combination of surface and rational motives plus a welter of subjective, idiosyncratic, and unconscious factors. The subsequent effects of living in the new land for years, however, took their own course and cannot be forever attributed to the sought-for goals of those who chose them. In similar vein, a person marries for a wide variety of reasons, conscious and unconscious, a kaleidoscope of internal motivating forces and external impingements. Not everything that happens thereafter, however, is what he wished, hoped, or bargained for.

Central to the willingness to commit oneself to a decision is the capacity to anticipate its consequences. The anxiety signal is not the only outcome of the capacity to anticipate. The nature and quality of decisions result from the same capability. However, included in this capacity is the knowledge of its limitations, of the fact that not all consequences and consequences of consequences can be foreseen. This is part of the developmental task which goes along with the relinquishing of infantile omnipotence. The extent to which this is achieved determines the ability to accept the limitations imposed by reality and the willingness to proceed always to some extent into the unknown. Trust in consequences beyond the foreseeable depends of course on the genetic history of past satisfactions and successes.

Decision-making thus involves planning. Nonanalytic psychologists and other workers in the field of decision theory speak of utility and probability variables, i.e., of the capacity to predict the utility of a particular considered decision and the probability of the utility coming about (Edwards and Tversky, 1967). Psychoanalysis adds the level of unconscious mental functioning, with its scanning for memories of previous psychic traumas, by which the utility of anticipated decisions are judged. The scope and accuracy of predictions are thus enormously amplified by bringing into play previous experience and the entire sweep of the genetic past.

In the sequence of anxiety-choice-decision, both affective and cognitive elements accompany and follow each other and are actively operative at the unconscious level. Various authors have concentrated on specific aspects of these processes, such as Arlow (1969) on unconscious fantasies; Beres (1960), Kohut (1960), and Rosen (1960) on the process of imagination; Schur (1953, 1958, 1963, 1967) on unconscious anxiety and unconscious affects in general, a concept which Freud showed some reluctance to accept. Gehl (1970) questions the relationships between indecision, doubt, and uncertainty. I would say that uncertainty obtains when the cognitive search for the anticipated outcome is incomplete or unsatisfactory; indecision is the unwillingness or inability of the ego to commit itself to a course of action either because of this or even after the cognitive consequences are known; and doubt is the affective state accompanying either or both of these cognitive conditions. Piaget (1970) speaks of the simultaneous operation of "the affective unconscious" and "the cognitive unconscious." Just as secondary elaboration works over a latent dream into an integrated manifest product (Freud, 1900), so does thinking, of elaborate and accurate nature, with the equivalent of secondary process decision-making as a final outcome, take place completely at unconscious levels. Indeed, problem-solving of highly sophisticated degree, on an unconscious or preconscious level (E. Kris, 1950), is known to take place in acts of discovery and creativity, wherein dreams or reverie states impinge on consciousness.

This brings me to an important consideration that I would like to submit to close inspection. It is one of theoretical, philosophical, and technical interest; might well lead to a new emphasis and orientation; and also serves as a bridge between theory and clinic. The very factor I have stressed—that of active unconscious decision-making, of the exercise of control and of "chosen" direction—also brings with it the opposite side of the coin of ego autonomy, the important and subtle issue of "responsibility." The privilege of autonomous choice brings with it the responsibility for making it. It is in fact this very coexistence which often brings about inhibition, withdrawal, and indecision. Because of its crucial relevance to today's psychosociopolitical human scene, I would like to demonstrate what I mean by examining the role of this factor within both psychoanalytic theory and technique.

As psychoanalytic theory developed, the general thrust of its implications, on an individual and social basis, varied according to which element within it was being described and highlighted at the particular time. Thus during the early period, at the time of the discovery of the unconscious and the emphasis on the role of the instincts, the stress was on psychic determinism, and on the relentlessness and inevitability of the unconscious inner forces which shaped and influenced overt behavior. This was stressed unduly, for a long period of time, to the exclusion of all acknowledgment of freedom of will, of choice, and of responsibility. The next phase in our history balanced this one-sided emphasis by adding the counterforces of defense, control, and adaptation which the ego contributes.

The extent of behavior now encompassed and the scope of explanatory power of psychoanalytic theory were enormously widened, and moved psychoanalysis further toward its claim of being a general psychology.

The ego function of decision-making carries psychoanalysis further in this direction. The delineation of an intrapsychic choice conflict spells out a moment in intrapsychic life in which the human psyche is confronted with the opportunity, and the necessity, to exercise its own directive potentials and to determine its own active course. Psychic determinism, which at the time of its inclusion added a dimension then unknown, is now not to be replaced but added to in its turn. Taken by itself psychic determinism is incomplete, unless it is viewed in the context of the role played by the individual himself in controlling and shaping his own destiny. By adding the conflict-free and autonomous aspects of ego functioning, Hartmann (1939a) made available to psychoanalytic theory and observation aspects of human life that until then had been less the focus of attention. The close study of the function of decision, I submit, moves the psychoanalyst's interest, concern, and armamentarium further in that direction because it makes explicit the methods by which the patient utilizes his autonomous functions and guides his life toward goals and areas determined by his own decisive ego. Composite external behavior consists of forces passively endured, fused with a spectrum of active, controlling, and deciding elements ranging from unconscious to full conscious control. It is this which makes for the "mutuality" of internal and external, of parent and child interaction, which Erikson (1950), Winnicott (1957), and other clinicians and theoreticians have come to as an inclusive formulation.

Although active ego decision-making, as stressed here, takes place in the unconscious as well as in the conscious and preconscious, analysts have generally tended to assume that responsibility begins to apply only as such activity approaches the border of conscious control. If the "free" of "free will" is limited to conscious freedom, however, the "will" is now seen to have a wider base and to exist in the deepest unconscious elements of ego and drive activity, as much as in their conscious derivatives and additions. Is action which is under conscious control, although there is also a world of unconscious motivation, to be considered fully responsible—and action which is unconsciously planned and premeditated but which, because of its impact, has been separated from external awareness to be considered free of responsibility? Clearly, simplistic criteria in this area of transition and ambiguity have become anachronistic.

The borderland and gray shadings which exist here have long made this an area of discomfort and uncertainty to psychiatrists and psychoanalysts who are in various ways asked to translate "responsibility" into practical and pragmatic terms. There is, or should be, a spectrum of responsibility from none or little through partial to full. It is this spectrum, as contrasted to the duality represented by the poles at either end, which is at the bottom of the dissatisfactions, uncertainties, and debates on the parts of many with regard to the legal aspects of responsibility and the dubious role of psychiatrists and psychoanalysts in the court room. It is from the fact of this spectrum that Szasz (1961) proceeds to his exaggerated position that there is no such entity as mental illness and that psychiatrists are the modern imposers of conformity. On the other hand, it is from these same considerations that Karl Menninger (1966) and others derive the more sober and scientific view that since all actions are a combination of less and more responsible elements, psychiatrists should not be called upon to assess right or wrong but should confine themselves to understanding and treatment.

TECHNICAL CONSIDERATIONS

This same issue, of a scale of responsibility, and the fact that it is subject to change, is reflected in the psychoanalytic situation as well. Mr. A., in spite of years of reconstruction, interpretation, insight, and reliving, continued to perpetuate the state of suspended indecision to the mounting frustration and exasperation of all about him. His vacillations were such as to exhaust everyone, tried the patience of all, and seemed to have become permanent and structured. His goal was to react, not to act. He invariably waited until others were forced to act, in which case he could react, with opposition and panic, no matter which way they had turned. Yet nobody broke. His wife screamed and stayed. His mother and brother became sicker but remained patient. As ambivalent and erratic as he acted in each position, his employers kept him and never forced an issue. He had a knack of stretching the rubber band longer, tighter, and further, without it breaking, than anyone could imagine.

The analyst, after I too had been stretched to my capacity, was then confronted with the task of dealing with this global resistance, the patient's inability, hesitation, and refusal to decide and act. All three were involved and blended together. The situation was akin to that obtaining in the phobic patient who, after extensive and intensive analysis of the components of the neurosis, hesitates similarly to strike out and be well, to confront and master the phobic object. It was at this one point that Freud (1919a) is often quoted as having recommended that activity on the part of the analyst is in order. I should like to submit, however, that while this therapeutic maneuver derives from a piece of insight first noted in a specific clinical situation, its applicability needs to be considered on a more general level. The need for an active ego move toward consolidating the gains of analysis exists not only in a localized phobia, but is present in many other types of cases, including states of more diffuse anxiety. In this context it is of course possible to look at Mr. A. in another way and to characterize him as a person who suffers from phobic anxiety—the phobic element in this case being concerned with the avoidance of choosing and completing a significant task.

At any rate, in such instances, the analyst is confronted with the patient's failure to propel the dynamic process further. Correct interpretation alone is not enough. The analyst's interpretations need to be followed by the patient's absorption of them, integration, and necessary action. What is involved now is the full acknowledgment of the patient's role in the duality of the psychoanalytic process, the operations of the executive segments of the patient's ego which, after analysis, insight, and sufficient working through must decide, test, try, and do. Psychoanalysis dissolves many of the ties which, operating from the unconscious, are strangling the progression to choice and action. After such work is accomplished, voluntarily executed action, by providing examples of safety rather than danger, of mastery rather than trauma, is the final test and the final confirmation of the absence of danger.

Psychoanalysis, by increasing the patient's width of choice (making the unconscious conscious), places the "responsibility" increasingly on him to effect them. This is implicit in Erikson's (1964) title *Insight and Responsibility*. Similar to the phobias, but extending as I suggested to a more general situation, many analyses reach a point where, after extensive loosening of the unconscious soil, the patient's capacity and willingness for experimental action is necessary to carry the analytic process further toward its goals. This is a crucial and often sensitive point in the therapeutic advance, at which faltering, even failure, may take place, and about which more needs to be said than I can say here. One must be alert, of course, to the danger of the analyst misusing this necessity to cover up a host of other reasons for blockage or incompleteness, such as inadequate or insufficient analytic understanding, failure of emotional insight or working through, or a variety of limiting factors stemming from the countertransference.

I wish, however, to add this particular dynamic situation, which I believe is a common occurrence, not only in the instances of "interminable analysis" but also as a transitory resistance during the course of average analyses. When, as in the case of Mr. A., this mechanism becomes a nodal point for interminability, it is to be separated from the repetition compulsion or a negative therapeutic reaction. The compulsion to repeat stems from the id, and the negative therapeutic reaction owes its origin to the superego, while this type of failure to act derives from a specific ego incapacity, a timidity about trying, experimenting, and taking a chance. What is centrally involved in this residual state is neither instinctual pleasure nor super-ego guilt, but a specific ego insufficiency. Where this particular ego function has been involved, by neurosis, or deficiency, or maturational neglect, it must also be looked into, cared for, and nurtured during the course of the treatment pro-cess.

A patient's failure to make such final necessary decisions and to carry out trial actions gradually and increasingly causes anxiety to back up and mount. As long as Mr. A.'s indecision went unchallenged and was allowed to remain chronic, anxiety was kept at bay. His own acceptance, via analysis, of the necessity for choice, coupled with his inability or unwillingness to effect it, made for a situation in which anxiety returned in an increasing and spiraling degree. To the extent that he himself as well as his environment felt increasing impatience with his state of inertia, calm ineffectualness was superseded by anxiety and agitation at the necessity but incapacity to act. But this failure itself now needed to be constantly rationalized and defended against, thus augmenting the anxiety which was then used for defensive purposes. When the patient, continuing to fail to choose, instead constantly bombarded the analyst with the physical evidences of his mounting anxiety, to the point of almost a hypochondriacal orgy, the technique was now to interpret to him that it was his own failure to choose, again and still, which determined this inner state. The manifest "I can't" meant the latent "I won't." In his complaint that he could not choose *because of* his anxiety, he was now putting the cart before the horse. Unlike the original intrapsychic sequence as given above, it was now the failure to choose which was causing the anxiety to mount, rather than the other way around. He could not do this or that because he did not want to—which was confirmed by the continued outpouring of contempt for whatever alternative came up for imminent consideration. In the meantime he had indeed chosen—to stay on the fence between both or all worlds, to have the indirect benefit of all. This was concretized in his concoction of a drink consisting of vodka and milk, which he took as a nightly sedative and which he also recommended highly to the analyst.

The steady persistence by the analyst along this line, particularly the insistence within the stream of interpretations that the patient and only the patient must come to face the factor of his own basic choices and of the consequences of his own deepest decision processes, finally produced a felicitous direction of change in the patient. Although the validity of the reasoning and the main points and principles which I am making in this paper do not depend on the therapeutic outcome of a particular case, nor really on therapeutic outcome at all, I am happy to be able to add the following clinical progress note to date.

The condition of the patient has taken such a marked and dramatic turn for the better as is rarely given to us to see in our work. After a series of events and circumstances, the patient was able to forge for himself a rather new and unique role in his professional life which combined the entire scope of his training and preparation in a creative and integrated way. It seems fair to say, however, that opportunities of this type had been within his grasping distance many times before, and that only a psychic readiness, stemming from the resolution and the putting at rest of deep unconscious conflicts, finally enabled him to put together "a winning package."

The patient is scarcely recognizable to his incredulous friends and pinches himself at the change in his life, his demeanor, and his material success. His relationship to his wife has undergone a similar improvement in the direction of increased positive feelings and a lessening of his state of balanced ambivalence. His sexual life has improved concomitantly, and he has spontaneously told her for the first time in years that he loved her.

The patient has changed during the past year from the

most abject misery, from a state where a physician who saw him on one occasion at the height of his illness offered "to use his influence" to have him accepted immediately for hospitalization at the Menningers, to a position where he has recently been told that he brings prestige and honor to his profession. With it his physical appearance has changed remarkably, and many psychosomatic symptoms which at the height of his anxiety I had assured him, with some trepidation on my part, were reversible have indeed reversed themselves. He had, for example, been unable to produce tears, and for months would regularly be seen to put drops in his eyes from a supply of artificial tears which had been given him by an ophthalmologist. One day during an outburst of joyful and appropriate laughter in my office, to his great pleasure and surprise his eyes began to tear, and he found himself wiping his wet eyes with a handkerchief.

This description is being written after a long period of steady progress which has never before been the case with this patient, and which includes the overcoming of a number of touchy and disturbing realistic occurrences. After many cautious misgivings, I judge this clinical course now to be on solid and reliable ground.

Another factor which is related to the technical analytic stance is the analyst's philosophical attitude to the question of finiteness of a piece of analytic work, whether related to the analysis as a whole or to any specific circumscribed interpretation. Although theoretically the unconscious is more or less infinite, and I myself consider analysis quantitatively comparable to shining a flashlight into the Grand Canyon, operationally and technically speaking analytic work must be looked upon as finite with respect to a particular symptom or a specific interpretation. Although theoretically a dream is never interpreted or understood completely but ultimately dips into "a nexus of obscurity" (Freud, 1900), for practical and operational purposes its message can be encompassed and utilized. In 1966, I pointed out that the central method of analysis, the resolution of the transference neurosis, must be considered reasonably attainable from a practical and pragmatic point of view because otherwise the possibility of ending an analysis would be inconceivable.

While acting out is generally watched for by vigilant alertness on the part of the analyst, the opposite condition, failure to act in appropriate ways and to an appropriate degree, has been less stressed in analytic literature and technique. I am referring not so much to major decisions and actions as to small ongoing decisions, forward movements, changes in attitudes to spouse, children, or parents, which are often indicative of the status of the analytic work. With regard to acting out it is a technical mistake when the analyst assumes a moralistic or authoritarian attitude; he should adopt as analytic an attitude toward this complication as to all other unconsciously motivated phenomena (Rangell, 1968c). This same point was made by Vanggaard (1968), and affirmed with clinical material by Zetzel (1970), Atkins (1971), and others. The same, however, is also true of the opposite state, an inhibition of action or of the decisions leading to action. The analyst must then adopt and maintain an equally vigilant analytic attitude and vigorously pursue the phenomena of inaction. To this end the relationships between anxiety, decision, and action deserve constant and careful attention, which must extend to the changing order of their sequence and the reciprocal moves of cause and effect. The consequences of failure to observe and to deal with these changing internal relationships lead to a widely held criticism, quoted most recently by May (1969), that "psychoanalysis is a systematic training in indecision."

RELATIONSHIP TO THE PRESENT AND FUTURE ROLE OF PSYCHOANALYSIS

In response to the vicissitudes and pendular swings of psychoanalysis in relation to the outside intellectual world, there are many within and without our field who, believing it necessary to increase its "relevance," emphasize research *on* psychoanalysis and the application of psychoanalytic knowledge to the issues of the day as the most pressing areas for the use of psychoanalytic energy at this moment in our history. While I feel that both of these are necessary as continuing lines of thought and research, I have stated on a number of occasions that continued research *by* psychoanalysis, applied to the psychology and psychopathology current today, continues to be the unique contribution of psychoanalysis to understanding the tenor of our times and the one which only it is capable of providing. I would like to add at this time that the detailed study of the psychology of the decision-making process not only gives the psychoanalytic method a new dimension but also opens up crucial new areas of its fruitful application.

Among the areas of increasing interest during this age of chronic crisis is that of the decision-making characteristics of world leaders and policy makers. With physical equipment standing ready which can explode the world, it is the silent as well as the explicit hope of all mankind that those whose fingers can set them off can think, judge, decide, and plan with cool rationality and with no influence, if that is possible, from contaminating, idiosyncratic, subjective motives which can move a person this or that side of reason. Recent psychopolitical studies have demonstrated that this is no mere academic question, and have documented such influences leading to recurrent wars from ancient to modern times. One such study, conducted by Stanford Studies in International Conflict and Integration (1963), compared the crucial intrapsychic and interpersonal patterns in two international crises of this century, the fateful decisions of the German Kaiser which triggered World War I and the Kennedy-Khrushchev confrontation over the Cuban missile affair in 1962.

Scribbles left by Kaiser Wilhelm in the margins of state documents indicate that he went through a personal crisis.

He was seized by attacks of panic resulting in distorted perceptions, loss of control, and irrational judgments which plunged the world into catastrophic war. With two quite different types of leaders at the helm half a century later, the cool though dangerous game which unfolded between them had an opposite outcome. Though close to the brink, but with neither causing the other to have to lose face, the world breathed easier when both men, with calculated risks but unambiguous moves, were able to survive the eyeball-to-eyeball confrontation off the Cuban coast (Robert Kennedy, 1969).

The affective and cognitive reactions of political and military leaders have always been important, but are perhaps only now beginning to receive their full recognition. Events in this country in these past few years have again brought to the fore a deep concern about the psychology of decision-making.[2]

To the growing interest in decision theory to which I have referred, I have added the role which psychoanalysis can play, and indeed which it has already played for many years without this aspect of its functioning having been explicitly studied until now. I do not wish to imply that there can be any greater leap from painstaking psychoanalytic studies of individuals to an effective application to world politics in this or any other aspect of man's psychic functioning. I share Freud's pessimism about psychoanalysis and a Weltanschauung, and the sober caution expressed by many subsequent writers up to Waelder (1967b). Nor do we often have a chance to analyze decision processes that result in such momentous consequences. But the elucidation of basic psychological principles hammered out from studies of their impact on relatively smaller instances of everyday life is what psychoanalysis has always provided and from which lessons

[2]This lecture was delivered a few weeks after the invasion of Cambodia by American troops and at the height of the national unrest and the general pall which followed this event and the subsequent Kent State shootings.

and applications have always derived. Decision-making is of central interest in many analyses and of some interest in all. It is also of interest to all of mankind. The findings from psychoanalysis need to be added to those of all other disciplines sharing an interest in human decisions.[3]

[3]A later paper not included in this volume but connected with this major theme concerns the age of 17 (Rangell, 1989). The age of 17 is presented as an important year of the consolidation of intrapsychic developments coming together to crystallize crucial life patterns. The decisions one makes at 21 are prepared at 17. Attitudes take shape—unconsciously are decided upon—about major crossroads and dichotomies which determine vital character traits as well as external decisions. Where one chooses to live, occupational decisions, and the nature of one's love objects made at this developmental phase can determine the direction and course of life. The roles played by these decisions support Freud's succinct aphorism about the central impact of work and love.

CHAPTER 14

Choice Conflict and the Decision-Making Function of the Ego

A Psychoanalytic Contribution to Decision Theory

I was very pleased to have been invited to contribute to the celebration of this important anniversary. *The International Journal of Psycho-Analysis* has served for 50 years as one of the major representatives of psychoanalysis to the scientific and literary world. I wish to congratulate last year's outgoing Editor, John D. Sutherland, who has continued and developed further the tradition and value of this important vehicle, and to wish well to Joseph Sandler at the end of his first year as Editor, for through him we can look forward with confidence to the future.

As my own contribution I wish to highlight one idea, namely, a decision-making function of the ego among the inventory of ego functions. Although I have expressed this thought several times before, this has occurred each time within

Published in *Internat. J. Psycho-Anal.*, 50:599–602, 1969.

a larger work (on intrapsychic conflict, the psychoanalytic theory of anxiety, psychic trauma or the "intrapsychic process") in which it was submerged and in which it occupied only a peripheral and tangential position. To extract this function and treat it on its own, and to establish its centrality in psychic life, is not only for the purpose of adding what I consider a vital link in our theoretical framework, to explain more fully the sequence of intrapsychic events, but also because it is a nodal point of enormous external and applied importance. With the latter I am referring to a contribution which I believe psychoanalysis can and should make to understanding the decision-making process of man. However, these thoughts on the unconscious roots of decision-making will be stated here in only the barest form. To exploit them fully and to elaborate on the roles which they play in the conscious and manifest aspects of human decision-making will require and will be left for a future much larger work.

The importance of this aspect of human behavior need hardly be belabored. While its centrality and utility would be obvious at any time, at the present moment of our history to understand it as a process as fully as possible has become imperative. As a token of the high order of priority which this subject occupies on today's human agenda, a large literature has recently developed on the subject of human decision-making. While this includes a cooperative effort by a wide spectrum of disciplines, psychoanalysis remains conspicuous by its absence. The discrepancy is in fact curious. Decision-making theory has become the domain of workers in a wide range of disciplines, including economists, mathematicians, and various behavioral scientists, sociologists, philosophers, game theorists, statisticians, and experimental psychologists. Although no analyst would be unmindful of the relevance of psychoanalytic thinking to this topic, what psychoanalysis has to offer has to this day not been included. In fact, in general until recently "decision theorists look to the current situation rather than to the past experiences of the decider" for the variables that control the decision. With increasing sophistication the role of past events, or what psychoanalysts encompass as the genetic point of view, has gradually been added to a growing dynamic decision theory, resulting in attempts to combine historical with ahistorical explanations of behavior. Although past history is thus being added and an awareness of its role appreciated, the missing ingredient to a psychoanalyst and the one which only he is capable of adding is the role of unconscious factors.

It is these which I wish to emphasize and to add now to decision theory. I did not set out to do so originally, but rather have come to this pairing-up, so to speak, by serendipity and from the opposite direction, from being engaged in examining microscopically the sequence of events which takes place in the unfolding of the unconscious intrapsychic process. It is from this direction and by coming upon the choice dilemma of the ego in its role in intrapsychic dynamics, that the importance of the ego's capacity for decision-making has become overtly apparent and its role and vicissitudes in this process have become manifest.

The crucial and relevant aspects of this intrapsychic sequence as I have reconstructed them in previous writings are as follows. In a typical and model situation, the ego, having permitted a small amount of instinctual discharge to take place experimentally (Hartmann and Loewenstein's "tentative temptation"), experiences a reactive response from the superego, and from other judging aspects of the ego itself, in accordance with the latter's evaluation of the nature of the discharge and its permissibility to these internal censors. This evaluation is accomplished by an internal scanning process in which the ego screens the present partial gratification through its filter of past memories, to see whether or not any past traumatic memory is revived, associatively connected with the experimental discharge. On the basis of the response received, the ego experiences either a feeling of safety and security, or a signal of anxiety, indicating the danger of punishment or disapproval by the superego, and/or of the external world. In the latter case, a tentative, experimental and signal conflict has been followed by the signal of anxiety.

Following the experience of anxiety the ego is confronted with a choice of what to do next, whether to permit further discharge, or how not to, or how to effect a compromise or some other adaptive response. Possessed of an awareness of cause and expected effect, of impulse and anticipated punishment, the ego is confronted with an internal, intrasystemic decision-dilemma as to what to do next, which path to choose, how to find a way out. What is important here is that another type of conflict is being recognized and introduced at this point from the usual type envisaged in the conventional use of the term "intrapsychic conflict." As a result of the estimate of danger accompanying the presence of signal anxiety, the ego is "in conflict" as to what to do next. To the traditional meaning of psychoanalytic conflict as an opposition between forces, as exemplified in the classical oppositional ego-id conflict, is added a second meaning of conflict as a "choice," a "decision-dilemma" type of intrapsychic conflict, a crucial type of intra-systemic conflict within the ego. This is now a competition between alternatives, a dilemma over which a decision must be made or, as given by Webster, conflict involving "competition or opposing action of incompatibles—antagonism, as of divergent interests." I am elaborating on the literal meaning of this type of intrapsychic conflict, not for the sake of semantic complete-ness but because of its clinical relevance to the subject under discussion. In spite of the ubiquity of this type of conflict, both in clinical material and in psychic manifestations in everyday life, the formulation of this type of being in conflict as a regularly occurring phase of the intrapsychic sequence has not been described in explicit terms and is not generally thought of in our metapsychological theory, to the detriment of a complete theoretical and clinical approach.

From this point on, a myriad of possibilities unfold as to possible outcomes. One possible outcome along the way, or more typically one possible transient phase, consists of the usual type of intersystemic, intrapsychic conflict between the ego and the instincts, with countercathectic ego energies being deployed in an oppositional confrontation to id discharge. At any rate, the unstable internal state continues striving toward a point of internal stability, either with or without resort to symptom formation. Further choices are involved along the way, of types of defense, action or inaction, choice of symptom, etc. The history of previous internal solutions lays down facilitating pathways which guide future choices, to the point of making the latter appear at times to be automatic. All of these result in predictability and become incorporated into enduring and structured character traits.

To return to the internal process, at the center of this sequence is seen to be the question of intrapsychic choice and decision. A corollary of the new type of intrapsychic choice-conflict which has been described, and in fact the opposite side of the coin, is the ego function which goes hand in hand with it and is specifically designed to confront and solve it, i.e., the decision-making function of the ego. While the role of the ego as a mediator between id and superego, as well as with an eye toward the external world, has always been assumed as a central function and even as the *raison d'être* of ego activity, the specific role of the ego in decision-making has not generally been explicitly stated. Just as intrapsychic choice conflict, although it might seem now so commonplace as to be taken for granted, has not been explicitly listed as a ubiquitous and theoretically crucial type of intrapsychic conflict, so is this ego function which goes along with it peculiarly omitted from any listed inventory of ego functions. Such is the case, for example, in several recently published dictionaries or encyclopedias of psychoanalysis, or in a tentative listing of ego functions recently compiled by the Committee on Indexing of the American Psychoanalytic Association. What Anna Freud did for the mechanisms of defense has in fact not been done in a comparable way for the remaining gamut of ego functions. While defense, perception, motility, affect, and the synthetic, integrative, and organizing functions of the ego receive their due place in any such listing, such compiled lists do not generally include what is probably the central function of all, i.e., to decide and to choose between contending and conflicting forces. Such decision-making is indeed a necessary preliminary activity, as described in the intrapsychic sequence given above, before defense or other actions can be electively instituted.

The elucidation of this point in the intrapsychic process, of the ego not only having a choice but being confronted with the obligation to make one, illuminates a large aspect of human behavior and adds an important dimension to our understanding of a complex and important problem of human functioning. The qualitative and quantitative aspects of this capacity to make decisions is an important determinant in character formation, and runs an individual developmental course quite apart from the history of other accompanying psychic functions. The vicissitudes of this line of development vary between individuals, including siblings, and within the individual acquire a crescendo of characteristics and determinants during the successive developmental phases of life. Spitz, Benjamin, Greenacre and others have described some of the very earliest experiences in life and their respective results, constitutional and early neonatal determinants, which play decisive roles in determining where on the spectrum an infant will already take its place, from early ease in deciding (for example, whether to cry or wait) to complete helpless passivity. These relate to the growing organism's capacity to bear, deal with, and adapt to anxiety and its facility with the means of combating it or putting it at bay. Further early vicissitudes of this line of development have been annotated and described in the classical early papers on the oral and anal phases, by Freud, Abraham, Jones and others, and the delineation of the important early elements which go into the child's first opportunities for decisive mastery, and for exerting at least some control over the mass of stimuli coming his way. The accumulated psychoanalytic literature since then has dealt with various aspects of such problems during the successive developmental stages of life, with the typical configurations and challenges of latency, puberty, adolescence, and of late the contributions to the problems of the later phases of the life-cycle by Erikson, Therese Benedek, Grete Bibring and others. The various maturational sequences, together with the vagaries of individual human life, make for the infinite variety of life's challenges, among which are decisions, decisions, decisions.

In addition to the genetic point of view and with the psychoanalytic theory of behavior and of character formation, unconscious determinants play a large and even decisive role in human behavior, the more so to the extent that the latter touches upon conflict situations. Such is very much the case in decision-making. The above-described process of internal scanning goes on at all times, is characteristic of the human psychic apparatus, and follows the ingress of impinging stimuli. It varies, however, from a token activity with negative results in states of relative quiescence, as in times of solitude or reflection or even in sleep, to states of acute emergency and psychic demand at times of crises, internally or externally induced. But from all indications there is a constant baseline vigilance maintained by this intrapsychic sequence which preserves the stimulus barrier and gives it its qualitative selectivity characteristic for the particular individual.

The more, however, that any external decision is related to situations which are uncertain, ambiguous, or conflict-laden, the more does its final solution depend on its ability to resolve or avoid inner dangers. Such is the case whenever an external decision is associatively connected with memories or fantasies relating to past anxieties or episodes of psychic trauma, thus eliciting a warning response from the protective anxiety mechanism. While a multitude of choices and decisions turn out to be related more to external than to internal factors, and have little psychic meaning or significance, many others, which may appear from the manifest content to be on an equally conscious, external and rational base, may well derive their motivation and direction from deeper intrapsychic sources.

I can only mention the clinical implications of this broad subject, which are myriad. While problems of choice and decision-making course their way, in a spectrum of intensity, through everyday life, and play a role in almost all types of symptom formation, there are patients whose pathology is localized to a difficulty at precisely this point in the intrapsychic arc, in the capacity freely to make an active choice. Instead, the ego hovers in a vacillating state, looking this way and that, or making transient, partial and tentative action-decisions, satisfying alternately both sides of its demanding structures, id and superego. The early classical papers contributed our first major insights into the deep origins of such problems, in discovering the elements which are at play during the anal stage of development. Such difficulties, however, are not limited to the consequent obsessive states, although they may rage in their fiercest forms during an acute obsessive-compulsive ruminative crisis. In addition to the role played by anally oriented instinctual impulses, further knowledge has increased our understanding of subsequent developmental contributions, which depend on the growing capacity of the ego and the quality and characteristics of superego development. It is the total interaction between these forces, and the specific capacity of the ego, after weighing all incoming influences and pressures, to cast the die and make a choice, which determines the composition of this important character trait. Alongside of ego functions of perception, judgment, and integration, the fate of its decision-making function is a major factor in determining ego efficiency and ego strength and in characterizing an individual in his course through life's problems.

It was Freud who said that in small decisions we may offer advice whereas in the large decisions of life one must leave it to a person's own deep intuitive feelings. A large part of psychoanalysis deals, either prospectively or retrospectively, with the major decisions of life, such as marriage, career, and where and how one has chosen to live. Even when these choices have already been made prior to the start of an analysis, as is typically the case with an adult patient, the exploration of their deep unconscious roots occupies a large part of the analytic work and such major decisions remain always open to question, analysis, and change if indicated.

Finally, there is a major applied aspect of this subject to which I wish to allude, namely, the contribution it can make to the decision theory being elaborated by social scientists. Motivated by the existence of nuclear weapons combined with the tensions of our age, there is a deep interest, in our current sociopolitical milieu, in all aspects of decision-making, particularly its predictive aspects in the character structures of our leaders. Living as we do at a time when a finger can trigger a world-destructive weapon, and when national leaders can face each other in eyeball-to-eyeball confrontations, as did John Kennedy and Krushchev off the Cuban coast in 1962, it is the concern of all that people in such positions have cool, rational, and externally oriented, rather than hot, subjective, and internally oriented decision-making processes. It has already been shown in the psychological-political literature that there have been instances in modern history where the world has gone to war because of idiosyncratic reactions, responses, and decisions of policy-making individuals.

There have always been special problems about applied analysis, and wide gaps between our increases in understanding and any possible quick utilitarian outcomes from such advances. Nor are such problems about to be solved. Nevertheless there is no substitute for understanding. On the occasion of this anniversary of *The International Journal of Psycho-Analysis,* I wish only to indicate what I believe psychoanalysis can add to our understanding in depth of the decision-making function of man.

CHAPTER 15

A Psychoanalytic Perspective Leading Currently to the Syndrome of the Compromise of Integrity

Man advances his knowledge in two directions. With the electron microscope he narrows down past the cell toward the molecule and atom. Standing next to a space ship, with the widest angle ever achieved by man, he can now see the earth as a globe. Both views have one thing in common: neither see a man.

Psychoanalysis was the breakthrough which provided a lens to see the size of a man. Sitting alongside a human mind the psychoanalyst sees in both directions as well, how a man does, and does not, look inward, and why he reaches for the sky. I have chosen to take a long view, of the forest rather than a tree, to look back at the state of our science from the beginning and to bring it up to this current pressing moment in

Presidential Address to the 28th International Psychoanalytic Congress of the International Psychoanalytic Association, Paris, July 23, 1973. Published in *Internat. J. Psycho-Anal.*, 55:3–12, 1974.

our history. I also wish to relate our field to its neighboring terrain. Contrary to opinions often held, an analyst is never without seeing and being exquisitely in touch with the outside world. But his is a unique view, an inside-out one, through the intrapsychic process in man.

Approaching the end of its first century of existence, psychoanalysis has undergone an uneven, stormy, never-uninteresting history during its eventful life. Stamping its time as "the century of Freud," it shared the history of the twentieth century: expansion, diffuse application, use and misuse, explosion, disaster.

THE ANALYSIS OF LIFE

From the point of view of clinical practice, psychoanalysis over the decades has moved both imperceptibly and yet with steady increments from the analysis of symptoms to character to the analysis almost of life itself. The relation between the analysis of the Rat Man or the Wolf Man to a psychoanalysis of today is as the relationship of the first electric bulb to Times Square or Piccadilly—or of Edison's first gramophone to a modern sound studio.

In each case there is as much nostalgia for the old and for what was as there is pride and awe in the technological advance. Psychoanalysis has moved from circumscribed, encapsulated, and therefore enucleable syndromes to diffuse and amorphous states without boundaries. Patients enter analysis today not with a phobia or an obsession but because they are "nervous," or, as one young patient recently put it, "My problems are just in two areas, my work and with girls."

It may take years during the analytic process for such complaints to become concrete and, at the end, termination is often equally indeterminate and hard to arrive at. Correspondingly, analysis takes not 11 months but more like 11 years.

To a great extent this expansion in treatment bespeaks the deeper aims and the increased reach of analytic technique which itself stems from an increased knowledge of the complexities of mental functioning. The anxiety mechanism is not confined to a brief period preceding symptom formation but is a constant filter which influences the actions and moods of everyday life. Imprinting from the outset occurs not only in the first weeks of life, and not only to the feeding figure, but to all animate and inanimate objects which people the child's early world. The tachistoscopic findings of Pötzl (1917) and Fisher (1954) on subliminal perception apply not only to the experimental situations which they studied but to the continuous movie frames of the daily waking existence of each living human.

The result is that each individual has his unique style of perceptual distortion burned into him like a tattoo. The number of neurons in the human brain is matched only by the number of memories in the psychic system. And just as Freud (1900) observed that the associations to any dream converge back into a "nexus of obscurity," the same obtains with any symptom, or to the free associations of any hour.

If we put it all together, the following proportion holds: an interpretation is like pointing a flashlight into the Grand Canyon! With this perspective as a reference point, it is amusing to listen to a clinical presentation where "the interpretation" is given and the class—or the audience—await the cure. If not, the teacher and then the class ask what went wrong.

The theory of multiple function with its centrifugal spokes, the theory of overdetermination relating to centripetal influences, and the theory of the complementary series—a sleeper among our theories, first enunciated in response to bisexuality but which applies to much more—all attest to the complexity and multiplicity of psychic functioning. But these advances in theory and understanding, just as technological advances, bring with them complications and a need to maintain clarity. While there are false polarities, the spaces between which would be better considered as diffuse spectra, there are also defensively held continua. It is still necessary to distinguish differences, to be aware of finiteness and lines of differentiation.

Analysts may fall into the trap of failing to delineate the line beyond which the patient can go—and unwittingly move in an analysis into a prolonged indeterminate and unjustified waiting period. The analyst's arena is typically in the struggle between the ego and the id. Reality and the superego are agencies in the periphery which guide and admonish but are generally not at the center of analytic concern. (I shall comment later about the role of the superego.) But while it is understandable, with the increased appreciation of how the patient shapes his reality, that he can be expected to improve it, it is also of vital importance that the line between neurosis and reality be brought clearly into analytic focus.

As Hartmann (1956b) has pointed out, reality is more than the patient's unconscious. After years of analysis, it is of questionable validity to wait for a divorced or widowed woman of 45 to get her man, at least in the city in which I practice and I suspect elsewhere as well; or not to take into consideration the realities surrounding a youth who works in a field in which unemployment and killing rivalries abound. The lines must be drawn between the patient's psyche and irreversible or at least uncontrollable external conditions, the average expectable erosions, even tragedies of life, near and far societal conditions. There are analytic systems which officially teach an ignoring of reality, an attitude as curious as those which give only reality a place in psychic etiology.

An analyst must justify a treatment which goes on for an indeterminate number of years by more than rationalizing that the patient would be in a mental hospital without it. Constant self if not peer review is necessary. Analysis can come to be parallel to, or even, in some cases, instead of ordinary life and its responsibilities. The failure to establish necessary lines of demarcation can lead to deep concerns and justifiable questions about the practice of psychoanalysis.

THE SPLITS IN ANALYSIS

Once it survived the initial shock wave and took root, psychoanalysis was confronted from the very beginning by a series of explosions set off within its own ranks ostensibly to be more on the target of truth. Already in the small group which surrounded Freud, after the solidarity which came with the initial impact, strong-minded individuals began to chafe under the domination of a man or even of an idea and to be stirred by needs for independence and their own direction. There then followed the history of psychoanalysis which has been no different from the history of man.

In the last quarter century I have lived in, around, and through the "splits" in psychoanalysis, as they have come to be called, as participant, site visitor, arbitrator, and reconciliator. I have lived through the tensions of splits which have threatened, have seen some happen which should not have, and have seen some not happen which ought to have. My recent years as President of the International Psychoanalytical Association have given me an even wider and, I like to believe, deeper view of these recurrent and seemingly built-in psychoanalytic-sociological phenomena.

A psychoanalyst cannot be witness to repetitive acts without seeing patterns and even being able to predict. I know of splits now which are scheduled for three or four years from now. I once spoke to the first meeting of a newly accepted component society and told them I could see the pattern of their future split. There is also no reason not to extrapolate backward. I was not there when the great giants defected, when almost in an instant man's knowledge was changed from having no psychoanalysis accepted by the world to suddenly having three and soon four—each already with its passionate adherents: Adler, Jung, soon Rank. All of them separated from what was already called "the Freudians."

Erikson points out that history meets the man. The course of this recurrent history has always been the fusion of a man, a group, and an idea which could serve. It was, for example, not as the result of a rational process nor of any compelling methodological approach that certain important schools of social work in the United States became Rankian. Or that one particular continent became Kleinian. I have been privileged to learn of the particular concatenation of circumstances, of group movements, relations between key individuals, and even chance events which have been responsible for some of these outcomes. There is now one city in the United States, and only one, in which Kleinian psychoanalysis has established a substantial root. Since I live and, more importantly, analyze in that city, I know the roots which brought that about. Scientific dialogue and an open comparison of views have played the least part.

There are differences between organizational and "systems" splits. With regard to the latter and to the scientific issues involved, I would like to offer the following long-term observations about what has been a constant and perhaps is destined to be a perpetual trend.

1. In every case what kept the new systems going and gained them respect and durability when these were achieved was what they took with them from the main body: the unconscious, dreams, conflict, etc., i.e., they were analysts. A candidate in analysis, upon hearing a paper by a person from a new school which he considers in most respects absurd, was nevertheless disturbed and in conflict because "but she has a respect for the defenses."

In a book which attempts to filter out what various analytic groups have stood for over the years, Alexandra Adler (1973), discussing her father's Individual Psychology, pointed out that Adler was interested in ego psychology and that he emphasized as the main problems of man's existence work, friendship, and sex. (I was interested in the addition of friendship to Freud's original two because I had myself suggested this addition (see Chapter 30) without, to my knowledge, having become an Adlerian!) Horney in this same series is given credit for the holistic approach. Sullivan was concerned with the science of man, and the existentialist tries to see "the individual human being in the world and to do away with the artificial separation of inner and outer reality" (Wenkart, 1972)! The ingredients of vitality in all of these systems were always present in the main body.

2. What was indeed new or a special emphasis from any of these often original thinkers could have been added to the main body as an interesting paper or book and was indeed later so added by others without contradicting and with added value to the whole. Adler could have early added ideas of ego mastery, Jung new layers of understanding of the dream and of primary process thinking, Melanie Klein new and important facets of the child's earliest intrapsychic processes.

3. What each system gave up and turned its back upon from the main body was what gave the new system its limitations and built-in obsolescence. To the extent that Adler gave up the sexual, or Horney or later Rado the instincts, or that Klein minimized the role of the Oedipus complex and castration anxiety, each had a lacuna which gives the system a short, even if for a while a dazzling, life.

4. What each did add distinctive to itself which separated it from other systems ranged from the responsible but limited to the irrational, the untrue, even the absurd. Jung's mysticism does not belong to rational psychoanalysis. And more within the analytic body today, the interpretations of some about the earliest months of human life survive their absurdity for a while only by their shock effect. Primary process is interpreted not by secondary but by as primary a process. The human being becomes a pyramid standing on its point.

Anais Nin, who currently is in vogue among a large intellectual set in the United States, went to an analyst because of her interest in her unconscious. But why she particularly sought out Otto Rank was—Nin quoting Rank (Stuhlmann, 1966): "I go beyond the psychoanalytical. Psychoanalysis emphasizes the resemblances between people; I emphasize the differences. . . . They try to bring everybody to a certain normal level. I try to adapt each person to his own kind of universe. The creative instinct is apart." I cite this only as an example. Such facile assessments come from every direction, from patients, the public, but also from analysts themselves. If I quoted more, this essay would move on to a different level, away from the psychoanalytic.

5. But whatever their points of difference, in all cases the alternative systems utilize the mechanism of *pars pro toto*—and their followers prefer the part to the whole.

Just as outside of analysis Glasser's reality therapy picks only reality; and Carl Rogers's nondirective method lifts out one element of our psychoanalytic technique; and behavior therapy concentrates only on conditioning, which does have a place in our total psychology both in its theory and techniques; and just as one psychologist carries our genetic view back to, and only to, "the primal scream," while at the other end Gestalt therapy picks our "whole" concept (while leaving out its inner parts!)—so within analysis, does Horney pick the environment, Sullivan the interpersonal, Rado adaptation, transactional analysts only aspects of the transference, etc. None of these are wrong, but all of them are incomplete. Sullivan's interpersonal as later Fairbairn's object relations have a place and need to be squarely in the middle of it all—but never alone or separate. I never forget "object relations" in clinical work or analytic thinking. No analyst can.

One group lists itself as the Institute for Psychosynthesis! We should, in self-protection, change our name to 'bio-psycho-social-internal-external-analyst-synthesists'!

6. One feature in this whole field of splintered parts is that they are mostly beyond debate—that rational argument and scientific discourse do not generally prevail, lost in the face of group psychology. (I do not mean by this observation to overlook the valuable contributions and serious lines of thought which have come from many of these diverse orientations. But the characteristics I am describing occur with a sufficient degree of volume and regularity for me to wish to record them here.) The irrefutable pointing out of the *pars pro toto* mechanism has no effect. And if to the question "If instincts are eliminated, of what does intrapsychic conflict consist?" there is no answer, there is also no concern. When we were in Russia, a group of visiting analysts were told that psychoanalysis in our country is too biological, i.e., too instinctual, while in the United States, to organic medicine, psychoanalysis has always

been considered too environmental! But to worry about such inconsistencies is too intellectual. The ultimate ploy is an overt abandonment of the virtue of reason itself. Carl Rogers, who has a greater following in the United States than Freud, when pressed, told me that "Insight is not only not necessary but does harm." In the encounter groups a "head trip" is the worst cop-out of them all. And even to some analysts being human replaces insight, "is where the action is" (a false dichotomy again, a straw man; the two are not opposed but belong together). One analyst achieves world prominence by extolling the value of psychosis over present-day sanity. And in one analytic group there was a discussion recently of "the rational id and the irrational ego." The twist was now complete and the circle closed.

7. Other analysts have made more major contributions, about child dynamics and development (Spitz, Benjamin, Mahler, Greenacre)—contributors of this magnitude exist in each country, in every language; in naming a few I know I risk injustice to others; about that great and powerful and important ego (Hartmann, Kris, Loewenstein, Anna Freud, Rapaport); about that never-to-be-forgotten outside world (Erikson, Waelder, Eissler's essays on history) as much as did "the environmentalists"—without inviting or encouraging a separate coterie.

8. While I have been open and receptive to new developments over the years, I would say that there has been no contribution or cluster of contributions that deserves to start or to have started a new and parallel school of psychoanalysis.

Over the rubble, psychoanalysis still stands, like a colossus, ravaged and gouged but always there, to the relief even of those who attack it.

THE SYNDROME OF THE COMPROMISE OF INTEGRITY

Syndromes resulting from the compromise of integrity are endogenous to human life. Not just with income tax or marital fidelity where double standards are accepted norms—or with major or notorious frauds—but in the interpersonal transactions and daily traffic of everyday living—and at all levels of the social intellectual scale. Compromises of integrity—I do not mean "lack of"; these are just partial; any more than neuroses, or even psychoses, mean *no* normal behavior, *no* ego control over the id—forestages on the path to psychopathy or impulse disorders, are as diffuse in behavior and their ingredients as ubiquitous in unconscious mentation as are the ingredients which will result in neuroses.

People sit glued to the latest public drama of the Watergate hearings, much as they do to violence and sex. They are as much in it as with it. The interrogated today were the prosecutors of yesterday. When a prosecutor was sought for the trials of Watergate, it was announced that he would have to be a man "of impeccable integrity." A search ensued around the country which lasted for several weeks. It is no accident that sometimes in an obituary a man's integrity is especially stressed. And this is not occupationally bound. In a memorial service for a particular psychoanalyst, each speaker repeatedly pointed out his integrity. He was, incidentally, very unpopular in life. None of these facts are new. Diogenes went around with a lamp looking for an honest man 2,400 years ago. And the myth, which makes a point about the unconscious of man, survived.

What we see as psychopathology in complex human behavior is often a combination of neurosis and compromise of integrity which should be separated and dissected out. Many of the syndromes we automatically think of as neurotic are more accurately blends between the two, if not more the latter. There is another borderline than what we commonly mean by that term. Clinical and life experiences show that there is a grey area, a borderline between neuroses and compromises of integrity, as common as that between neurosis and psychosis. A psychic act to resolve intrapsychic conflicts can be a combination or a vacillation between the two.

I will allude only briefly to the intrapsychic dynamics of compromise of integrity. In the neuroses the analyst observes the struggle between the ego and the id; in compromise of integrity between the ego and the superego. Just as reality factors should come squarely within the purview of analytic observations, so does the same apply to the role and operations of the superego. The pressure from the id upon the ego is matched by a constant baseline tension between the ego and the superego. In petitioning for internal sanctions from the latter, the ego mediates not only instinctual drives but its own intra-systemic ego interests (Hartmann, 1950a), previously thought of as ego drives by Freud. In any particular psychic outcome one or another or some combination of the psychic agencies may yield. In the neuroses the id is sacrificed; in psychosis, reality; in compromise of integrity, the superego gives. In some outcomes, the ego denies or postpones its own interests. This may be in the service of, or counter to, adaptation.

Narcissism unbridled is the enemy of integrity. While in more overt criminal behavior instinctual pressures for gratification also play a strong motivating part, the stimuli to compromise of integrity are uncontrollable and unsatisfiable narcissism. Subsumed under the latter are the totality of ego interests, including largely the ego's function in preservation of the self (Kohut, 1971), and in the maintenance of what Erikson (1956) has called ego identity.

Perspective is necessary as always. Narcissism is as nodal a point in normal intrapsychic dynamics as are anxiety, sexuality, or aggression. And as the others, it ranges from positive to negative, is necessary for health, and prominent in breakdown. It is interesting that Freud originally postulated the self-preservative instincts. While his later revision in which these forces were shifted to the ego made for a more useful and pragmatic conceptualization, this did not reduce the recognition of their universal character and peremptory nature.

Instinctual pressures are then to neuroses as ego interests are to the compromises of integrity. And just as in the external world a "conflict of interests" is considered a threat to the exercise of moral responsibility, so does the same obtain intra-psychically. An internal conflict of interest between ego and superego may regularly exist, which, in the absence of a specific type of ego strength, may represent a similar threat and result in a compromise of the integrity.

The superego bridges from inside to out. Originally the introject from parental imagos, it remains in most open communication with external objects and most subject to their continuous influence. A patient, after doing something bad, felt uneasy after telling it to me. "I wish you would say something," he finally said, "I don't know how guilty to feel!" The superego is the least structured of the psychic structures. While this leaves an individual open to social progress, it also makes him an easy subject for the fickle whims of a crowd.

This fluidity of the superego enables it to serve as a bridge between the individual and the group. New mechanisms, or combinations of mechanisms, of defense or adaptation may need to be defined in this area of ego-superego, or ego–external world operations, at the border between individual and group action. What, for example, is "the crime of silence," whether of an individual in the street to a mugging or of a nation toward genocide—or for that matter, of onlooker nations as well—or of a populace toward an immoral war? Are these the crimes of the individual or the group? Are they a crime? A neurosis? Or some undissected and unarticulated combination of the two?

Is it denial, negation, repression? Are the factors all unconscious? Is there conscious suppression too? Is there identification with the aggressor? Perhaps we smother a fact with intellectuality when we try to transfer too readily from the individual to the group, or from ego-id to ego-superego interactions. I recall in seminars with what eager scholarship we tried to dissect introjection form incorporation from identification—or another exercise between denial, negation, and repression. Here, in contagious public behavior, it is all of these combined, one conglomerate aggregate which produces not only failure of action but even of reaction. Where, for example, is outrage? Why is it so late?

There are other phenomena in the public sector which

derive from a ping-pong effect between a leader and a group in which the superego floats suspended between them, and needs to be claimed by neither. I will mention a few examples only, it is their multiplication which is important. These larger movements antedated the acute volcano which has recently erupted—and perhaps were forerunners of the latter—and were what I had in mind when I referred in Vienna to the problems of sincerity and trust.

Consider, for example, that only a President whose entire political life was based on a virulent anti-Communism can attempt to claim his place in history on the achievement of a detente with China and Moscow! His defeated opponents who espoused these policies all along would never have been allowed to do so—by him. Or the fact that only a hawk could end the war—and incidentally continue to push to bomb.[1] A hawk turned dove is the stuff a hero is made of. Always a dove is no good. Ellsberg, by the way, was once a hawk.

A premature anti-Vietnam stand is a detriment to a record. When a candidate, Romney—others could be named—returned from Vietnam with an antiwar statement, he was finished. This mechanism is a sequel to a syndrome of the 1930s, of those who were "premature anti-Fascists." Subsequent history did not make them right. They were right too soon, therefore wrong! This mechanism, incidentally, is not limited to one political party. Nor to one nation. Nor even to a period in time. No country or population can take solace.

Flexibility, the ability to change one's mind, to admit one was wrong, to learn from experience would be a positive set of ego attributes. The sequence here, though, that one was always right, that not the mind but the times have changed, is a combined mechanism of distortion, denial, rationalization, deception of the self and others, and bridges across unconscious-

---

[1] In view of the swirling and rapidly changing events which have taken place since, it would be helpful to bear in mind the point in time at which this was written. The Vietnam War had just been ended. The bombing of Cambodia, however, was still going on; Congress had not yet forced the President to stop it. The Vice-President was still overtly clean and in good repute.

preconscious—and conscious. Is it neurosis, character trait or
compromise of integrity? Or the norm for the day? I believe a
case could be made for all. A mechanism even more in this
direction, which seems, however, more squarely planted in the
conscious, was recently offered from the top: "What I said
before is from this point on inoperative!"

The syndrome described is accepted by the population
because it satisfies both sides of the unconscious of the latter. A
consistent leader might leave one half uneasy—not only one
half of the people, but one half of each person—frustrated,
anxious, and guilty about the sole course chosen. There was a
motion picture whose advertising theme read, "Being in love
means never having to say you're sorry." The picture, incidentally, was a standout success. The mechanism offered counters
the superego value of consistency, the requirement to live up to
superego principles. With the behaviors described, this is
patently unnecessary. In an interesting variation, the Vice-
President of the United States recently went even further. To
grant amnesty to the war deserters stranded in Canada, he
demanded that they first say they were sorry. They felt he
should. There is no reckoning, no final court. The result is a
suspended state, which invites recurrences.

Another perplexing but important question presented
itself publicly during these recent hectic times. A candidate for
high office was disqualified from running when a history of
clinical depression was revealed. Is a severe superego, which
this bespeaks, more of a risk than one in the opposite direction,
which is hardly ever questioned? A scientific opinion could well
be rendered that the former is safer for the people.

The mechanisms described do not fail to have their counterparts within the psychoanalytic world as well. In a split city 20
years later, for example, the most honored and even endeared
is the one who joined the rebel group but remained classical.
Those who stayed to begin with were and still are "rigid." More
insidious, however, I must say from a plethora of experiences
and observations, is the too frequent presence in ongoing psychoanalytic life of the same mechanisms I have been describing:

the presence of internal conflicts of interest resolved in favor of narcissism at the expense of principles. These occur in small and larger committees, in the large society, in one geographical area as much as another, and at all levels of responsibility. Character assassination by a small number is made possible on a wide scale, if not by the crime of silence, by the sin of omission on the part of many. Impaired morale and ill-will, scientific deterioration, and even corruptibility are accompaniments too frequent to be ignored. That unconscious mechanisms are also involved does not absolve responsibility. The whole question of the relation between the unconscious and responsibility needs, in my opinion, a searching re-examination.

Psychoanalysts in training capacities, or in administrative positions of responsibility, dealing as they do in the evaluation of others, are frequently in tight and delicate situations, subject to crises of character of their own. Caught in conflicts between independent judgment and group pressures, attachments to charismatic or even just dominant figures, with the variety of attendant gains, or the same need to be a member of the team may often cast the deciding influence.

These observations, I repeat, are not by way of presenting a moral, or philosophical, essay but to pursue a scientific line of thought. Such problems bear a special relevance to the science of psychoanalysis. At the pre-Congress conference in Vienna held on the assessment of candidates, I pointed out that the goal of psychoanalysis was psychic integrity. The psyche, through its defenses, distorts, to deceive the self. Analysis, burrowing always toward the truth, aims at undoing these deflections and at producing as much straightness as possible. Every patient in analysis is in training toward intrapsychic integrity. A patient, after a piece of insight into a defense and discovering a new motive, observed, "Then I wasn't being honest with myself." Another confessed, "I haven't been honest lately," not about any large sexual suppression but about having held back a small but tender narcissistic hurt when she and her husband found themselves sitting alone at a banquet table and were not joined by others.

Analysis aims at turning out an honest man. To be more realistic, one as much free of compromise of integrity as neurosis, which is not complete in either case. It is no accident that the word "integrity" has several shades of meaning. Semantic usage usually reflects underlying insights. Moral integrity, in the sense of the superego, depends on ego integrity, in the sense of wholeness. The latter depends, importantly, on the sense of safety, freedom from anxiety, which stems from control over the id and the external world. All together result in integration, in the sense of togetherness, of the three internal structures within, and the internal-external linkages to without.

As important as this is in the general population, the achievement of intrapsychic integrity, the capacity for straightness, is imperative for future analysts and therefore in the analysis of candidates. I might say that problems of greed, envy, and gratitude play an important role, the success of which will often determine the atmosphere of the future psychoanalytic society. And I would add that the analysis of these traits belongs squarely in the main body—rather than that they remain unanalyzed and made into a new system instead. This, by the way, is an empirical observation from clinical data.

Candidates are selected to become analysts who have at least the potential of achieving this trait of intrapsychic integrity. Is this in fact not what we mean by character? Freud had it *de novo*. In a letter to Stefan Zweig, quoted by Schur (1972), Freud wrote: "in so far as [my] achievement is concerned, it was less the result of intellect than of character. This seems to be the core of your opinion and one in which I myself believe." Schur notes Freud's basic dislike of biographical studies written about him and his demand of them for strict adherence to the truth.

The analytic attitude is in its very essence the model—I hope not the last bastion—of relentless incorruptibility. To maintain this is its core. There is no analyst, subject to the daily spectrum of transference displacements, who does not know and feel the range of pressures to which this is put, from sexual to material to narcissistic. Basic trust is rightly tested and has to be earned. The capacity to use rather than to abuse transference cannot be taken for granted. Nor once achieved does it automatically continue for life. It needs to be worked at and constantly reaffirmed.

The dichotomy often made between transference and human factors is one of the most important to understand precisely because of its temptation and appeal. Both are necessary. The human alone, however, existed before the analytic. Unfortunately, by itself, it often carries with it human corruptibility as well. The scientific attitude of psychoanalysis is carried to the patient by a caring human. The capacity to achieve the proper blend between the two is one of the most difficult but necessary goals for training to impart.

While I am on the technical procedure, narcissism and its vicissitudes belong in the psychoanalysis of every man. This is the most recent area in which a tendency to separatism is observable, and where any valid contribution which may be made to this important subject may regrettably be lost in the psychology of a small stampede.

Through the perspectives and the distant haze, I see psychoanalysis as a distinct and separate entity, different from all others. While as a theory it faces life in open communication on all sides, it is also a finite procedure, with a beginning, a middle, and an end. To round out its periphery and complete its center, the reality without and the superego within must be added to its concerns and operations. Not with a sidelong glance, but with the same depth and full intensity as heretofore rendered the ego and the id. Only in this way will its role as a general theory be properly fulfilled. The full circle of forces impinging on the ego needs to be taken into continuous account. Together these encompass all contingencies of life and behavior. None of them can be minimized or ignored. With them all, no other theory is as comprehensive.

If you will permit me to conclude on a personal note: In 1950, as a graduating candidate, I read a paper to the last meeting of a society before it was to split. It was "The Analysis of a Doll Phobia" which shortly afterwards won for me the Clinical Essay Prize of the British Society (Chapter 2). A training analyst in the audience—mine, in fact, from whom I was separating; we were both choosing different societies— asked me in the discussion why I was seeing the patient five times a week, why not three or four or six? I gave him the reasons why I thought this was best from what I had been taught and learned so far. I went on to say, however, that some day, perhaps in 25 years, I hoped I could answer this and other questions from my experience.

It is now just short of those 25 years, but the views expressed here are finally those. They are my own views. They are on subjects which I consider at the moment of most importance. They are now the data of my own amassed experience. They are derived from the couch, which is from where a certain type of deep knowledge flows which can be extrapolated by an analyst to the wide world around us. I hope they stand the test of further time.

May I express to all of you my gratitude for the privilege of this unparalleled experience at the helm of this Association. Thank you.

CHAPTER 16

The Executive Functions of the Ego

An Extension of the Concept of Ego Autonomy

ADAPTATION AND EGO AUTONOMY

It has been common, almost routine in psychoanalytic writing, for an author to start with a passage of Freud's in which a subject has been laid down but incompletely developed which can then be further explored in depth. Hartmann (1956a) pointed out that Freud made "radical new departures" and reformulations up to his last papers, that he freely admitted to the quality of not being finished, and that there were a number of important chapters "he had not yet come round to" (p. 268). Freud himself continued to expand old ideas as he added new ones. But whatever Freud laid down during his lifetime, a seemingly endless mine was left for others to discover or appear to discover.

The same can be done, although it is far less routine, with

The Heinz Hartmann Award Lecture of the New York Psychoanalytic Institute for 1985. Published in *The Psychoanalytic Study of the Child*, 41:1-37, 1986.

the work of Heinz Hartmann. At the memorial service for
Hartmann, I pointed out that in 1939, the year Freud died,
Hartmann published his famous monograph which defined the
direction of psychoanalysis for the next three decades. "The
baton had been passed between the two men. Heinz Hartmann
stood on a mountain, built just before his time, preserved its
space, cleared its top, and built it almost twice as high." While
the language was fitting for a eulogy, the thoughts were meant
as a scientific assessment. "Each piece of comprehensive writing
about some aspect of human behavior was itself an abstract,
hard put to contain the ideas which were bursting from its
capsule in all directions."

I would like in this presentation to lift out one of the veins
exposed by Hartmann but insufficiently pursued since then.
Just as Anna Freud (1936) did not discover defenses, but
elaborated and systematized what her father had named, and as
Hartmann (1939a, 1950a) expanded ego psychology which had
also been set into place by Freud, so would I like us now to work
toward a deeper understanding and appreciation of the role of
autonomy in human behavior.

While writing centrally of the problems of adaptation,
Hartmann included the concepts of autonomy and conflict-
free. In the decades since then, however, the mechanisms of
adaptation became the primarily discussed theme. While Hartmann's contributions could have been utilized toward elucidating the human aim to shape as well as adapt, historically
adaptation—"fitting in" rather than sticking out—clearly became the central thrust. Both Anna Freud's work on the
defenses and Hartmann's on the adaptive functions converged
on the reactive, leaving an interest in the shaping activities of
man for future scientific concern. The ego psychologists from
the 1940s to the 1980s concentrated on the ego's reacting to
stimuli, stopping short of the immediately subsequent activities
of the ego to initiate and direct.

The problems of adaptation need to be followed by an
equal interest in initiation. It is into this area that I propose to
move. While this shift in direction might seem slight and the

movements small, there is a theoretical advance which in my opinion will carry us into a new dimension of relevance and understanding. It is most impressive that this area of human activity has been so slow in being exposed and developed. There has actually been a small but steady edge of crucial research at this border, but at a creeping rate of acknowledgment and acceptance compared to its significance.

Conflict-free and ego autonomy, named by Hartmann, were accepted if not pursued. While the psychoanalytic method is a treatment of conflict (Anna Freud, 1936; E. Kris, 1947; Brenner, 1979b), psychoanalytic theory as a general theory, in keeping with Hartmann's view, includes behavior surrounding conflict and independent of it as well. Hartmann (1950a) pointed out how primary autonomy can become embedded in conflict formation, and secondary autonomy can arise out of conflict and become reinvolved in it. While the first to formulate and elaborate autonomy, Hartmann himself also emphasized its limitations, leaving the issue of its executive functions still to be pursued.

Rapaport was one of the few who subsequently wrote of ego autonomy, solidifying its theoretical place in metapsychological theory. In two papers (1950, 1958) devoted specifically to this subject, Rapaport qualified the term "autonomy" as "relative," in the first as relative to the force and influences of the drives, and in the second by pointing to the equal restriction on ego autonomy by the pressures of external reality. Taking his cue from Hartmann, Rapaport's aim, while setting into place the role of autonomy, was to preserve the role of drives and of external factors pressing upon the ego from within and without.

The emphasis was to retain the basic discoveries of psychoanalysis and to underscore the limited role to be assigned to autonomous ego capabilities. Each side connected to the ego gave it a degree of independence from the other, but at the same time each impinged on the ego's freedom by its own demands. While the ego's roots in the drives diminished its dependence on the environment, and its connections with reality its dependence on the drives, it could also be said that the drives and the external world each reduced the autonomy of the ego from opposite directions.

With autonomy and conflict-free named but not pursued, the new adaptive functions became the key concept occupying the next decades. While the main viewpoint absorbed and stressed by this new emphasis had to do with the ego's interests and methods of adapting to the surrounding world, i.e., the process of socialization, which had heretofore taken second place in psychoanalytic theoretical concern, adaptation, in its strict sense, as meant by Hartmann, included the ego's dealing with inner conditions as well, with conflicts, restrictions, deficits, and limitations by a variety of adaptive rather than defensive methods.

The psychology of initiation, from simple to the most complex human activities, executed spontaneously or even subsequent to receiving stimuli from any or all directions, was left for the future, or to await another phase, perhaps when its time will have come after the previous new insights had been sufficiently consolidated. This has remained so since the 1950s, with a secondary role granted to autonomous factors. The concept of a conflict-free thrust of motivational behavior, set in place by Hartmann, requires further extension and elaboration to paint that element into the mental canvas in its full colors and to the full extent of its intrapsychic operations. This needs to be accomplished by a removal of the barriers to its more complete acknowledgment and study.

What I am speaking of is "will." This is a word not prominent in psychoanalytic terminology and which I feel is met by a quality of inhibition, as though it places in jeopardy the central contributions of psychoanalytic discoveries and understanding. A few isolated papers have appeared on the subject, especially long ago, such as by Knight (1946) and Lewy (1961), and a few in modern times, but its role has always been seen as an island and it has never received vigorous or persistent attention. One problem has been the automatic association of the word "will" with the word "free." I will discuss the subject of "free will" to which this subject leads, but I also propose that the automatic linkage between the two words be discontinued and that each word and concept be separately considered in the service of clarity.

In 1946, Robert Knight saw fit to address the delicate subject of free will. If we keep in mind what he felt was a strict determinism, which could not be denied or mitigated in the realm of psychology, Knight made room for a freedom of choice, which he saw as occurring in an ego not hampered by neurotic restrictions. While this was a subjective feeling, it was not a spurious one, based as it was on ego-syntonic, free choices made by well-integrated persons.

The same vexing subject was approached by Lewy (1961), centering primarily on responsibility, and secondarily but necessarily on the closely contiguous subject of free will. Confronted by the apparent contradiction of psychic determinism of psychoanalytic theory and the aims of psychoanalysis to develop and strengthen the patient's responsibility, Lewy felt he found the way out of the dilemma by the concept of relative ego autonomy which had emerged from Hartmann's ego psychology. Leaning on both Hartmann's concepts of adaptability and autonomy, and Rapaport's reasoning of the relative independence of the ego, Lewy felt he could support Knight's stipulation that "free choice exists to some extent, provided a person is healthy and integrated" (p. 266f.). This formulation of a limited free will did not interfere with but preserved the requirements of a strict determinism in psychoanalysis. Neither Lewy nor Knight pursued the problem in depth of how determinism was compatible with a relative freedom of choice, or with the free choice which they felt was possible only by the nonneurotic ego.

In a study of the metapsychology of activity and passivity, Rapaport (1953b) mentioned will a number of times, but, in a manner atypical for him, never pursued the subject with the depth and penetration characteristic of him. In fact, he tended each time to equate the concept with voluntary and by implication with conscious, and failed to follow up the complexities involved. In the same study, Rapaport mentions that Brenman had suggested to him that he might be speaking of the "metapsychological considerations of the freedom of the will" (p. 535). Freud (1901) wrote of a "special feeling of conviction that there is a free will" (p. 253) in a manner akin to Knight's description and formulation. In one of the few recent papers on this subject, Schwartz (1984) concludes with a formulation that, while intention exists in the unconscious as well as conscious, deliberate choice takes place only in the conscious and preconscious. While this also makes room for the concept of some degree of free choice, a topographic explanation is introduced with which I do not agree. The entire sequence, I hold, up to and including the final execution of choice, runs its course in the unconscious. Subsequent conscious behavior can then either be consonant with or opposed to the unconscious decision and action.

CONVERGING DIRECTIONS

I will bring to our minds the formulation that "thought is experimental action," a detour on the road to gratification. This is an insight arrived at by Freud (1900, pp. 508ff., 533, 535; 1911a, p. 14; 1933, p. 89f.), repeated centrally by Rapaport (1950, 1951b) in his monumental study of the psychology of thought processes, and noted prominently by Fenichel (1945) in his summary of the theoretical background behind psychoanalytic clinical work. This succinct formulation is now regarded as a truism in explanatory theory. Its avowedly teleological nature is accepted without concern. Philosophical and other psychoanalytic considerations may provide caution, but such an explanation fits in well with today's hermeneutic emphasis on meanings and purpose. As a forerunner, however, of my thoughts at this point, which I will develop further, questions are left open, such as who or what conducts the experiment? To what end? What follows and under what circumstances?

The same form of dynamic sequence, to be followed by the

same type of questions, is seen in another, even more central formulation of psychoanalytic theory, Freud's (1926) second, signal theory of anxiety. Here again an experimental intrapsychic operation is alluded to. Anxiety now is no longer a result of a build-up of tension resulting from repression. Instead the ego anticipates action to be taken by permitting a small, tentative, instinctual discharge. Anxiety is then a signal the ego produces—Schur (1953) and I amended this to "experiences"—which indicates danger from the direction of the superego or external world.

A third avenue of approach to the theory I am developing is what I described as the intrapsychic process. This was a more microscopic examination of Freud's anxiety theory. In briefest summary, the ego permits a small amount of instinctual discharge and samples the reactions of the superego and external world. If no significant anxiety ensues, the discharge can proceed to full and normal expression. If anxiety or other unpleasurable affect results, producing what I call the first phase, the tentative experimental phase, of intrapsychic conflict, the ego institutes defenses of some type to control the tentative and desired instinctual discharge. If this proves to be successful, stability results and the conflict is at an end. If the defense is insufficient to the pressing instinctual drive, the ego is confronted with a greater disharmony. This brings on the second or major phase of intrapsychic conflict, which challenges the ego for a more viable solution.

A fourth line of psychoanalytic thought I wish to cite is that when we examine ego functions to assess ego strength, we are apt to think of such ego functions as judgment, discrimination, differentiation, etc., but stop short of what happens after the ego judges. Synthesis and integration are usually included in the inventory of ego functions, but these come closest to being thought of as ego goals as well. As goals, however, they are incomplete and do not, in my opinion, accurately reflect the total sweep of ego aims and activities.

Upon what dynamic moment do these various paths converge? In each of the four sequences I have described, the line of reasoning leads in the same direction. What is the result of the experiment which thought represents? What does the ego do after the signal of anxiety has been received? What is the next move of the ego when its initial attempt at defenses proves insufficient? What follows the ego's judgment?

In each case something more is needed. A next step is necessary. An active, decisive move needs next to be made. This is the ubiquitous course of ordinary human life. Lest one feel at this point that I am drifting into a conscious psychology, I wish to state firmly that I am speaking of unconscious mentation, and of processes within the structural view, both hallmarks of central psychoanalytic theory and concern.

Gray (1982) has written of the lag between new theoretical formulations and their applications to technique. Besides historical and cultural inertia, Gray ascribed this to resistance to applying the new knowledge of ego psychology, in particular the necessity to analyze the defenses. I (1982a) have pointed to a wider set of resistances toward the progression of psychoanalytic theory, based on a variety of "transferences to theory," causing recurrent regressions in the steady advance of theory formation. This can take the form of resistances to specific aspects of existing theory, failure to develop or apply necessary advances, or the formation of new systems which abrogate much of what went before.

Such, I believe, has been the case in the failure of fruition of the concept of psychic autonomy. While the conceptual advances enumerated above all culminate naturally in the next necessary step, for the ego to proceed to execute what it is there for, to direct the course and activities of the total organism in its navigation through the surround of its life, furtherance of this understanding has for the most part faltered, or turned back, or has at least been delayed at the threshold of the ego's unconscious decision-making functions. This is exemplified by Hartmann (1947) stating that we do not yet have a psychoanalytic theory of action, as he himself was at the brink of taking that important and necessary step. Such a direction, however, was obviously recognized in its import for the future. He writes, "it seems probable that a theory of action based upon the knowledge of the structural aspects of personality . . . is the most important contribution psychoanalysis will one day be able to make in this field" (p. 38). Preceding action must be the decision to act. Hartmann (1950a) stopped short of describing the final mode of action of the ego's executive functions. Although he referred to ego apparatuses, following the ego's original differentiation from the id, as executive apparatuses, Hartmann (1939a) never went on to describe their definitive executive functions.

The unconscious decision-making function of the ego is a neglected although not completely overlooked point in the microdynamic series of events which takes place in the interplay of the psychic systems. The problem cannot be averted or better solved by reverting to the organism as a whole as the agent of decision, as is commonly held at this point. It is still the ego, not the self, or the self schema, or the whole person, or consciousness, or the existential "I," which stands at the threshold of executing an act at this decisive moment of the intrapsychic process. Perhaps the occasion of this Hartmann lecture is a fitting time to attempt to extend the articulation and integration of this next crucial step into the psychodynamic series of events, in what I believe can become an advance in theoretical understanding.

Freud, focusing on introducing and defending the crucial, innovative insight of psychic determinism, did not deny the existence of another type of mental activity during the intrapsychic sequence of events, but never gave this aspect his central attention. These organizing and executive functions of the ego were alluded to wherever they became descriptively necessary, although always briefly, glancingly, almost secondarily, and never coordinated into a cohesive and substantive section of theory. In his final *Outline*, describing the two fields of action with which the ego is concerned, Freud (1940) states that "the ego has voluntary movement at its command. It has the task of self-preservation. As regards *external* events, it performs that task by . . . learning to bring about expedient changes in the external world to its own advantage (through activity). As regards *internal* events, in relation to the id, it performs that task by gaining control over the demands of the instincts, by *deciding* [my italics] whether they are to be allowed satisfaction, by postponing that satisfaction to times and circumstances favourable in the external world or by suppressing their excitations entirely" (p. 145f.).

Freud (1940) describes the ego in childhood as "governed in all its *decisions* by the injunctions of a modified pleasure principle" (p. 205; my italics), and later governed toward the same decisions by the reality principle through the now internalized superego as well as the external world. Freud's (1927) emphasis on "the voice of the intellect" as soft but persistent can be taken to express his hope and expectation of ego control. And in 1923, while stating that "Often a rider, if he is not to be parted from his horse, is obliged to guide it where it wants to go" (p. 25), Freud also points out that psychoanalysis aims "to give the patient's ego *freedom* to decide one way or the other" (p. 50n.). In 1926 Freud cautions against making the strength of the id into a Weltanschauung, which would be "an extreme and one-sided view," and speaks for leaving room for independent functioning of the ego (p. 95).

Anna Freud's references to this point also are not copious, or consolidated, yet she takes the same view as Freud of the ego as an organizing and problem-solving agency. In a passage which is also made in passing, after stating that instinctual drives cannot be in conflict with each other but require a formed ego to institute conflict, she states, "the ego develops from a receiving station for dimly received stimuli, to an organized center where impressions are received, sorted out, recorded and interpreted, and action undertaken." Other opinions on the subject vacillate and vary. Rapaport grants freedom of choice to the degree that the ego is within the limits imposed by pressing internal and external events which play a causal role in behavior. Waelder (1960), who feels that Freud saw the ego as a problem-solving agency, also sees the ego as directing purposeful activity, and its processes as "task-solving," attempting solutions (p. 177). To others, e.g., Karl Menninger (1942), free will and responsibility apply only in a legal sense, or as a problem belonging to philosophy to which science can have no answer. Alexander and Staub (1956) consider free will an illusion, and Schafer (1976) regards it as having no place in psychoanalytic discourse.

Aside from such scattered and inconclusive references, the subject has either been unattended or opposed, but it did not remain completely undealt with. I now return to the intrapsychic sequence in the series I was describing above, which I interrupted at the point at which the defenses were failing to accomplish their intended function. Instead, mounting instinctual pressure leads to the next stage, the major phase, after the tentative, experimental one, of unstable, pressing, intersystemic conflict, as a result of which the ego is confronted with the necessity to choose. This introduces a second type of intrapsychic conflict, which I have called a dilemma or conflict of choice, in contrast to the usual conventional oppositional type of conflict.

Intersystemic conflict becomes superseded at this stage by an intrasystemic conflict of the ego, the necessity to choose between id and superego and/or id and external world. Intention, choice, decision, action enter the unconscious intrapsychic picture. The ego is forced to execute a plan of activity. Normal or pathological outcomes ensue, whether into the external world or the psychic interior, motor act or psychosomatic outcome, symptom, fantasy, or even affect. Or there is the decision not to act, to hold conflicting forces together as long as possible in a state of increasing unstable tension.

UNCONSCIOUS DECISION-MAKING

My own series of papers referred to on intrapsychic conflict and process culminated in a work explicitly on "The Unconscious Decision-making Function of the Ego" (see Chapter 13), a function not hitherto included in the official inventory of ego functions by Hartmann, before him by Freud, nor

by anyone following. Clinical data came from analysis and
everyday life. The vicissitudes of this factor were traced in a
particular patient in analysis where it was not an occasional
issue but coursed its way through the entire treatment process.
However, while the problem was followed in depth during the
course of analysis, the phenomenon was to be seen not only in
certain patients but in all patients and as part of normal psychic
functioning as well.

Autonomy and choice are not, as felt by Knight and Lewy,
limited to individuals without psychopathology. Choice of outcome needs to be made during the sequence of intrapsychic
events, whether the final external behavior is normal or pathological. Symptoms are as much an unconscious choice as normal
behavioral outcomes. While we speak freely of choice of
symptoms, we do not as readily acknowledge the unconscious
choice to have symptoms at all. I also do not agree with
Winnicott's (1958b) differentiation between a "false self" subject
to psychic determinism and a "true self" able to exercise free
will. Every "self"—or ego, to be more precise—functions with a
combination of the two, is confronted with deterministic neces-
sities, which are in conflict, following which it has no choice but
to choose.

In 1976, I focused on the role of the superego in intrapsychic conflict, especially as operative in group life, which is the
"average expectable environment" of everyday life (see Chapter
32). Before this, the "syndrome of the compromise of integrity"
(see Chapter 15) was described, in a scientific not moralistic
sense, as another resultant of unconscious ego decision-
making, on a par with neurosis in human affairs. Ego-superego
tensions and conflicts are as much to be solved, and compromises to be chosen, as between ego and id, or more accurately,
between id and superego as mediated by the ego.

Unconscious decision-making was introduced in these contributions as squarely anchored within the structural view, not
different from the "executive intention" formulated by G. Klein
(1970, p. 92) in his "clinical theory," or from the observations or
experiments of academic psychology. However, the opposition,

or, as I will suggest, the resistance to this concept which I described in the past, continued as before. In 1977, Kohut, as one justification for his superseding the structural view by his new self psychology, stated, "I could find no place [within Freud's model of the mind] for the psychological activities that go by the name of choice, decision, and free will—even though I knew that these were empirically observable phenomena. . . . I had to acknowledge that the theoretical framework at my disposal—classical, mental-apparatus psychology, which conceived of the mind as a reacting machine—could not accommodate them within its realm" (p. 244). This view was of course incomplete.

Other theoreticians concluded similarly that for the inclusion of intention it was necessary to dispose of Freud's metapsychological model, which included the structural view. G. Klein (1973, 1976), for example, and his followers, felt that Freud's model consisted of two theories, not one; that choice, intention, purpose, meaning belonged in one psychology and that Freud's metapsychological theory, which was an attempt to join psychology to the natural sciences, no longer obtained and needed to be abandoned. Schafer (1976) joined this group in discarding Freud's metapsychological views and developed an "action theory of psychoanalysis" to incorporate the need for intention and action, which he preferred, as did Klein, to attribute to the whole person rather than to a psychic system or part.

Other objections coming from analysts to the concept of unconscious decision-making take several forms. One source of concern is on a philosophical as well as theoretical basis, derived from Ryle's (1949) metaphor of "the ghost in the machine," against the concept of a homunculus as the agent of human decision. The latest to express this opinion, widely held by others, is Brenner (1982b), who, discussing Waelder's (1930) principle of multiple function, criticizes "Waelder's assumption that the ego is a steering agency—that it is like a little man, a homunculus in a sort of a driver's seat of the psychic apparatus" (p. 117). The same objection caused Klein, Gill (1973), Schafer,

Kohut, Gedo (1979), in different ways, to turn away from Freud's metapsychological, especially structural theory, to explanations of psychic decision and action by the person as a whole.

This objection is, in my opinion, a misunderstanding of the meaning of structural theory and a misleading application of Ryle's metaphor to psychoanalytic theory. Actually the opposite is the case. The ego is not the total organism, shrunken down, but an inner structure—a conceptual one, to be sure, but what the development of psychoanalytic theory has come to, for good reasons, over the years—to which this final directing function can be ascribed. The whole person, normal size or diminutive, whether in the new systems designed to replace the structural view, or as erroneously conceived in seeing the ego in this central function as a diminished replica of the total organism, reverses the explanatory power to understand clinical phenomena built up since the advent of psychoanalysis. A diminutive, whole person would still be in need of an explanation as to the specific agency within this new miniature whole which performs this active function. It is not the inert parts of the total organism, or organs or systems serving other functions, which are psychological agents of direction and will, but the psychic system which by agreement over the years has served to clear the way for this final function.

Another source of widespread opposition to this view of ego functioning can be seen in Brenner's (1982b) objection that "Waelder's picture of mental functioning impresses the reader as passionless, intellectual, almost mechanical. The ego he depicted could easily be replaced by a computer" (p. 117). This concern of overintellectuality has been used from the inception of psychoanalysis about other psychoanalytic formulations as well, to object to theory in general—see Fenichel's (1941b) discussion of the views of Reik—or to Freud's total metapsychological theory which culminated in the structural point of view. The fact is that there is no incompatibility between the most abstract psychoanalytic theory and the understanding of affects or a proper affective approach to clinical psychoanalysis.

The opposite is true, as the work of Brenner himself attests. Psychoanalytic theory and the psychoanalytic method each combines the theoretical and clinical. Psychoanalysis consists of a blend between scientific explanation and humanism, just as empathy resides operationally within the analytic attitude. While Brenner feels that Waelder, in presenting his formulation "made no special reference either to anxiety or to psychic conflict," the formulations I have described demonstrate the fusion between affective clinical material and the explanations tracing their course and fate within the operations of the psychic systems. Anxiety and psychic conflict are the material and fuel with which and for which the intrapsychic process continues its dynamic movement. Nor can anyone think that Waelder saw it differently.

What I have been concentrating on in this presentation is the extension of the ego's activities to its next level of functioning and the inevitable outcome and final result. Others react negatively to pursuing ego functions to this extent because of the feeling that extra baggage is being added to a structure already overburdened in a theoretical sense. For a system already credited with being the organ of thought, the seat of affects, the locus of memories, also to be considered the executive agent for the behavior of the individual has elicited a critical reception. Leites (1971), for example, points with strong disapproval to the almost limitless inventory of behavioral functions attributed to the ego, as if the ego becomes synonymous with the person. This shift is made explicitly when the self replaces the ego in a psychology of the self, which takes over for a psychology of intrapsychic structural systems.

The same objections to this persevering and inclusive pursuit of ego functions could be made in the somatic sphere to the organizing and integrative functions of the brain and central nervous system, with their labyrinth of neuronal trunks, pathways, tributaries, and connecting links. In spite of this theoretical asymmetry, however, and a failure to achieve an aesthetic architecture of theory, psychoanalytic theory, with its central executive role of the ego, fulfills its purpose, and has proven useful as a coherent, explanatory system to encompass observational data, which is always the basic foundation upon which theory receives its definitive test.

Still others fail to respond to this aspect of ego functioning out of the feeling that it comes too close to a description of the problem-solving methods of conscious mental life. To this I would point out that the opinions by Freud, the views of Anna Freud, the explicit description of a steering agency by Waelder, the data and reasoning I have presented—all point to the existence of a problem-solving function in the unconscious ego that applies to the repressed mental content. Problem-solving is too often met by analysts in a pejorative sense. Such activity takes place in the unconscious routinely, is affected adversely by neurosis, and is to be encouraged and freed from its encumberments rather than regarded with a negative view. The exposure and the stimulation of motivation to seek solutions to unconscious problems do not stand in contradiction to other affective achievements and hermeneutic pursuits.

Freud (1923a) initiated this level of insight when he pointed out that not only the id but the ego is unconscious. From there we have come to know, empirically, unconscious defenses, unconscious anxiety and other affects, unconscious fantasies, completely formed and viable, operating outside of consciousness. Then symptoms, character traits, and the most complex psychic formations can be held in repression, even if it is basically the drive components at the heart of each which may provide the central impetus for such global defense.

The topographic divisions into conscious and unconscious do not precisely overlap with Freud's (1911a) two principles of mental functioning or primary and secondary process mentation. I have been describing secondary process functioning in the unconscious ego. In a discussion of the ego with Anna Freud, Sandler (1983) notes, and Anna Freud agrees, "The more we know about how the mind works, the more we see the extent to which there is unconscious functioning which involves secondary process" (p. 136). Other writers who have contributed ideas and opinions contiguous to these views include

Hendrick (1942) on ego mastery, the Bühlers (1951, 1954) on ego effectance and ego pleasure, Harrison (1984) on the ego as prime mover, and others who have pointed out the intricate operations of the unconscious ego.

The opposite also is the case—at times and under certain conditions, there are residuals and derivatives of primary process activity operative during conscious life. Contradictions exist and live together in conscious as well as unconscious life. There is no fine line separating the two systems in this regard, even though the preconscious connects them in a neat theoretical sense. People drift, daydream, fantasy when awake, as they can create, be on guard, and solve problems while asleep. The unconscious fantasy, so thoroughly anchored into mental life by Arlow (1969), Rosen (1960), Beres (1962), and others, is more than a cognitive construct. Operative unconsciously during sleep and the waking state, it is an organized cognitive-affective mental complex composed of elements of all three psychic structures and inputs from external perceptions as well.

There is a spectrum from the dream, and even here between deep dream states and REM dreams, hypnopompic hallucinations between sleep and waking, primary and secondary process operations during the day, waking fantasies, alert states, daydreams, and hypnagogic phenomena as one is falling asleep again (Isakower, 1938). All of these mental products, at all stages, during the night and day, are treated by secondary revision as they approach the preconscious and then conscious and alert state. And all are composites of cognitive and affective contents, derivatives of drives and defenses, miniature or intermediate compromise formations, all brought together into one running thought or image as a final, more macroscopic, compromise formation.

Can there be special receptivities and separate creative capacities at the various stages of consciousness from unconscious to conscious? Creativity may be optimum when the two are mixed, perhaps with different types of outcomes with different proportions of each, such as during free imaging, i.e., the admission of primary process thought and affect in the waking state, and secondary process functioning operative during sleep. Einstein, assessing his own creativity, ventured an opinion that his ability and insights came not so much from his capacity to think or remember as to fantasy, i.e., to permit unconscious drive discharge within his waking fantasy life.

The autonomous ego, especially in its unconscious aspects, plays as necessary a role in the creative process as in planned activity. The creativity of which man is capable cannot spring from the conscious alone. Whether the painting of a gifted artist, or a dream created by any individual, or a chemical or mathematical formula arrived at by a creative scientist, the contribution of the unconscious is indispensable, and within this the secondary process revision and integration also are necessary and available at the unconscious level. Creativity is in fact associated with the greatest amount of autonomy, to the point where it can be antiadaptive—an empirical finding which lends evidence to the fact that autonomy and adaptation, both ego functions, do not necessarily overlap.

Individuality, as expressed both in a creative and more planned sense, springs from and rests upon autonomy. In the total fabric of a human life the degree of autonomy, unconscious as well as conscious, is what determines an individual's motivation to develop his own ego style, and directs and propels him along his unique path. From the time of self-object differentiation, this is in fact the pathognomonic determinant toward the development and preservation of the self. Self-differentiation and integration are achieved and maintained by this function of the ego within the self. This can be less understood in the psychology of the self, which obscures this factor by substituting the self for the independent ego.

While all mental functions interrelate, there are specific developmental determinants which may influence the fate of this central measure of ego strength—the ability, when all the data are in, not only to integrate or necessarily to adapt, but to elect to foray, or to strike out anew. This capacity for self-expression—to judge, discriminate, differentiate, and then choose—may spell the difference intrapsychically between what in oversimplified terms are called winners and losers. This ability, nurtured or injured from early life on, begins at the earliest stages, is tested constantly, is confronted strongly at certain critical times and ages, and undergoes as many vicissitudes as any other aspect of mental functioning. Its developmental history consists of progressions and regressions accompanying separations and rapprochements (Mahler et al., 1968, 1972, 1975, 1982), and emerges in a form characteristic for the individual. Hanly (1979) stresses the developmental aspects of the acquisition of relative ego freedom. While the developmental or vertical history of this function is of considerable analytic importance, the function also exists and is under test during each horizontal moment of human existence.

Many or perhaps most people remain attached to their surround, as figure to ground, self to object, or individual to the inevitable group, sacrificing or minimizing this trait in favor of security. Reality, inner and outer, defines the area within which choices can be made. Within this area, the ratio between choice by compulsion and choice with a variable latitude of freedom separates one individual from another. Weakness or strength in the capacity to choose or create, whether in a practical or aesthetic sense, stamps the individual character. While the necessity and therefore the ability to choose are part of all human life and mentality, the capacity of the ego to roam freely and allow a creative process to come to pass is achieved by a small minority of individuals. In the larger perspective, given the restrictions of everyday life at all levels of society and cultural development, the capacity to choose with a significant degree of security and freedom is limited and not given to many.

Decisions can take place in the unconscious and remain unconscious. Rationalization is then an unconscious defense made after the decision which obscures the motivations upon which it was made. Hartmann (1950a) points out that both insight and rationalization take place in the ego. I would add that both can take place at the unconscious level. Just as man "knows" more than he knows he knows, i.e., from memories and thoughts not permitted into consciousness, so does he decide more than he allows himself to know he decided. A patient, or people outside of analysis, may decide and not know it, say they have decided when they have not, and say they have not decided when they already have. The analyst, attuned to the unconscious of the patient, often knows that the patient has decided when the latter does not yet know it, or that he has not yet decided when he thinks he has. Contradictions are observed routinely in patients between conscious decisions and behavior which belies them, and the reverse, actions and behavior which indicate decisions have been made before or without their being consciously acknowledged.

These clinical-theoretical observations have important consequences, including shedding clues as to the explanation of the negative reactions they elicit. It is in this connection that I wish to point out that the ambivalent and contradictory reception accorded this subject since the onset of psychoanalysis can best be understood by psychoanalytic insights themselves. The original opposition to Freud's discoveries and to early evolving psychoanalytic theory was based on the injury to man's narcissism, that he was no longer master of or in control of his behavior. The present theme adds simultaneously an opposite mechanism, affecting not control but responsibility for one's actions. Lewy's (1961) point of departure for his study of autonomy and will was the question of how responsibility was affected. A new resistance to psychoanalytic understanding stems from the fact that man now becomes responsible not for less but for more than he knows. With respect to narcissism, man is traumatized; with respect to an unconscious decision opposing his superego and the external world, he is made anxious and guilty. Both mechanisms of course can and do coexist.

The question of responsibility, which flows as a natural extension of the theme I am discussing, moves on to an issue of the widest ramifications in human behavior. A number of applied aspects come into consideration, such as, from the standpoint of the psychoanalyst, the role of responsibility in the therapeutic process, and from the broader perspective, its place in a spectrum from the social relationships of ordinary life to the crucial and ambiguous position of responsibility in the psychosociolegal area. These important applied aspects will be pursued in a separate paper, and only the more theoretical stream will be developed further here.

WILL, FREEDOM, AND PSYCHIC DETERMINISM

If the fear of increased responsibility and accountability is the dynamic behind the resistance to autonomy seen in patients and large segments of the public, the lag among analysts in accepting and using this aspect of theory stems from another source as well. Here the conflict involves the need to preserve the concept of psychic determinism, so central a tenet of psychoanalytic theory. Autonomy and determinism have been seen from the start as mutually contradictory, each canceling the other out. Yet just as determinism stands upon an unassailable theoretical and clinical base, the same holds, from both clinical observations and theoretical persuasiveness, with regard to the need for formulations about autonomous functioning. The two appearing to be immiscible, the result has been a theoretical lag. Empirically, from the order of the chronological development, determinism had priority, and autonomy has therefore remained relatively undeveloped.

But continuing phenomenology presses for expansions of theory to accommodate the findings. Observational data leading to a conviction of the presence of both determinism and autonomy are of such ubiquitous and compelling nature as to make any theoretical reasoning which would eliminate either one of them untenable if not absurd.

Theory usually catches up, even if after long periods of time. Of many studies along the lines I have been describing which have not yet coalesced or been brought together, I would mention in particular two centers of such research, one on each coast. Weiss and Sampson (1982) in San Francisco have come to similar theoretical conclusions, of the routine operation of high-level secondary process functioning in the unconscious ego, from a long-term, experimental approach involving detailed clinical analysis of process notes. On the opposite coast, A. Kris (1977, 1982, 1984, 1985) has postulated the routine presence, stemming from similar observational phenomena, of what he calls divergent conflicts, either-or conflicts, or conflicts of ambivalence, akin to what I have called choice or dilemma types of conflicts. In his case, the same conclusions which from my line of approach stemmed from a microdynamic analysis of the "intrapsychic process" derived from a study of the process of free association.

It would not be amiss, and confirms an aspect of my thesis, to point out that the authors of these studies have felt, not without reason, that their findings have not only been disagreed with, but have been considered controversial. Both have aroused an affective opposition. The reactions to the subject, however, are not negative but ambivalent. There is, in my opinion, a widespread feeling of something having been omitted or at least underplayed. Esman (1985) has elevated Rapaport's 1953 paper on active and passive to the status of a "neglected classic." Noting its immense contribution as well as its fate of having remained unheralded, Esman points out how Klein, Schafer, and others have utilized Rapaport's insights in their own subsequent formulations—in Klein's case, specifically toward a psychology of will—without sufficient reference to Rapaport's contribution. Transported back by Rapaport's paper to the "heroic age of ego psychology," Esman found this work helpful not only in his general clinical experience, but specifically in conceptualizing the nature of healthy adolescent development. He also singles out the light it sheds on understanding artistic creativity, "to emphasize the active role of autonomous problem-solving ego functions as opposed to the more conventional notions of passive 'inspiration' based on regression, even if 'in the service of the ego'" (p. 69).

The same combination of special importance coupled with a strange and inexplicable inhibition in furthering the concept is seen at the source in Rapaport himself. In an introduction to the posthumous publication of Rapaport's paper in 1967, Gill notes the surprising fact that Rapaport never published this paper, although it was in careful, finished form since 1953. This was attributed by Gill to "the extraordinary scope of the concept of activity and passivity in Rapaport's mind, [which] he regarded . . . as at the very heart of an adequate conceptualization of the human psyche" (p. 531). It is interesting that Gill himself, a few years later (1973), to achieve the same inclusion of active intention into psychology, joined Klein in abandoning Rapaport's and Freud's abstract metapsychological views.

From the arguments and line of reasoning I have adduced, I share Rapaport's opinion of the centrality of the active and directing function of the ego in mental functioning. I also agree with Esman about "the rich, complex, and many-veined lode that Rapaport began to explore" (p. 69) in this paper, which was left aborted. The thrust of this theoretical advance was toward what Brenman recognized as the metapsychology of will. The importance as well as the ambivalent reactions demonstrated to this subject are part of the observable data, and stem, in my opinion, from a push toward and a pull away from deep contradictory unconscious motives which this issue evokes.

I believe that the relationship between autonomy and psychic determinism needs to be clarified and revised. Observational data, the final arbiter, dictate that both need to be fitted together in a harmonious, coherent, and unified theory. Previous studies which have made room for both have not settled on a satisfactory or coherent relationship between the two. Knight, Lewy, and others, for example, include the existence of free will side by side with what they continue to feel is a strict or rigorous determinism in its original sense, without regard for the mutual relations between the two or eliminating the apparent incompatibility between them. I would like, particularly in line with what I believe are subtle new developments since then, to offer a way of thinking about this dilemma which I believe achieves theoretical and scientific consistency.

First, will does not automatically mean free will, as conventional phraseology routinely and literally links the two. Just as

I have previously separated conversion from hysteria (1959) and suggested (1982b) that we dissociate self from the concept of borderline or narcissistic, so does the automatic linkage between the pair of words "free" and "will" also need to be discontinued, if clarity of thought in this difficult field is to be attained. As autonomy is relative, so is "freedom" of will. As "free" associations are only relatively free, the same applies to "free" will. Will, as autonomy, is always relatively free and relatively restricted. Hanly (1979) speaks similarly of "grades of freedom."

The concept of autonomy, which is accepted, brings with it the concept of will, which is resisted. Perhaps the recognition and automatic limitation of the human will to the degree of freedom it actually has, while contiguously linked and intimately responsive to its surrounding psychic elements, would reduce or eliminate the immediate rejection it otherwise arouses. I have described with great care the inputs from drives and superego impinging routinely upon the ego before its autonomy can come into its area of functioning. Will has the characteristics of any ego activity, exerts itself after the ego has been subjected to and taken into account motivations from all other sources from within and without.

Will is to be differentiated from the instinctual wish, the wish of early psychoanalytic theory. It is also to be distinguished and separated from a superego demand or requirement. The human will is an ego faculty, a directing capacity following and combining motivations from the three psychic systems, external reality, and the goals and intentions of the ego itself, of which will is its culmination.

The relationship between autonomy and psychic determinism is a complex one, and must take into account the stages by which insights into this area were established. As Freud first discovered the determinism exerted by drives and the unconscious (Breuer and Freud, 1893–1895; Freud, 1900), the role of the latter over what was then known about the ego was the dominant and overriding insight, to be protected and preserved against any minimalization. As the counterforces of the ego in relation to the id were elaborated, the deterministic influence of the id, and later of the superego, on the ego were maintained, while the wider scope of ego functioning was increasingly mapped out (Freud, 1923a).

While the developments from then on led Freud to a fuller appreciation of the active in addition to reactive activities of the ego, these were never consolidated into an equally cohesive summary form as had been his earlier discoveries. The way was clearly open, however, for the subsequent work of Hartmann to add the adaptive and, more importantly for my theme, the autonomous functions, without violating, but complementing, what Freud had laid down. From the content and spirit of Freud's writings in this connection, I would say the following. If Freud had done with this subject what he did with anxiety (Freud, 1926), i.e., attempted to coordinate and unify his views of psychic determinism and his cumulative new understanding of the active, directing role of the ego, he might well have come to the same conclusion as he did with the two successive anxiety theories. He could have felt that both views applied, that they seemed to be mutually inconsistent, yet that he did not feel either should be discarded, and that, for the time being, *non liquet*.

And just as I concluded with regard to Freud's two anxiety theories that both the first physiological theory and the second psychological signal theory needed to coexist in a unified theory (distinctly a minority view, I might say), I would conclude the same about determinism and autonomy—evidence exists that both concepts apply, and both need to coexist in one harmonious theoretical whole (which also might or might not turn out to be a minority view). Jones (1924), while adducing arguments from philosophy to atomic physics to cast doubt on the scientific credibility of free will, quotes Kant's two forms of truth, his "critical reason" and "practical reason." From psychoanalysis, there are similarly two unconscious truths on the matter of free will and inevitability, from which Jones sees one day "a chance of reconciliation between the two in place of regarding them as an insoluble antimony" (p. 187).

But each concept needs to be clarified on its own, as well as the mutual relationships between them. As autonomy came to be seen as relative, the same can be said to apply to determinism, at least in the original sense of automaticity and compulsion in which Freud introduced the term and concept. Each, in fact, limits, modifies, and influences the other, again thinking of determinism in its original sense. The failure to see this relativity and reciprocity in perspective has led to the usual sequelae of one-sidedness and *pars pro toto* in this area which has been characteristic of the history of psychoanalytic theory during its entire course. Thus Kohut (1977) came to see classic theory as "the domain where the authority of absolute determinism holds sway [as] unlimited" (p. 244), an observation he used in support of his replacement of ego by a new, more flexible self psychology. I do not think that Freud viewed any phase of his discoveries of mental functioning as absolute, as his many changes and modifications attest, but all as a series of checks and balances and interconnecting links. That is why dualism and conflict remained his center. Kohut is correct, however, to the extent that the admission of ego autonomy into psychoanalytic theory and its clinical applications have remained limited and restricted. It was not necessary, however, in order to introduce and integrate choice and intention, to replace ego by self psychology, nor to abandon metapsychology and the structural view in favor of any of the psychologies of the whole as agent, as Klein, Schafer, and others have done.

The subjects of free will and determinism have been among the most debated issues in the intellectual concerns of man from earliest times, occupying the minds of philosophers, religious theorists, ethicists, logicians, and the great psychologists before Freud. The related group of issues woven together in a melange of sophistic and elliptic arguments have included causation, freedom, responsibility, necessity, and that most elusive subject of chance. The opinions offered are all definite, eloquent, well-fortified, and equally convincing on opposite sides of each question. They range from William James's (1897) conclusion for the necessity of free will, espousing pluralism, chance, and indeterminacy in the service of making possible optimism and a moral sense, through Hospers's (1950) arguments against the logical existence of free will, to Wood's (1941) strongly presented conclusion that "a capricious free will—capable of acting independently of antecedent conditions—is a philosophical absurdity" (p. 46). I would like to reflect briefly on how the opinions I have offered from the psychoanalytic viewpoint, most specifically on the function of ego autonomy, relate to these various questions and concerns, and what light they may throw on this perennial area of intellectual controversy and debate.

Autonomy and will are not without motivation, and neither is contrary to the concept of causation. Both take their place as sequences within the causative chain, maintaining the continuity with nature stressed by Hanly (1979), and consonant with Hume's characterization of causation as "the cement of the universe" (in Wallace, 1985a). Thus neither runs counter to the tenets of science as demanded by biologists and psychoanalysts alike. Nor are autonomy and will contradictory to the concept of psychic determinism. In keeping with Knight's requirement that an absolute determinism is intrinsic to science and nature, autonomy, as I have described it in the intrapsychic sequence, also is a psychic determinant of action and thus resides within the domain of psychic determinism. Behavioral outcomes are as much determined by the role of the final autonomous inputs of the ego as by the underlying formative pressures of the drives and superego.

The concept of determinism, however, is seen to have been widened. This is not determinism in the original "id" sense of compulsion with no room for choice and decision, but determinism which includes the ego as well and its final autonomous will and act. Just as external constraints are always present, but are also always circumscribed to a greater or lesser degree, so are internal restrictions always present, but only to a finite degree. Freedom of the will lives and exerts itself between these limiting borders. Anchored to its own past history, it is caused and is itself a cause. It is no more capricious, magical, free-floating, or unanchored in history and a surrounding milieu than other psychic elements or agencies, but has its function and power to choose, even if at times it elects to limit, postpone, or abrogate that power.

Will does not make behavior indeterminate, but adds to determinism by compulsion the determinism of choice. Neither does the substitution of probability for absolute predictability impair the concepts of determinism or cause. Probability does not negate causation, but also takes its place among the links of the causative chain. Predictability, another prerequisite demanded by philosophers of science, is present, but in a relative, not absolute sense. Doers fall into groups, which lends some predictability, and within the individual, actions are not independent of antecedent factors, which again provides a means of prediction. But if we follow these preparatory determinants, the autonomy as to final choice, not only within the control of, but required of each separate human individual, prevents predictions from being absolute.

Autonomy, however objective a position one wishes to take toward it, makes for a softer determinism, introducing the factor of human individuality, of choice and direction instituted by an agent of decision. The most elegant expression is contained in Waelder's (1934) concept of ego "transcendence." Referring to man's capacity to rise temporarily above his instinctual and environmental demands, Waelder notes the ability for "objectification of one's self, the attainment of a position above one's own ego" (p. 104). Elsewhere, in a psychoanalytic survey of the entire sweep of human history, Waelder (1967b) notes the claims by some of the universality of dominance and aggression in the animal kingdom, from which they would conclude that despotism is a universal law of nature. He states, "Even if this condition were universal, however, it would not prove that man cannot alter it; for man, though rooted in nature, can transcend it to a large degree. As Denis de Rougemont put it: 'Man's nature is to pass beyond nature'" (p. 47).

With the evolutionary development from animal instinct, through intermediate forms to human will, with its intention and direction, a factor is added to biological determinism, coming now from the psychic determinism of the human will, which retains the scientific status of determinism while making it more complex and complete. Human nature, by the combined attributes of intelligence and will, can slow, hasten, prevent, or abort processes in the physical world around it. Waelder (1967b) states, "man has since time immemorial changed his environment and disturbed the balance of nature" (p. 285). These capacities have been incrementally accelerated in modern times. Softer deterministic characteristics introduced into physical nature by human nature alter the absolute predictability of the present and future of the physical universe as well as of the human condition contained within it. Wallace (1985b), speaking in favor of a strict determinism, distinguishes determinism from predetermination. The nature of the universe may therefore be not only not predetermined, in the sense pointed out by Wallace; but, now that a relative uncertainty has been introduced by the acts and influence of human nature, it is not subject to determinism or predictability in an absolute sense.

Whatever causative events and determining influences have preceded ego choice in the intrapsychic sequence, it is precisely man's ego autonomy, and the degree of freedom this bespeaks, which defines and makes room for his subsequent assumption of responsibility. Without the possibility of autonomous choice, responsibility for one's actions or behavior is theoretically nonexistent, or in an untenable or ambiguous role, no matter how ardently but inconsistently the opponents of independent will try to include it within their formulations of causation. The factor of responsibility is included by the proponents of all shades of opinion in this area because, by observation and logic, it cannot be left out. Yet its inclusion within the system of reasoning is without a logical and consistent base.

Responsibility, however, is also a gray area, and relative, not absolute, not all or none. Responsibility is directly related to the ratio between psychic compulsion and autonomy, between automaticity and control, however difficult a problem this is to measure clinically or in life. The degree of autonomy and the resultant responsibility are not to be contrasted with the presence of conflict, nor sharply equated with the conflict-free. Will based on autonomy is exercised for cause, expresses motivation, and is instituted equally after the ego is confronted with conflicts as in the absence of these. Nor are this function and capacity related specifically to the degree of psychopathology or its absence, as both Knight and Lewy have suggested. The problem of assessment, of degree of autonomy with its attendant responsibility, exists in all behavioral functioning. Accountability may not overlap or coincide with responsibility, but may be wider or narrower than the latter. Society and legality add their own criteria. A person may be held accountable even if not responsible, and in some instances the reverse.

Will power, a colloquial expression which resonates with meaning to the average person, connotes an intuitive recognition of this decisive ego force. It is man's will which gives him the power to direct the path to be taken by the self, to decide, to execute, to do, to act. The role played by "the will to recover" in the psychoanalytic process has been traced by Nunberg (1926). The "will to win" is well known as it influences outcomes, from competitive sports to the games of business and living. It is recognized how, in times of severe crisis, the "will to survive" can determine life or death. "Brainwashing," a term used to connote the elimination of this force under conditions of oppression, is not a solution of cortical cells of the brain, but a dissolution of the will while the brain remains intact. The decision of the victim to allow this to happen is a psychological defense, typically preconscious, or unconscious, or even conscious, in the service, in fact, of preserving the existence of body and brain somatically. The uncritically accepted and commonly agreed-upon misnomer for the syndrome of submission, making it instead a physical process, defends and excuses the ego decision, with which all can identify, made by the captive against odds.

Freedom and necessity, both of which occupy a central

place in the reflections of philosophers, are reciprocally restricting, and both are relative, not absolute, even in more fortunate societies. Necessity is relative, not absolute, even in an oppressive environment. Heroic acts, choosing for or against self-preservation, point out that from the mundane to the extreme, even after necessity comes the necessity to exercise choice. To execute this, the will of the ego takes its place in the sequence of the instinctual wish and superego demand as an element in the causative psychological chain.

Democracy is also "free" only to a certain degree, within the boundaries of rules and restrictions necessary to preserve an orderly and sufficiently predictable life. Predictability is subjected to a softer view from this line of observation and reflection. As Rapaport and Gill (1959) point out, although autonomy has an antecedent history of its own, it actions cannot be predicted as the sum total of its history. No matter how much is known of an individual's previous patterns of behavior, the outcome to a current, particular combination of stimuli is always uncertain, even more so in an environment which prides itself on the attainment of a "free society." Given the fresh confrontation and exposure to the ego's will, the result can never be predicted in an absolute and infallible sense. This is characteristically human.

Limitations of predictability have recently been indicated by scientific reflection even in the physical and biological worlds, where causation and predictability had previously held absolute sway. Much has been made in recent years by social scientists, philosophers, theologians, and ethicists who wish to preserve man's freedom of choice, of the introduction of unpredictability into the world of physical matter by Heisenberg's (1958) principle of uncertainty in the movement from Newtonian physics to quantum mechanics. Random occurrences among subatomic particles have been assumed to be paralleled by random, or at least independent, choice by whatever each psychological system considers the human agent to be. While I agree with Hartmann (1959) that psychoanalysis, or psychology for that matter, need not be bound by the laws or requirements of the physical, including the somatic, world, similar end points, arrived at independently by research in each field, each by their own paths and criteria, would seem to convey a special impact.

Waelder (1967b) includes the role of chance in his thorough list of the determinants of history. Chance is part of nature and of science, Max Born is said to have said to Einstein. Social scientists, with the concurrence of nuclear physicists interested in applying their new knowledge, have stressed the role of accident and chance, some to the point of developing the chaos theory of social progress and regress. And Darwin has demonstrated the role played by chance in the random mutations along the course of the evolutionary scale. Chance is minimized but not eliminated by active choice, and continues to play a causative role outside of ego control. This applies to an equal degree to the physical, biological, and psychological chains of events impinging on the course of human history. Not all illnesses, for example, are psychosomatic, nor all accidents brought about by an accident-prone victim. Reality, as Hartmann (1956b) points out, is more than man's unconscious.

The history of an individual life is not determined entirely by causative events within the psychic self, without influence by physical occurrences external to it and outside of its control. Conversely, with man now having within his power the capacity to unleash energy of a magnitude to significantly alter the physical arrangements in the external world, the history of the physical world is to a certain extent dependent on the vicissitudes and choices of the human will. The latter, I have been saying, cannot be predicted with certainty. As a culmination of these views about the sequence of thinking and affect within the intrapsychic process of man, the influences which play upon it and those which derive from it, I would say that human history, individual and collective, results from a combination of determinism, random occurrences, and the guided event.

Freud discovered that unconscious forces determined psychological history more than was known. This never proceeded to an opinion by Freud that determinism, in the sense of compulsion in which it was first considered, was thereby absolute. Nor did it follow that all aspects of behavior are determined outside of the control of the subject doer, a fallacy fallen into by many who erroneously attributed this view to Freud. There is no evidence that Freud ever set himself against what strict determinists call "nonnecissitated choosing." Autonomy and will are part of the chain of psychic determinism, as I have described. Both are included in unconscious mentation, as well as the conventional association of these with conscious functioning. Just as defenses are unconscious, so can decisions be equally kept from consciousness. The motive, as always, is to ward off anxiety, in this case from the unconscious ego decision and action having been made counter to the interests of the superego, with the usual fear of punishment resulting. Consciously, in such instances, either the person denies that a decision has been made, or its external presence is attributed to other motives. Such a sequence of decision-making and rationalization is commonplace in life.

While improved choices on a conscious basis are expectable and acknowledged as an outcome of analysis, a more subtle achievement is an effortless solution of intrapsychic conflicts by autonomous activity of the unconscious ego. The psychoanalytic process makes the intrapsychic process less disturbed and disruptive, and more efficient during its entire course. Changes after insight do not take place automatically. With the increased freedom available to the ego, the patient needs next to act. Waelder (1960) is one of the few authors on technique whose formulation leaves room for the factor of choice, although this is not elaborated upon in an explicit way. After insight, the patient has "a *possibility* of working out a viable, nonneurotic, solution" (p. 46; my italics), Waelder states. Glover (1949) writes of "freed will." The decision, however, then remains with the patient to proceed with the possibility. While some patients do, others introduce further difficulties at this point, which may either be dissolved or, with further analysis, open new possibilities, which may then be chosen to effect a change.

Without the inclusion of unconscious forces, cognitive

psychologies limited to conscious intention are incomplete. Without the inclusion of the role of ego autonomy in the unconscious, psychoanalytic theory also remains incomplete. Such an omission adversely affects the analytic situation and the theory of therapy which guides it. A psychic determinism which does not include the roles of unconscious decision and choice makes psychoanalytic treatment untenable and incomplete, and defeats its goals from the start. I cannot visualize practicing psychoanalysis without having within my therapeutic armamentarium the interpretation that "you have a choice," or "you had a choice, and chose this or that," or at least that "you set up the conditions which made such-and-such a decision necessary or inevitable." Without the inclusion of such concepts and tools, understanding the past and influencing and guiding the future life of the patient must remain incomplete.

Clinical psychoanalysis decreases the determinism emanating from id and superego and increases the scope within psychic determinism of unconscious ego autonomy and choice. This expanded view of Hartmann's ego autonomy, which, in my opinion, has been aborted in psychoanalytic theoretical development, is necessary to achieve the full meaning and applicability of the concept in psychoanalytic theory and practice. With its successful inclusion into the total psychoanalytic goal, psychoanalysis joins other conscious psychologies in including deliberation and direction in the chain of causative events. It would then, however, be the only psychology which also includes its unconscious scope of operation. Without an unequivocal role given to autonomy and choice, with their attendant assumption of responsibility for behavior, the Sartrean existential criticism of "bad faith" leveled at the psychoanalytic view of psychic causation acquires credibility. The widespread acceptance of this critique of psychoanalysis is at least partly due to the awareness of this common omission in psychoanalytic theoretical and practical discourse.

A patient expressing repetitive, uncontrolled anger against indiscriminate targets, displaced from repressed rage against his father, comes to see the irrationality of his behavior, not only of the present inappropriate objects of his aggression but even in the part he played in the original development, what he contributed to bring about his father's aggressive acts. During the progressions and regressions of this insight, the patient himself introduces a metaphor to reinforce his accumulating insight, "You can't blame the caddy for giving you the wrong club. In the end, it was I who swung the club." As he returns to this repeatedly with each new incident, we are awaiting the time when he solidifies this insight and learning, that he should and can swing the club differently, and finally that he does so. His affects as actions will also then be under greater control.

To return to a colloquial phrase I referred to above, one might say that psychoanalysis increases "will power," an equivalent of Freud's, and Fenichel's, pointing to the increased operation of the rational ego. Hartmann (1956b), pointing out the "bewildering . . . complexities [behind each] basically simple question" (p. 267), hoped for such a time when "we may reach a decidedly more beautiful and satisfactory stage, when simple formulations will become of equal or superior value" (1958, p. 313). That time has not yet come and, in view of the history and course of the applications of psychoanalytic insight, may be far off. For the time being, limiting ourselves, as an example, to the subject under discussion, recognition of the autonomous functions of the ego has had a greater effect on the conduct of an analysis than their discovery has had on psychoanalytic theory.

I will end with a passage of Freud's quoted by Hartmann (1950a, p. 141), in connection with Hartmann's "synchronization and reformulations" of Freud's psychoanalytic theory of the ego. "There is no need," writes Freud (1926, p. 160), commenting on his own changes in the theory of anxiety, "to be discouraged by these emendations. They are to be welcomed if they add something to our knowledge, and they are no disgrace to us so long as they enrich rather than invalidate our earlier views—by limiting some statement, perhaps, that was too general or by enlarging some idea that was too narrowly formulated."

CHAPTER 17

The Decision to Terminate One's Life

Psychoanalytic Thoughts on Suicide

Anyone moving out on a ledge to talk to a would-be jumper had better have at least an intuitive idea of the psychological aura into which he or she has been cast. The police officer, psychologist, friend, or stranger entering the drama at this crucial moment represents the object world to a person who, often for the first time in his or her life, occupies center stage. One need not and cannot have an informed knowledge of the psychodynamics that have led to this moment. But an effective identification, often borne of and surprisingly present in crisis, cannot fail to be of help. External advice or exhortation when the suicidal intention has taken such hold is of no value because external objects have been

Plenary Address to the Combined Meeting of the American Association of Suicidology and the International Association for Suicide Prevention, San Francisco, May 27, 1987. Published in *Suicide and Life-Threatening Behavior*, 18:28–46, 1988.

devalued. The last thing one should show now is a tone of insincerity. Rescuers instinctively know and feel this.

My approach to this subject that rivets the attention, that commands intense and universal interest, is from the experience and vantage point of a psychoanalytic generalist. I do not speak from a special interest, nor from having been involved in any controlled experiment or focused research on this specific subject, which might in fact result in a skewed, exaggerated, and especially highlighted view; rather, I speak by virtue of my general data base. From this vantage point, I look at the suicidal impulse, or wish, or fleeting thought, as it resides in the general psychology of the population. In an active general psychiatric practice of well-nigh 50 years, I have not had an experience with suicide that would enable me to make claim to being a specialist. Anyone who did would be inclined to cover it and hide his or her expertise. On the other hand, any long-time psychiatrist who has had no experience with suicide is like a surgeon or internist who has never had a patient die because they turn sicker patients away to others.

I have seen suicide and overseen it. Perhaps of more universal applicability, I have observed its aborted, controlled, and redirected forms in a huge sample of general psychopathology. Looking over nearly 50 years of daily, continuous practice, in which my patients and I operated at the psychic depths for what I once calculated as well over 100,000 hours of free associations, I would say in an overall way that suicide as a universal fantasy occupies a discernible but small place in mental life. I do not attempt to quantify, but hope to arrive at an impression of its importance by descriptive and dynamic exploration.

THE LATENT AND QUANTITATIVE QUALITY OF SUICIDE

As a bridge to my assertion that suicide is latent and quantitative, and that under certain circumstances it can become commonly operative, the experience comes to mind that is connoted to us by the name "Jonestown." This natural experiment of astonishing proportions has, in my opinion, never been sufficiently absorbed or its grim psychological lessons extracted. About 980 persons quietly administered a lethal dose of poison to themselves and their children (some 250 of them), with no compelling internal or external reason except loyalty to their leader and to each other. Surely there was no convergent past psychodynamic history in all these victims, as much as they were tied and united by this common external bond and condition. What the act gave testament to was the power of followership, passivity, submission to charisma, and identifications upward and laterally (to the leader and to peers); the universal "need to belong" was not given up even at this price.

That such pathological behavior is not limited to ardent and overt cultists, but can affect a wider-based "normal" population, can be reflected upon and validated by an even worse example of submission to authority—in this instance, complying with aggression outward rather than toward the self. I am referring to the experience of another gripping "natural" experiment in our lifetime—this one of an entire nation, and more than one nation, passively enduring and permitting (if not actively participating in) genocide and torture. These two grim "natural" experiments did not need the official and more academic experiment performed by Milgram (1975) at Yale on "obedience to authority" to confirm these conclusions. These two polar examples—phenomenological manifestations of mass behavior in the service of genocide and suicide—are linked to the theoretical concept of the aggressive instinct, directed outward in one instance, and turned toward the self in the other. As an empirical observation that ties the two together, about one-third of all homicides include suicide.

To trace and understand the origins and vicissitudes of what can be called suicidal content in general psychology, one has to take into account gradations, structural aspects, and the developmental progression of mental constructs. In suicide, perhaps more than with any other mental content, the distance between the conscious intention offered verbally and what actions and attitudes reveal about more significant unconscious intention is a crucial datum for explanation and understanding. A suicidal thought is not a suicidal wish. Every thought is a trial action, itself a compromise of instinctual impulse and defense. A suicidal wish is not a suicidal intention. Not every wish is intended for action. A suicidal intention is not a suicide attempt. Intentions are subject to further intrapsychic testing—actually, a series of tests. A suicidal attempt is not yet the act of suicide. Indecision and compromise formation continue. Even a suicidal act is not yet suicide. The intention is still not unequivocal, or its results assured. Finally, there is suicide. Even here there is not always finiteness, especially now that there is a question of when death actually occurs.

Anyone who wishes totally to die, with no ambivalence or indecision, has the means of bringing it about. No one lacks the power to do so. A gun or a jump assures death with most certainty. Gas can be stopped, a telephone off the hook can lead to help, even the gruesome head in the oven can be taken out. It is remarkable what creativity can go into leaving loopholes in otherwise most ingeniously contrived methods. No method assures an unequivocal decision. There is a joke in which a man looks out of his window in the middle of a skyscraper and sees a body hurtling downward. "How's it going?" he asks. "I don't know yet," replies the plunger. (It is strange that I heard this as occurring in San Francisco. Maybe that is because I live in Los Angeles.)

Even the jump, and probably the gun, do not eliminate the opposite wish while one is still alive. At the 50th anniversary celebration of the Golden Gate Bridge, a rare jumper who survived the leap from the bridge described his experience: "From the instant I saw my hand leave the railing, I knew I wanted to live. I was terrified out of my skull." He remembered waking up swimming. "I was screaming, 'Oh, God, save me! Oh, God, I want to live.'" When one intends the act of suicide more completely, a news item such as the following appears: a woman, age 27, walked into a schoolroom, went to the front of the class, said, "I'm sorry I have to do this," pointed a gun at herself, and pulled the trigger. It misfired. She then shot the gun at the wall, pointed it again toward herself, and this time died before the bewildered class.

THE CONTRIBUTION OF DECISION THEORY

The theoretical armature of my running formulation is based on my concept of decision theory. Although psychoanalysis has contributed knowledge of the complex workings of the unconscious, this has not involved to an equal degree all aspects of unconscious mental activity. Because of the sequence of psychoanalytic discoveries, human beings were seen first in their reactive aspects, reacting to instinctual drives from within, and the effects of external traumatic events from without. During the second half of the psychoanalytic century, ego psychology was added, but this too at first mainly in its defensive aspects. With Hartmann, Rapaport, and the ego psychologists who followed, active ego functioning was finally seen in its adaptive and nonconflictual aspects.

Psychoanalytic decision theory, however, has always lagged behind. Decision theory has been left to mathematicians and game theorists, the military, logistic experts, and players and gamblers at games of chance. But human decisions are as much about emotions as about numbers and things. As a background to the analysis of the decision for suicide, I utilize a description of psychoanalytic decision theory developed over decades, on the subject of unconscious choice and decision. From a background unconscious intrapsychic process—always operative in human mental life, during the course of thought as trial action and the testing for signal anxiety, at various points in the intrapsychic sequential chain—the ego selects action or defense; brings about an acute affect or chronic mood; and chooses a symptom, perversion, or act, or other discrete or complex compromise formation, to give expression to the conflicting forces impinging upon it.

I pass over the decisions of everyday life every minute, day, and night (in my theory, even during sleep) to come to the big one, the monumental decision of universal interest. The decision to terminate one's life, leading to the most violent and finite of human acts, considered the most pathological of decisions, has more recently been recognized as encompassing some exceptions. This is an aspect only beginning to receive conscious social attention. Although the broadening of humanitarian motives poses the possibility of an arguable rationale in favor of the termination of life, I consider first the greater and still pathological segment of suicide, the most malignant of clinical conditions confronted by those dedicated to the maintenance of mental "health." Health is in quotation marks because of never-absent subjective aspects. We do, however, aspire to objective standards and criteria as much as the "soft" human sciences are capable of achieving.

THE RANGE OF MOTIVES FOR SUICIDE

Human behavior, as complex a final product as exists in the animate or inanimate world, can be pared down from complexity to relative simplicity, whether with respect to phenomenological observations or explanations as to origins, which can be both parsimonious and complete. Studying the subject of dreams, Freud (1900, 1916–1917), with characteristic virtuosity, followed them in all their ramifications, and performed an opposite task as well—condensing their infinite variety into an observation that dreams are built up out of a few universal basic elements. Just as a few numbers or integers or a short musical scale can be elaborated into infinite possibilities, dreams are also concerned at bottom with a few irreducible items. Freud said about dreams that the range of subjects is rather simple: the human body, parents, children, brothers and sisters, birth, death, nakedness, and sexual life. In a similar vein, the range of motivations for the extreme resort to suicide is also not wide. The moment of decision always rests on deeper states: on the relative degrees of satisfaction or frustration; on hopes and expectations of the satisfaction of instincts (loving and aggressive), or their opposite; on the possibility of ego mastery or its unlikelihood; on superego tranquility or savagery toward the ego and the self. Again, the range is not wide. A small number of crucial ratios are the determining factors.

CONSCIOUS VERSUS UNCONSCIOUS INTENTION: THE ROLE OF AGGRESSION

The decision about one's birth belongs to others. The decisions in life about one's life are one's own. In the current period of our history, the decision about one's death has been added as a subject of discussion. In retrospect it has always been there, but is only now being talked about.

The decision to terminate one's life is not an accident, unknown or unpredictable, if the life be known. Human decisions span from survival to destruction. From the impulse side, aggression—more easily defined and widely accepted than death as an instinct—can be turned inward as outward. The ego, acting for the organism, can master, even conquer the external surround, or, identifying with the surround, can turn its armament and effectiveness against the very organism it represents. The superego, guiding the ego, can exert its influence for or against the self. The body cannot count automatically on the protection of its ego. The aggressive instinct may line up with the ego against the self.

Suicide, however, can be at least partly accidental. In assigning responsibility to or thinking of the individual's active role in the decision-making process, it is well to bear in mind that the events following a decision, large or small, conscious or unconscious, are not necessarily or even typically based on long-range intention. The decision does not always count on its ultimate consequences, on the continuous stream of effects that may follow. A quick marriage to satisfy a sexual need or any other impulsive urge does not necessarily intend, in a longitudinal sequence, to bring about the long miserable life that may follow. A suicidal attempt, undertaken for one or many reasons, may result in a suicide by accident. A person going to bed under the influence of drugs and alcohol does not count on the cumulative lethal effect of the combination of both, although there could have been self-destructive or self-stimulating wishes from one or both.

Not everything that follows a decision was intended by it. In addition to the gray area of intention is the factor of ego judgment. The ego, in its intrapsychic operations, may not accurately assess the long-range occurrences that may inexorably result. There have been many suicides brought about in this ambivalent and uninformed way. Perhaps a metaphoric example of how the ego can misassess the future, how judgment and calculations can be off, is the suicide of van Gogh in 1890 in dire poverty at the age of 37. Until then, he had sold one painting in his lifetime, for $30. One of his "Sunflowers" sold almost 100 years later for $39.9 million![1] In the dramatic situations we are confronting today, the ego's choice, even if it fails in its precise intent or accomplishes its mixed intent but leaves a loophole of inefficient outcome, can be an irreversible one.

The area of responsibility for conscious or unconscious intention with respect to what follows is not an unlimited one. Intentions are complicated questions to assess. From how deep do they come? A young woman whose twin infant children died in a car of heatstroke while she slept with a man next door in a mechanic's shop was spared a verdict of involuntary manslaughter because of her good intentions; that is, "she did not mean to fall asleep but only to lie on the bed to rest for a few minutes." She also stated that the man she was with had agreed to listen for the children for her (*Los Angeles Times,* April 17, 1987).

The most insightful look into the psychodynamics of depression, the most frequent prelude to suicide, comes from Freud's (1917) division between mourning and melancholia. To mourn for a loss is normal and reparative, whereas melancho-

---

[1]Since this was written, his "Irises," inspired by the gardens of the mental hospital in which he spent the last year of his life, sold for $53.9 million!

lia, also a reaction to loss, is pathological and destructive. The latter syndrome shares dynamics with a significant percentage of suicidal conditions. In such a pathological state, which is what presents itself typically to a psychiatrist as "a suicidal patient," the ego loathes the self; that is, the mental agent or system in which emotions are felt holds the entire self or person in abysmal disregard. Aggression or hate is actually in both directions. It does not originate toward the self, or in a postulated internal death instinct, but as aggression, anger, or hate toward others, resulting from disappointment by loved ones or from failure of love. As in melancholia, where mourning is converted into psychotic depression, aggression is also turned upon the self. Nor is its original intention outward lost or always unclear. Suicide is also a threat to others, to whom the threat is often made overtly long before the act. The moment of its execution can be unconscious murder turned inward. That this is unconsciously recognized as such may be seen in survivor guilt, which can also reach the point of danger to its bearer.

SUICIDE AS A PLEA FOR LOVE

But not all suicide is anger toward others turned against the self. Pathological syndromes, particularly those that eventuate in a single dramatic act, are most liable to generalizations and cliches. The causes of suicidal impulses and even acts vary. Suicide can also be a misguided plea for love—one that, to be sure, has gone too far. In the recent rash of adolescent suicides, this is frequently one important component.

Adolescence is a time when the need for approval, love, and reassurance against the ferocity of inner impulses is at its height. Coupled with a lack of efficiency, skills, or judgment, or a lack of ability to reflect, postpone, or apply perspective, it is more an acute swell of helplessness, a crisis of hopeless expectations, than a chronic state of self-hate. There is a fragile and unstable tolerance of the self, compared to the pressures and intensity of the drives. It is the gulf between the two that constitutes the etiology, not internally directed aggression.

Cultural influences have been at work toward this. More is expected of adolescents, by others and by themselves.

The suicidal act can be sudden and unexpected, as from an acute humiliation, not a chronic psychotic lowering of self-esteem. There can be an acute crisis of impotence or its revelation—literally in a failed sexual experience in one's early, immature love life, or figuratively or symbolically, displaced onto the need to demonstrate young or early success. A high school student made a suicidal attempt after he lost an election, in part because of what the loss would mean to his parents, but more because of what it meant to himself. Suicide or homicide is not uncommon at the revelation of homosexuality to one's peers.

THE ROLE OF HOPE

Alongside the chronic or acute lowering of self-regard (E. Bibring, 1953), or outburst of aggression against the self (Freud, 1917), the ultimate but crucial dynamic spurring the suicidal impulse to destruction of the self is the status of hope—the ego's deep, pervasive unconscious assessment of the potential for overcoming the conditions that have brought about the present internal condition of a traumatic state with no expected path of escape. The differences among anxiety, depression, and a suicidal state have to do with the status of the complex ego affect of hope. Anxiety, however intense and out of control, has two faces—one facing a traumatic state, and the other the possibility of avoiding or overcoming it. There are both present danger and the potential for escape; the future is uncertain, but there is a future. In depression, the trauma is here, and the hope of averting it is gone or diminished. But this is for now. There is still a time factor and a possible change. With a suicidal urge, there is no future. Hope neither is present now nor will ever appear.

A type of ego affect described by Erikson (1950)—hope, related to trust (in objects)—assumes a dominant, diagnostic, and prognostic import. It can be a thin line from an expectation of the temporary nature of traumatic helplessness to giving up that hope. The specific dynamics that propel the ego toward the dramatic action of the termination of life, while externally kaleidoscopic, can be pared down to certain features in common. If I can attempt to be even more parsimonious than Freud was about dreams, on a subject of such individual variability, the signposts on the road to suicide can be focused and converged on the status of love, hate, and hope.

This has nothing to do with what appears on the surface. The crucial affects can be easily forgotten/repressed. Klaus Barbie, at his trial in Lyon in 1987, said that he had no hatred against minorities, Jews, gypsies, or homosexuals. "I do not know the word 'hate.' . . . . I had nothing to do with the Jewish question. That was the work of a special committee."(*Los Angeles Times*, May 14, 1987).

Loss of love or of one to love, as occurs in mourning, leaves aggression to dominate over libido. This leads to a hopeless distance between the ego and the ego ideal. The ego has failed the superego, leading to guilt and to the need for and the feeling of deserving punishment. Narcissism, so much maligned when excessive, is deficient or nonexistent; the self has lost the love or protection of the ego. Or, paradoxically, is it still excessive, such as in the omnipotence in Tom Sawyer's (Twain, 1875) fantasy of returning and enjoying his own funeral? "Disturbed" patients, as suicides are considered to be, are thought of as highly narcissistic. Suicide in this respect is akin to delusions, which, as in the case of Schreber (Freud, 1911b), similarly stem from omnipotence, megalomania, or a feeling of influencing and being influenced by the world.

SUICIDE AS A PATH TO GLORY

There can also be an opposite path to the same tragic result. There is even at times something attractive, heroic, or positive about the suicidal attempt. In San Francisco, the magnetic attraction of suicide has been increased immeasurably by the beauty, nobility, and dignity of the Golden Gate Bridge, whose 50th anniversary was recently celebrated. Its strength and majesty are visualized as the background in the jumping subject's mental picture of the event. The same result can occur from other types of psychopathology besides depression, such as from manic excitement. Derring-do unto death, in a manic or hypomanic state, can be just another way to go—to defy nature, God, fate, parents, and all their surrogates. With patriotism added to the meaning of the act, along with fantasied adoration by the nation and heroic membership among the martyrs of the ages, a kamikaze pilot carries these national values to his death with the greatest pride. Or the same aristocratic tradition leads to a virtuous end by hara-kiri.

In its accompanying unconscious fantasy, the act of suicide can achieve immortality, the same result as the poets strive for, sharing in common the essence of religion. The opposite of shame is an exhibitionistic defense, a counterphobic acting out into the offending environment. The treasurer of the state of Pennsylvania (*Los Angeles Times,* Jan. 22, 1987), under indictment for criminal behavior, called a press conference, declared his innocence, pulled out a gun, placed it in his mouth, and pulled the trigger. The moment of horror appeared in photographs in newspapers across the country. The act, symbolically and in its posthumous sequelae, restored mastery over traumatic helplessness, in the only way the individual felt was possible.

DISTINCTIONS BETWEEN "SUICIDAL" AND "SUICIDE"

"Suicidal" is not a diagnosis but a descriptive statement of a mental state. It can be present across the nosological spectrum—from the most malignant and ominous diagnostic categories, to cognitive-affective states that some claim are the epitome of sober rationality. My only current patient who is a distinct suicidal risk is otherwise functioning exceptionally well in life. His suicidal content is a loculated area of pathology, although one that threatens his life. The suicidal act itself is a symptom, not a diagnosis, stemming from and grafted upon a developmental history that needs its own specific understanding and interpretation. Each has a current, horizontal, acute meaning, as well as a chronic longitudinal one leading up to it. As final as its effects may turn out to be, its psychological motivation is an individualistic one, not always parallel to the severity of the outcome to which it leads.

There is an important distance between "suicidal" and "suicide." Whether or when one crosses it is not always easy to predict, and at times difficult to understand. The dynamics of "suicide" may be similar to, but not the same as, "suicidal." Not many patients have free-associated in depth about the dynamics of the suicidal act. A suicide note is not the same. Those patients an analyst knows in depth do not commit suicide. Those who do, the analyst does not know in depth.

One does not know the panorama before the mind in the seconds before death, by any cause. Most thoughts about what the dying person is thinking are projections of the survivor. A patient arrived in time to see his comatose father once more just before he died. He reports without question that his father, toward whom he had lifelong ambivalence, squeezed his hands and had tears in his eyes. In a rare clinical instance, a patient on the couch associated about what went through his mind one afternoon during the Battle of the Bulge, as he crouched in a trench, with a German soldier in sight over him holding a dangling bayonet. This patient did not confirm the myth of one's entire life passing before one at such a moment of pretermination.

The state of being suicidal can be analyzed; the act of suicide cannot. One cannot analyze a dream until after it has happened, if one is to include everything up to the last precipitating stimuli. Some who commit suicide may not have been suicidal in a chronic or prolonged sense, as is the case with some who commit murder. Others have been suicidal and then commit suicide; the act then does rest on the etiological base. A profile of the subject after the fact is never the same or the equivalent of a psychodynamic depth study. I think of two patients in whom the suicidal state was turned around and averted. Were these the analyses of suicide about to happen, or only of the suicidal state? Is "suicidal" sufficiently different from "suicide"? One of these two patients was trying to calculate mathematically how many seconds it would take from jumping off a high-rise building at a certain floor until he reached the ground.

Is the analysis of a suicidal patient the averting of a suicide? Does one ever really know? A patient, during a long analysis, stated that he went through a suicidal period, which I as the analyst never thought of as such. The patient, in an acute period of combined anxiety and depression, and acute panic mixed with hopelessness and helplessness, stated that that was the closest he ever came to the actual possibility of committing suicide. I, working in my own mind on understanding the causes of the anxiety and depression and the nature of the defenses against them, and feeling sufficient confidence in the patient's ego strength, adaptive capacities, and ultimate hold on reality, did not feel a suicidal state to be a real danger, and did not respond with medication, extra hours, or the sense of an emergency. The patient always chided me after that for not caring, or for not being able to do anything about it. Was this an experience of the treatment of a suicide successfully averted, or a more typical regression during treatment? Was it a correct assessment, properly treated with a good outcome, in spite of the patient's negative residual feelings, or a therapeutic lapse (or error) that the patient himself rescued from disaster? The patient said that he could have committed suicide, that I did not care, and that I could do nothing to help him anyway. He had better not trust me in case of such a crisis occurring again.

We must be suspicious of analysts who claim many analyses of suicides, just as we must be of an analyst who claims to have analyzed 50 or 100 homosexual patients, with each analysis taking 10 years, more or less. I also hesitate to claim many such analyses on other grounds as well.

CONTAGION IN TEENAGE SUICIDES

The rash of teenage suicides today has become an epidemiological problem of major proportions. David Hamburg (1987), the president of the Carnegie Foundation, places its social importance ahead of nuclear war as the most pressing subject of human concern. Suicide is the second leading cause of death in the 15- to 24-year age group. Of four New Jersey teenagers who died in a garage in a suicide pact, which shook middle America recently, only one had a severe and overt suicidal history. The others, although disturbed and irregular in their previous behavior, mainly "went along" (*The Record,* Northern New Jersey, 1987). The need to belong, operative for a decisive moment but with a fantasy of permanence, outweighed the instinct to live. Attachment behavior, a powerful antidote against separation anxiety, took precedence over the pressure of instincts whose satisfactions dwindled into an indeterminate future. The decision could have been made in a flash; it took hold temporarily but for an irreversible moment; the instinct to live was momentarily but fatally repressed.

Contagion, characteristic of hysteria, also takes hold. Four young people in the same circle of friends had died by various "accidents" in the 9 months before the group suicide. Several of them were mourning the loss of one of their leaders in a "fall" from a New Jersey palisades cliff. Three of the victims had fathers who had died by their own hands. A series of other youths identified with the event, and as "copycats," imitated the incident, influenced by the media, fame, and other short-range but fantasied long-range goals. Two others attempted suicide in the same garage the next week. A series of "copycat" suicides and suicide attempts in the same age range appeared across the nation.

THE DYNAMICS OF ACUTE ONSETS

Quick decisions about life and death can be made in opposite directions. Some people reflexively and automatically turn away from a mugging, or even from a murder. Others are instinctively willing to take a risk. One's own life is not always the highest or the only priority. In a group skydiving maneuver, a woman and a man skydiver collided in midair. She was knocked unconscious. Another man jumped from the plane without opening his parachute, reached the unconscious woman diver, pulled her string first, and only then pulled his. Both survived, where 10 seconds later both would have died (*Los Angeles Times,* May 10, 1987). The dynamics of valor, of heroism or altruism, are not well known in the psychoanalytic literature.

There are writings about the organic, chemical, or structural causes or facilitators of the suicidal state or act, just as there are about depression. These include genetic and constitutional factors, and postnatal somatic and psychic structures; the latter are built upon early mother-child and other object relations, and later organic occurrences or inputs. Whatever roles, however, are played by neurotransmitters, endorphins, the neurochemistry at the synapse, the state of the limbic system, or early structural defects from postnatal and infantile experiences that have predisposed to depressive reactions, such chemical-metabolic changes as do take place during depressive and suicidal mentation are set off in life by acute or erosive cognitive-affective experiences that accompany loss, exposure to ridicule and humiliation, and fragility of the ego feeling of self.

A common mechanism behind an acute onset is sudden shame. We have seen this in recent years in events in the public domain, as a result of the power of modern technology and the news media to publicize worldwide what would heretofore have had to be faced and mastered within the confines of one's own personal social sphere at most. Robert Macfarlane's suicidal attempt early in the Iran–contra disclosures was the latest of such public happenings, occurring as the light of publicity was descending upon him. The strength of his superego was clearly visible, pitted against the morass of involvement in which he was trapped. Having studied the problems of Watergate in depth (1980a), I could not help but be aware of the confluence of the nature of Macfarlane's dilemmas with those of his Watergate counterpart, John Dean. Both were pressed from within by a conflict of values—what we call an intrasystemic conflict of the superego, truth versus loyalty, a clash of principles. Both were confronted by the same anticipation of a sudden exposure, to the aggregate of their peers, of behavior of which they themselves did not approve.

Their decisions were not quite the same, however; the psychic outcomes or solutions were different. Dean, in a staccato delivery that many who heard it will never forget, told it all, and toppled the government. Macfarlane was also as truthful as he could be; he told the facts, but protected and praised President Reagan and Oliver North. During Dean's months of indecision, he resorted to serious alcoholism, as opposing forces within him fought for dominance and a solution. Macfarlane made a suicidal attempt. He recovered well; at one point, he told his questioners not to consider him fragile, but to fire their biggest questions at him.

PARTIAL SUICIDES

There are also the common experiences and observations, in the clinic and life, of what can be considered "partial suicides," in keeping with the concept of gradations: not "all or none," but the sacrifice or abandonment of a significant portion of the functional pleasures and activities of life. These are brought about in a myriad of ways, psychological and somatic: by severe restriction of object relations; by a narrowing of the criteria for sexual object choice that makes satisfaction or fulfillment unavailable; by limitation of occupational attainments; or by somatic equivalents limiting the full range of life. Examples of these last include anorexia and emaciation, or obesity, which take one out of the stream of social relations; and chronic, habitual, ego-syntonic alcoholism (one patient had blackouts every night, so that he would not have to sit up and talk to his wife, for a period of years).

RATIONAL SUICIDE

Although the acute problems of adolescence constitute a social peak, the period of adolescence arrives from childhood and points to adult life. Comparable problems exerting an impact on suicidal conditions precede and outlive the adolescent years. There are also relevant developmental factors at other specific age periods in life, pathognomonic stamps of particular developmental phases. Although problems are statistically at a peak during adolescence and young adult years, there are also midlife crises and the relentless and irreversible erosions of old age. In middle life, the more mature development of skills, experiences, and resources makes for greater adaptability and capacities for sublimation, and there is less likelihood of being overtaken by critical periods or unexpected demands. A change in jobs, or even of a spouse, is not necessarily the end of one's self. There are also, however, unusual external events at any age—war, the military, a holocaust; the feeling of being overwhelmed can never be counted out. And there is always serious illness.

Problems of old age, and the question of terminal illness at any age, have brought to the fore the subject of "rational suicide"—a concept that not too long ago was regarded as internally inconsistent. The burgeoning technology that has permitted the prolongation of life (however close this may be to the mere functioning of a heart-lung machine), coupled with increasing pressures for human rights wherever these are applicable, have made this a subject of pressing and impassioned debate. Suicide today is not a proof of psychosis. Opinions have changed from when I grew up in psychiatry—from the belief that the moment of suicide was always psychotic, if psychosis was not there before, to the thought that sometimes the act is the epitome of sober rationality. The problem of rational or voluntary suicide, although it may occupy a small percentage and an atypical segment of the total suicide problem, must be worked through theoretically, as clinical and life situations become more complex.

The arguments of the Hemlock Society for voluntary euthanasia, and for "living wills," that provide permission for the removal of life support systems under certain stipulated extreme conditions, are persuásive to many, and embody high ideals and humanitarian motives. From the sympathetic play *Whose Life Is It Anyway?* (Clark, 1979), to the same libertarian considerations in support of abortion (whose body is it anyway?) or the argument in regard to involuntary commitment (whose mind is it anyway?), the argument is made to preserve the rights and freedom of the individual in an increasingly democratic and fair society. The right to end one's life, common-sense suicide, is seen as the final right—to choose a painless over a tortured, pain-racked death.

Those against the movement for secular humanism feel that this aims to legalize crimes against humanity, crimes against the whole basis of our Judeo-Christian culture. They see a correlation between increased euthanasia and "mercy" murder cases under the same banner. There were 14 occurrences nationally in one year of suicide in pairs, or of "mercy" killing and/or suicide of elderly couples. An elderly Florida man who shot his wife in the brain as a "mercy" killing is now serving a long jail sentence for his "crime." Others see the pressure for euthanasia as being encouraged for economic reasons, to cut down on the money needed for health care for the aged.

A patient was called upon recently to decide whether to sign permission for surgery for his comatose 95-year-old sister, who had gangrene of the leg, for which amputation was recommended. He decided not to, but to let her go. Many doctors view such decisions and actions as counter to their Hippocratic oath. Physicians are uncomfortable about being forced to do what they morally object to, to take actions they consider unethical, to be executioners rather than to sustain life. These feelings are pitted against the rights of patients or families to halt life-sustaining care—the right to death, if they so choose, for the irreversibly ill. The solution is often to leave the decision and even the act to the patient's spouse or children, with no advice or even opinion provided by the physician. With increased technical progress, new medical questions arise spanning life from birth to death, with subtle moral and legal implications yet to be solved. From who are the parents in a surrogate birth (whose child is it anyway? whose womb? whose ovum? whose semen? there are now so many variations and unknowns) to agonizing dilemmas about the termination of life, the human and ethical dilemmas confronted are bewildering and often tragic.

SUICIDE AS A DEFENSE AGAINST CASTRATION

Although the decision for suicide appears on the surface to be the most pathological decision in life, or at least the most negatively motivated, we should consider and keep in reserve what I hear from a patient who, in relating his anxieties, speaks often of "a fate worse than death." Alongside the fear of death, and at times of equal valence, is the fear of survival. In an avant-garde art work by Terry Allen (1985) entitled "Grace," a tribute to the Vietnam war, the artist includes the phrase "fear of survival" as one of the most frequently experienced horrors. As far back as World War I, when traumatic neurosis was separated for the first time from the syndrome then called "shellshock," Ernst Simmel (1944)—then a young psychiatrist with the German army, who later moved to Los Angeles and lived there until his death—wrote an early paper on the war neuroses in which he stated that the fear of death in combat was a revival of and defense against castration anxiety.

This mechanism is present in less traumatic situations than combat in war. An analytic patient, reconstructing the composite experiences behind his lifelong castration anxiety, often stated that he had a feeling of "a fate worse than death." This is the feeling of the danger, which may become inescapable, of having to endure the unendurable. The pain of castration will be superimposed upon castration anxiety. The traumatic event will supersede the fear of anticipating it. The physical will combine with the mental; the total self or person will suffer; the castration trauma will radiate to annihilation of the self. To think of enduring this is worse than the concept of death. This has a developmental background as well. Infants experience fears of bodily injury, physical invasion, separation, and destruction of the self, leading up to castration focally and specifically, before any concept of the end of life (or, with it, the fear of death).

Death by one's own hand is at times a defense against the possibility of castration—castration at the hands of another, or castration by a lingering death. The process of dying is feared more than death. During the Holocaust, surviving victims have attested to incidents in which their tormentors wished to kill them slowly so they could feel and experience it more. A patient frequently associated to his horror at the concept of Jews in concentration camps digging their own graves, in order to prolong life for a few minutes, before they themselves were shot to be pushed into those same graves. He would never do that, he angrily averred, and if he had to, he would in some way or other have taken a few Nazis with him. In his own life, he considered it a triumph when he could muster up courage to speak back to a loudmouth or bully who had spoken to him harshly in an elevator or on a tennis court.

Death is not necessarily the greatest fear, nor is its avoidance the highest priority. A mother will save her child from drowning before herself. In a poll taken of Olympic athletes, they were asked whether, if a pill were available that would help them toward victory but make death likely within 5 years, they would take it; 61 percent responded that they would. In sentencing the Billionaire Boys Club's Joe Hunt to life in prison without the possibility of parole, a juror explained, "We decided that the death penalty was too quick. Joe Hunt needs time to sit and think about the things he did" (*Los Angeles Times*, 1987). Alongside the experience of Jonestown I alluded to in our times, we should recall that about the same number of people, 960 defenders of Masada in 70 A.D., committed suicide for a very different reason—because they preferred death to capture and slavery under the Romans.

CONCLUDING REMARKS

Thought is experimental action. Human mental life, consisting largely of unconscious fantasies, contemplates action, assesses the consequences thereof, and filters its acts accordingly. Among drive wishes entering into the compromise formations that constitute human fantasies and actions, suicidal impulses find a place in a far wider segment of thoughts than those that are called psychotic, borderline, malignant, or even pathological.

In common to this stratum of motivation is a deep unconscious will to die, however much this is kept in check and prevented from the execution of its full purpose by the strength of the opposing life instincts. The further development of this antilife force is perhaps visible in the marasmic infants studied by Spitz (1945), who, in the face of the actual absence of maternal or other external nurture, do go on to death. We may also think in these connections of the deep resistances of the id against recovery, described by Freud (1937a) as operative behind interminable analyses, and reaffirmed by Stone (1973) in chronic, intractable cases.

This is to be compared with the opposite trend in the always dichotomous human psyche, the "will to recovery" described by Nunberg (1926)—the ally of the analyst in the analytic process. The longest surviving heart transplant patient, who lived with his second heart for 18 ½ years, died recently in Marseilles, France, at the age of 67. Asked about his longevity as a transplant recipient, he once said, "It is perhaps because I have a passion for life, that I have slammed the door on death. . . . I get an extra thrill out of everything I do. . . . I am the happiest man in the world. . . . That's how I live with my old chassis and my Formula One motor" (*Los Angeles Times,* 1987). This force opposes death, and suicide.